# Caribbean
# Transformations

# Caribbean
# Transformations

Sidney W. Mintz
*The Johns Hopkins University*

ALDINE PUBLISHING COMPANY, *Chicago*

ABOUT THE AUTHOR

Sidney W. Mintz is Professor in the Department of Anthropology at the Johns Hopkins University. He received his B.A. in Psychology from Brooklyn College and his Ph.D. in Anthropology from Columbia University. He has taught at Yale University, the City College of New York, Columbia University, Queens College, Wesleyan University, the Massachusetts Institute of Technology and the École Pratique des Hautes Études, Paris. He has done extensive field research in Puerto Rico, Jamaica and Haiti, as well as in Iran. The author of more than 100 articles and sections of books, Sidney Mintz is co-author of *The People of Puerto Rico* and author of *Worker in the Cane,* the life history of a Puerto Rican working man.

First published 1974 by
Aldine Publishing Company
529 South Wabash Avenue
Chicago, Illinois 60605

ISBN 0-202-01125-9 clothbound edition
Library of Congress Catalog Number 74–82602

Printed in the United States of America

*Dedicated to the memory of my mother and father*

# Contents

# Preface

The following chapters were originally written during a period stretching over two decades, most of them as independent essays, and deal exclusively with the Caribbean region. That region was the earliest focus of European colonial development in the New World. Sugarcane, African slaves, and the plantation system were introduced into it within twenty years of the "discovery." The Caribbean was to become a principal locale for the African slave trade, and one of the three major centers for the growth of Afro-American cultural syntheses in this Hemisphere.

I am indebted to Eugene Genovese and Jacqueline Wei Mintz, both of whom suggested to me separately that I attempt to put some of my essays into one easily accessible collection. This turned out to be a more difficult and time-consuming task than I had expected, both because I wanted to impart some unity of theme to studies that had originally been written for diverse purposes, and because no single essay seemed satisfactory on rereading. I also found that I had to make choices in deciding which to revise and include, and which to omit; I now recognize that no such undertaking ever leaves one very content.

Two good friends were kind enough to read through an entire early draft of the manuscript and to comment at length upon it: Jerome Handler and Alexander J. Morin were especially careful in their criticisms, though neither has any responsibility for the results. Peter Wilson read and commented helpfully on the original preface, which was later incorporated into the introductory chapter which follows. A. T. Wall prepared the index. I am very grateful to these friends for their patience and help. The editors who worked on the manuscript at Aldine did much to improve the text, and were unfailingly kind and dependable.

Most of the work embodied in these pages was originally prepared while I enjoyed the support of such institutions as the Social Science Research Council, the Guggenheim Foundation, the Laboratoire d'Anthropologie Sociale and the École Pratique des Hautes Études, Sixième Section (Paris), and Yale University. Proper thanks should also go to those students, colleagues, secretaries—friends all—who over the years tried to make sense of my ideas, spoken and written, and to help me clarify them. The list would fill many pages, however, and I can only hope they will recognize that my gratitude to them is far greater than these perfunctory words must make it seem.

Lastly, I want to thank the people in Puerto Rico, Jamaica, and Haiti with whom I worked in the field. Anthropologists enjoy a special—and perilous—freedom. "We *impose* ourselves unasked," Fredrik Barth has written, "and in many ways incompletely perceived on other people in other countries and societies. There are no standards in those worlds for the intellectual and moral operation of making an anthropological study; and as 'marginal natives' we are free of many of the constraints of society—both ours and theirs. This entails that we must ourselves set the standards and impose the constraints, and that we carry full responsibility for what happens." (1974: 100). Unfortunately, there is a blitheness among anthropologists that sometimes goes by the name of "scientific objectivity," other times by the name of "dilettantism," and that becomes more dangerous, particularly to one's informants, with every passing day. While it is certainly presumptuous to suppose that we anthropologists know what is good for those whose friendship, trust, and help we depend on in the field, it is less presumptuous, perhaps, to try to recognize what is likely to be bad for them. In this book, as elsewhere, I have done my best to do these friends no harm; if, in any way at all, what I have learned can do them some small good, so much the better.

# Acknowledgments

All the chapters in this book have previously appeared individually in various publications. Each, however, has been considerably revised and rewritten here. The following gives the original publication information.

Chapter One is a revised version of the "Foreword" in *Afro-American Anthropology,* edited by N. Whitten and J. Szwed. It was published in New York, by the Free Press, in 1970.

Chapter Two is revised from "Slavery and the Afro-American World" and a review of *Slavery,* by S. Elkins. The former appeared in *Black America,* edited by John W. Szwed, copyright © 1970 by Basic Books, Inc., Publishers, New York. The book review appeared in the *American Anthropologist,* Volume 63 (1961), pages 579 to 587.

Chapter Three is a revised version of "The Role of Forced Labour in Nineteenth-Century Puerto Rico," published in *Caribbean Historical Review,* Volume 2 (1951), pages 134 to 141.

Chapter Four is a revised version of "The Culture-History of a Puerto Rican Sugar-Cane Plantation," published in *Hispanic American Historical Review,* Volume 33 (1953), pages 224 to 251.

Chapter Five is a revised version of "The Question of Caribbean Peasantries: A Comment," published in *Caribbean Studies,* Volume 1, Number 3 (October 1961), pages 31–34. Reprinted by permis-

xii        CARIBBEAN TRANSFORMATIONS

sion of The Institute of Caribbean Studies. Copyright 1961, by The Institute of Caribbean Studies, University of Puerto Rico.

Chapter Six is adapted from "The Historical Sociology of the Jamaican Church-Founded Free Village System," published in *De West-Indische Gids,* Volume 38 (1958), pages 46 to 70.

Chapter Seven is a revised version of "The Origins of the Jamaican Internal Marketing System," with Douglas Hall, published in *Yale University Publications in Anthropology,* Volume 57 (1960), pages 1 to 26.

Chapter Eight is a revised version of "The Jamaican Internal Marketing Pattern: Some Notes and Hypotheses," published in *Social and Economic Studies,* Volume 4 (1955), pages 95 to 103. Reprinted with the permission of the Institute of Social and Economic Research.

Chapter Nine is a revised version of "The House and the Yard Among Three Caribbean Peasantries," published in *VIᵉ Congrès International des Sciences Anthropologiques et Ethnologiques,* Tome II (1ᵉʳ Volume), 1960, pages 591 to 596, Paris.

Chapter Ten is based on the "Introduction" in *The Haitian People,* by James G. Leyburn, Revised Edition. Copyright © 1966 by Yale University.

Chapter Eleven is a revised version of "Caribbean Nationhood in Anthropological Perspective," in *Caribbean Integration: Papers on Social, Political and Economic Integration,* edited by Sybil Lewis and Thomas G. Mathews. Third Caribbean Scholars' Conference, Georgetown, Guyana, April 4–9, 1966 (Rio Piedras: Institute of Caribbean Studies, 1967), pages 141 to 154. Reprinted by permission of The Institute of Caribbean Studies. Copyright 1967, by The Institute of Caribbean Studies, University of Puerto Rico.

# 1

# Afro-Caribbeana:
# An Introduction

In the course of the nearly five hundred years since the "discovery" of the New World, millions of migrants from every corner of the earth became "Americans." In the process they transformed aboriginal American life, such that even the most isolated and self-sufficient Native American communities of the Hemisphere were profoundly modified. "Becoming American," that is to say, has been a process of change defining the history of the Americas and affecting every inhabitant of the Hemisphere. Though the people of the United States persist in regarding themselves as *the* Americans, all who live in the Americas have a proper claim on that title, and those to our south commonly refer to us as *"Norteamericanos"* to make the point.

If we ask what, in some essential sense, makes one an American, the first answer is likely to be geography; however, only the Amerindians, of all Americans, can really lay prior claim to a world that was to become "new"—in total ethnocentric innocence—in 1492. But if this answer fails to satisfy, we may seek to specify further. We who are Americans live in societies and bear cultures whose origins are elsewhere, transformed by the migrations of our ancestors and by the novel challenges this New World imposed upon them. Today, the consequences of transplantation and of adjustment during a period nearly five centuries long define us, even those of us who are Native Americans.

Such a definition may seem irrelevant when one considers the profound gaps—cultural, economic, linguistic, political, physical— that divide New World peoples, both within the component American polities and among them. But from the point of view of those of the Old World we are, in some fundamental way, of the New. That even slight additional qualification may appear to dissolve the contrast—we are rich and poor, Spanish-speaking and Quechua-speaking, Haitian and Canadian, black and white—does not really alter so central a historical feature of the New World reality.

From one vantage point, then, we of the Hemisphere are peoples whose ways of being share the common quality of a foreign past. From another, this reality seems unimportant in our daily lives and in our social relationships. We "Americans"—in this widest sense—share too little. That we are all in part from somewhere else fails of itself to provide us with any sense of common identity or destiny. In fact, some would even argue that the lack of understanding arising from an acknowledgment of the shallowness of our own roots typifies the American experience, dividing us rather than bringing us together. From the vantage point of an Egypt, a China, an India—or even a Europe—we of the Americas are raw and callow, the bearers of diluted civilizations. Our awareness of such disdain is often blurred, but the Limeño in Madrid, the Bostonian in London and the Martiniquan in Paris—not to mention the Trinidad-born Indian in New Delhi—share some knowledge of what it means to be an American, in this most ample of senses. That we more commonly experience our "Americanness" as something else—Blackness, Indian-ness, Third-Worldness, antiyanquismo, or North American xenophobia-at-large—is a reflection both of the highly differentiated character of the peoples of these continents, and of the relative rarity of social situations in which some generalized hemispheric identity might take precedence over other allegiances. In other words, what is implicitly shared by all Americans is usually ignored in the midst of more pressing priorities of consciousness.

And yet it should be within this widest context—the Hemisphere and its five short centuries of newness—that North Americans begin to explore Afro-America. The very word is a hybrid, expressing symbolically the linkage of two worlds—but it is innocent, as is Euro-America, or Mestizo-America (Service 1955), and no more hybridized. We who think of ourselves as athwart the American tradition may claim to feel no need for hybrid words and hyphens, and to resent their implications—except, of course, on St. Patrick's Day, Columbus Day, and certain other Days, and in memories, dreams, and subtly persistent insecurities. Hyphens are supposedly laid aside, together with old languages, old costumes, and old habits of thought. Shiny new unhyphenated North Americans— gringos, the Mexicans might say—usually prefer the image of a past uncluttered by any realities, and marked by such cozy symbols as Washington's hatchet, Franklin's kite, Boone's bear, Crockett's coonskin cap, and Teddy's Rough Riders. We claim to honor a past; yet we have difficulty in admitting that it ever had a beginning, for particular persons among us.

This unease, this nervous joy, is part of a very North American style; Henry Ford's dictum that history is bunk is a North American dictum. We do not question the American past, most of us, in part because we covertly recognize that we are not altogether part of it. It is a seamless past, summed up in Jamestown, Sturbridge, and Freedomland; we make the Pilgrims' Pride our pride and our reality; it is Ellis Island and the village slums of Europe that become the fantasy. Nor should it surprise us that new and insistent demands that the Afro-American past be identified and explicated excite a certain amount of resistance. After all, if ancientness of pedigree were enough to win membership in the D.A.R., those worthy ladies might be aghast at the company they would have to keep. How much more anxiety-provoking, then, to the Johnny-come-latelies, is a pedigree search by the anciently disinherited!

### Africa and Afro-America

But a genuine search for that hidden past has begun, and it requires of the interested that they think through seriously what "Afro-American" can mean. The term implies two backgrounds, or some kind of interpenetration of one background by another.

This book is largely concerned with just such implications as they apply to the Caribbean region[1]; their meanings are various and complex. Terms like "Afro-American" and "African"—or any comparably geographical term used adjectivally—are not self-explanatory. When one speaks of an "African" food, an "African" dance, or an "African" custom, for instance, one may mean any of several quite different things. An African food may be a crop domesticated in Africa or native to Africa—such as okra (*Hibiscus esculentus* L.) and akee (*Blighia sapida* Koen.). Or an African food may be a food processed in a distinctively African fashion, such that certain sorts of cassava cakes—the Haitian *bambouri* or

1. An agreed-upon terminology for ethnic and "racial" categories does not exist for the Caribbean region, and geographical terminology for the region itself is highly variable. Terms, the meanings of which appear self-evident when used in the United States, may not exist, or may lack acceptable equivalents, in the languages of many Caribbean societies, and vice-versa. Accordingly, the terminology employed in this book should be understood as arbitrary, and readers ought to feel free to substitute their own favorite words as necessary.

"Antilles" and "Caribbean" are used interchangeably. "West Indies" is generally employed to refer to the polities now or formerly within the British colonial system (e.g., Jamaica, Barbados, Trinidad and Tobago, Grenada, etc.), and that is how the term is used here. The terms "Española" and "Hispaniola" refer to that island where today's Haiti and Santo Domingo (the Dominican Republic) coexist. Before 1697, it was a single Spanish (and hispanophone) colony. Thereafter the western third became (French) Saint Domingue and, in 1804, Haiti. That is how these names are used in this book.

Where appropriate, and according to ethnic separateness—as defined either by group "members" *or* by outsiders—terms such as "Chinese" or "Javanese" are used to describe particular Caribbean populations. The term "East Indian" is used in the anglophone Antilles to describe persons whose origins are in India, not in the East Indies; it is usually replaced in this book by the term "Indian." Those descended from the original inhabitants of the Caribbean region are also (though rarely) referred to as "Indians," and more commonly as "Amerindians," "Native Americans." or as indigenous or aboriginal peoples.

Persons of African ancestry may be so referred to; commonly, they are here called "Afro-Americans" and sometimes "black Americans." The term "Negro" is only rarely used, as is the term "colored" ("coloured"); like terms meant to describe genetic "intermixture" such as English *mulatto*, Spanish *pardo* and *moreno*, and French *gens de couleur* and *griffe*, these words occur principally in citations from the works of others. As far as possible, an attempt has been made to be clear in these usages; but that is not always easy.

the Jamaican "bammy"—might justifiably be considered African, even though the cassava is a New World cultigen and was only diffused to Africa after 1492. Conceivably, an African food could be a food eaten regularly by a group of Africans working at the United Nations—in which case one assumes that it would be a food they typically ate in Africa, and now continue to eat in a new setting, rather than that anything eaten by people from Africa thereby becomes African. One might be impelled to wonder, though, whether anyone feels that pigs' ears, turnip greens, and grits—items from the cuisine called "soul food" in the United States—could qualify as African, even if these foods are not (or were not) eaten in Africa. Most reflective persons would, one supposes, think not; but the confusion here is real, even if its implications are not wholly intellectual in character.

If we turn from such things as foods to human beings, the confusion is compounded. When a person is described as an African, one is prepared to assume that this means someone born in Africa, or a citizen of an African country or colony—that, at least, is parallel to the way we North Americans define an American. The term *African,* that is, refers to someone from a definable geographical area, the African continent. But if that is the meaning, are not the children of Kenyan Indians, Nigerian Lebanese, and Dutch voortrekkers Africans all? And, this of course, is part of the confusion —because, for at least some people, the term *African* carries clear overtones of physical type. Such confusion inevitably returns us to puzzles of culture such as cuisine, to ask again whether a food might be classified as "African" according to the physical type of those who eat it.

For most of those interested in defining the field of Afro-American studies, the term *Afro-Americana* has to do with culture—that is, with patterns of socially learned behaviors expressed in artifacts, languages, traditions, values, and the like. In the case of Afro-American cultures, the patterns of socially acquired behaviors and their consequences are principally—though by no means exclusively—carried in time and space by those descended at least in part from African slaves whose histories involved enslavement, forced transatlantic migration, protracted servitude, and persistent social isolation and exclusion. But the physical type of the individuals who maintain the behavioral patterns, hold the values, and use the languages is a relevant datum only to the extent that it affects behavior socially—that is, through the perceptions of the persons involved in social relationships. There is, in other words, no genetic relationship between a particular mode of learned behavior —eating turnip greens, dancing the frug, standing or gesturing or intoning in some patterned way—and the physical type of those who exhibit it.

Yet there is a noticeable readiness on the part of contemporary observers to attribute such behavioral patterns to heredity rather than to learning. In the case of white North Americans observing Afro-Americans—and it needs remembering that some Afro-Americans are phenotypically white, while some white North Americans are not—such attributions cannot be explained purely on grounds of a lack of observational keenness. While we may expect to see English children dance morrises, we are neither startled nor amused to see them dance a waltz or even a mambo. Polish children do dance polkas; but the news that they knew how to dance the watusi and preferred it probably would be received calmly by most of us. And yet, when we see black North American children dancing, too many of us expect them to dance in ways that are *somehow* connected to the way they *look*—even though we are not always prepared to admit this.

The implications of an assumption that socially learned behavior is really genetically transmitted are immensely important, and not only because of the intellectual errors that flow from this assumption. Here, however, the assumption concerns us only with reference to the study of Afro-Americana. In recent years in the United States, this assumed or imputed connection between physique and behavior has become more rather than less widespread among Afro-Americans; its presence among North American whites is ancient. Malcolm X tells us in his autobiography (1966: 57) that learning to dance appropriately was difficult for him at first; but soon his African ancestry—his "long-suppressed African instincts," as he put it—"broke through." There may be a full circle here: from the imputation of "inborn rhythm" to Afro-Americans by whites who cannot (or will not) distinguish between physique and culture, to the pseudoscientific question of the difficulties of finding "a gene for rhythm," to the assertion of "an African instinct" for dancing by a black militant. To some extent, this conceptual merging of physique and behavior is expressed in common parlance by the use of such terms as *black* and *soul* without any clear attempt to specify that African or Afro-American cultures are socially learned and socially perpetuated phenomena. Discussions of Afro-Americana and Afro-American studies today thus must take into account the fact that terms like *Afro-American* may be used in ordinary discourse with either physical or cultural associations, or both, in mind.

The distinction between physique and culture was once drawn carefully by Afro-Americanists, as in the work of Melville Herskovits (1930: 145–55). The apparent linkage between physique and culture is difficult to dispute, however, in regard to such items as intonation, facial expression, gesture, and posture—items of the sort Herskovits himself once labeled (1945: 22) "cultural imponderables." It is easy to see why these aspects of behavior might be thought to be innate or genetically transmitted, since their manifestation seems "automatic" or "natural"; but the socially acquired character of these traits is demonstrable. The learned and patterned motor habits that we usually pick up unconsciously and at very early ages from our parents and other kinsmen, and carry into adolescence and adulthood, are both difficult to become aware of and difficult to change; the covert and unnoticed character of the social transmission of such habits is of course the principal reason why they are commonly perceived as "innate" rather than learned. Motor habits of speech are similarly learned, in good part unconsciously, and carried unnoticed; these, too, though to a lesser extent, may be perceived as "part of" a person because they seem to be linked phenomenologically to the very way in which he or she is defined.

It is of interest that these seemingly minor behavioral patterns are also closely tied to the expressive media, such as music, dance, drama, voice, and the like, and that it is in these aesthetic spheres, once again, that linkages between physique and culture are often imputed to Afro-Americans. However, rather than "explain" such behavioral patterns by vague reference to racial or instinctual responses, we should view them as continuities with the African past, and as evidence of the success of Afro-Americans in conserving cultural materials that could not always be conserved in other aspects of life. Patterns of socially learned motor behavior are probably not readily destroyed, even by extremely repressive conditions; and the aesthetic and creative possibilities implicit in these traditional patterns and their cognitive accompaniments may have been among the cultural traditions most readily maintained under slavery.

Nonetheless, there is a strong predisposition to view the connections between physical type, learned motor behavior, and aesthetic expression as genetic rather than cultural, and it is not difficult to see why. What is more, the perceptions of persons who assume a genetic connection between perceived physical characteristics and learned behavior become cultural data themselves, by virtue of the effects such perceptions may have upon behavior. That is, physical type and culture are not biologically linked, but certain kinds of social behavior, based on the assumption that they are, can produce clear correlations between them. This assertion in no way qualifies a historical reality—that those African peoples torn from their ancestral homelands whose descendants are today's Afro-Americans both carried with them elements of different cultures, and were of different physical appearance, from those who frequently became their masters. But the assumption that the linkage is biological rather than social lies buried beneath the whole of Afro-American social history and is—in some deformed and refracted way—the mirror image of the Afro-American tradition itself. In what sense this may be so will become clearer at a later point.

The first African slaves to be transported to the New World arrived during the first decade following the "Discovery," and slavery did not end in the New World until Brazilian abolition was decreed by the imperial government at Rio de Janeiro in 1888. Hence the involuntary servitude of Africans and their descendants in this Hemisphere lasted nearly four centuries; its initiation predated the North American Declaration of Independence by nearly three centuries. The precise number of enslaved Africans who reached the New World alive will never be known—nor will the numbers who died in slaving wars and in the hideous coffles to the coast, during the Middle Passage, or before being debarked in the Americas. Even if we accept the radically reduced estimates of the number of African slaves who reached this Hemisphere (Curtin 1969), New World slavery may well have been the most massive acculturational event in human history (Mintz 1961b: 580).

Aside from special circumstances—as when hispanicized slaves of African origin served as subalterns and assistants to the conquistadores—nearly all the slaves were allocated in terms of the needs of large-scale agriculture. This was especially the case for the production of subtropical commodities, such as tobacco, sugar, and spices, which were finding large and sometimes new markets in Europe. Hence the African slave trade and slavery itself were intimately bound up with the spread of European military and colonial power and with commercial developments, especially in overseas capitalistic agriculture.

New World plantation organization during the sixteenth century and the subsequent two centuries, though of course agricultural, had a very modern—even industrial—cast for its time. This was particularly true for sugar production, where mill operations were tied closely to those of the field, and capital investment in equipment was necessarily heavy. Slaves were used extensively for sugarcane cultivation and sugar production in Brazil and the Hispanic Caribbean in the sixteenth century; in later centuries, similar patterns developed along the Guiana coasts, through the Caribbean islands, on the Pacific coast of Peru, on portions of the Caribbean littoral, in Mexico, and in Louisiana. The relatively highly developed industrial character of the plantation system meant a curious sort of "modernization" or "westernization" for the slaves—an aspect of their acculturation in the New World that has too often been missed because of the deceptively rural, agrarian, and pseudo-manorial quality of slave-based plantation production.

Moreover, the development of plantations to produce commodities for European markets was a vital first step in the history of overseas capitalism. Even more than the exploitation of mines, the plundering of native treasures, or the development of trade patterns with viable indigenous societies, as in much of Asia and parts of Africa, the establishment of the plantation system meant a rooted overseas capitalism based on conquest, slavery and coercion, and

investment and entrepreneurship. The stimulus to overseas commodity production originated in European developments accompanying the accelerated breakdown of European feudalism, the
growth and unification of international trade, and the disfranchisement of vast rural European populations as part of the creation of
factory cities. Thus, the growth of slave-based economies in the
New World was an integral part of the rise of European commerce
and industry, while European factory workers were in a position
structurally parallel to that occupied by the enslaved and forced-
labor strata of New World colonial societies.

Finally, it should be pointed out that the slaved-produced commodities of the subtropical areas outside Europe, particularly in
the Caribbean region, were sold to Europe's working masses and,
at a later time—especially with the growth of factory-based production of cotton textiles and of other industrial fibers—to local
populations in the "underdeveloped" world as well. Here, again,
we discern direct relationships between New World slave-based societies and the growth of European power and influence.

Hence the development of slave systems outside Europe was
important to European development; the slave economies were in
fact dependent parts of European economies; and slavery itself, as
it grew in the New World, was an essential ingredient of that westernization of the world outside Europe that has typified the last
four centuries of world history.

## Afro-American Cultural Creativity

While the demographic spread of peoples of African or part-
African ancestry has not been determined solely by the demand
for labor, their spread through the centuries has been dominated
by that demand. Though granting the provisional nature of his
data, Zelinsky (1949) demonstrates that peoples of African origin
are still concentrated heavily in the Antilles, coastal Latin America
(particularly the Caribbean and Atlantic coasts, but also along
the Pacific littoral), and in the South of the United States. Morse
(1964: 3) points out, in spite of the obvious inexactness of such
calculations, that in 1950, 95 percent of the Negroes and mulattoes
in Middle America were in the Antillean islands, while 76 percent

of the Negroes and mulattoes in South America were in Brazil: "In short, of the 33 million Negroes and mulattoes in Latin America in 1950, 27 million were in the Antilles and Brazil."

In any case, however, the distribution of *peoples* must be carefully distinguished from the distribution of *cultures,* even though cultural elements of demonstrable African provenience will probably turn out to be concentrated in the same areas in which peoples whose ancestry is in some degree originally African are found. When we turn to the distribution of cultures we are, of course, dealing with phenomena that can diffuse freely between individuals, and from group to group, without genetic change of any kind. Folklore, dance forms, cuisine, music, aesthetic traditions, language, and all else that is cultural require no genetic transmission —only a readiness to learn new forms. These forms, moreover, may be taken on with their old meanings or with new meanings added; in fragments (a word, an exclamation, a gesture) or in "complexes"; to replace or supplement older forms or, perhaps most commonly, to intermix in some way with them. Even if the word *goober* (from Kongo *nguba*) does not displace *peanut* in everyday speech, its use may lend a sentence regional flavor; "creole" cookery can combine African and European and other elements in a new and distinctive cuisine that differs from all the traditions that sired it; Br'er Rabbit may learn new tricks, some of them European; and the blues may incorporate a few European elements—instrumental, melodic, rhythmic—that seem to serve the musician's purposes.

The ancestors of Afro-Americans could not transfer their cultures to the New World intact, but in this regard they differed from other migrants only in degree. With few exceptions (see, for instance, Pierson 1942: 73; 1953), enslaved Africans were systematically prevented from bringing with them the personnel who maintained their homeland institutions: the complex social structures of their ancestral societies, with their kings and courts, guilds and cult-groups, markets and armies, were not, and could not be, transferred. Cultures are linked as continuing patterns of and for behavior in such social groupings. Since the groupings themselves could not be maintained or readily reconstituted, the capacity of isolated representatives of African societies to perpetuate or to re-create the cultural contents of the past was seriously impaired. In addition, the slaves were usually unable to regroup themselves in the New World settings in terms of their origins; the resulting cultural heterogeneity of most slave groups limited that which could be shared culturally. It was not, after all, some single "African culture" that was available for transfer. Moreover, the ancestral African cultures, like cultures everywhere, were neither unchanging nor unresponsive. They shared the dynamic quality of all cultures. Thus, at the same time that cultures were transmuted in the New World, they continued to change in the societies of the Old.

Inevitably, Afro-American cultures would take on their characteristic forms under the social and physical conditions with which the slaves themselves had to deal. To probe the consciousness of those millions of Africans as they sought to survive as functioning human beings in the settings into which slavery thrust them is a task which will concern (and, it is hoped, intimidate) generations to come of serious students of Afro-Americana. Surely these human beings, like all others, sought to make comprehensible the destinies imposed upon them by brute force. The daily job of living did not end with enslavement, and the slaves could and did create viable patterns of life, for which their pasts were pools of available symbolic and material resources.

These creative processes had a two-way character, however; not only did the cultures of the slaves come to implicate features of other, non-African origins, but the cultures of nonslaves also assimilated important materials from the African heritage. Such assimilation was especially strong in the expressive aspects of culture, as in Brazilian, Cuban, and North American music, dance, and folklore. So interpenetrated did the heritages of Afro-Americans and other Americans become, in fact, that in many cases it is difficult (if not impossible) to speak of an "Afro-American culture" that is rigorously distinguishable from the wider national culture. This assertion has been put so eloquently by Ralph Ellison (1964: 247–49) that he must be quoted at length:

> Slavery was a vicious system, and those who endured it a tough people, but it was *not* (and this is important for Negroes to remember for the sake of their own sense of who and what their grandparents were) a state of absolute repression.

A slave was, to the extent that he was a *musician,* one who expressed himself in music, a man who realized himself in the world of sound. Thus, while he might stand in awe before the superior technical ability of a white musician, and while he was forced to recognize a superior social status, he would never feel awed before the music which the technique of the white musician made available. His attitude as "musician" would lead him to possess the music expressed through the technique, but until he could do so he would hum, whistle, sing or play the tunes to the best of his ability on any available instrument. And it was, indeed, out of the tension between desire and ability that the techniques of jazz emerged. This was likewise true of American Negro choral singing. For this, no literary explanation, no cultural analyses, no political slogans—indeed, not even a high degree of social or political freedom—was required. For the art—the blues, the spiritual, the jazz, the dance—was what we had in place of freedom.

Technique was then, as today, the key to creative freedom, but before this came a will toward expression. . . . Negro musicians have never, as a group, felt alienated from any music sounded within their hearing, and it is my theory that it would be impossible to pinpoint the time when they were not shaping . . . the mainstream of American music. Indeed, what group of musicians has made more of the sound of the American experience? Nor am I confining my statement to the sound of the slave experience, but am saying that the most authoritative rendering of America in music is that of American Negroes.

For as I see it, from the days of their introduction into the colonies, Negroes have taken, with the ruthlessness of those without articulate investments in cultural styles, whatever they could of European music, making of it that which would, when blended with the cultural tendencies inherited from Africa, express their own sense of life—while rejecting the rest. Perhaps this is only another way of saying that whatever the degree of injustice and inequality sustained by the slaves, American culture was, even before the official founding of the nation, pluralistic; and it was the African's origin in cultures in which art was highly functional which gave him an edge in shaping the music and dance of this nation.

The question of social and cultural snobbery is important here. The effectiveness of Negro music and dance is first recorded in the journals and letters of travelers but it is important to remember that they saw and understood only that which they were prepared to accept. Thus a Negro dancing a courtly dance appeared comic from the outside simply because the dancer was a slave. But to the Negro dancing it—and there is ample evidence that he danced it well—burlesque or satire might have been the point, which might have been difficult for a white observer to even imagine. During the 1870's Lafcadio Hearn reports that the best singers of Irish songs, in Irish dialect, were Negro dock workers in Cincinnati, and advertisements from slavery days described escaped slaves who spoke in Scottish dialect. The master artisans of the South were slaves, and white Americans have been walking Negro walks, talking Negro flavored talk (and prizing it when spoken by Southern belles), dancing Negro dances and singing Negro melodies far too long to talk of a "mainstream" to which they're alien.

Ellison is making an exceedingly important point, not only about the innovative resiliency and creative integrity of the slaves, but also about the nature of culture. When we speak of Afro-American cultures, we are speaking of disturbed pasts; but those pasts were carried by successive generations, each dealing with the daily challenges of oppression. The glory of Afro-Americana inheres in the durable fiber of humanity, in the face of what surely must have been the most repressive epoch in modern world history. It depended—had to depend—on creativity and innovation far more than on the indelibility of particular culture contents. Such creative adaptation is, of course, a form of culture change, in which the individual, or a whole mass of individuals sharing certain traditions and values, develops new forms. In one sense, those new forms are American, more than anything else—but "American" here means *new,* means of the New World. We need to discover what actually happens when such new forms—be they musical, linguistic, political, or whatever—take shape. In the case of music, the clues are especially plentiful.

Richard Ligon, an English sugar planter whose remarkable *History of Barbados* (1657) appeared when its author was languishing in debtors' prison, provides us with a moving example of the ways in which the new music was created by the slaves:

> In the afternoons on Sundayes, they have their musicke, which is of kettle drums, and those of several fifes; upon the smallest the best musitian playes, and the others come in as Chorasse; the drum all

men know, has but one tone; and therefore varietie of tunes have little to doe in this musick; and yet so strangely they vary their time, as 'tis a pleasure to the most curious eares, and it was to me one of the strangest noyses that I ever heard made of one tone; and if they had the varietie of tune, which gives the greater scope of musick, as they have of time, they would do wonders in that Art.

I found Macow [a slave] very apt for it of himselfe, and one day coming into the house (which none of the *Negroes* used to doe, unlesse an Officer, as he was,) he found me playing on a Theorbo [archlute], and singing to it which he hearkened very attentively to; and when I had done took the Theorbo in his hand, and strooke one string, stopping it by degrees upon every fret, and finding the notes to varie, till it came to the body of the instrument; and that the nearer the body of the instrument he stops, the smaller or higher the sound was, which he found was by the shortning of the string, considered with himselfe, how he might make some triall of this experiment upon such an instrument as he could come by; having no hope ever to have any instrument of this kind to practise on. In a day or two after, walking in the Plantine grove . . . I found this Negro (whose office it was to attend there) being the keeper of the grove, sitting on the ground, and before him a piece of large timber, upon which he had laid crosse, six Billets, and having a handsaw and a hatchet by him, would cut the billets by little and little, till he had brought them to the tunes, he would fit them to: for the shorter they were, the higher the Notes which he tryed by knocking upon the ends of them with a sticke, which he had in his hand. When I found him at it, I took the stick out of his hand, and tried the sound, finding the six billets to have six distinct notes, one above another, which put me in a wonder, how he of himselfe, should without teaching doe so much. I then showed him the difference between flats and sharpes, which he presently apprehended, as between *Fa,* and *Mi:* and he would have cut two more billets to those tunes, but then I had no time to see it done, and so left him to his own inquiries.

We recognize that the Sunday slave-musicians Ligon was describing played music that was wholly or in good part African in origin. But we also recognize with what skill and interest Macow was preparing to make new music out of old—both European and African—resources. Ellison's assertion that these inventions were perfected ruthlessly, "without articulate investments in cultural styles," is particularly illuminating. Enslaved Africans carried their cultural heritages into the inferno of slavery with a very different commitment to their ancestral societies than that of the unenslaved. Those heritages, in fact, could be maintained in the new settings only by innovativeness and flexibility. This is what Ellison means when he says that there were no articulate investments in cultural styles; for surely, as he knows well, the cultural styles themselves were already there, embodied in the repertoires of slave musicians as they set out to create a new music.

Language provides us with another such example. A category of languages called "Creoles" is represented by many tongues spoken by Afro-Americans, in such New World areas as Haiti, Surinam, the Dutch Leeward Islands (Aruba, Bonaire, and Curaçao), the British and French Lesser Antilles, and Louisiana. These languages usually have lexicons that are readily attributed in large part to one or another European language, such as French or Spanish; but the ancestry of their grammars is not so easily determined. Some authorities believe that the grammars are—on at least some levels—African, though there is considerable controversy about this point; in any case, the grammars are not clearly and unmistakably Indo-European. Many linguists believe that the majority of creole languages originated under special conditions of contact between Europeans and Africans, either on the West African coast or in the Caribbean colonies. In a number of cases, however, the creole language eventually became the language of a whole people or nation. Thus Haitian Creole is the national language of Haiti, even though French has always been its official language.

Though it serves useful scientific purposes to determine the origins of particular words and usages in the case of each creole idiom, other scientifically provocative questions concern the nature of creole languages themselves, and the processes of their emergence. Thus, to give a single example, Haitian Creole has numerous words (such as *akansan, marassa, ouanga, afiba,* and the names of many plants, religious ceremonies, and gods) of clearly African origin. But the phrase structure of Creole gives us examples that may or may not be African, yet are not certainly Indo-European. The processes of creole language-formation were in one sense social, involving the interaction of small numbers of people who spoke European languages with large numbers of people who spoke different African languages. In another regard, these processes were linguistic, involving the adaptation of old content to new uses. As in the case of music, people were busily creating new, synthetic forms out of older materials, both their own and those they borrowed.

Though they may have begun as a means of communication between masters who spoke one language and slaves who spoke several or many different languages, pidgin tongues of this kind eventually came to be the native (read "creole") languages of whole slave communities and—as in the case of Haiti—even of whole countries. One linguist has called such languages the "unwanted step-children of linguistic science," but he has also noted their unusual linguistic character and the even more unusual social circumstances under which they arose (Lounsbury, 1968: 205–6). What is so remarkable about these languages is that they could develop under repressive social conditions until they became the first or native languages of millions of people, even becoming literary languages in some instances. It is not their particular historical roots alone, but also the ways in which they grew, that makes them especially interesting to the Afro-Americanist. And in this perspective, it is not the precise historical origins of a word, a meaning, a phrase, an instrument, or a rhythm that matters, so much as the creative genius of the users, molding older cultural substances into new and unfamiliar patterns, without regard for "purity" or "pedigree."

Misunderstandings about the nature of culture and "cultural purity" occur within the contemporary dialogue of Afro-American studies. If three and one-half centuries of acculturation in the New World have diluted and "contaminated" once pure African cultures, it might conceivably make good sense to argue for the reconstitution of their original purity. But this would mean, among other things, the reconstitution of cultural forms that have in many cases vanished in Africa itself. Nor is this the only difficulty; here is an example of another. In much of West Africa—doubtless the principal source of the ancestors of today's Afro-Americans—islamization of native peoples was an ongoing process during centuries of the slave trade. Such islamization meant, of course, the

supplanting of ancient indigenous African religions by "foreign"—
originally non-African—religious beliefs and practices. In the abstract, this implies that in the interest of consistency a quest for
African cultural purity would require a rejection of Islam among
West Africans, and a reversion to pre-Islamic belief and practice.
Yet surely such an idea would be poorly received by the Muslims
of Northern Nigeria, for instance, who no doubt consider themselves quite as African as their "pagan" (that is, non-Muslim)
neighbors.

Or consider a parallel New World example. In many Afro-
American religious groups, elements from African religions and
from Christianity have been synthesized into new bodies of belief.
Thus, for instance, Catholic saints are merged with African gods,
as when the Yoruba Ogun, the Dahomean god of iron and smiths,
Gun, appears as St. George, St. Peter, or St. James the Apostle.
In Hispanic Afro-America, St. James is sometimes called Santiago
Matamoros—St. James the Moor-killer—since he is supposed to
have appeared miraculously during the Reconquest, fighting on the
side of Catholic Spain. It would be difficult, one supposes, to con-
vince those who believe Santiago Matamoros and Ogun to be one
and the same god that he should be expunged from their religion
because his presence dilutes or "contaminates" the African past.

The argument here, then, is that we must conceptualize Afro-
American cultures not simply as historically derived bodies of
materials, as patterns of and for behavior, but also as materials
actively employed by organized human groupings in particular social contexts. Without the dimension of human action, of choices
made and pursued—of maneuver—culture could be regarded as
a lifeless collection of habits, superstitions, and artifacts. Instead,
we see that culture is *used;* and that any analysis of its use immediately brings into view the arrangements of persons in social groups,
for whom cultural forms confirm, reinforce, maintain, change, or
deny particular arrangements of status, power, and identity.

But such validations or denials through the employment of cultural forms depend upon the symbolic associations—the meaning
or significance—of each usage for those who hold positions within
a given social system or subsystem. Whether it be drinking tea,
wearing an Afro hairstyle, or employing certain idiomatic expres-

sions, usages are endowed with meanings apparent to those who habitually practice them, acquire them, or invent them; and appropriate practice confirms a network of understandings, of symbolic accords, corresponding to the networks of social relations within which persons define themselves, act, and interact.

In attempts to trace or recapture the history of a particular culture, both the employment of cultural materials for social maneuver and the symbolic meanings of the forms themselves may be ignored. Yet the social and symbolic significance of such forms in maintaining or changing a society, or the relative positions of the individuals and groups within it, is of primary importance. In fact, the very search for the "origins" of cultural forms may itself be part of social maneuver; if we seek to "prove" that the North Americans invented political democracy, there is implicit in the search the premise that political democracy is a good thing to have invented. Much the same holds true for monotheism, the phonetic alphabet, and the internal-combustion engine; few polemicists set out to prove that their ancestors invented blood sacrifice, the sexual double standard, or the ambush, unless these practices have been either ennobled or repudiated in the interim.

This is by no means to say that the study of historical origins and diffusion is empty of intellectual meaning. Demonstrating that the aboriginal peoples of the New World, Asia, and Africa have contributed massively to the world's total repertory of skills and resources—for example, in terms of domesticated plants and animals, engineering and the sciences, philosophy and aesthetics—has had tremendous influence, both intellectually and politically. Such findings have done much to restore a sense of balance and modesty to the Western view of the world outside.

But the history of a particular skill, artifact, belief, plant, or food is not the same as its employment and the symbolic meanings it has for the members of a continuing society. Culture has "life" because its content serves as resources for those who employ it, change it, incarnate it. Human beings cope with the demands of everyday life through their interpretive and innovative skills, and their capacity for employing symbolism—not by ossifying their behavioral forms, but by using them creatively. Thus, quite aside from the question of historical origins, the cultural resources of

Afro-Americans and of Afro-American cultures are by no means
limited to those elements or complexes that are provably African
historically; such origins are far less significant than the continuing
creative employment of forms, whatever their origins, and the symbolic usages imparted to them.

## Afro-America and the Caribbean Region

At an earlier point in this chapter, it was suggested that the assumption of a direct linkage between physique and behavior underlay the whole of Afro-American social history, constituting, in
some twisted fashion, a reflection of the Afro-American tradition
itself. In practice, and throughout the Hemisphere, the perceived
physical differences between Afro-Americans and other Americans
has served as a basis for social and economic exclusion and isolation. In turn, this enforced separation, probably clearer and more
inviolable in the United States than anywhere else in the Americas,
has simplified the oppression of Afro-Americans and limited their
access to mobility within the wider society.

The social and economic exclusion of Afro-Americans has been
by no means complete, even in the United States, nor are the people who call themselves Afro-Americans in this country genetically
homogeneous, or even necessarily identifiable in individual cases
as having any African ancestry. Hence, if there is a community of
Afro-Americans in the United States (in the widest sense of the
term *community*), then it is bound by social ties and by cultural
affinities. It is not "race," that is, *but the perception of race differences by the majority,* which has provided an apparent genetic
underpinning for the Afro-American community in this country.
Since in the United States the cultural development of Afro-Americans has in most cases been accompanied both by the majority imputation of an inherent linkage between physique and behavior, and
by the social and economic exclusion of Afro-Americans from
large sectors of the national society and its institutions, Afro-
American culture in North America has of course been significantly
affected by these accompaniments. Consequently, the sociology of
prejudice, economic exploitation, and discrimination based on perceived physical differences illuminates the arena within which Afro-

American culture in this country has taken on its characteristic shape.

In the Caribbean region, however, the operation of racial bias has generally been more subtle and more complicated than in the United States. Moreover, the Caribbean region, with its more than fifty island and assorted mainland societies, embraces a wide range of local codes of race relations. Even a casual observer will be struck by the differing tenor of social relations in, say, Puerto Rico, Haiti, and Jamaica; were one to add Trinidad and one of the very small, historically somewhat untypical islands, such as Saba or Aruba or Providencia, the picture would be even more complex. It might be possible to chart the differences according to such criteria as the changing relative proportions of Africans and Europeans in each society through the centuries, the varying slavery codes and their varying effectiveness, and the importance or unimportance of the plantation system in each local case; but such is not the point of this presentation. Rather, it needs to be stressed that the perception of race differences by the majority, which has so consistently shored up the operation of racial oppression in the United States, simply has not functioned in the same ways in Caribbean societies. To begin with, in many Caribbean societies—in Haiti or Jamaica, for instance—phenotypically black people *are* the majority. Again, great variations exist in the local codes of social assortment by which persons of intermediate appearance are perceived and treated as members of one social segment rather than another, and in no Caribbean case may one confidently assume a bipolar "racial" system—"white" and "Negro"—of the sort operative for white North Americans. Finally, it should be noted that many Caribbean societies have waged political struggles against their European colonial masters, and problems of race have usually been embedded in wider questions of colonial exploitation, rather than the other way around. There are many other reasons why the Caribbean cases must be viewed differently from that of the United States; but these will be taken up later.

For the purposes of this book, the definition of the Caribbean region has been restricted to the islands extending from Trinidad, Aruba, Bonaire, Curaçao, Margarita, and others off the coast of Venezuela in the south, to Jamaica, Cuba, Hispaniola, and Puerto

Rico—the Greater Antilles—in the north, including all of those islands which stretch in an arc nearly 2,000 miles long from Trinidad to westernmost Cuba, and a few outliers, such as San Andrés and Providencia. We are dealing here with more than fifty inhabited island societies, ranging in size from a few square miles—as is the case for Dutch Saba, English Carriacou, or French Marie Galante—to Cuba, with its 44,000 square miles of area. In terms of contemporary populations, we go from Cuba's more than 8 million inhabitants down to local populations of a few thousands or less.

All of the Caribbean islands lie within a subtropical zone, Trinidad just north of ten degrees north latitude, Cuba at approximately twenty-three degrees north latitude. With climates that may truly be described as "balmy," and possessing soils of unexampled fertility when first invaded by the Europeans, it is hardly surprising that the Caribbean islands were to become the first major sphere of Western colonialism outside Europe itself, the site of the first important overseas capitalist experiments, and the starting place for tropical estate agriculture, the plantation system, and the large-scale New World enslavement of African peoples.

The social history of the Caribbean region shares much both with the South American mainland societies stretching from Brazil northward and with the United States South. Yet the meaning of the Caribbean for Afro-America may be considered apart from these other grand regions, which, together with the Antilles, constitute the core area of Afro-America itself. It was in the Antilles that European force of arms—not to mention European diseases—first put down and destroyed large aboriginal populations; it was in the Antilles that the sugarcane was first imported for world market production; it was in the Antilles that plantations were first established in the New World; and it was in the Antilles that New World slavery reached a dreadful pinnacle of intensity. Even today, the Antilles symbolize, in their variety and complexity, the whole of nearly five full centuries of European hegemony. Here we have the site of the first significant European colony outside Europe itself—Santo Domingo, settled by men from Columbus's crew on the first voyage; and on the same island we find the Republic of Haiti, the first black republic and the second independent nation in the Hemisphere. In the Antilles, some colonies—such as Barbados, from 1625 until 1966—remained the wards of European masters for the whole of their post-Columbian history. Others were the sites of some of the most brilliant and terrifying revolutions in the modern world. The first American Indian rebellion against the European invaders and conquerors took place on Santo Domingo, as did the first armed resistance of African slaves against their masters.

Within this setting, we seek to define the significance of Afro-Americans for the Caribbean, and of the Caribbean for Afro-Americans. Lowenthal (1960) has stressed effectively the very considerable variability of scale in Caribbean societies. Of the approximately 21,000,000 people in the Caribbean islands, perhaps 85 percent live in societies of more than 1,000,000 inhabitants; less than 10 percent live in societies of from 100,000 to 1,000,000; and only a small fraction in societies of less than 10,000. Though more than half of all Caribbean societies have populations of less than 10,000, the combined populations of islands with under 10,000 people make up only a trivial proportion of the population of the entire area. Thus, the Caribbean region is a highly divided, insular, and small-scale region, as compared with much of the rest of the world.

Let us examine these figures from the point of view of language, in order to fill in further the nature of Caribbean diversity. The major official languages are the European languages of the conquerors: English, French, Dutch, and Spanish. Yet we have noted that the first language of the bulk of the Haitian people is a Creole. The language of the people in the Dutch islands of Aruba, Bonaire, and Curaçao is Papiamento, likewise a Creole. The language of Martinique, Guadeloupe, and their outliers is a French-based Creole, as is the language of a substantial part of the populations of Grenada, Dominica, St. Lucia, and Trinidad. Lucumí, a dialect of Nigerian Yoruba, is still spoken by a number of Cubans. In Trinidad, as in Jamaica, Hindi is still important to most of the descendants of migrants from India, at least for special purposes, while the same is true of Tamil in Martinique. This linguistic diversity reflects not merely the history of the colonial powers but the history of the Caribbean peoples as well—they came from all over, and they either brought their languages with them or developed new modes of communication in new settings.

If we turn to physical type—to "race," as it is called—we confront a comparable diversity. In dealing with physical type, we began by noticing that local standards of racial classification varied widely in the Caribbean, but nowhere fit neatly with the prevailing United States stereotypes of "white" and "Negro." Hence the use of census figures as a source of description of Caribbean peoples requires care and prudence, and rarely leads to more than obvious generalities. Moreover, since the code of social relations varies from island to island, no confident inferences about behavior can be made from census data.

Speaking very generally, it can be said that among the independent nations people at least in part of African origin predominate numerically in Haiti, Barbados, and Jamaica; they are numerically significant in Santo Domingo and perhaps less so in Cuba. They are still less significant numerically in Puerto Rico, but wholly predominant in nearly all of the Lesser Antilles, with some minor exceptions, and with the major exception of Trinidad, where the population of East Indian extraction makes up nearly one-half of the total. Put another way, the population of discernible African origin in the Antilles as a whole—a matter always subject to local norms of perception and assortment—probably makes up at least 75 percent of the total. The importance and meaning of racial identity in these societies varies significantly from one to another and, to a considerable extent, within the social fabric of each component society. Allowing for all of these qualifiers, the fact remains, however, that the Caribbean region is a core area of contemporary Afro-America.

If we turn from physique to ethnicity and culture, the picture grows yet more complicated and diverse. Some elements of the aboriginal Amerind cultures of the Antilles are still perpetuated in local life—thus, for instance, certain words, foods, and beliefs are attributable to the cultures of the Native Americans who lived in the islands before the Europeans came. Again, much of the content of the local cultures of the Antilles may be traced to Europe, since the Europeans first conquered and colonized the islands, enslaving or killing off or assimilating genetically their Amerind predecessors.

A third and highly diverse source of Caribbean cultures was, of course, Africa. African peoples began to colonize the Antilles as slaves, soon after the islands' "discovery" by the Europeans, and the African contribution to contemporary Caribbean life has been massive. But there were many other sources besides these. Over the centuries, an endless search for plantation labor was carried on by the Europeans, who, in addition to Africans both enslaved and free, imported vast numbers of Indians (from India), Chinese, and Javanese, and even the impoverished of Europe itself to man the mills and plant the fields. As a result, the Caribbean islands early became settings in which peoples of very different pasts but fairly similar presents jostled together in new social settings. The cultural accompaniments have been heterogeneity and diversity, as well as a remarkable amount of innovation in style.

Most North Americans think of the Antilles as "black countries" because their populations are in large part of African origin. But in almost every island, different gradations coexist and interpenetrate, and all of the Caribbean societies reveal blendings and separatisms, side by side. Thus, a search for Africa in the Caribbean is among other things, an exploration of the nature of cultural disguise. Here one sees a wide variety of usages that appear to be rooted, in one way or another, in the African past; but such usages are often interpenetrated by others. The result is neither a seamless synthesis nor a potpourri; and the different blendings (and nonblendings) that typify Caribbean culture cannot be explained or summarized in a few sentences. Above all, it is important to separate out what people do from what they think about what they do —a distinction too rarely drawn in the study of social history. Only rarely do people invest their consciousness and their daily energies with a concern for the historical origins of one or another belief, practice, value, material object, tradition, or skill. It is usually only when an ideological—in such cases, often political—significance attaches to the interpretation of the past that people seek deliberately to identify or specify the provenience of particular bits of culture. And, as suggested earlier, such searches are often accompanied by an interpretive predisposition on the side of cultural intactness, or purity, even though culture is typified precisely by its capacity to change and to accommodate.

In the Caribbean region, East Indian, Chinese, Javanese, black, and white live side by side. Though they do not share a common culture indiscriminately, their lifeways crisscross and interdigitate; those interested in origins must tease out single elements of belief and practice, and often enough the findings are not wholly or clearly attributable to any specific place or time. Occasionally, such attributions are firm and—since they are rare enough—resoundingly satisfying. Thus, for instance, when Bascom (1952) compares Cuban (Lucumí) and Yoruba (Nigerian) divination ceremonies, he offers us overwhelming evidence of their African origins; what is more, the tribal attributions are reasonably precise and may be accepted with confidence. A great many specific elements and even complexes—that is, interlocking small systems of culture traits and practices—are as readily and surely attributed, including Herskovits's (1929, 1932) distributional study of the game called *wari,* or *adjiboto,* found in so much of Afro-America. Words, phrases, names (including gods' names and rich theological lexicons), foods, musical forms and practices, and a great deal else can be traced with reasonable success to the African past.

But the main difficulty with studies of cultural origins has rested with the majority of cases in which a confident attribution is not yet possible. Thus, to take but one example, the nine-night mourning ceremony of the Jamaican people (Beckwith 1929: 77 et seq.; Simpson 1957) might be attributed to either Europe or to Africa. It is not particularly useful to explain its popularity by resort to the postulation of a common Euro-African cultural substratum underlying the diverse and complex cultural traditions of both continents (Herskovits 1941: 18, cited in Smith 1965: 29). Searches for origins, if they are to serve scientific purposes, need to distinguish among form, content, and symbolic meanings, and to attempt to document the processes by which change can occur in the form, content, and meanings of particular traditions. Otherwise, such studies run the risk of becoming only celebrations rather than documentary interpretations of the past, sometimes of a past made mythical by careless history. Perhaps a trivial example can clarify this.

While doing fieldwork in Haiti, I undertook to collect lexical materials to cover the terminology for domestic animal anatomy, butchering, and cooked foods. These three lexicons, if complete, should reveal something about the way rural Haitian folk perceive their animal food sources, and much else. But at the outset, I was only interested in learning and recording new words and—in a very amateurish sense—their meanings. As my lists grew, I began to notice a very curious feature: words of possible or probable African origin were entirely absent from the anatomical and butchering categories, but occurred with some frequency in the cooked-food category. This feature may contrast usefully with changes in English following the Norman Conquest, when French terms for cuts of meat and for cooked foods entered the language—their meanings partly changing in the process—but French anatomical terms apparently did not. In the case of the Norman influence on English, it is generally assumed that the conquerors' culinary prestige led to the adoption of such terms as beef, veal, and mutton but that French butchering practices and terminology were not borrowed. In the case of the Haitian people, it may be that the slaves learned French terminology for animal anatomy and cuts of meat, consonant with their acculturation to plantation life, but that when they were able to prepare their food in their own quarters, the African names could persist. This, at any rate, is a guess I have made; but it will take far more research than I have done to confirm or disprove it. Again, the emphasis might better be on the innovative skill and resourcefulness of the people, than on any automatic fidelity to tradition.

In recent years, scholars interested in the African tradition in the Americas have unfortunately grown less patient, not more, with the tedious documentary and field research required to pin down specific origins for words, traits, beliefs, values, and material objects. There has been a growing tendency to postulate general "African" traditions or origins for a wide variety of contemporary phenomena: family structure and familial authority patterns; religious content and form, as well as specific symbolisms; life-attitudes and cosmologies; and much else. Frustrated by the painstaking (and often inconclusive) research that detailed searches for origins requires, some students of the African tradition have found

it easier to project an African "ethos" or "epistemology" to which
the widest possible variety of contemporary cultural forms may
be articulated.

The foremost exponent of this approach is probably Janheinz
Jahn, whose book *Muntu* has exerted an unusual influence on
Afro-Americanists. In *Muntu,* Jahn sets forth to his own satisfaction an integral picture of African culture that embraces the Old
World and the New, the present and the past. This exposition requires some suspension of critical historical judgment by the
reader, and the author justifies the need to "risk the leap to Africa"
(1961: 26) by reference to his prior examination of New World
contemporary Afro-American cultural manifestations. Several quo-
tations may help to clarify Jahn's (1961: 26–27) methodology:

> We must make this leap, for philosophy, which is presented in the
> fourth chapter, *Ntu,* is the foundation of African culture. . . . Ka-
> game, Ogotommêli, Tempels have expounded and systematized the
> philosophy of the Bantu, the Ruandese, and the Dogon. Their basic
> principles agree, although the peoples from whom these ideas stem
> live in different parts of Africa. Thus we are presenting here that
> common denominator which allows us to interpret the whole of
> African culture, both old and new.

Or, again:

> The concepts are taken from the language in which they are first
> mentioned. Thus, *Magara* is a concept of the Kinyaruanda, *Nommo*
> a concept of the language of the Dogon. If a term has once been used
> it is retained even though the thing it designates has an entirely dif-
> ferent name in some other area. Since African culture appears as a
> unity, it makes no difference from which African language a term
> is derived. Nor do the terms need to come from a single language;
> thus we are able in each case to choose terms that are easy to re-
> member. The reader should not be alarmed if, for example, Bantu
> and Dogon concepts are used in speaking of a Yoruba mask.

Contained in these passages are a number of postulates concerning the nature of culture—and its relationship to language—that
would not prove equally acceptable to all. Moreover, the concept
of a unified or common culture not subject to qualifications of time
and space raises serious questions for the historically minded social

scientist, questions not readily resolved by postulation. These and other questions inevitably arise when the cultures of entire large areas, such as aboriginal North America, or Africa, are treated as homogeneous, or as samples of one culture. While it is not the purpose of this introduction to attempt definitively to refute such concepts, the theoretical questions they raise must at least be mentioned, with particular reference to the Caribbean region and its history.

It is essential, finally, to take note of the relevance of culture and cultural origins to political ideologies and ethnic consciousness. Stress has been laid here on the difference between what people actually do and their expression of what they do as a measure of their identity. This difference becomes particularly acute in political situations in which people struggle to define themselves vis-à-vis some other society or social group. In the simplest terms, people can be rallied to a political position in terms of perceived needs and goals, and this commonly occurs around some set of values or beliefs. Political solidarity requires the expression of a common interest, at least for specific purposes, and such an interest can be made to adhere to the perception of a common past, a common consciousness, or a common code of behavior. Culture, in the widest sense, is a repository of practices, values, and ideas into which political leaders can dip in creating loyalties and infusing their organizations with purpose. But such undertakings must build on felt needs and, in growing, on the awakening of like needs in others.

The manipulation of symbols is an important part of the consolidation of political positions, and of the extension of such positions to embrace more adherents. Symbols—expressed in such items as flags, slogans, catechisms, modes of dress, hairstyles, foods, rituals, modes of speech, gestures, and postures—serve to make visible the solidarity of political groups and to intensify the search for additional supporters. In the growth of political movements, symbols may either arise out of the traditional cultural content of the carriers, or they may be postulated as part of the past—as in the case of the National Socialist swastika, the double-headed eagle, or the Stars and Stripes. In political terms, it does not seem to matter much whether the item behind or through which the symbolism operates is indeed an authentic part of the past; what matters is the effectiveness of the item as a means of galvanizing and dramatizing support and solidarity.

Yet, inevitably, when culture is employed in these fashions for political objectives, heated discussions about origins and identity will follow. In the case of Afro-American cultures, such discussions have been more common in North America than in Latin America, including the Caribbean. The reasons for this are by no means entirely clear; but an important reason may be that much of the political history of the Antilles has been a history of anticolonial struggle, in which the identity of peoples was put primarily in terms of the local island society versus a European (or North American) colonial oppressor, and only secondarily in terms of the real or postulated common identity of local peoples. Thus, Caribbean political symbolism in good part has been phrased on the basis of an assumed or understood common identity, rather than in terms of a struggle to prove that identity. It may well be that this contrast embodies one of the most important differences between Afro-Caribbeana and Afro–North Americana.

At the same time, there are very important ways in which the Afro-Caribbean and the Afro–United States are becoming more alike, in spite of vast historical differences and the very considerable internal differentiation of both Caribbean societies and the United States. However, such emerging likenesses—of the sort largely manifested in ideological assertions, intellectualizations of political positions, arguments for new kinds of common consciousnesses, the identification of new "enemies," the use of physical type as a rallying-base, and so on—are too frequently seen by their protagonists as stages in an unfolding one-way process. The fact is that Caribbean social history is littered with analogous movements, ideologies, and developments; the realities of power in the region have changed, while many of the ideological views have tended to remain surprisingly similar. Such views are invoked and reinvoked at different points in the history of particular Caribbean societies: pan-Africanism, pan-blackness, pan-non-whitism, anticolonialism, Marxism, Trotskyism, antimetropolitanism, proindigenism (in the sense of a local cultural authenticity), proaboriginism (in the sense of an original African cultural authenticity), and so on, are all employed at one time or another by Antillean leaders and political groups as ways to make the world intelligible and the solutions to life's problems possible. Any such attempt to explain what is wrong and how it may be repaired will vary, of course, depending on the particular society in which it is invoked, and the circumstances of its invocation. But the problems which political ideologies have sought to explain in the Caribbean region are, in certain senses, cruel, ancient, and obvious—though often far less obvious than the proposed solutions.

It was argued earlier that the uses to which African slaves were put in the Caribbean region between its "discovery" and the total abolition of slavery were "industrial" uses, even though they often were concealed within a rural setting. After slavery, the same major modes of labor use persisted; the Caribbean region continued to serve as an arena of European imperial power, its economic character largely framed by the plantation system, its governments the puppets of the metropolises, its labor drawn from elsewhere by a variety of schemes, all marked by elements of coercion and deception.

Whereas certain other parts of the colonial world—in Africa, Asia, and mainland Latin America—changed significantly in their relationship to European centers of power, the colonial position of the Caribbean region tended to remain depressingly unchanged. Thus there is no ground for surprise that the more radical solutions proposed by Caribbean ideologues should appear and reappear, somewhat modified by locale and circumstances, but essentially as responses to the profoundly disadvantaged position in which Caribbean peoples have for so long been confined.

The three crudest, yet most important, ways in which Caribbean politics differ from North American politics are the colonialism of the Caribbean region, the smallness of its societies, and the predominance of nonwhites in its populations. It is perfectly true that these societies lack "a tradition of democratic procedures" on the highest political level, and that their populations are poor, rural, and illiterate. But such background circumstances do not explain Caribbean political ideologies so much as they attest to the consequences of European colonialism over nearly five centuries of rule. Indeed, political leaders and would-be leaders must take poverty, rurality, and illiteracy into account in the development of their positions; but these are precisely the conditions that evoke the need for political action in the first place.

## About this Book

The following chapters attempt to put some of these wider political and economic issues into more homely, local, and everyday contexts. They deal with matters more conventionally anthropological and matter-of-fact, both viewed in the past and in the present. It seems to me immensely important to maintain an insistence on the sociopolitical significance of the tyranny of everyday life— whether we analyze contemporary black power movements, slave revolts, or the growth of a nation. Throughout history, the massive struggles of whole peoples to discover and claim their own destiny have been waged against a background in which love, hate, personal loyalty, the rewards of propinquity and familiarity, and the ordinary pleasures of existence continue to make irrevocable claims upon the human spirit. The peoples of the Caribbean, predominantly poor, rural, agricultural, and illiterate, have been as subject to these claims as any other peoples in world history. Crops must be planted, cultivated, and harvested; babies must be conceived and born; young people must fall in love; old people must be cared for. The animal and spiritual needs of all human beings demand satisfaction, no matter what the convulsions of history.

This, we have said, has been as true for Afro-Caribbean peoples as for any other. In fact, most struggles for a decent life in the Caribbean region have originated in perceived deprivation in these very regards. Thus, to attempt to document some aspects of everyday life is no more than to etch in some of the background conditions against which so-called important events occur. This, at any rate, is what the following chapters hope to suggest. They were originally written during a period stretching over nearly two decades, and deal exclusively with the Caribbean region.

In the last decade of interest in Afro-Americana in the United States, however, too little account has been taken of the significance of Afro-American societies and cultures elsewhere in the New World, such as the region I deal with here. The United States experience, however, is but one case in many, and one that will become better understood when the social histories and contemporary societies of Afro-Americans everywhere in the Hemisphere have been fully analyzed. Some useful purpose may be served, then, by describing certain major historical processes that affected the growth of Afro-American societies in another part of the Americas. Where my own understanding has permitted, I have attempted to specify certain contrasts between the Antillean and North American experiences. The interested reader may be stimulated to reflect on such similarities and differences—and it was partly with this end in mind that the present book was prepared.

The islands of the Caribbean Sea and the colonies and countries of the adjacent mainland were, and to a noticeable extent remain, instruments of Euro-American policy. Their histories have been marked by contact and clash, amalgamation and accommodation, resistance and change. Such histories, however, have both political and cultural coefficients. From a political perspective, one sees the near-monopolistic exercise of military and administrative power by the European colonizers at the outset, and then the successive changes in the nature of that power, and its erosion over time. Not surprisingly, political histories of the Caribbean region have largely been written with the view from Downing Street or the Quai d'Orsay in mind, and their major distortions have flowed from this limitation. If the intent is to provide a cultural perspective, Caribbean history not only should not, but cannot, be written from a metropolitan vantage point. The region has been one of the truly great arenas for the interpenetration of African, European, Amerind, Asian, and other traditions, and the values, life-styles, attitudes, and behaviors of its peoples reflect that fact.

In recent years, however, it has become fashionable to speak of writing Caribbean history "from the inside" (e.g., Patterson 1967; Williams 1970). Such a view was at one time a badly needed countermeasure to imperial historiography. Too much of the Antillean past was made by its own peoples for the imperial view to prevail. Yet the best of future Caribbean histories will probably exclude neither the colonial powers on the one hand nor the peoples of the Caribbean on the other. Caribbean history has been characterized primarily by encounter, difference, and differential power—

it has been a history, if one wishes, of fighting back. Since the Caribbean peoples, Afro-Americans included, had no time for the luxury of jousting either with windmills or with specters, their history must deal both with themselves and their antagonists. In various chapters of this book, I have therefore attempted to view the Caribbean past from both the inside and the outside. The balance between these approaches has been determined by the nature of the themes themselves, rather than according to any abstract principles.

It was not, in any case, a primary concern with Africana or Afro-Americana that led me into Caribbean research. Rather, I was fascinated (if also repelled) by the effects of what has variously been called "westernization," "industrialization," "modernization," "imperialism," "colonialism," and "economic development"—depending to some extent on what one has in mind and where one stands politically—on small, poor, dependent, predominantly rural, and agrarian societies. Such effects may be seen in stark relief in the Antilles. But because of the particular history of the Caribbean region, it was inevitable that the cultures with which I was dealing were in good part African in ultimate origin— as were many of the people with whom I worked and lived.

Though I have visited many Caribbean societies briefly, I have only worked in three for lengthy enough periods to allow me to feel I know anything about them: Puerto Rico, Jamaica, and Haiti, and in that order. The significance of both cultural materials and of peoples perceived as Afro-American is different in each instance, and I can only touch on those differences here in terms of some very shallow distinctions.

Puerto Rico was a Spanish colony for nearly four centuries, and has been a United States colony for nearly seventy-five years. Though African slaves were part of the island's history for about three and one-half centuries, they never figured as importantly in Puerto Rico's history as they did in that of Jamaica and Haiti. As compared with plantation development in those societies, Puerto Rico's sufferings were relatively minor until long after slavery was abolished. While many aspects of Puerto Rican culture today are probably of ultimate African origin—rather more, I suspect, than even the most enthusiastic Afro-Americanists suppose—in contrast with Jamaica and Haiti, Puerto Rico lies on the margins of Afro-Caribbeana.

From a sociological standpoint, while physique and class distinction tend to run parallel in Puerto Rico, as they do in much of the rest of the Caribbean—those perceived as black are usually poor, and a disproportionate percentage of the poor are those perceived as black—such distinctions are much less starkly revealed here than elsewhere. From a cultural standpoint, the Afro-American component is subtle, interwoven, and reworked, even in such categories as terms of racial reference, dance and other expressive media, and language. The reasons for such subtlety are complicated and do not originate solely in the demographic history of the island. The genetic and social interpenetration of whites and blacks, the tempo of manumission over the centuries, and the ideology of a single Puerto Rican culture—even in the presence of discriminatory racial attitudes—militated against any kind of black consciousness, any harking back to the African past, any politically rooted perpetuation of separateness on the part of Puerto Rico's people of color. And it is worth remarking that—from the point of view of the politics of color—this still holds true in Puerto Rico itself, though much less so for Puerto Ricans living in the mainland United States.

Jamaica provides a startling contrast. Between its conquest by the Spaniards and its seizure by the British in 1655, Jamaica remained a Spanish imperial backwater; under Britain, it became the queen of sugar, slavery, and mercantilism. When Emancipation was declared, in 1838, only a small fraction of Jamaica's population was white, while another small fraction was of "mixed" ancestry and free. In the subsequent 124 years before Independence, Jamaica evolved social forms that allowed tiny white and "coloured" minorities to maintain their dominance over a massive Afro-American society. But the prevailing distinctions among black, "coloured," and white were traditionally conceived of in terms of colonialism and class, while race—and, hence, "Africanism"—was viewed as a corollary of exploitation and dependence, rather than as its cause. Hence, whereas Afro-Americana in Puerto Rico seems subtle and diffuse, in Jamaica it was often concealed (or, at least, unnoticed), partly because of the nature of the social structure, partly by ideological considerations that put colonialism before color, partly by class and urban-rural distinctions.

Haiti offers yet another sharp contrast. Like Jamaica, Santo Domingo was a Spanish colonial hinterland, for the most part, until the western third was ceded to France, in 1697. From that year until the Haitian Revolution, at the close of the eighteenth century, French Saint Domingue became a thoroughly "africanized" society, ruled by a small group of French colonial masters, and a comparably small but aggressive and gallicized group of freemen of color. After the Revolution, the plantation economy in ruins and most members of the controlling classes dead or in exile, Haiti "re-africanized" itself in culturally important ways. But this process did not become a matter of self-conscious concern until the United States occupation, 1915–34, when the African component of Haitian culture became a thing of pride for many Haitian people. The pre-1915 culture of Haiti was quite sharply divided by considerations of class and race, its ruling group distinguished by its lighter skin color, its use of French, its conventional Catholicism, and its admiration for French civilization. The African elements in popular Haitian life were recognized but not valued. But the North American occupation exposed the weakness of Haitian francophilia, and demanded of Haiti's elite a recognition of their African, as well as of their European, cultural roots. This new tendency is symbolized by Jean Price-Mars's magnificent *Ainsi parla l'Oncle* (1928), the creation of an ethnological tradition, the appearance of creole poetry, and much else in Haitian life after 1915. Whereas Afro-Americana in Puerto Rico is subtle and diffuse, while in Jamaica it was ignored or buried, in Haiti it has long been everyday and matter-of-fact for most people. However, it became politically relevant only when the ruling group faced the consequences of the impositions of North American culture and power.

It is extremely difficult to perceive such differences in the field, to attempt to study and document them systematically and objectively as parts of everyday life. The study of other cultures poses a common problem expressed in the different perceptions of the observer and the people he seeks to understand. In societies such as those of the Caribbean, this problem is complicated in part by the way its observers look and think, by their images of themselves and the images others may have of them. Thus, a difficulty present in any field study of a culture conducted by an observer whose cultural background is different may be compounded by the presence of superficial similarities between the observer's culture and the one which he or she wishes to describe. The very westernness of Caribbean cultures can contribute to their enigmatic quality, concealing their distinctiveness under apparent likeness.

A white North American, for instance, is likely to perceive any Afro-Caribbean culture as a variant of Afro-American culture in the United States; a black North American may do the same, though with significant differences in perception. Each will probably be influenced by stereotyped thinking, rooted in preconceptions transferred from the dominant tenor of race relations, culture, and the quality of racism in the United States itself. It may be some time before any North American visitor—of whatever physical type—gets to recognize Afro-Caribbean cultures on their own terms, rather than in terms of dominant contrasts or similarities with the North American experience.

But this difficulty does not hinge solely on questions of physique and race relations. North Americans often see Caribbean societies as startlingly small in scale, archaic, poor, and poky—sometimes, as rather tawdry imitations of the European master-societies (in the case of Puerto Rico and the United States Virgin Islands, of the North American master-society) that forced their creation or perpetuate their past. This misperception has little to do with racism as such; its far wider relevance is the fundamental contrast between the so-called developed and underdeveloped worlds, and our disposition to use so crude a binary division in attempting to make the world interpretable. Race, surely, is one dimension of the difficulty; but it is by no means the sole explanation of the outsized mote in the North American's (or European's) eye.

The fact is that the Caribbean region, as the first overseas outpost of European imperialism and capitalism, was "westernized," "modernized," and "developed" before most of the colonial world had even become colonial, and that the peoples of the Caribbean—whatever their physical type—are the peculiarly disfranchised beneficiaries of centuries of Western capitalist solicitude. They are illiterate rather than nonliterate; countrified rather than rural; urbanized, but nearly without cities; industrialized, but without factories—and, often, agricultural, but without land. Their poverty, rural styles, and agricultural dependence make them look like most of the Third World; but the similarities are deceptive and untrustworthy. Within these terms, however, one perceives another reason why outsiders—and, sometimes, even insiders!—have trouble seeing what Caribbean peoples and cultures are really like.

As I have tried to suggest, every culture in the Americas is a newly mixed, or "mongrelized," culture; but since every culture in history has been "mongrelized," the Americas merely dramatize in this regard what has sometimes been carefully concealed elsewhere. What may be less easy to grasp is that Caribbean cultures, in this context, are as integral as any others in the Americas, and that all of them are in some fundamental sense American. Hence I believe that none of the following chapters deals with anything that one could properly label "African culture." All however, deal with Afro-American cultures—that is, with cultures whose repertoires include substantial profoundly altered materials of positive, probable, or putative African origin. Our uncertainty about origins is caused in part by the transmutation that typified the transfer of Old World cultures to the New—broken, disordered, fragmented, in disrepair—and this was as true for the cultures of Europe as for those of Africa and Asia.

The point is important. Because African peoples reached the Hemisphere under horrifying conditions and were thereupon thrust into lifelong servitude, the seemingly inadequate or imperfect or much-modified transfers believed to typify Afro-American cultures seem completely understandable. What is not so clearly recognized is that *any* people forming distant colonies faces the problems inherent in such transfers, and that the solutions never provide a mirror image of the motherland, no matter how faithful the memories of the migrants. Because in most cases the carriers of European cultures came to the New World under conditions far more favorable than those faced by enslaved Africans, there is an understandable tendency to suppose that European cultural continuities are reasonably clear and intact. The facts are otherwise.

In the view of older, more consolidated cultures, all New World peoples are—in some basic cultural sense—callow, uncritical restless and innovative. Moreover, we New World peoples who are white, or who too eagerly accept our European cultural continuities, tend to be biased accordingly. Thus, when we seek to account for a particular habit, practice, belief, usage, attitude, or material object by saying that its origins are both European and African, there is a tendency on our part to suppose that the European origins are in some way decisive—or even (this view is not remarkable, but it is worth watching it slip in by the back door) that the moral or aesthetic value of the item in question depends on the "percentage" of European versus African elements it displays.

Much of the anthropological and culture-historical research conducted in the Caribbean regions has dealt with the question of African origins and the remolding of African cultures, as exemplified best in the studies of Melville and Frances Herskovits and their students (see, for instance, Herskovits 1941; Merriam, Whinery, and Fred 1956; Waterman 1943; Price 1955; and Bascom 1941, 1951). This valuable and stimulating body of research is little touched on directly in the following chapters, however, since their conception was not guided by any primary concern with origins. That such origins do, indeed, matter greatly in our understanding of Caribbean culture goes without saying. But most of the following chapters are concerned more with particular types of synthesis or reconstitution than with the specification of some proven, probable, or putative African component.

This book has been organized in terms of several themes, each of which I regard as of some importance for the understanding of contemporary Caribbean life. It could be argued with justice that such principles of organization are largely arbitrary; the chapters might have been grouped geographically instead, or according to some other rule of assortment. But the sequence of categories bespeaks my own view of Caribbean social history. From the moment of the initial clash of European and Amerindian in the region, the central problem of the colonizer was that of controlling supplies of disciplined labor. A variety of legislative subterfuges were invented, often in covert opposition to metropolitan policy, to keep labor defenseless and obedient; modified forms of control reminiscent of the European past—indenture and debt-peonage, for instance—were employed for this purpose. But the major means of labor control was slavery, and I, at least, am convinced that the slavery of Afro-America was qualitatively different from any previous mode of bondage known to history. The first part of the book therefore deals primarily with Caribbean slavery and only incidentally with other modes of labor coercion in the region.

Though slavery typified whole sectors of Caribbean societies and, in a few cases, underlay the entire social structure, its principal mode of implementation for economic purposes was the plantation system. That system, which the Trinidadian historian Eric Williams once described as combining the worst features of feudalism and capitalism with the virtues of neither, is dealt with in the lengthy final chapter of Part I. The plantation system, however, survived slavery; hence that chapter deals with both slavery and postslavery plantation adaptations.

The counterpoint to slavery and the plantation system was provided by a wide variety of small-scale tenure arrangements, ranging from illegal squatting on crown lands to genuine freehold, and from almost total agricultural self-sufficiency to a lively involvement with national or world markets on the part of the small-scale producer. Within this range of variable responses to the hold of the plantation system and all it stood for, the most important social types were the peasantries. The term *peasant* has hardly any currency in North American thinking, and it has been restored to its former sociological significance only in recent years (e.g., Wolf 1966; Landsberger 1970; Shanin 1971; Mintz 1973). Not only is there a continuing lack of clarity about the definition and significance of the peasantry as a sociological category, but the term itself is used loosely, and with various meanings, in social science literature. When we turn to the Caribbean region, the confusion is confounded. Sometimes "peasant" is even used to mean any country dweller who works the land; such sloppiness of usage has typified both Right and Left, for instance, in debates over the Cuban Revolution and its roots (Mintz 1974). But a new concern with the myriad meanings of rural life is now growing, and serious scholars can no longer so easily employ broad terminological labels to conceal their fogginess.

In Part II, I have attempted to set forth some assertions about the origins of peasant groupings in the Caribbean region, and about the typology of such groupings as well. I have also tried to deal in some ways with the inner workings of peasant life. Here we turn wholly away from the plantation system as sociological "revelation"—that is, as a unitary explanation of Caribbean societies—to its logical and historical opposite. The peasantries, once defined, deserve to be described in terms of their life-styles, their ways of coping, their modes of adaptation. Here, perhaps more than in other parts of this book, a sense of "the African" may be conveyed. It is not at all the intent of this part to document, in some mechanical fashion, elements that can be certainly or probably attributed to Africa, but to make a more general point about the rationality, enterprise, and resourcefulness of Caribbean peoples. But these are folk who have preserved (some might say who have been doomed to) ways of coping whose history and quality reveal a substantial isolation from the wider world. This isolation may help, in part, to explain the seemingly archaic and traditional nature of their life-styles. However, there is an ampler meaning to the Caribbean peasant adaptation. The world—the West—looked to the Antilles for the gains that might be extracted from them. Peasant life-styles show us some of the ways in which the people respond to such demands, just as the lives of the rural proletarians on the plantations reveal others.

Finally, in Part III, I seek to describe some of the wider political and economic forces that have affected the shaping of Caribbean nationhood. Here the discussion deals less with culture, and more with the social structures of Caribbean societies: By what means have Caribbean peoples begun to identify themselves, and to draw from their pasts a richer meaning of what, and who, they are? How have the traditional social arrangements—in terms of economic classes, political groups, sociological categories—positively or negatively affected the emergence of a sense of autonomy, of belonging without dependence? I tread here on very shaky ground, particularly with regard to the significance of the African past in the

Caribbean present. But these chapters must be seen as tentative ways to ask new questions—none of which has been satisfactorily answered as yet.

The categories employed in this book are also meant to suggest something about the historical evolution of Caribbean societies. In a rough and qualified way, the categories constitute a sequence, from the enslavement and forced transportation of Africans to Caribbean plantations, through various modes of adaptation, to the emergence of nations where there were once only colonies. Having used a topical basis of grouping, I have attempted to make the chapters in each part more relevant to one another and to the central theme by supplementing, abridging, or rewriting large portions of the essays from which most of them were drawn.

Each part of the book is preceded by a brief introductory essay, the intent of which is to suggest why its theme may be significant for Caribbean social history. These are, of course, only a few themes out of many. I stress this particularly for any readers who may be trying to discover for themselves whether the study of Afro-America raises "genuine" intellectual problems. The answer to that question is—for this student, at least—emphatically affirmative; and this book is in a sense really no more than a series of suggestions justifying that response.

# I

## SLAVERY, FORCED LABOR, AND THE PLANTATION SYSTEM

By any comparative measure, Caribbean island societies are small in scale. Cuba, the largest independent Antillean country and the largest by far of all of the islands, has an area of 44,000 square miles—about the size of Pennsylvania. Haiti and the Dominican Republic (Santo Domingo), which share the region's second largest island, have a combined area of less than 30,000 square miles. Jamaica is one-tenth the size of Cuba, and Puerto Rico is even smaller; among the larger of the Lesser Antilles, Trinidad and Tobago together are slightly more than 1,000 square miles in area, while Martinique, Guadeloupe, and Barbados are far smaller. Dozens of inhabited islets are no more than a few-score square miles in total area.

The smallness of these societies, and the distances which separate them from each other, have always militated against any integrated economic or political development, against federated solutions to regional problems, and against strong feelings of common identity, even in the face of commonly felt needs. The main reason, of course, for the lack of any regional coherence has been the complicated colonial history of each territory, the persisting influence of metropolitan power, and the highly conflicting political pressures to which Caribbean peoples have been subjected for so long.

But smallness of scale and a protracted colonialism are by no means the Caribbean's only problems. These are poor places, with scanty resources in minerals, fuels, arable land, technology, and capital; labor is the only truly plentiful resource, and even labor is unevenly distributed, largely unskilled, and not well prepared for industrialization. Hence few regions exhibit so richly as do the Antilles those diverse aspects of backwardness and poverty associ-ated with the "underdeveloped world"; that this is to some extent a spurious association will become clearer, perhaps, at a later point.

Despite this background of smallness and poverty, the Carib-bean region once comprised some of the most lucrative colonies in world history. During the eighteenth century, French Saint-Domingue and English Jamaica were the richest dependencies in the world; in the nineteenth century, Cuba bid fair to occupy a similar status. Of course, in speaking of richness in such cases, one refers to the yields accruing to the metropolis rather than to the accumulation of wealth or capital within the colonies themselves. The economic successes of colonialism in the Caribbean colonies had much to do with the growth of the European "motherlands" and with the enormous expansion of European industry in the eigh-teenth and nineteenth centuries.

However, the "economic development" of the islands was largely responsible for their "underdevelopment" at a later time. The pe-culiar mix of agriculture and industry, as developed by the Euro-peans, was adapted to the assimilation of the Caribbean territories to their metropolises only in ways that made the territories them-selves increasingly backward, relative to the economic growth of the metropolises. Even while investments in Caribbean-based enterprise were growing and the Caribbean labor force steadily mounted, the situation of Caribbean peoples remained poor and often grew worse. These economic processes, which have by no means come to an end in the Caribbean region, confront us with no paradox. Rather, they express certain contrasts—often, contra-dictions—that commonly typify the spread of political power from stronger, more heavily capitalized societies to areas that are po-litically defenseless and poor.

The keystone of Caribbean "development" in past centuries was, of course, labor. As Eric Williams has pointed out (1944), without labor the Caribbean islands would have been deserts in spite of European arms, European capital and technical knowledge, and European ambitions. Yet the labor necessary to "develop" the Antilles could not be had simply for the asking. These were not pioneer revolutionary societies, drunk on newly won freedoms, to which the oppressed of other countries might come in search of the right to pray, to be economically independent, to secure their children's futures, or to become like their oppressors. They were, it is true, pioneer societies; but their frontiers were carefully closed to free men whenever possible, to prevent "uncontrolled" settlement. Hence, for most of the islands during most of their post-Columbian history, labor had to be impressed, coerced, dragged, and driven to work—and most of the time, to simplify the problems of discipline, labor was enslaved. In employing terms like *slavery* and *enslavement,* one must distinguish between technical and literary usages. Wage labor may be called "wage slavery" at times, and this imagery is understandable; but in fact free labor is not slave labor, and normally there are no wages for slaves. Slavery was but one mode of relating Caribbean labor to the land, and while other modes serving this purpose also contained elements of coercion, this did not make them identical with slavery.

Following the conquest of Santo Domingo (Española) and its neighbors, the aboriginal populations were concentrated, for the most part, in subject villages, so that their labor could be exacted efficiently by the Spanish conquerors in mines, on farms, and elsewhere. Legally, Native Americans who accepted Spanish rule and Christianity could not be enslaved; they were, technically, vassals of the Crown. To hundreds of thousands who died in vain, and from disease, overwork, and maltreatment, it could not have mattered in the least whether they were "legally" enslaved or not. But, in fact, Spanish imperial policy grew out of the Caribbean experience, and that policy evolved only after considerable struggle in the metropolis.

It was also the Spaniards who first employed African slaves on Caribbean enterprises, beginning within about a decade of the "discovery." Since there was no effective territorial challenge to Spain in the Caribbean until about 1625, Spanish policy reigned alone in the islands for perhaps 135 years, in spite of the clandestine trade, the smuggling, the attacks on ports and fleets, and the constant diplomatic pressures exerted by Spain's enemies. By and large, the local long-range effects of this first epoch of European rule in the Americas—the rule of Spain in the Greater Antilles— were the destruction of the aboriginal island populations without their effective replacement by any other, and the founding of the West's first important overseas colonies. However, this statement must be qualified. What distinguishes the Caribbean colonies is not only their ancientness, but also their function as areas of settlement, their role as hosts for migrant subject populations, and the particular forms of agro-industrial enterprise that flourished so early within them. They were not, in other words, ports of trade, of the sort common in the Mediterranean and in Asia at an earlier time, but parts of Europe in what was, from the fifteenth century onward, a qualitatively different variety of colonialism.

Beginning around 1625, however, France, Britain, and Holland began to challenge Spain's Caribbean hegemony effectively, first in the lesser islands and, by the middle of the century, in the Greater Antilles as well. Ultimately, Spain's rivals took the islands far more seriously than had Spain itself. The Spanish conquest of the mainland, starting with Cortes's mastery of Mexico, had justifiably diverted imperial ambitions from the islands, whose importance seemed slight in comparison with that of the mainland colonies, which extended from what is today the southern United States to the southern tip of South America. For the rest of Western Europe, the Caribbean islands continued to loom importantly, however; and Spain's three major rivals would see those islands fulfill their promise.

Again, labor was the crucial factor in development, and the first such labor, once the fast-dwindling supply of aborigines was exhausted, was European—not enslaved, but "transported." The indenture system, as employed by both Britain and France, was a thinly veiled form of coercion, but it was not slavery. Soon, however, enslaved Africans supplanted the English indentured servants and the French *engagés,* first in the smaller colonies (such as Bar-

bados and Guadeloupe), and later in the larger (such as Jamaica
and Saint-Domingue). Beginning about 1650, slave labor became
identified with Africa and Africans. Thereafter, the major means
for relating labor to Caribbean land was slavery, and this remained
true until well into the nineteenth century, when revolution and
emancipation brought new "solutions" in their wake. The last
Caribbean slaves achieved their freedom in Cuba in 1886, nearly
400 years after the first Caribbean slaves, Indian and African, were
driven into the mines and onto the plantations by their Spanish
masters. Thus slavery—and particularly the slavery of Africans—
marks almost the entire span of post-Columbian Caribbean history.
It should not be surprising, then, that the saga of the Caribbean
has always been so much a saga of slavery, and of the plantations
upon which slaves were principally concentrated.

The chapters that follow approach these themes from somewhat
different vantage points. Several basic contentions are set forth.
First, Caribbean slavery shared much with slavery in other parts
of the colonial New World, but far less with slavery elsewhere (for
instance, in pre-European Africa, imperial China, or aboriginal
America). It is certainly useful and necessary to formulate a general definition of the institution of slavery that will facilitate comparisons in time and place; but the distinctive characteristics of
European slavery in the New World need special emphasis. Though
slaves were used for many purposes in this Hemisphere—for instance, as artisans, musicians, concubines, domestic servants, subalterns, and scribes—their primary function was to serve as manual
laborers engaged in production, in production in excess of consumption, that is, in the production of market commodities, in production for the gain of the master and the metropolis. Slaves were
not *primarily* a source of prestige, of sexual gratification, of the
satisfaction of sadistic impulses, or of anything else but profit—and
of profit within a frankly capitalistic system, even though the curious view that slavery and capitalism are mutually exclusive still
persists. The slaves of the Caribbean, like those of the American
South and Brazil, were used for the creation of wealth in enterprises intimately related to world trade. These were no serfs toil-
ing on isolated manors, no captives of war endowing their masters
with prestige, but industrial workers whose work was principally

agricultural. They differed from the proletarians of Europe because they were unfree, because they were subjects in colonies rather than citizens in mother countries, and because they were rooted in vastly different cultures. Yet, in both their status and their economic function, they resembled the proletarians of Europe more than is often conceded. One may justly question the use of the term *freedom* to describe the status of the children chained to the looms of early industrial Britain. But it should not be supposed that the status of slaves and proletarians was identical because both were miserable. British mill workers were not slaves; Caribbean slaves were neither free nor Englishmen. Misery no more made these sufferers alike than their different complexions made them different.

Second, slavery was an answer to a felt need for labor. Just as the function of Caribbean slaves cannot be explained in terms of their masters' temperaments, so the need for slaves cannot be explained in terms of the masters' emotional needs. Many masters, in fact, bemoaned slavery and called it evil. Slavery did not need to be good just because it was necessary; but that it was viewed as necessary justified it more than if it had been good. It was necessary because the New World, and particularly the Antilles, lacked sufficient populations at the outset to provide the entrepreneur with a labor force whose numbers and hunger would discipline it. Since such a labor force would not materialize "freely," it would have to be dragooned. That is, the coercion employed, rather than being exercised through the "free" play of market forces, would have to be explicit and overt. In other words, if the slaves had been free, they would not have yielded a corresponding profit to the entrepreneur; indeed, had they been free and landed, they might not have done his work for him at all. So although slavery may have been considered an evil, it was considered a *necessary* evil. The received wisdom of European capitalism was often explicit on just this point. Though many slaveowners defended slavery by recounting the misfortunes of free proletarians (who had no master to look after them)—free to starve, at times—the abolitionists were equally aware of the free laborer's buying power, an economic advantage with moral implications that the slave generally lacked. Nearly everyone seemed prepared to suppose that a free man could easily outwork a slave, other things being equal;

the problem was that there were not enough hungry free men to spare the planter the need to buy slaves.

Yet the distinctiveness of New World slavery should not conceal the general motives which underlay all the modes of labor exaction in the Antilles. The third point is just that: just as the speciality of slavery deserves stress, so its similarities to other forms of coercion merit our reflection. Events occurring in the course of Caribbean history reveal clearly the underlying motives of those who made things happen; labor history is perhaps particularly enlightening in this regard. In comparing cases, one looks from similarities to differences and back again, just as one moves forward and backward in time, seeking cases that are truly comparable. There were many periods in the Caribbean past when slavery and other forms of labor coercion were hardly distinguishable.

A fourth point may be made about the physical type of the victims of coercion. Most of Caribbean history is black history; Europeans carried Africans to these little islands by the millions, to be used like animals to produce wealth. This process of enslavement and transport "blackened" the islands, "africanized" them, so that their cultures and their peoples are to this day in good measure African in origin. But the Europeans also oppressed peoples of other physical types as enthusiastically as they oppressed Africans—and this is the fourth point. Caribbean history is not only black history, but also yellow history, red history, brown history, and—not surprisingly—white history, so far as the testament of oppression is concerned.

Finally, a point is made about the slaves themselves. Without slaves there is no slavery; in the Caribbean, the slaves were mainly African. Though a few so-called scientists and substantial numbers of laymen may still believe that Negroes are hereditarily inferior, the saga of Caribbean slavery provides rich evidence of their attainments in the face of incredibly difficult obstacles. In Saint-Domingue, for example, within less than a century of the establishment of the French plantations, a very substantial number of freedmen of African origin owned and managed hundreds of plantations manned by scores (and possibly hundreds) of thousands of slaves. These *affranchis* were zealous in their search for legal equality, and repeatedly demonstrated themselves to be the equals, if not the superiors, of the French colonists who had spawned them upon their slave mothers. In fact, the Haitian Revolution—which ended as a servile revolution—was sparked by the attempts of the French *colons* to limit the *affranchis'* share in the benefits of French culture and plantation slavery.

But even where the blacks failed to achieve the privileges of the Saint-Domingue *affranchis*—after all, it was unusual for people of color, no matter how great their capacities, to be permitted to own slaves—they demonstrated their wit, their resourcefulness, and their insight in myriad ways. Since the resistance of slaves to slavery itself was far more typical of the chronicle of Caribbean slavery than were the accomplishments of the *affranchis,* this is the fifth point: servile resistance may take many forms, some of them by no means readily identifiable as such. In order to comprehend what made up that resistance, it is essential to set aside a variety of preconceptions about the nature of resistance. The real point here may be to spare the past the need to live up to the interpretations we impose upon it—at least long enough for us to try seriously to discover what, indeed, *did* happen.

The two chapters which follow take up these points. In the first, a general overview of New World slavery is offered, within which the Caribbean experience is embedded, and a critique is presented of the supposed distinction between "North European" and "South European" slavery. This distinction has a long history, but has proved central to the arguments of such contemporary scholars as Frank Tannenbaum (1947), Stanley Elkins (1959), and Herbert Klein (1967). While it is difficult to escape entirely the persuasiveness of the distinction, many students continue to feel that something other than ideology was at work in creating it. Elkins—against whom the critique is principally directed—concerned himself primarily with one aspect of the problem: the creation of a so-called Sambo personality within the North European (in this case, North American) institution, and its supposed absence in the South European institution. But this supposed difference rests in turn on the idea that the slave possessed a "moral personality" under South European slavery that was denied him by the North Europeans. The wider issue, then, is whether all slaves in the North European colonies lacked a moral personality, while all those in the South European colonies possessed one—or whether we are in fact dealing with a significantly different problem.

We must also ask to what extent, and in what ways, the nature of slavery was related to the geopolitical facts under which it occurred—since the emancipation and post-emancipation experiences of locales such as Haiti, the United States South, and Brazil were so different, as had been their experiences under slavery. It is of the greatest importance, even in interpreting the racial attitudes of contemporary peoples, to recall that only in the United States was the slavery issue resolved by a civil conflict occurring in a truly sovereign country, rather than in the colony of a European power. The implications of this difference are suggested, at least in passing.

In the third chapter, the relationship of slavery to other forms of oppression is approached through the use of a particular historical example. This example concerns a structural change in nineteenth-century colonial power relations on the island of Puerto Rico, a change intimately connected with the use of labor. The victims of this change were neither African in origin nor slaves; but their labor was needed at a time when neither slaves nor a sufficiency of hungry freemen was available. The importance of the case lies in the fact that neither their status as free men nor their European (and, hence, white) origins were permitted to interfere with the contribution these victims were forced to make toward Puerto Rico's "economic development."

Chapter 4 deals with the history of a single plantation, and is based on research conducted over twenty years ago in a plantation area of the south coast of Puerto Rico. At the time, anthropological research on plantations had not yet begun; the dissertation resulting from that fieldwork (Mintz 1951b) was, to the best of my knowledge, the first ever written by an anthropologist on the subculture of plantation workers. In the same year, Elena Padilla, a member of the same field group, completed a doctoral dissertation dealing with the same theme (Padilla 1951), based on her research on a government-owned plantation. Since that time, other anthropologists have done considerable additional research on plantations.

The reasons for this growth of interest are easy to identify. Plantations, as I have sought to suggest, have been a major form of "economic development" imposed on subject peoples by the West.

This has been true in the New World since the first decade of the sixteenth century, when tiny sugar plantations worked with Indian and African slave labor were established in the Greater Antilles by the Spanish conquerors. In view of the lengthy career of plantations as Western institutions, studies of their history and sociology can provide considerable data on the workings of capitalist enterprise, and on the responses of subject populations to its pressures for change, particularly in tropical colonial and quasi-colonial areas.

Another basis for the growing interest in plantations is the continuity of form in plantation regions. The scale of enterprise, technology, and the scope of the market have changed, as have the institutional arrangements relating the laboring populations to the land they work. Often, the political ties linking subject and dependent areas with the metropolis have been altered. Nevertheless, significant features of present-day plantation organization and plantation life are startlingly similar to those of earlier centuries. Close ties still exist between field and factory, as in the case of sugarcane, which must be cut when ripe and ground as soon as it is cut. The regimen of daily plantation labor still requires some overarching authority to make all production decisions, with the assurance that they will be swiftly executed. There are still sharp social distinctions between those who labor in the sun and those who direct their labor, distinctions expressed in such matters as income, prestige, and living standards. There is still the factorylike organization of agricultural labor into large-scale, highly coordinated enterprises. Moreover, in most cases there is still the rather rigid social order of the plantation hierarchy, and the sharply limited opportunities it offers those at the bottom to change their relative position in the social system.

These and other continuities make plantation areas "laboratories" of a kind, within which observers can formulate and test hypotheses about the relationship of life-style to the demands of the plantation system. That studies of this kind have continued to prove fruitful in the social sciences is suggested by the recent work of such scholars as Jayawardena (1963), Benoist (1968), Knight (1972), Jain (1970), Beckford (1972), Best (1968), and the students of Julian Steward (1967)—working in such diverse societies as Guyana, Martinique, Colombia, Malaysia, the erstwhile British West Indies, and Peru.

Another important reason why plantation communities are of interest to the social sciences is that they have almost always been frontier communities in which populations of differing ethnicity confronted each other. The sociologist A. G. Keller took note of this feature long ago (Keller 1908). Edgar Thompson, one of the best and earliest sociologists of the plantation, made the point with considerable elegance in his first papers (e.g., 1932); Ida Greaves treated it in her important *Modern Production Among Backward Peoples* (1935); and others have since made the same discovery (e.g., Wagley 1957). As contact communities—settings of ethnic and "racial" encounter—plantations have provided rather rigid, sometimes oppressive, contexts within which newcomers had to work out a different style of life.

With the exception of certain early plantation experiments in the Mediterranean zone, antedating the "discovery" of the New World, the Caribbean plantations of the sixteenth century were the first such theaters of encounter and adaptation. The first subjects—one might better say "victims"—were Native Americans. These were soon followed by Africans. Later, Europeans faced a similar crisis of adaptation. In each new plantation area—as when the first plantations were established in Santo Domingo (Española) within two decades of the Conquest—the process of adaptation was pristine, almost without parallel. But in succeeding periods, as when Indians from India, Chinese from the mainland empire, Javanese from the East Indies, and other newcomer populations were thrust into the plantation framework in the Antilles, the models for the new styles of life of the later arrivals were provided in some measure by their predecessors. One of the best examples is that of Hawaii, where the plantation system produced an "ethnic succession" (Lind 1938) that lasted for nearly a century, and involved in turn at least six ethnically distinguishable migrant populations.

The parallel processes in the Caribbean, however, involved many more different peoples and extended over a period nearly five times as long. As in Hawaii, these processes affected populations that differed not only in culture—in ethnicity—but in physical appearance; and to the extent that such differences were perceived and made socially relevant, these acculturational situations were also "race-relational" situations. Thus, even before the growth of the great plantations of the eighteenth century, and even after the end of slavery in the nineteenth century, the plantation system has always been the main setting for the cultural demography of the Antilles. In this sense, slavery, which powered the plantation system for centuries, was but one stage in an unfolding process of control that began in 1492 and has not yet ended for much of the Caribbean region.

Those of a generalizing turn of mind find the plantation system of interest because it has been so effective a mode of colonial "development," for so long, in so many places, and for so many European powers. But it would be a mistake to think of these enterprises as nothing more than tightly organized "large estates." Since most plantation products involve a measure of processing or treatment at the point of production, the plantation almost always includes a processing plant or a factory and developed transport facilities as part of its organization. Accordingly, the plantation is often as much a factory as a farm, and the labor force is likely to be both agricultural and industrial. Moreover, the lines of organization and the forms of production are likely to have an industrial character, even though the agricultural basis of the enterprise is everywhere more obvious.

This curious cloaking of industry in agriculture may account for our unawareness of the rapidity with which the same forces that created an urban proletariat in Western Europe also created a rural proletariat in the Caribbean islands. Imperialism is commonly viewed as a late stage in the history of European capitalism, but the slave plantations of the West Indies imposed an important (if admittedly very variant) form of capitalist industrial organization upon subject peoples beginning in the sixteenth century, long before European industry itself had taken on a modern form. This parallel process was concealed, in part, by the colonial character of the Caribbean societies; by their lack of large cities; by the fact that plantation products are thought of as "agricultural" rather than as "industrial"; and by the unfree character of the laboring populations on plantations during so much of their history. The supposition that imperialism grew only after the consolidation of European capitalism at home obscures the role of colonies, slavery, and the plantation system in the evolution of capitalism before the eighteenth century.

However, the development of the plantation system occurred in a series of steps, not instantaneously; and these steps were neither unidirectional nor irreversible. In fact, the immense complexity of Caribbean history flows in good measure from the multiplex development of plantations during five centuries. In some cases, it is even possible to establish that the plantation system was declining in one society precisely when it was expanding in another—as, for instance, when one compares Jamaica and Puerto Rico at the start of the nineteenth century (Mintz 1959). In spite of this complexity, however, it has seemed useful to attempt to specify the developmental steps involved in plantation growth in a general fashion, so that systematic comparisons of developmental sequence might be made; this has been a task for historically minded Caribbeanists. One such sequence is suggested in Chapter 4, in which three stages of development of Puerto Rican plantations are set forth. After this way of looking at the data was first used by the author (Mintz 1953a), it was adopted by Hutchinson (1957) and Wagley and Harris (1955) for Brazil, and later it proved useful for Steward's students elsewhere in Latin America.

However, the main purpose of the chapter is not to detail the stages of plantation history but to show how the acculturation of Afro-Caribbean folk proceeded in a plantation setting. In Puerto Rico, as elsewhere, each stage of plantation development implicated the laboring classes in new kinds of acculturational processes. In the Caribbean region, once the introduction of fresh slaves had ended (in the British and French areas, by the early nineteenth century; in the Spanish areas, after about 1860), these acculturational processes could no longer be linked to a continuous flow of African cultural features into the zone, but became more purely "creolizing" in character. Later, the introduction of newcomer populations from other parts of the world further complicated the ethnic and cultural picture.

In the case of Puerto Rico, however, the major sources of plantation labor, after the elimination or genetic absorption of aboriginal populations, were Europe and Africa. The acculturational setting was also typified by continuous Spanish rule during slightly more than four centuries of colonial history—that is, from the Conquest until the North American invasion in 1899. Moreover, the history of the Puerto Rican plantations was significantly different from that of such colonies as Jamaica, Martinique, or French Saint-Domingue—since plantations on the grand scale were not created in Puerto Rico until the eve of the nineteenth century, after nearly three centuries of colonial rule without an expanding plantation system. These circumstances and certain others—such as the growth of large free colored and European settler populations—gave the Puerto Rican case a somewhat distinctive character, which must be taken into account in any history of its plantation system.

The fieldwork on which this chapter is based was not undertaken primarily to unravel local history, nor to study the plantation system as such, but to describe analytically the present-day culture of people living in a specific plantation community. The community exists on the periphery of a large United States–owned plantation that stretches over nearly a dozen different municipalities and manages or owns many thousands of acres of prime-quality sugarcane land as well as several enormous grinding mills. In this region, one cannot help noting many vestiges of previous eras in plantation history; and local people are eager to describe the changes that have affected their lives. Ruins of the tiny sugar mills of the past dot the landscape. Stories about the former owners, the hacendados, abound. Though the fields are now numbered, and are generally known by their numbers, many old-timers refer to them by names as well—names that mark the past of the land and of the tiny haciendas that once flourished there. There is, in other words, a strong sense of local history, and a complex of feelings about the past, both bad and good, that is readily evoked.

The past reveals itself in other ways as well. Local people vary widely in physical appearance, and in the cane communities of the coast Puerto Ricans of all physical varieties live and socialize freely with one another. There is no visible "color line," no fixed separation of people into groups of differing colors, no exclusion on the basis of appearance, and no *expressed* sense of group difference or of group solidarity on the part of the darker members of these local communities. It is, in fact, a population that looks as if it has been mixing freely for a very long time—even though there are many people who look entirely "white" and many others who look entirely "black," by North American standards. On this subject, too, people are prepared to talk about the past—but perhaps with more reluctance and, occasionally, even unease. Nor is the presence of individuals of highly variant appearance and the lack of any color line to say that there is no *consciousness* of color —there is, and it is sociologically demonstrable in the vast local terminology of color, hair form, lip form, and so on.

Thus the Puerto Rican situation suggests both an awareness of differences and a relative lack of assortment along the lines of such differences, at least among working-class people on the plantations. When the past is discussed, all sorts of small clues to "race" history are suggested, and these clues relate to matters of status, work skills, social mixing, and other areas in which the substance of race relations can be studied. It was inevitable, perhaps, that the availability of these kinds of materials should lead the writer into historical reconstruction. At any rate, such a reconstruction was attempted, and it dealt not only with the stages of plantation development as such, but also with the history of peoples, the human materials that the plantation system engulfed in its spread and consolidation.

In a very general sense, the darker people of Puerto Rico are more commonly found in the coastal areas of the island than in its highland centers. This impressionistic distribution accords well with the geographic spread of the plantation system, which was substantially confined to the alluvial floodplains of the coast, first in the north of the island, later along the south coast. To this day, there are curious bits of cultural evidence that accord with the demographic picture. Thus, for instance, the south coast town of Guayama, well known as a "black" town, named its baseball team "The Witches" (*Los Brujos*), in accordance with the still-common Puerto Rican association of darker-skinned persons with witchcraft. The dance called *"bomba"* (also the name of the drum played at such dances) is associated with the south coast, as are the song forms called *"plena"*—both bomba and plena are thought of as "African" (that is, are associated with people of color). In these and other ways, a serious visitor to the south coast is brought to realize that, beneath the surface of social association, there is an awareness of certain kinds of cultural (and, less directly, "racial") difference that does not interfere in any very noticeable way with the conduct of life but that remains a part of the consciousness of local people. It would be folly, however, to overemphasize these elements, just as it would be ill-advised to ignore their existence. The research direction is one of teasing out the past as fully as possible, and relating it to the present; that is partly what is attempted in Chapter 4.

From the Afro-Caribbean perspective, we are concerned with what happened to those Puerto Ricans whose origins were wholly or partly African: how they were brought into the Puerto Rican setting, how they adapted, what kinds of social relationships they were able to work out with other Puerto Ricans. We discover that such people not only "became Puerto Rican," as had other migrants to the island, but that at a later point in history they played a special role in acculturating highland immigrants of European ancestry to local plantation life. We further discover that many skilled jobs on the plantations were more commonly the responsibility of black men than of white. And we get some hints that the local culture of the plantation region became Afro-Caribbean—in terms of daily activities, aesthetics, and possibly cuisine, for instance—just as people of African ancestry mixed into the general population in which they found themselves.

These blendings and mergings seem to have occurred for the most part within a single class grouping, that of the plantation working people. But within that grouping, any very significant distinctions between black and white do not seem to have persisted, in spite of strong color consciousness, some clearly detectable feeling of prejudice, and the certainty that darker-skinned Puerto Ricans, as a group, has always been at some disadvantage in national life. In a concluding section of the chapter, an attempt is made to suggest some of the reasons why a color bar could not be made to function effectively in Puerto Rico, as it has in certain other parts of the New World.

A great deal of further research will have to be done before the sociology of the Puerto Rican plantation past can be depicted completely. Chapter 4 is intended merely to suggest the distinctiveness of the Puerto Rican case and to point the way to additional research.

# 2

# Slavery and the
# Afro-American World

Though there is some doubt about the initial date, we know that enslaved Africans were probably transported to the New World—the Spanish colony of Española, today's Haiti and the Dominican Republic—no later than 1505 (Sauer 1966: 207). That would be only 13 years after Columbus's arrival in this hemisphere and 271 years *before* the Declaration of Independence.

The date of the last shipment of African slaves to the Americas is also uncertain, because the slave trade was eventually outlawed by the governments of all the participating powers, and thus reduced entirely to smuggling. We do know that the last shipload of smuggled slaves reached this hemisphere well into the second half of the nineteenth century—that is, more than three and one-half centuries after the trade had begun.

Easily within the memory of North American adults, the last of our citizens born as slaves were interviewed and memorialized in a touching account by an American folklorist-historian (Botkin 1945). Less than a decade ago, the Cuban Academy of Sciences published the autobiography of a Cuban ex-slave, then living, who had escaped from his masters and had become a *cimarrón,* or runaway, in that country (Barnet 1966). The eightieth anniversary of the abolition of Brazilian slavery, the last such system to disappear in this hemisphere, was celebrated in 1968. The links between the New World and Africa are ancient, and contact between these two great regions has been protracted. Moreover, the nature of this contact has been prevailingly unidirectional and of one sort: from Africa to the Americas, the vast majority of newcomers having come as slaves rather than as free men. The exceptions to this process—the return of Brazilian ex-slaves to West Africa to acquire medical training that would enable them to treat their Brazilian clients more effectively; the use of a few thousand Africans as free contract laborers in the Antilles after the end of slavery; the modest colonization of West Africa by freedmen or freed slaves during and after slavery—are extremely interesting, but they never involved any substantial numbers.

In marked contrast, the scale of the forced westward movement was staggering. We will never be able to specify numbers with any precision, and in the light of important new work (Curtin 1969) earlier estimates of a total transportation of 12 million or more enslaved Africans now seem excessive. But even Curtin concludes that more than 9 million slaves were imported into the Americas from Africa. Curtin's revisions are prudent, for the most part, and well-argued; they reveal that the French colony of Saint-Domingue imported 790,000 slaves in 90 years; the British colony of Jamaica, 662,000 slaves in 109 years; while Brazil, the largest of all New World slave colonies, received 3,646,800 slaves during the course of the entire slave trade. Spanish America received 606,000 slaves, according to Curtin, between 1811 and 1870—but we must note that, by 1811, Spanish America consisted essentially of Cuba and Puerto Rico, so far as the slave trade was concerned—tiny colonies, to have received 10,000 slaves a year for sixty years.

Viewed in terms of transoceanic travel during the seventeenth, eighteenth and nineteenth centuries, and remembering that this was a forced migration, the Atlantic slave trade may well have been the most colossal demographic event of modern times. Surely it eclipses any comparable event that preceded it, while putting in perspective the oft-recounted horrors of European immigration to the Americas, including the admittedly dreadful experiences of the more than 250,000 European indentured servants sent to the British New World possessions during the colonial period. And the sufferings of free European immigrants to the United States in the nineteenth and early twentieth centuries, of which a great deal has been said lately, can hardly be compared in scale or intensity with those that typified the Middle Passage for more than 350 years.

But if the Atlantic slave trade was significant as a demographic phenomenon, the institution of slavery itself was far more so, as a social and cultural phenomenon. The culture history of the New World had begun to change from the moment of Columbus's first landfall. Thereafter, the New World was viewed by Europeans as a gigantic frontier area into which vast numbers of people from the Old World could pour, seeking their fortunes, escaping the confines of European institutions and European societies, and remaking their lives. In this process, the fates and social histories of the peoples of African origin were to be set apart—often harshly and completely, in other cases less extremely—from those of the other newcomers. And, of course, the fates and social histories of the indigenous peoples of the New World, the Native Americans whose ancestors had been the real discoverers of the Americas, would differ as well, and depressingly so, from those of the European newcomers.

The distinguishing feature of the Afro-American and Amerindian experience was, of course, the extent to which these peoples were subjected to the will and intent of the European colonizers, and this subjection is clearly revealed, in the case of Afro-Americans, by the institutional history of slavery in the Americas. This topic, which once preoccupied some of the best Western minds, dwindled in importance, especially in the United States, during Reconstruction and received surprisingly little attention from historians and sociologists between the closing decades of the nineteenth century and the end of World War II. Frederick Jackson Turner, the great North American historian of the frontier, suggested serenely that North American slavery would someday turn out to have been only a historical incident; the sociologist Albert Galloway Keller postulated that slaves of African origin were naturally fitted by temperament to servitude (Keller 1908: 145, 282); while U. G. Weatherly would write—unchallenged—that "the Negro belongs perhaps to the most docile and modifiable of all races" (Weatherly 1923: 242). Not only was the history and importance of slavery in New World history played down, but its very origins were rationalized and concealed by musings upon the supposed inherent plasticity and passivity of temperament of Afro-Americans. Nor was literary stress on the docility and malleability of Afro-Americans always innocent. In the United States, such stress served to reduce popular awareness of the sufferings of black freedmen and of the continuous terrorism employed to maintain or intensify racial inequalities. Moreover, if Afro-Americans were "naturally docile," then their legitimate protests could be viewed as temporary aberrations or, in some cases, as the awakening of dormant "primitive instincts." Even so significant an event as the Haitian Revolution, which led to the establishment of a black New World nation (James 1963 [1938]) and this hemisphere's second sovereign polity, was little studied—or written off as a "nightmare."

And yet the historical record of slavery in the New World is clear enough. Over a period very nearly four centuries long, millions of human beings were dragged from their ancestral homelands, put in chains, transported across an ocean, and sold. If the yield of this accumulated labor power, stretched over centuries and wrung from defenseless millions, could be accurately measured, we would be stunned by its magnitude. We might be struck as well by the breadth and depth of the embedding of the slavery institution in the social fabric not of one, but of many different New World societies—an embedding so intimate and persistent that the aftermaths of slavery still endure in the social forms and perceptions of New World peoples, including those of the United States.

Slavery is much more than a matter of economics, more than solely a means of controlling the labor of others. It is one of the most important inventions in human history, and it has formed part of the institutional system of myriad societies. The anthropologist Tylor wrote: "The greatest of all divisions, that between freeman and slave, appears as soon as the barbaric warrior spares the life of his enemy when he has him down, and brings him home to drudge for him and till the soil" (1946 [1881] II: 156). That "greatest of all divisions" involved in every historical instance a way of life, a conception of the human condition, an ideology of society, and a set of economic arrangements, in short, a cultural apparatus, by which slaves and masters were related. The slave systems of the New World were the last chapter in a story some millennia old.

The economic arrangements which bound slave and master postulated that the master had the right to appropriate something which was the slave's—his time, or the products of his labor, his skill, often his children, perhaps his life. All definitions of the slave condition contain as a nucleus the idea of the property rights of one person in another. In certain circumstances, such rights take the form of capital. For the anthropologist, whether or not the slave is a capital good, a source of capital accumulation, a commodity, or something beyond these, is very relevant. Kroeber has written that "the fundamental thing about culture . . . [might be] the way in which men relate themselves to one another by relating themselves to their cultural material" (1948: 68). The relationships between slaves and masters in any particular historical instance are an illustration. As for capital, it may be viewed concretely, as some store used to undertake fresh production, or as a social aspect of the productive process. "Capital is not a thing," states Marx, "but a social relation between persons, established through the instrumentality of things" (1939 [1867], 1: 791). And, in a peculiarly relevant footnote, he adds, "A negro is a negro. In certain circumstances he becomes a slave. A mule is a machine for spinning cotton. Only under certain circumstances does it become capital. Outside these circumstances it is no more capital than gold is intrinsically money, or sugar the price of sugar. . . . Capital is a social relation of production." The similarity between Kroeber's definition of culture and Marx's definition of capital springs from no common intent other than to describe something characteristic of human behavior.

But both of these definitions compel us to reflect upon the extent to which slavery as a system for the unrestricted exaction of labor can operate without reference to the undeniable humanity of the enslaved. All slavery may be slavery, but not all slaveries are the same, economically or culturally. Through slavery, human beings, their labor, their lives—that is, their production and reproduction—become commodities. In capitalistic societies in which a proletarian labor force sells its labor on the market, the price of labor is supposed to be determined in some large measure by the relationships of the labor supply to opportunities for employment. But slavery represents an investment by the capitalist in the purchase not of labor alone, but of the laborer as well. It was the combination of slavery—from the capitalist perspective, an archaic form of labor—with European overseas capitalism that gave to the New World situation its special, unusual, and ruthless character.

Slavery is a complex term with many meanings (Davis 1966; Finley 1968; Genovese 1969). Fundamentally, however, slavery rests upon coercion; the slave is, in certain important senses, the property of his master—as is, for instance, the master's land and the master's mule, though not the master's wife or child. In one way or another, the slave is defined in such fashion that he is not a person—at least, not a person in all of the senses that a free man is a person in the same society. But of course the slave *is* a person —and both masters and slaves, in all of the slavery systems of the New World, knew this, even if they were not always willing to admit it or able to say so.

## Slavery in the Americas

The economic advantageousness of slavery in the New World was based on the relative scantiness of other forms of labor supply. The New World stretched from Tierra del Fuego to the Arctic, accessible to those who would plunder it; only the aboriginal peoples of the Hemisphere stood in the way. In areas of dense aboriginal concentrations, such as the Andes and highland Mexico, imported labor was not necessary or, at least, was not so commonly enslaved. But in all areas where the aboriginal population was sparse or soon destroyed, slavery provided one sort of answer for the European colonizers. Thus it was that an institution already dead or dying in the metropolises could be spread, sometimes with remarkable speed and intensity, through the subtropical lowlands of the New World, particularly on the Atlantic periphery. In the Danish, Dutch, English, French, Portuguese, Spanish, and Swedish colonies, and in the United States, the slave trade and slavery played an important role in the economic development of the "mother country." Thompson (1932) has shown how this Western industrial slavery, slavery within capitalism, was basic to a pioneer institution, the plantation. The developmental problem was one of bringing into production large tracts of fertile land available for the asking, or little more than the asking, but in the absence of an adequate labor supply. The thrust toward such development grew ever stronger as plantation products were transformed from the luxuries of the rich—sugar, coffee, tobacco, rum—into the daily necessities of the urban proletarian masses in the metropolises.

Yet from the entrepreneur's perspective, free labor would not do for plantation development since land itself was free or nearly so. Free men provide opportunities for the garnering of entrepreneurial profit when they have no direct access to the means of production, particularly land, and must therefore sell their labor at the going market price. In the absence of coercion from above and of organization below, this price is determined by supply and demand; where supply far exceeds demand, the price is low. Such is the situation which that much-neglected ethnologist, H. J. Nieboer, called one of "close [*sic*] resources" (1900: 420–22). But the pioneer situation prevailing in the New World lowlands was one of ample free land and scarce labor; the entrepreneur could appropriate neither profit from the employment of needful laborers nor rent from scarce resources. Nieboer called this situation one of "open resources." In one instance, as Thompson put it (1932: 21), two would-be employers chase one laborer; in the other, two would-be laborers chase one employer. The baldness of this formula does not rule out its usefulness for understanding the economic basis of slavery in the Americas. Slavery provides the entrepreneur with a guaranteed, controllable, and disciplined labor force. There are, it is true, decidedly uneconomic aspects to such an arrangement; but slavery made good sense, along the Atlantic littoral from Brazil to the United States South, and especially in the Antillean islands, where the decimation of native populations had left empty lands, and where climate, soil, and topography provided a superb locale for plantation agriculture of all kinds.

It was within this region that a single classic mode of economic development, based on European capital, American land, African slave labor, and a large-scale agricultural estate system—usually described by the term *plantation* (Mintz 1951b, 1968)—flourished. This was not by any means the only way in which slaves were profitably employed; nor was plantation organization limited exclusively to the subtropical American lowlands. Slaves were used in workshops and factories; they dug diamonds and gold; and in the fully developed New World slave economies, the slaves occupied many other economic niches. But the basic relationship of African slave labor to plantation production underlay and predated almost every other mode of employment of peoples of African origin in the New World. That relationship has not been entirely eroded to this day, even though eight decades have passed since slavery itself ceased to exist in the Hemisphere.

It should be stressed that the relationship between slavery and Africans was rooted fundamentally in demographic and economic forces, not in the physical type of the slaves themselves. The European colonists and investors demonstrated repeatedly, and in manifold ways, that they were color-blind—so far as getting the job done was concerned. The aboriginal lowland people—for instance, in the Greater and Lesser Antilles—were almost entirely exterminated by the Europeans, forced labor and maltreatment being among the major causes of their extinction. Indentured servants from Britain and France were also immolated on the plantation pyre; in all, an estimated quarter of a million English indentured servants were brought to the New World colonies (Jernegan 1931), many of them to the Caribbean islands, and most of them worked—for a time, alongside African slaves—on the plantations. English convicts—who included petty thieves, debt-prisoners, Gypsies, and labor organizers—were deported to the plantation colonies in large numbers (E. Williams 1944); and Cromwell found the Antilles a convenient dumping ground for thousands of Irish revolutionaries (J. Williams 1932). At a much later time, as the institution of slavery came under attack in the Americas, new sources of plantation labor were tapped, and hundreds of thousands of Indians, both Muslim and Hindu, Chinese, Javanese, free Africans, and others were shipped to the New World, ostensibly as free plantation laborers, but bound in most cases by repressive contracts (Mintz 1966).

Nonetheless, the major source of forced labor—that is to say, of slaves—was Africa. The word *slave* still brings the visual image of blackness to North American minds. This association of forced labor and degradation with peoples of a particular physical type is a powerful symbol of the extent to which social perceptions are historically conditioned. And it much needs emphasizing that this consciousness, these perceptions, are peculiarly—if not exclusively —a New World phenomenon. It is fair to argue as much, since slavery, during its nearly four centuries of existence in this hemisphere, normally involved the forced interaction of two groups of people who differed in their cultural and physical origins, in their access to power, and in their ability to affect their own destinies. The monumental tragedy of this involvement has for long been central to the artistic consciousness of many of the New World's poets, novelists, and essayists; today, it has once again claimed the center of the political stage as well.

And yet, while the slavery of peoples of African origin in the Americas can for many purposes be treated as a single case, any attempt to carry the analysis further requires that comparisons be made: between and among different historical periods, different slave codes, and different colonies. For even though some common values and attitudes may have underlain the slavery institution throughout the New World, local circumstances varied widely. Systematic comparisons of slavery systems have become the concern of many contemporary scholars, particularly historians and sociologists, in the last ten years—a concern excited in part by a reawakened consciousness of the importance of Afro-Americans and their history in this hemisphere. But it should be stressed that such a theme is not really new. While slavery still flourished, and while proslavery writers and abolitionists struggled to win adherents and to expose the weaknesses of their antagonists' arguments, serious and impressive comparative analyses of slave systems were in fact produced. One thinks, for instance, of the French Antillean Creole Emilien Petit, whose two-volume comparison of the British, French, and Spanish slavery institutions was published in 1777. Herman Merivale, the British political economist, whose lectures on colonization—first published in 1841—are still read, also devoted considerable attention to the comparative aspects of slavery. In his prejudiced but pathbreaking work, *The Negro in the New World,* published in 1910, Sir Harry H. Johnston considers (albeit not very carefully) the differences among the slavery institutions of the Spaniards, the Portuguese, the Dutch, the French, the British, the Danes, and the Americans.

In the United States, a new period in the comparative study of slavery was initiated by the appearance of the Trinidadian historian Eric Williams's *Capitalism and Slavery* in 1944 and of Frank Tannenbaum's *Slave and Citizen* in 1947. These two books reopened the questions of the nature of slavery and of differentiation in the slavery systems of the New World. Could it be said that different systems of slavery had operated, such that the peoples of African origin in the New World differed significantly in their relationships with their fellow citizens in the various countries of the Hemisphere for reasons attributable to the pre-emancipation past? Or had slavery merely created the same social conditions everywhere, such that no significant differences among post-emancipation social circumstances could be detected?

Tannenbaum's answers put heavy emphasis on the differential readiness of slaveowners, and of a slave society, to acknowledge the humanity and individuality—the moral personality—of the slaves. In his view, the institutional systems of the New World slave societies created by the South European Catholic powers stood in marked contrast to those that were produced by Protestant North Europe. He implied that in the case of the United States, the question since the Civil War had been one of when and whether the North American Negroes would be accorded a *moral* status equal to their *legal* status. In much of the rest of the Americas, particularly in Catholic-Latin lands such as Brazil, Tannenbaum argued, the moral personality of the slaves was never lost, so that emancipation constituted a change in civil status but not in moral personality. Tannenbaum also weighed heavily the lengthy South European experience with slavery before the New World was discovered; North Europe, he felt, had had no truly comparable experience. According to Tannenbaum, the Catholic slave did not stand outside his society by virtue of his enslavement; the Protestant slave did.

This view has been sharply contested. Several authors have asked whether a single analytic distinction of this sort can in fact be drawn between the Catholic and the Protestant slaveholding powers. Some, accepting the distinction, have wondered whether it can be so readily and completely attributed to ideological and/or institutional considerations. The plantation economies of the different slave powers matured at different rates, in different parts of the New World; and the particular demands of plantation operation very clearly affected the treatment of slaves in the colonies. Moreover, the European powers varied greatly in their rigidity of control over the colonies. The English, for instance, appear to have given their colonists maximum local authority—which in practice could mean maximum power to abuse the slaves and to bypass any imperial concern for their protection. In contrast, the Spanish colonies were administered from the metropolis with considerable rigor, and the Crown conceded local authority to its colonists only slowly and grudgingly. Slavery under Spain, consequently, was more subject to control from afar. Here, in a curious way since reconfirmed in much of the colonial world, the imperial presence both underwrote and limited exploitation—at least in some cases and to some degree.

Finally, critics of Tannenbaum's position have insisted that the experiences of New World plantation slavery cannot be summed up in so polar a fashion. The Spanish colonies varied considerably in their use and treatment of slaves, and the Spanish picture changed with time, scale of plantation development, and much else. Cuba is a particularly interesting case, since plantation slavery on the grand scale developed there very late in the history of such slavery in the New World, yet achieved unusual levels of intensity before abolition, toward the close of the nineteenth century. William Law Mathieson (1926: 34) may have been the first writer to point out that Spanish slavery seemed to start and to end very badly, though he did not really explain why: "Spanish slavery in the West Indies was a century older and lasted considerably longer than that of any other European power. It began and it ended as probably the worst in the world; but there was an intermediate period, happily of great length, during which its reputation for mildness was fully deserved." If this is so, we have to ask ourselves what happened in the first and final periods of Cuba's slave-based economy to the institutional framework which presumably kept the slaves' moral personalities intact. Admittedly, institutional restrictions might have hampered the full maturation of slave-based agricultural capitalism in Cuba; that they could in no sense prevent its development is painfully clear from the record.

On the one hand, then, there were Latin societies in which economic changes appear to have radically conditioned the slaves' status. Yet, on the other hand, the argument that there was no working tradition for slavery in the non-Catholic New World is not entirely convincing. There was an English legal, and to some extent even institutional, background for British West Indian and North American slavery. Madden (1835, 2: 131) notes that "a commission was appointed by Queen Elizabeth in 1574 to take steps for the manumission of English slaves, even while her Majesty's fleet was ravaging the coast of Africa for negro ones." In 1537, the House of Lords rejected a bill for the manumission of villeins (Lipson 1945, 1: 130) and, according to the same author, there is documentary evidence in the form of surveys, court rolls, and manumissions, proving the existence of sixteenth-century villeinage. While it is true that the villeins are estimated to have numbered but one percent of the population, this still meant many thousands of persons.

The Rev. G. W. Bridges, a racist proslavery writer of nineteenth-century Jamaica, cannot be entirely discounted when he writes:

> The Negro slave-code, which, until lately, governed the labouring classes of Jamaica, was originally copied from that of Barbadoes; and the legislature of that colony resorted, for a precedent, to the ancient villeinage laws, then scarcely extinct on British ground. They copied thence the principles which ruled, and the severity which characterised, the feudal system under the Saxon government.
>
> Not seventy years prior to the settlement of Barbadoes, a remarkable badge of servitude had been imposed on British subjects, by the statute against vagabonds, which adjudged them, expressly and absolutely, to positive slavery; inflicting violent punishments on the disobedient, stigmatising runaways by branding, and, for the second offence, decreeing death. The same law empowered the master to rivet an iron ring around the neck of his slave, affixing the penalty of ten pounds upon the person removing it; and it repeats the word *"slave,"* so odious to British ears, no less than thirty-eight times.
>
> Such remained the effective law of England in the year 1553; and it was only thirty years after that period that Barbadoes fell into

the possession of the Lord High Treasurer. The enactments regarding negro slaves in the colonies were therefore, naturally enough, transcribed from these late precedents at home, where the name and character of slavery was thus familiar (1827, 1: 507–8).

In commenting on this quotation, no less an authority than L. C. Gray concludes: "It appears probable that colonial lawyers seeking precedent for their legislation found it in this statute, as well as in other vagrancy laws" (1941, 1: 343).

Slaves had numbered 9 percent of the population in the Domesday Book, but slave status had been gradually assimilated to villeinage thereafter. Villeinage at its simplest involved an obligation to enforced labor, both regular and extraordinary (the *precariae*), as well as contributions in kind or in money to the lord; normally the villein had no legal security, but he was given some protection by custom and tradition and in the manorial courts. It would certainly be defensible to argue that the legal suppression of personality was never present in villeinage, and this assertion should occasion no surprise. Slavery of the British West Indian, North American, and nineteenth-century Cuban sort was probably without precedent, legal or otherwise, anywhere in modern times.

The issue, then, does not seem to hinge on the presence of a tradition in one case and its absence in another, but on the effective transfer of a tradition in one case and its nontransfer—or incomplete transfer—in another. The Spanish colonies in the New World were no more and no less pioneer settlements than were Barbados, Jamaica, and North America. Why did metropolitan institutions travel effectively with the South Europeans and only ineffectively with the North Europeans? It is hard to suppose that only religious and other ideological systems of the metropolises, were important while their economic and political structures were not. England's tradition of representative government meant that, as likely as not, slave laws would be made by slaveowners, and so they were. In the Spanish colonies, such laws emanated from the mother country. But Elsa Goveia (1960: 81) shows that when Cuba's slaveowners became politically powerful, as plantation slavery there became capitalistic in a fuller sense, they handily defeated the intent of the 1789 laws designed to ameliorate the slaves' condition, and that humanitarian tradition, universalistic religion, and past practice did not prevent them from doing so.

The upshot of these arguments is that there *was* a legal precedent for slavery in the North European colonies, and that the institutional apparatus of the South European countries did *not* always protect the slaves—or, for that matter, the freemen—in their slaveholding colonies. Notable differences between these two kinds of colonial situation were the varying effectiveness of metropolitan political control and the differing rates of emergence of capitalist plantations. Furthermore, the principal powers which had colonies in the New World differed in the degree to which representative or self-government was possible on the local level. Representative government and quasi-autonomous legislatures were apparently firmer in the British colonies than in the French, firmer in the French colonies than in the Spanish.

The slave plantation, producing some basic commodity for the mother country, was a special, emergent capitalist form of industrial organization, which appeared earlier, and with more intensity, in the colonies of the North European powers than in the colonies of Spain. (Omitted from consideration here are the earliest Spanish plantation experiments in Santo Domingo, Cuba, and Puerto Rico, which soon declined.) Industrial slavery of this sort effected a more complete dehumanization of the slaves than did other forms of slavery. (And, of course, even domestic slavery in Jamaica, French Saint-Domingue, or the American South was less crushing in its impact on the individual than field slavery.)

The differentials in the growth of the slave plantations in different colonies are to be understood as resulting from different ecologies, different rates of maturation of metropolitan markets and industries, and different political relationships between creole governing bodies and the metropolitan authorities. The rate of growth of the slave plantation, then, did not hinge on matters of race, civil liberties, protection of the rights of individuals slave and free, or the presence or absence of particular religious codes.

The rates at which existing norms of behavior with reference to "social inferiors" were changed or reversed depended to a considerable extent on the power of the planter class in the creole society, and on the capacity of this class to influence or to immobilize political decisions made in the metropolis. The power of the planter class of course varied. But the capital for plantation development usually originated in the metropolis, and the moral force of capital's sacred right to reproduce itself was felt in metropolitan legislatures.

At the same time, it must be noted that the South European countries and their colonies gave up slavery later than did those of Northern Europe. Spain's Antillean colonies Cuba and Puerto Rico declared emancipation, respectively, in 1880 (effective 1886) and in 1873 (effective 1876) (not 1867, the date Tannenbaum gives for both, 1957: 62). From this, it might appear that the North European powers were the first to recognize the moral failure of slavery and responded selflessly. By and large, that does not seem to have been the case; the difference seems to have been more economic and political than ideological. Once emancipation was accomplished, moreover, there is a striking similarity between the adjustments to freedom of the South European and the North European colonies and countries. Jamaica, British Guiana, and Trinidad imported Indian indentures, and the record of their employment is not pretty. Cuba, having at last achieved emancipation in 1880 (followed by six years of "guardianship" for the ex-slaves!) imported Chinese—approximately 125,000—with few institutional protections of any sort, and thereafter judiciously kept the price of free labor low by massive importations of Haitians and Jamaicans. W. Kloosterboer (1960) has demonstrated that, where slavery came to an end too soon—that is, before the labor pool had increased to a "closed resources" level—various sorts of forced labor arrangements, usually justified by "vagrancy" laws, were used.

These laws have lingered longest, not in countries of a particular institutional background, but in those of a particular level of economic and demographic development. A prime example—as South European as one would like—is provided by Harris (1959: 50–65) for Mozambique, and Kloosterboer (1960: 67–78) deals with a similar instance in Angola. In much of contemporary Latin America, indigenous peoples are still driven into wage labor by an array of laws which permit no feasible economic alternatives. Can it be possible that the South European ideology recognized the moral personality of the slaves but could not adjust to the idea of the moral personality of the freedmen? Be that as it may, it does appear that capitalism matured more rapidly in the colonies of the North European powers and that emancipation was an aspect of this maturation. Without questioning the motives of the abolitionists, it needs to be asked again whether the growing awareness of the dignity of freedom may not have been accompanied by the belief that, other things being equal, free workers produce and consume dramatically more than slaves.

An investment in slaves, after all, means that capital is being held in a particularly inelastic form. Whether or not this will be brought home to the slaveowner depends on the degree to which he considers his human chattels an investment. On the plantations, ecological conditions and the nature of the crops grown meant that the slaves were substantially nonproductive—in terms of maximizing a cash profit—for some part of the year. Unlike the wage earners of early capitalism, slaves represented a cost to the entrepreneur when they were not working. This helps to explain the truly desperate efforts of some slaveowners to increase their profit margins by compelling slaves to grow their own foodstuffs, by enabling them to become artisans, by renting them out in labor gangs, and so on. The more capitalistic the slavery situation, the more the businessman's view prevailed—the deliberate purchase of slaves with the intention of expanding production and hence profit, the borrowing of capital at interest in order to buy slaves, and other practices associated with the developed slave plantation. The very definitions of idleness, stupidity, and even humanity differed accordingly. On the capitalistic slave plantation, humanity was an obstacle to the maximization of profit. In other, less economically committed situations, this was not necessarily the case. The degree of social commitment to a capitalistic mode of production based on slavery is an essential determinant of the slaves' status. Consequently, even in situations where slaves were used for gain, such use alone does not adequately explain the status of the slaves.

Can it be contended, however, that the differences among the slave codes, the various ways of viewing and treating the slaves, the variety of circumstances in which the slaves found themselves, were so great in magnitude that one cannot generalize at all about

New World slavery? Such a contention would be ludicrous; the fundamental fact about slavery—that it arbitrarily places some human beings in the power of others, legalizing inequality among men in perpetuity—was true of all New World slavery systems. Hence, while different circumstances, different times, and different slave codes all doubtless affected the details of the slaves' condition, slavery was an inherently degrading institution. This does not mean that differences under slavery were unimportant; but it does mean that they should be viewed as variations within an institution that rested upon a fundamental rejection of the idea of human equality. In the New World, that rejection became linked with considerations of physique, such that an association between degraded status and physical type came to typify slavery in this hemisphere.

## Slavery and the Slaves

How did the slaves themselves view their plight? The record, though by no means absent, is meager—there were few opportunities for the enslaved or their immediate descendants to put their experiences down on paper. Almost as rare are accounts by the free men of New World societies who were truly interested in finding out what slavery meant in human terms to its victims. This issue has come back into intellectual and political discourse with sudden and almost violent significance, as the winds of social change have once again risen. How did the slaves cope with slavery? How did slavery affect the slaves, in terms of their preparedness to deal with emancipation? That such questions have considerable intellectual relevance has become self-evident; the argument must now be advanced by careful historical research on case after case.

If a rhetorical vantage point is employed, the story of slavery will be said to demonstrate unending and invariable resistance to slavery by the slaves, resistance both to the demands of their condition and to the culture of their masters. The truth, history suggests, is more complicated than that. There was resistance, to be sure, and in a variety of forms: malingering, self-induced abortion, suicide, feigned stupidity, armed revolt, self-mutilation, sabotage, poisoning, and myriad other ways. But there was also accommodation, submission, degradation, and self-hatred. Moreover, it is clear that some of the most effective forms of *resistance* were built upon prior *adaptation,* involving the slaves in processes of culture change and retention of a complicated kind. To write off all adaptive mechanisms as a loss of will to resist is tantamount to the denial of creative energies to the slaves themselves. The intricacies of resistance and accommodation are only now beginning to receive the attention they deserve, as in the works of Frederickson and Lasch (1967), Genovese (1967), Patterson (1967), Brathwaite (1971), and Price (1973)—though a now-classic paper by two students of Melville J. Herskovits pointed the way a quarter of a century ago (Bauer and Bauer 1942).

Once the complexities of resistance and survival are acknowledged, it becomes obvious that the struggle of the slaves was a subtle, involved, and delicate phenomenon. To take but one example, to which we shall advert more fully at a later point, was the readiness of Jamaican slaves to grow their own foodstuffs on plantation uplands to be written off as "nonresistance"? Through such activities, the slaves acquired skills in cultivation and marketing that greatly increased their ability to escape plantation labor after emancipation; traveled freely to the marketplaces, where they learned much of value (some of which may have been essential in fomenting rebellion); demonstrated to observant visitors their capacity to function independently and intelligently; and acquired liquid capital for various purposes. Yet no one would call subsistence cultivation and marketing mechanisms of "resistance," for the very good reason that they were not resistance as such, but forms of accommodation. At the same time, suicide—since it deprived masters of their labor—is correctly labeled "resistance," even though, once dead, one does precious little resisting.

At the same time, it is easy to see why the whole issue of resistance raises almost inescapable ideological questions that are very hard to answer. On the one hand, one wishes to document the truly hideous nature of slavery, destroying as it did almost every opportunity of the slaves to organize their lives in a manner befitting human beings. On the other hand, if the institution had been *entirely* successful, this would mean that it completely dehumanized the slaves, thus denying them any capacity to maintain their humanity in the face of total oppression. In fact, slavery *was* hideous; but it failed to dehumanize the slaves utterly because human beings are not things, and because contradictions built into the slavery system were as inescapable for the masters as they were for the slaves. Every plantation must have had slaves who clung to their own definition of the human condition in spite of everything. The social organization of the slaves was surely more complicated and differentiated than is commonly supposed; different slaves must have had different stakes in accommodation and in resistance. And the same slaves who accepted the status quo one day might reject it violently the next.

But there are no easy answers to the puzzle of slave resistance. Ideology continues to haunt research in this area more than in most others. Why, a century after abolition, are there those who apparently need to believe that North American slaves—in general —were happy with their condition? And why are there those who need to believe that no slave, ever or anywhere, accepted the state of slavery? Such vantage points simplify the tasks of the historian and the social scientist by obviating them; they add nothing to our understanding of the real nature of slave systems or of man. That slavery is inherently degrading, that it degrades both master and slave, goes almost without saying. But this does not mean that men are incapable of living in degraded conditions, nor does it guarantee that they will wage an unremitting struggle against them. In slave societies, as in other societies, the task confronting the scholar is that of discovering how a particular social arrangement persists both because of and in spite of the way it is viewed in the minds of men.

Within the structure of a slave society, the slaves were required to engineer styles of life that might be preserved in the face of terrible outrage. The daily demands—to eat, to sleep, to love, to grow, to survive—do not become less imperious because their satisfaction is persistently thwarted by oppression. Men organize themselves to resist according to their estimates of the distribution of power and the potential for changing it—sometimes coolly, at other times in a blind rage. To divest them for ideological reasons of their capacity to calculate risks and defer action is to vulgarize the function of intellect and to strip struggle of its inevitable complexity. An act of cruelty that succeeds in breaking one human being's resistance may spark the will to resist in a dozen others. An act of concession or submission, undergone to win time or trust or adherence, may contribute to the creation of a new situation in which effective resistance becomes possible. It is curious that a tolerance for complexity in the present may be accompanied by an insistence on simplicity in the past—since this runs counter to the conventional way in which men seek to understand and to interpret human affairs.

Reawakened interest in such questions has brought back into view a number of unjustly neglected works on slavery and slave resistance, including Herbert Aptheker's pioneering *Negro Slave Revolts* (1939) and *To Be Free* (1948). But few North Americans have shown comparable interest as yet in hemispheric slave resistance elsewhere than in the United States, except for an occasional acknowledgment of the Haitian Revolution as one of the New World's most striking historical sagas. This lack of interest originates in an insufficient understanding of the panhemispheric character of slavery and of the panhemispheric social history of Afro-Americans.

The "black republic" of Os Palmares, a palisaded community of perhaps 30,000 runaways with its daughter villages, flourished for nearly a half-century in the Brazilian interior in open defiance of the slaveholder society—though with its own slaves—before being destroyed by an army of 7,000. The Bush Negroes of Surinam and of French Guiana, who still maintain special relations with the colonial powers, are descended from other successful runaways. Runaway communities were important in Jamaica and in Cuba; in French Saint-Domingue, a runaway band captured in the late eighteenth century included in its membership men who had been born and had grown old in freedom (Bastide 1965; Debbasch 1961–62; Moreau de St. Méry 1958 [1797]). These cases of slaves who made good their escapes and maintained their freedom are significant; in each of their respective slave societies, they represented to the still-enslaved something that was *possible*. Usually, runaway communities lived in constant peril of attack; their civil liberties were guaranteed not by law, but by the force of their own arms. The very existence of such communities is immensely important to our understanding of slavery, of the proslavery ideology, and of the capacities and perceptions of the slaves themselves (Price 1973). If, as some historians and sociologists have suggested, Afro-Americans were inherently predisposed to enslavement, how explain their spirited resistance to it? The doctrine of New World plantation slavery required a regimen that would crush the slaves' will to resist. The slaves' triumphs over that system are a tribute to their indomitable humanity; the rarity of those triumphs attests to the brutal oppressiveness of the slave system. Resistance gave the lie to the claim that the slaves were uniformly contented with their condition; and the existence of runaway communities made it possible for those still enslaved to question the institution that manacled them.

We have seen that the principal purpose of slavery was to supply labor, considered unavailable otherwise, for the plantations. But the institution of slavery in societies such as Jamaica, Saint-Domingue, and Cuba, where its success at various times encouraged further expansion, demonstrated its peculiar internal capacity to grow at the expense of free labor. The process of plantation growth and the concomitant decline of free institutions typified three centuries of Caribbean history, as small-scale farmers of European origins were uprooted and disfranchised by the spread of great estates and their slave-labor squads (Mintz 1961a). A comparable process occurred in the United States South, though local differences created a wider variety of economic and social adjustments.

But the spread of plantation slavery was also accompanied by the penetration of slave labor into economic sectors formerly occupied by free artisans and craftsmen. Domestic service, for instance, could not easily remain the work of free men and women when slave labor became widespread. The design of slave societies, in fact, militated against the free man's doing any manual task—and the ideology of slavery tended to justify this state of affairs. Since slave labor was chronically less efficient than free labor, it followed that the more and more widespread use of slave labor in local economies would result in a decline in individual productivity. Thus, we have accounts of the many slaves needed to maintain a household that could have been cared for more efficiently by fewer free servants—but the blame, characteristically, is put not upon slavery but upon the slaves.

The slaves, simultaneously denied some part of their humanity and usually defenseless before their masters, were blamed for more than stupidity and indolence, however. They were also charged with licentiousness, with lack of feeling, and with cruelty. Surely, it must be one of history's deftest ironies that oppressors have always sought to rationalize their oppression by blaming the oppressed for the state to which it has reduced them. If the slaves were licentious, surely the historian must ask who was sexually omnipotent and who was defenseless against sexual advances; if the slaves were lazy, surely the historian must ask who worked and who did not; if the slaves were cruel, surely the historian must ask who were the tyrants and who the tyrannized. But reproaching the victim for the consequences of his victimization antedated slavery and has outlasted it.

The vigor and voracity of the slavery institution was its most virulent characteristic. Like many social institutions that serve one interest group by disadvantaging another, slavery, once instituted, usually became its own reason for being. Writing of the British Leeward Islands, Elsa Goveia, one of the finest modern historians of slavery, has said it well:

> Originally the slave system had been intended to relieve the shortage of field labor for the plantations. But by the end of the eighteenth century its influence had created a pattern of profuse consumption of relatively unproductive forced labour, as well as of wealth, which was already proving ruinously expensive to maintain. In spite of its heavy cost, however, slave labour was being used not only in cane cultivation but in all types of domestic and manual work, in the towns as well as on the estates. Slavery had spread from the fields into the plantation house and sugar factory, and from the country into the town houses and workshops, and into the very streets and harbours of the islands (Goveia 1965: 150).

And here, to underscore her point, she quotes the words of the late eighteenth-century West Indian planter and politician Clement Caines:

Was it necessary that slaves should be artisans and mechanics, as well as labourers? Was it necessary that they should wait in our houses and on our persons? Was it necessary that they should follow us, when we mounted on horseback, to hold our bridle or our stirrup, as we alighted at the end of our journey? Was it necessary that they should be made playfellows to our younger, and confidants and companions to our older children? Was it necessary, that they should minister to our passions and become subservient to our lusts? Was it necessary, that they should do the work of cattle, horses, and mules? Was it necessary, that their hands should be substituted for every implement of husbandry, for every engine that economizes labour, and saves the sweat of the human brow?

Caines, Goveia tells us, detested slavery as he knew it; and yet he gave an answer to his own shameful questions that Goveia herself calls sufficiently just. "No," he said, "it was not necessary. Yet it had been done, and perhaps blamelessly too." And Goveia concludes that Caines "at least understood that the institution of slavery had a certain grim logic of its own." That logic, may it be said, is still relevant—one cannot degrade another without degrading oneself.

# 3

# Slavery
# and Forced Labor
# in Puerto Rico

The supreme importance of slavery in Caribbean labor history
has sometimes concealed from view the subtler varieties of coercion used to maintain an adequate labor supply in the region.
Reference has been made to the European indentured servants
who peopled the early British and French plantation experiments
in the Lesser Antilles in the seventeenth century, and to the Asian
contract laborers who arrived in large numbers after (and sometimes even before) emancipation on various islands. But Puerto
Rico provides us with a very special instance of forced labor—an
instance that throws real light upon slavery itself and, to a lesser
extent, upon the relationship between race and social structures.
The Puerto Rican case is not unique in all particulars. In Cuba,
for instance, Chinese contract laborers were imported in very large
numbers before emancipation and worked alongside slaves on the
same enterprises. In Barbados in the seventeenth century, European indentured servants and enslaved Africans and Amerindians cut cane together under British masters. Thus the Puerto
Rican experience, in which African and Creole slaves and freeborn
"white" Creoles worked side by side, is but one of several. Each
such case shares certain features with the others. In all, acknowledged ethnic and/or "racial" differences tended to separate those
of one status (for instance, the slaves) from those of another (for

instance, the indentured servants). In all, those of nonslave status were complementary to the slaves—at least, until final emancipation erased that category from the Caribbean region, island by island. Accordingly, differences in status among categories of forced labor illuminate the local code of race and ethnic relations, and say something as well about the intrinsic characteristics of each such category. Just as the presence and status of enslaved Africans in Cuba threw light upon the position of the Chinese contract laborers, so too those laborers, by their presence and status, help to enhance our understanding of Cuban slavery.

Hence the Puerto Rican case, while only one of several, may be worthy a somewhat closer look, not only for what it reveals to us about Puerto Rico itself (and its allegedly benign slavery), but also for what it suggests generally about the exaction of labor power in colonies of this kind. In addition, it may be worthy of notice because, *unlike* the other cases, it involved the deliberate and systematic disfranchisement of free white citizens, in the nineteenth century and before emancipation, who then joined enslaved Africans in doing the most onerous and debased labor.

The Puerto Rican case is also of interest because it marks the late development of the plantation system and of slavery—long after these European innovations had first been introduced by Spain into the Antillean region. Spain's hegemony in the West Indies lasted more than a century; but its early experiments with the sugarcane did not flourish. For a very long period, Spain ruled the Antilles alone—but did little with them.

Early Spanish colonial exploitation in the New World was typified by a stress on the extraction of precious metals, and this emphasis was important not only in its effects upon the economy of the metropolis, but also upon Spanish colonial policy in later centuries. Extractive exploitation soon led to a concentration of Spanish colonists and colonial interest in the highlands of South and Middle America, areas of advanced aboriginal social and political organization, dense populations, and enormous mineral wealth.

But the Antilles were the first American lands to fall to Spain. Less heavily populated than the highlands of Tierra Firme, characterized by less complex and less well organized aboriginal societies than those of the highlands, and endowed with only a limited supply of ores, these islands soon lost their immediate exploitable appeal for the conquerors. After the conquest of Middle America, the insular colonists sought every chance to migrate to the mainland, where opportunities for direct gain were greater. Except for small enclaves, the islands' native populations were decimated by warfare, maltreatment, starvation, and disease.

Modern Antillean populations, particularly in the areas of early Spanish settlement, still carry some of the genetic heritage of Arawak ancestors; and many cultural features—for example, technical processes, agricultural practices, foods, house types, folktales, and lexical items—can be traced to these aboriginal antecedents. But for the greater part, the insular aboriginal populations were crushed and their cultures obliterated by the impact of a more powerful society, bent upon a kind of specialized plunder.

With the virtual destruction of the insular Native Americans and the depletion of gold resources, Spain's exploitative interests in the Antilles also waned. First to introduce the sugarcane, the plantation system, and African slaves to the islands, Spain failed to maintain its early support of a sugar-and-slave pattern in the Caribbean. Bourne, an early North American historian of the region, writes (1904: 272):

> The development of the sugar industry and the growth of slavery were dependent upon each other, especially after the mines in the Antilles gave out. Each trapiche, or sugar mill, run by horses or mules, required thirty or forty Negroes, and each watermill eighty at the least. Had the commerce of the islands been reasonably free, plantation slavery on a large scale would have rapidly developed, and the history of Hayti and the English islands would have been anticipated a century by the Spaniards.

Bourne anticipates too much. It was not the absence of free trade alone that inhibited the development of a large-scale slave plantation system in the Spanish Caribbean of the sixteenth century, but the entire character of contemporary metropolitan Spanish society. One might well argue that, even with free trade, Spain's early plantation experiments in the islands would probably have grown slowly. In fact, the Spanish economy of the sixteenth century was apparently not prepared to absorb the products of large-scale plantation production. The same forces which inhibited the sustained growth of the plantation system in the Spanish islands also deprived that system of the expanding metropolitan markets it would have needed in order to flourish.

Those islands which remained Spanish until the nineteenth century thus provided a significant contrast to the insular possessions or former possessions of Britain, France, and the Netherlands, the preeminent Antillean sugar producers before 1800. For nearly three centuries, the Spanish West Indies stood guard along the routes of the fleets carrying gold and silver from mainland America to the metropolis, and quicksilver and finished goods from the metropolis to the New World. But they fulfilled their military and supply function with an absolute minimum of internal development. Puerto Rico, for instance, was governed by a civil administrative hierarchy dispatched from the metropolis and supported by funds provided by the Crown from its income in New Spain. A military outpost and provision station, Puerto Rico played a largely passive and defensive role for centuries. Its population was sparse—Negro slaves in limited numbers, many freemen of color, squatter subsistence farmers of different backgrounds, militia and government officials, and a few Native Americans. Legal trade, funneled entirely through the one port of San Juan Bautista (Puerto Rico), was very limited, though smuggling early became important, and remained so during the eighteenth century.

It was not until the start of the nineteenth century, however, that Puerto Rico entered a period of rapid change, markedly different from the stasis of the preceding 300 years. Meanwhile, the Caribbean region and the European world had changed greatly. In the preceding century, France had won out over Britain in the sugar market, only to lose its advantage in the Haitian Revolution: "In less than two months, 2,000 Europeans had been massacred; hundreds of plantations had been laid waste; and the world's supply of sugar was suddenly reduced by over a hundred million hundredweights" (Mathieson 1926: 9). The locus of commercial power in Britain had shifted from the West Indian sugar planters to the cotton manufacturers; free trade had largely supplanted commercial exclusivism, and the British West Indian planters were sped upon their decline by the development of sugar production in competing areas, the increasing tempo of slave revolts, high interest rates, and the wastefulness of their own productive arrangements (Williams 1944).

## Forced Labor and Economic Development

It was in the starting decades of the nineteenth century that the growing merchant and landed classes in the Spanish Antilles began to make themselves heard in the metropolis. Cuba, larger and more populous than Puerto Rico and Spanish Santo Domingo, took the lead in the struggle for accelerated economic freedom and internal development; but Puerto Rico was not far behind. In 1808, the Spanish Crown invited Puerto Rico to name a representative to the central governing council of the Empire (de Hostos 1949: 72). The purpose of this grant of limited representation was to reduce separatist pressures in the colony. The grant led inevitably, however, to demands for even greater commercial independence and freedom from royal restrictions. As early as 1797, the merchants of San Juan had petitioned the Spanish king to open San Juan as a free port, on the model of the Danish establishment at St. Thomas (de Hostos 1949: 74). And when D. Ramón Power went forth to the Spanish Royal Council as Puerto Rico's first deputy, he carried with him a list of twenty-two propositions, which delineated the economic aspirations of his merchant and landed countrymen. The list included petitions for the end of church dues; the abolition of payments for the construction of military facilities; the encouragement of free trade; an end to nepotism (particularly where it favored the *peninsulares* over the Puerto Rican *criollos*); and demands for the exclusion of the landless from Crown lands, together with control of the labor of landless citizens (Ramírez de Arellano 1936: 39–41; *Boletín Histórico* 1923: 10, 117). It is these final demands, and their satisfaction, that constituted the basis for a new labor policy in Puerto Rico. It is clear that the Crown's submission to economic pressures in the island represented not only a shift in economic policy, but also the basis for significant changes in the distribution of political power—and hence of force—in island affairs.

D. Ramón Power returned to Puerto Rico with much to show for his efforts. The emergence of new structural features affecting the relationship of Crown land to private land, of landless persons to landed persons, and of capital-poor enterprise to capital-rich enterprise, signified that the subsequent development of island society, both in economic and in political terms, would be radically different. The effects of the new policy took their shape from the prior disposition and life-style of the island's inhabitants. The lack of a developed plantation system and the very uneven economic development of the island had resulted in the absence of any large number of slaves (Díaz Soler 1957; Curtin 1969: 30–34). At the same time, the irregular development of plantations and the institutional arrangements by which slaves might win their freedom contributed to the growth of a substantial population of free men of color; in fact, almost from the start of the colony, the number of colored freemen had equaled and often exceeded the number of slaves on the island. Figures for the period before 1800 are not plentiful, but reports for 1777 and 1787 give some idea of the distribution of free and unfree of African origins (Brau 1904: 199; Steward et al. 1956: 46):

|  | 1777 | 1787 |
|---|---|---|
| Whites | 31,951 | 46,756 |
| Indians | 1,756 | 2,302 |
| Pardos—free | 24,164 | 34,867 |
| Negroes—free | 4,747 | 7,866 |
| Mulattoes—slave | 3,343 | 4,657 |
| Negroes—slave | 4,249 | 6,603 |

The category *"pardo"* is significant, for the term was used here to describe anyone who was not classifiable as "white" or "black." The absence of a "free mulatto" category makes clear what is otherwise concealed—that free pardos were those of mixed genetic origin not classified in these censuses as "white." Thus, for the respective dates, the numbers of freemen of color and of slaves would be: 28,911 and 7,592; and 42,733 and 11,260.

The "white," "free pardo," and "free Negro" groups were not isolated from each other socially. Though such commentators as

Iñigo Abbad make clear that the lot of slaves was often miserable, the extent of genetic intermixture was such that the majority of the population in the eighteenth century is believed to have been of "blended"—that is, European and African (and Native American) —ancestry. The original European settlers included not only colonists from Spain who came with the intention of settlement, but also shipwrecked sailors, deserters, adventurers, and convicts. By the start of the nineteenth century, a very substantial part of the island population appears to have disassociated itself from the control of the insular civil and military administration by seeking refuge in the highlands, where squatter subsistence farming on unattended Crown lands was possible. The royal decree permitting private inheritable property in land was not enacted until 1778, by which time the squatter highland pattern was firmly established. A number of such settlers attached themselves to colonists already working highland land, either farming on some kind of share basis or offering their labor to others. In 1775, the number of such dependent settlers, called *agregados,* exceeded the number of slaves (Abbad 1954 [1788]: 153). Fernández Méndez (1969: 351) has drawn a useful distinction between the truly landless, who had no working arrangement with other landholders, whom he calls *desacomodados,* and the agregados, who worked, on share arrangements, land that they did not own.

But it would appear that, for both groups, the control exercised by the landed or by the state was minimal before the Power reforms initiated after 1809. In his instructions to Power, the mayor of San Juan, D. Pedro Irizarri, wrote:

The magnanimity of my countrymen, or rather the abundance of uncultivated lands whose owners are unable to develop them, is in my opinion a great obstacle that forcibly retards the development of population, limits harvests, and stimulates vice and hooliganism among many who could be useful citizens, valuable to themselves, the country and the state. To begin with, the abundance of uncultivated land holds back the people because its owners, lacking the power to cultivate it, make it available to the poor so that they may break land and clear pasture for livestock. Those who receive the land (who are called agregados) need not report to the owner on any regular basis, nor pay rent, nor render the owner any service in recognition of his ownership; on the contrary, the owner almost always gives the agregado a half dozen cows, and they share equally in the profits of raising them. Build in the waste of these uplands an improvised little shack, dilapidated, poor and contemptible, of boards and branches such that, without any exaggeration, a man can finish the job in eight days, better called a bird's nest with its straw roof, or a wild animal's lair with its pitiful materials, than the home of rational beings. Settled here, these workers in name only, together with wife and children, desirous of having land but without spending money for its acquisition, and with no other source of income, might be expected to apply themselves to cultivation: on the contrary, they reduce the harvests, because even if they clear a *cuerda* of land in the bush, that is, 75 Castilian *varas*, they only cultivate corn, beans, rice or potatoes, basic staples that hardly last out the year; but they never plant coffee, plantains, cane, cotton or any other crop that bears repeatedly, and from the lack of these things the harvests decline, since they are unconcerned and do without, and the landowners get no benefit therefrom . . . and those without cultivated land readily abandon it to take up other land, which they do frequently, and it is rare that they stay a year in one place, some staying only a month, always vagrant, wandering, without a fixed residence, neither knowing nor following the conduct of a settled serious worker. . . .

The lack of labor, what can it bring to agriculture but its ruination? All landowners lack labor, and some see no solution. What does it matter if others want to increase the labor force, if they lack the means? The best-manned sugar haciendas do not have 50 Negroes whom they can put to work; the small number of resident peons, much reduced since the shipments of those who are militiamen to serve in the city, cost more in wages, and there are more than a few hacendados who suffer the loss of a good part of their crops for the lack of harvest hands (Fernández Méndez 1969: 351–52).

Irizarri understood that the economic development of the island would depend ultimately on the availability of labor, and he was equally aware that the securing of such labor might involve some delicate adjustments:

This lack could be corrected in part by the putting to work of those who have none; but to perfect our agriculture, these are not enough, and it will be necessary to secure others, either free men or slaves:

whether it be one or the other, and to which of the two may be given
preference, either being a delicate and unpleasant matter, should be
decided only after a serious, profound and scrupulous discussion,
and with prudence (Fernández Méndez 1969: 353).

Thus the situation facing the agricultural entrepreneurs of Puerto
Rico in 1809 did not differ substantially from that faced by the
British and French plantation pioneers 150 years earlier. But there
were two fundamental differences: Puerto Rico already had a substantial population of landless (and politically defenseless) free
men; and the slave trade to the Spanish Antillean colonies was
about to come under intense pressure from the English. Hence the
landless freemen of the island, no matter what their complexion,
were of very considerable interest to Puerto Rico's embryonic captains of industry, and the instructions to Power neatly summarize
their plans for their landless fellow citizens. In substance, the availability of land on the island meant that a free laborer was able to
produce his own subsistence without entering into significant relationships of dependence on landowners or the state. Agricultural
entrepreneurs, in turn, found the cost of labor "high," by virtue of
its unavailability. And so much undeveloped land was available
for squatter use that plantation owners and landowners generally
could not appropriate, in the form of rent, a profitable proportion
of the surplus of free farmers. Such was the situation in Puerto
Rico at the end of the first decade of the nineteenth century.

That century opened, as we have seen, with France's loss of the
sugar markets, while Britain and other powers were not able immediately to fill the resulting gap in the world's sugar supply. The
sale of the Louisiana Territory—conditioned by the loss of French
Saint-Domingue—and the wave of revolutionary activity in Spanish
America followed soon after. In 1815, the Spanish Crown, anxious
to retain its few remaining possessions in the New World, and
pressed for more concessions by the landed and merchant classes
in these colonies, issued the Cédula de Gracias, or Decree of Bene-
faction. This decree opened Puerto Rican ports to legal commerce,
allowed royalist refugees from the mainland and Catholic entrepreneurs from other areas (including Louisiana and Haiti) to enter the island with their slaves, permitted the importation of sugar

processing machinery tax-free, and arranged for liberal grants of land to newcomers. In the following year, 324 foreign Catholics came to Puerto Rico from colonies outside the United States. Eighty-three additional settlers came from the erstwhile Louisiana Territory, bringing their slaves, their technical knowledge, and their wealth (Brau 1882: 1·6). Thus the Cédula de Gracias set in motion a series of internal economic changes so far-reaching in their effects that the early decades of the nineteenth century have come to be known as Puerto Rico's "Golden Age"—though it was hardly golden for those who toiled in the sun.

## Tightening the Screws

In 1812, Puerto Rico had only 17,000 slaves, and the planters who arrived after 1815 brought few slaves with them. In 1817, the Crown submitted to British pressure and agreed to abolish the slave trade in three years. The subsequent half-century was marked by the most complicated maneuvers on the part of the Crown, which sought on the one hand to satisfy the insatiable demands for more slaves on the part of its Cuban and Puerto Rican hacendados and on the other to avoid open conflict with Great Britain (Williams 1950: 22–45; Corwin 1967). The expectable happened: the earlier demands embodied in Power's mission were met by the systematic, legalized coercion of free fellow citizens, whose only real sin was their landlessness. This coercion came about through the legal institutionalization of a worker-landowner relationship that had operated previously through force of custom; the difference inhered in depriving the landless of their access to land. Strict regulation of the labor of free but landless citizens was initiated in 1824 (*Boletín Histórico* 1915: 2, 33; art. 8), fourteen years after Power's mission. Between 1824 and 1827, the number of agregados increased from 14,327 to 38,906 (de Córdova 1831–33: 6, 431). In the same period, the number of slaves increased from 22,725 to 28,418—some part of which increase was probably natural, rather than from importation. In 1837 the screws were tightened. El Bando de Policia y Buen Gobierno, enacted under the authority of Governor-General D. Miguel López de Baños, compelled all landless unemployed to go to work on local plantations. All workers had to register their names on municipal rolls (Brau 1904: 246; *Boletín Histórico* 1917: 4, 129–30). In 1849, as the planters further reconsolidated their power, Governor-General D. Juan de la Pezuela extended the law so that workers were compelled to carry workbooks (the infamous *libretas reglamentarias*) recording their services, and maintained by the plantation owner or manager who employed them. Workers were forbidden to change their place of employment if they had contracted debts at the plantation where they were already employed; and it is worth remarking that these laborers were plainly less able to produce their own subsistence than before, since such debts were often contracted. Loss of the workbook was punished by forced labor without pay, repeated loss by six months' imprisonment (Brau, ibid.). Information on pay rates is expectably scanty; but the lack of alternatives for the landless freeman suggests that salaries could hardly have depended on collective bargaining.

The overt intention of the 1849 decree was to bind landowners and municipal administrators, as well as the landless laborers, to a just system of labor practices. But the redistribution of power symbolized by these various decrees makes it plain that the landless were deprived of any means, economic or political, of defending themselves. A modern Puerto Rican historian writes:

> Vagrancy spread through the whole island, among the free and freed, making necessary regulations to compel the idle to work. Although logically one understands "wage earner" [*jornalero*] to mean anyone who lives by a wage, Governor López de Baños defined *jornalero* as any person, free or freed, who had neither property, profession nor position by which to live. Such a "wage earner" was left obliged, as a result, to work as a hired hand for some employer (Morales Muñoz 1949: 72).

That forced labor legislation was used, together with slavery, and that such legislation was based on property and not in any way on the physical type of its victims, is of great importance in interpreting the evolution of race relations in Puerto Rico, and the way in which racial identity and national identity are linked in the island's culture. Turnbull, writing in 1840, defined the agregados as "considered of pure European descent, holding the station of cottiers on the plantations, and contributing a certain portion of labor in place of rent" (1840: 556). Endowing the category of agregado with a racial label is extremely questionable, even though Turnbull is careful to say "considered of" European origin; but it certainly suggests the presence of nonslave workers on the plantations, many of them at least not wholly African in ancestry. Turnbull notes that five years earlier (1835) there had been 40,785 agregados and 34,336 slaves in Puerto Rico. Turnbull states very explicitly that free "whites" worked alongside slaves on the plantations—that fields were cultivated and sugar manufactured by white men.

Some historians do not regard the legislation of the period as a basis for forced labor. Morales Muñoz (ibid.) writes:

> This administrative method was not an intervention in free labor, as has been believed through error, but rather a legitimate intervention of authority in the generalized vagrancy or idleness, which was always the cause of frequent delinquency. In our days, vagrancy is a punishable crime in most of the states of the American union, and to avoid it, the "work book system" (*sistema de las libretas*) was extended. This labor legislation had, as its only end, to prevent the effect by attacking the cause: that is, it prohibited vagrancy or idleness, mother of all vices, making work compulsory. It converted the potential delinquent into a worker, useful to himself as well as to the society in which he was living.

It is remarkable how closely Morales Muñoz agrees with Mayor Irizarri, who prepared his instructions for D. Ramón Power 140 years earlier. Such an interpretation wholly avoids the vital political issues that flow from all such practices, temporary or permanent, as in the case of those countries where an elaborate penology is profitable to the state, at the same time that it suspends the political rights of its "vagrants." In some cases, such practices fall most heavily upon population segments of a certain ethnic or physical type; in the Puerto Rican nineteenth-century case, the state showed itself capable of rising above such tawdriness, coercing black and white alike to achieve "economic development."

Until all laws affecting the legal rights of landless workers to work where they chose, when they chose, and for whom they chose were revoked in Puerto Rico, the significant distinctions between slave and free—at least with regard to the growth of the plantation system—were deliberately blurred. The laws were repealed in 1873, the same year that slavery itself ended in Puerto Rico. It is perhaps significant that El Grito de Lares, the revolutionary spasm of 1868, was marked by a call both for the emancipation of the slaves and for the burning of workbooks—suggesting that the nature of these twin oppressions was well understood by the revolutionaries. Thus ended—legally, at least—an almost unique chapter in the history of labor in the Antilles. It is instructive in that it demonstrates the color-blindness of the planter class—so far as getting the cane cut was concerned—at the same time that it offers further proof that white men can indeed plant, water, cut, and grind cane beneath a tropical sun. It also throws into relief the functioning of slavery in the Hispanic Antilles—or, at least, in Puerto Rico—where the treatment accorded slaves may well have been conditioned by the existence of a large, free, landless, and politically defenseless labor supply. Finally, it suggests that the history of Antillean labor will only be fully understood when slavery, contract labor, forced labor, and all other means for relating labor to the instruments of production are seen in relation to one another in any particular locale or historical period. Such an approach may shed fresh light on the limitations of slavery studies that emphasize racial differences or moral considerations only.

# 4

## The History
## of a
## Puerto Rican Plantation

This study of a sugar plantation is an attempt to combine information from historical documents with data collected from elderly informants for purposes of historical reconstruction. The subject is the changing way of life of people living in a community on the south coast of Puerto Rico; the aim, to show the relationship of social forms to economic organization: in this case, to the prevailing agricultural system. Fieldwork in 1948–49 provided firsthand materials for describing the system at the time. But data collected for historical reconstruction were scanty, necessitating frequent inferences in interpretation. A collateral source of information was provided by the reminiscences of ten chief informants of advanced age.

Though the materials raise more questions than they can answer, we suggest here a threefold typology for the history of large-scale agricultural enterprises in the region. Significant changes over time in the life-style of local people fit clearly with the successive stages of plantation history. This typology has two points of reference. On the one hand, it is based on determinable changes in the economy of a single region of one Caribbean island, which we shall undertake to describe in some detail. On the other, it suggests something about the relationship between such changes and the patterning of local life, a relationship that may be further tested against comparable histories in other regions, such as the northeast coast of Brazil and the Guianas. Hence the wider intent is to formulate a developmental schema marked by regularities that may hold for other cases.

## Stages of Development of the
## Puerto Rican Sugar Industry

The plantation has been defined as "a capitalistic type of agricultural organization in which a considerable number of unfree laborers were employed under unified direction and control in the production of a staple crop" (Gray 1941: 444).

This general description of the plantation as a type was formulated for the North American antebellum South, but it may be applied usefully and appropriately to the pre-emancipation plantations of the Caribbean islands, Brazil and the Guianas, and certain other New World areas. In its operation, according to Gray, the plantation system was marked by four principal distinguishing characteristics: (1) the roles of the laboring and employing classes were set sharply apart; (2) the aim of the system was continuous commercial (that is, market-oriented) agriculture; (3) the trend was to specialization in monocrop production; and (4) the enterprise was capitalistic in character in that the value of slaves, land, and equipment required the investment of money capital, frequently in large sums and frequently borrowed, while the planter tended to assume the role of businessman, testing success by the yield of income relative to the capital invested (Gray 1941: ibid.).

While additional characteristics undoubtedly distinguish various plantation "types" from each other in terms of the amount of equipment required for processing, the annual or perennial character of the crop, and so on, Gray's treatment provides a typological (and variably chronological) baseline. That most plantations arose in the New World tropics, and that these were prevailingly staffed with African and Amerindian slaves, are features incidental to the organization of the system itself and not essential to it. Plantations as defined above have existed mainly in the tropics because tropical areas have long been an accessible economic frontier, particularly suited to expanding capitalistic agriculture, and this agriculture has been most profitably expressed in plantation organization (Thompson 1932: 13–14). Most plantation crops are raised in subtropical areas. More significant, however, is the fact that these crops were essential to the development of European consumption patterns and industry and that raising them facilitated the early overseas expansion of European capitalist enterprise.

The means used for relating labor to the land, in situations where labor was scarce and land plentiful, was basic to the plantation system, while the racial character of unfree and coerced labor was only an incidental aspect of this relationship. During the history of the New World slave-based plantation, forced European labor was commonly employed; toward the close of the slavery period, contract labor—European, Indian, East Indian, Chinese, and African—became popular. Hence the essential features of the plantation system in its early stages were its dedication to commercial monocrop production and the unfree or contracted (and partly coerced) character of its labor supply: climate, geography, and "race" were incidental to the plantation form. Though most plantation crops can be grown only in tropical or subtropical climates, these same crops can be grown by the use of nonplantation forms of organization. And plantation organization has not been restricted to tropical and subtropical areas (Thompson 1932; Wolf and Mintz 1957).

From 1815 until 1876, a full-scale plantation system using both slaves and coerced (but nonslave) laborers called *agregados* (Mintz 1951a) operated in Puerto Rico. In 1876, with the abolition of slavery and legally sustained forced labor, a modified form of plantation organization developed, persisting until the end of the nineteenth century. In 1899, after the United States invaded and seized Puerto Rico, radical changes in the organization of sugar production were introduced, creating a new "stage" in plantation history.

I have labeled these three periods as follows: (1) the slave-and-agregado plantation period; (2) the family-type hacienda period; and (3) the corporate land-and-factory combine period. Subsequent writers (Hutchinson 1957; Wagley and Harris 1955) have applied other labels to different New World plantation areas; but the three "stages," whatever their labels, seem to have succeeded each other with some regularity, though by no means invariably. In each period, it is possible to describe the prevailing organization of plantation production in terms of a number of traits which, taken together, stand for a type or model. Such formulations are necessarily abstract, incomplete renderings, but here part of the picture will be filled in by describing the historical development of agricultural organization in a particular south coast Puerto Rican community.

Though the sugarcane, slavery, and the plantation system were first introduced into Puerto Rico as early as the beginning of the sixteenth century, it was not until after the start of the nineteenth century that commercial sugar production was undertaken in earnest. At this time, the Haitian Revolution had reduced the most advanced sugar-producing area in the world to a largely self-contained peasant society; the sugar-producing British West Indies had fallen upon hard times; the revolutions in South America had restricted the scope of Spanish colonial rule, increasing the proportionate importance of Spain's Antillean possessions; royalist emigrés from South America needed a place to settle; and Spain was eager to secure and develop her remaining holdings in the New World. These conditions, taken together, were responsible in the main for the subsequent development of Puerto Rico as an important sugar producer and for the maturation of the plantation system on that island.

The Cédula de Gracias of 1815 (*Boletín Histórico* 1927: 14, 3–24; López Domínguez 1927) permitted the entry of Catholic entrepreneurs who were granted land from the royal domain in proportion to the number of slaves they owned; provided for the tax-free importation of machinery; removed taxes on slaves and agricultural implements; established free commerce with Spain; and allowed direct commerce with foreign nations. Anyone familiar with the traditional mercantilism of Spanish policy can imagine the revolutionary effects of these changes on Puerto Rican agriculture; both sugar production and the number of slaves rose rapidly (Puerto Rico, Department of Agriculture and Commerce 1939–40: 116; Blanco 1948: 74). Illicit slave trading, in defiance of treaties with Great Britain that became effective in 1820, continued during the first half of the century (Williams 1950). And, as we have already seen, the shortage of labor power was also compensated for by legislation compelling landless citizens (agregados) to work as plantation wage earners alongside the slaves (Mintz 1951a).

*Table I.*

| Year | Sugar (in tons) | Year | Number of slaves |
|------|------|------|------|
|  |  | 1812 | 17,536 |
| 1827–28 | 9,391 | 1824 | 22,725 |
| 1834–35 | 21,928 | 1834 | 41,818 |
| 1846–47 | 52,089 | 1846 | 51,216 |
| 1860–61 | 65,517 | 1860 | 41,736 |

The slave-and-agregado sugar plantation was a tiny enterprise by modern standards, ranging in size from perhaps less than a hundred to as much as four hundred acres in total extent, with about one-quarter of its land in cane (Bagg 1851–52: 38–40). Steam or cattle provided the power for the crude grinding mills, which consisted of vertical iron rollers. Sugar processing was also crude, and the *moscovado* sugar "logs" or "heads" or "cones," produced by successive boiling, evaporation, and draining, were typical of much earlier developments in the sugar-making industry. Fertilizing was limited to the use of animal manure, and manuring was not always practiced; rudimentary hook-type plows were employed in field operations. Potential profits were lost in badly ground cane, poorly manured land, low-quality sugar, and high interest rates. The plantations were usually owned by individual families, with agents or single members of the family supervising the operations. The system expanded, however, during the first part of the period 1815–76 because the market remained generally favorable during this time, and a constant profit could be assured without additional investment in irrigation, improved technology, or enlarged operations. Highly important for the momentum of a newly reorganized sugar industry, even in the absence of technical advance, was the opportunity created for small-scale individual producers to launch themselves on a plantation career—Namier's "planters on the make," in contrast to the older established planter class—and the eventual political consequences of this new opportunity.

But the slave-and-agregado system was eventually doomed by the development of more advanced productive techniques and the employment of more efficient free labor in other regions. What might have been interpreted as a reluctance to invest in increasing the size and efficiency of plantations in the 1840s and 1850s had by 1870 become sheer inability to do so (Mintz 1951b).

The most important distinction between the slave-and-agregado plantation and the family-type hacienda which succeeded it was the latter's use of free labor, rather than slave labor and forced labor. To this distinction are attached many cultural features having to do with the style of life and the social relationships of the plantation working classes. Emancipation came relatively easily to Puerto Rico; but its enaction involved the pledge of certain guarantees to the planter classes. The nature of these guarantees suggests that the "saturated planters"—again to use Namier's terminology, this time for the older, more established estate owners—were confident of their ability to compete successfully in the labor market against the smaller-scale newcomers. Thus, for instance, it was the larger slaveholders of the south coast (those owning twenty-five slaves or more) who pressed hardest for emancipation, partly because they expected to benefit from indemnities, but also because of their probable superiority in attracting free labor after emancipation (Sanromá, quoted in Blanco 1935: 88).

The terms of employment arranged for the ex-slaves on the eve of emancipation help to explain this optimism. The labor contracts for *libertos* (freedmen) for the three-year period 1873–76 stipulated that the liberto must get his ex-owner's permission to leave the municipality and that he must reside on the farm of his contractor. The gradual increase in population and the related decrease in available land per capita for peasant farming also helped to "stabilize" the labor power of the sugar industry after 1873. Indeed, the ex-slaves and the agregados, formerly bound by harsh contracts, had both won an important political victory in 1873; but the ex-slaves were still bound by the subsequent legislation and by the need to eke out their survival on soil they did not own. In effect, the end of forced-labor laws and of slavery brought agregado and liberto into keener competition in the labor market. We know too little of the social consequences of these changes for the relationships between ex-slaves and agregados; but some of the features will be described in a later portion of this chapter.

Barring the all-important distinction between enslaved and free labor—even granting the reservations noted above—the family-type hacienda was only a continuation of the slave-and-agregado plantation. The functions of workers and employer were still, of course, kept sharply distinct, with labor provided predominantly by resident agregados, many of the slaves merely becoming agregados in name when they were emancipated; the system, based on commercial agriculture, was still a capitalistic enterprise requiring money investment (in fact, the elimination of slavery may be said to have deepened the commitment to a capitalistic mode of production); and monocrop production for markets still prevailed.

Technologically, the Puerto Rican sugar industry lagged far behind the sugar industry in the British and French West Indies and elsewhere. The industry had been revolutionized outside of Puerto Rico by the creation of great centralized grinding mills, to which the cane of many former small-scale plantations now flowed. This "factory central" system enabled small-scale producers to contract to provide the central with all the cane they grew, so that losses inherent in the use of outmoded and inefficient productive methods could be reduced. In the period 1876–99, Puerto Rican producers made repeated efforts to establish such centrals, but nearly all of these efforts ended in failure for lack of the necessary capital (López Domínguez 1927; Mintz 1951b). The inability to convert to more efficient production led to widespread deterioration of the industry. In 1899, 81 of the 289 plantations in forty-five Puerto Rican municipal districts were no longer in cultivation (Carroll 1900: 116).

Immediately after the North American invasion, however, capital began to flow heavily into the sugar industry, re-creating a "sugar way of life" in radically different form. By 1899, a mill rendering 5,000 tons of sugar annually required an outlay of $500,000, and control of cane-producing lands in sufficient quantity to keep the mill operating efficiently during the harvest was of course essential to economic success (Davis 1900: 37–38).

The new land-and-factory combines developed first in the south coast zone of the island, seat of the early expansion of the slave-and-agregado plantation of the preceding century. During the periods of the slave-and-agregado plantation and the family-type hacienda, capital investment was mainly restricted to slaves and machinery, and the machinery was comparatively inexpensive. Land was cheap, often granted by the Crown as a gift; cultivation was unscientific, investment speculative. In the third and still-continuing period, however, capital investment shifted from labor to machinery and land; labor could now be hired, rather than represent a fixed charge in the form of chattel slaves. Agriculture became intensive and scientific. Perquisites were no longer supplied to workers in place of wages, and efforts and techniques became standardized. "Permanent investment and a long-term interest in a defined area of land" typify the modern plantation (Greaves 1935: 170).

Some of the changes in Puerto Rico after 1899 can be demonstrated most dramatically by simple statistics. Between 1909 and 1919 the number of holdings increased from 6,816 to 8,839; the total percentage of arable land in cane in the island rose from 9.3 to 17.5. In the same period, the number of sugar factories belonging to individuals decreased from fifty-one to twelve, while the number owned by corporations increased from twenty-three to thirty-three. In 1909, there were forty-eight enterprises in sugar with a capital of less than $5,000; in 1919, not one of this size remained. In 1909, there were three enterprises (all established after 1899) with capital investments of $500,000 or more; in 1919 there were thirty-two. Individual ownership in 1909 was valued at $1,328,809 and corporate ownership at $13,129,453; in 1919, individual ownership was valued at $3,333,521 and corporate ownership at $45,925,205 (López Domínguez 1927: 223).

The corporate land-and-factory combine is a logical continuation of earlier agricultural systems, but with notable differences, largely produced by changes in size and technology. The functions of laborer and employer are even more sharply distinct than before—the "employer" is corporate, and contact between the corporate personality and the laborers is completely impersonal, wage-based, and mediated through an employed managerial hierarchy. The new system is similar to the older ones in that commercial agriculture prevails, but whereas the older forms tended to fall back on subsistence production in times of depression, the corporate land-and-factory combine can maintain its production even in the face of a worldwide contraction of markets (Gayer, Homan, and James 1938: 159). This is the system of sugarcane and sugar production that now prevails in Puerto Rico.

### The Development of Hacienda Vieja:
### Regional and Municipal Setting

The municipality in which Hacienda Vieja was located, called here "Cañamelar," was a *barrio* (subdistrict) of the Villa de Coamo until 1842 (*Boletín Histórico* 1917, 4: 93). Between 1842, when Cañamelar was established as an independent municipality, and 1899, six sugar estates operated within the municipal limits. Five of these began operations long before emancipation, but probably not as early as the start of the nineteenth century. No record of the exact dates when these estates began operations could be secured. The mass baptism of fifteen African slaves by one plantation owner in 1844, however, suggests that his plantation may have already been in operation at that time. In 1852, the baptisms of African slaves by another Cañamelar plantation owner were recorded, and by 1855 all four plantation owners who could be identified were baptizing newborn slaves in Cañamelar. These baptismal dates suggest that by the year 1855 all four plantations were probably in operation. Of the four documented slave-holding plantations, one was started by the son of a Venezuelan royalist emigré, another by a Spaniard from the Canary Islands, the other two by Spaniards whose exact origins are not known. These four estates operated until a few years after the start of the twentieth century. Very little is known of the other two estates. One could be identified only by name. The other seems to have begun operations somewhat later than 1855. Of the four known plantation owners of the slavery period, only one is definitely described in municipal records as living outside the municipality.

The cane acreage cultivated by the six plantations is difficult to estimate for the period before 1880. Cultivation on the south coast was limited by the need to exploit the poorly drained lowlands (*poyales*) and river floodplains. Irrigation before the United States occupation apparently depended mainly on the plantation owner's capacity to construct and improve water facilities. In some cases, deductions in taxes were granted by the Crown to plantation owners who invested in irrigation works. Although severe droughts were frequent in this area, the 1899 census states that the Ponce District (of which Cañamelar was a part) had the largest acreage in cane that year and the highest average hacienda area—115 *cuerdas* (United States War Department 1900: 154. The cuerda is slightly less than an acre in size). The first Governor's Report issued after the United States occupation (Allen 1901: 39) gives the average size of a Puerto Rican sugar hacienda as thirty-five acres (i.e., about thirty-four cuerdas), so that south coast estates in the Cañamelar region remained relatively large at this later date.

While all of Cañamelar suffered from the severe and persistent droughts which characterize the south coast, groundwater was most accessible in Cañamelar in the eastern lowland parts. It was in this eastern section of the *municipio* that the four main slaveholding plantations developed. Settlement of the western section of Cañamelar came later, and was much sparser. The only sugar mill to be built in the western part of the municipality in the nineteenth century was built later than those in the east and is said to have failed for lack of water. This important local variation in surface water supply in the municipality had considerable effect upon its later development. Agricultural wealth and population remained concentrated in the east as late as 1880; population increases and concentration of holdings in the west did not occur until after the American occupation, when the expansion of the cane industry and the development of irrigation systems made the potential productivity of the western half of Cañamelar as great as that of the eastern half. Municipality records for 1880 illuminate the local situation. In that year the estimated value of property in the municipality was 121,585 pesos, nearly half of which (57,326 pesos) was classified as agricultural wealth. A census of the town's workers by name and barrio is provided. Three hundred and ninety-five workers were living in the municipality in 1880, the largest aggregates, as would be expected in view of the hacienda distribution, in the two easternmost barrios. The barrio adjoining the town on the east contained two haciendas and had 131 workers; Barrio Poyal, the easternmost barrio of the municipality and the subject of study in this report, contained two haciendas and had 95 workers.

The two barrios with the highest land valuations were also to the east: the land of Barrio Llanos, which adjoined the town, was valued at 32,137 pesos; and that of Barrio Poyal, on the eastern border at 22,204 pesos. While the twelve farmers in Llanos and Poyal represented agrarian wealth of over 54,000 pesos (52,000 pesos of which was represented by the four haciendas), the twelve farmers in Cañamelar's northwest barrio owned a total agricultural wealth valued at but 1,179 pesos. Wealth in cattle, owned by forty-seven farmers, came to 17,678 pesos. Apart from the cattle-raising hacienda owners, who needed animals for draft use and for food, cattle owners were concentrated in the northwest of the municipality. Although cattle raisers were numerically important, their invested wealth was comparatively limited. There were also in Cañamelar twenty-six taxable businesses, with a total valuation of only 2,215 pesos, and other valuations were likewise small in comparison with the total land valuation.

These records provide another hint about municipal history. In the 1880 local census, sixty-four workers bore the surnames of the four original plantation owners in the east of Cañamelar. That is, about one-sixth of the *agrupación de braceros* (laborers' census) for that year had the surnames of the original plantation founders. Twenty-five of these workers carried the surname of Cañamelar's wealthiest hacienda operator, nineteen the surname of the second wealthiest. The baptismal records for 1863 show that slaves in that year had begun to acquire the names of their owners. There is little doubt, then, that these laborers of 1880 were, at least in good measure, the children of freed slaves or themselves freedmen. It remains a commonplace in Cañamelar that people of color are concentrated in the eastern barrios and in the districts along the eastern fringe of the town. That the eastern half of Cañamelar was more fully developed than the western has meant greater demographic stability as well. Between 1920 and 1940, Barrio Poyal, to the east, gained only 109 persons, while two western barriors gained 863 and 442, respectively (United States Bureau of the Census 1942). Clearly, in 1880 Cañamelar was a "sugar town," as it had been in 1855, and its center of development lay in the eastern barrios of Llanos and Poyal, in terms of agricultural wealth and rural labor supply.

We surmise that Cañamelar changed little from 1880 until the turn of the century. Local hacendados, though aware of the threat of outside competition in the sugar industry and their own weakened position, could do little; a statement from the town fathers, submitted to the government in 1888, underlines their position:

> The only agriculture now functioning here consists of four cane haciendas, if we take account of the prolonged droughts that have punished this area, reducing to insignificance the cultivation of minor crops. These haciendas, corroborating the theories of Ricardo, were founded on lands of first quality; and thanks to their amazing fertility and the high price of sugar at the time [1835–1855?], they could bear the substantial costs of machinery, buildings, irrigation, etc. . . . Today these selfsame haciendas maintain themselves, thanks to the remarkable and costly cultivation and manuring they use; but if production is more or less the same, the yield is far less. We cannot hide from ourselves the fact that profits have declined from what they were ten or twenty years ago, even without taking into account the decline in the value of sugar in recent years due to the tremendous stimulus to sugar-beet production in Europe and the extension of cane production to countries that were consumers before. Another cause of damage to our industry are the usurious rates of interest.

About ten years after the American occupation a modern central was built with local (i.e., Puerto Rican) capital in Cañamelar, but this central sold out to the expanding American corporation in the area in the 1920s. The south coast swiftly became typified by unified land-and-central productive units, rather than by the contractual relationships which obtain between independent landowning cane farmers and factory administrations in other areas, such as the north and west coasts. Cañamelar demonstrates through its history the simultaneous development of large estates and factory centers, as parts of the same productive process.

The almost complete absence of small, independent cane farmers (*colonos*) in Cañamelar has had an important effect on local social structure. As the great centrals replaced the local, outmoded haciendas, old-time hacienda owners, to a man, sold or rented their land to the large corporations. These hacienda owners and their descendants, living off the interest on the capital received for their fertile lands and reinvested, moved to urban centers and left a social vacuum in the municipality. In other areas, such as the west coast, these same hacienda owners frequently became colonos of the mill and continued to be a social force in their communities. One possible determinant of the difference was the water factor. American corporations, and a few Puerto Rican corporations as well, paid good prices for dry range at the turn of the century and afterward. Corporate organizations of this kind had sufficient capital to build their own wells and irrigation systems, and by 1920 a vast insular irrigation system was supplementing private works. Construction on this scale was never feasible for the nineteenth-century hacienda operators of Cañamelar and its neighbors. At the present time there are probably no irrigated farms on the south coast smaller than five hundred acres.

Around 1905, Cañamelar hacienda owners began to buy range-land near their haciendas, serving in fact as commission agents for an expanding American corporation. Cañamelar land was resold in large tracts to this and another corporation. Other extensive holdings were leased. Between 1905 and 1930, over 700 cuerdas of land were bought outright by a single mill-owning corporate entity in Cañamelar; another 5,000 cuerdas were leased by the same organization between 1909 and 1929. During the twenty-five year period from 1905 to 1930, the productive control of more than 12,000 cuerdas was marshaled under a single corporate owner-lessee in this single small municipality.

As Table II demonstrates, all data from 1897 on point to the progressive spread of sugarcane cultivation throughout the community.

*Table II.*

| Year | 1897[1] | 1910[2] | 1940[3] |
|---|---|---|---|
| Number of farms | 141 | 77 | 16 |
| Cuerdas in cane | 1,328 | 3,071 | 6,031 |
| Cuerdas in minor crops | 193 | 169 | less than 25 |

1. Carroll 1900:118.
2. United States Bureau of the Census 1910.
3. United States Bureau of the Census 1943.

The effects of the invasion of capital in the municipality of Cañamelar are many. From 1910 to 1940, the average farm size in Cañamelar increased from 162.8 cuerdas (United States Bureau of the Census 1910) to 1,405.1 cuerdas (United States Bureau of the Census 1943). Production of tobacco, fruits, and minor crops, never extensive in Cañamelar, became negligible after 1910. The concentration of ownership reached an extreme which it is never likely to exceed. Out of sixteen farms reporting in 1940, seven were owner-operated and six manager-operated. The average size of the seven owner-operated farms was 5.9 cuerdas, while that of the six managed farms was 3,731.8 cuerdas. Owner-operated farms controlled 0.2 percent of the crop area; managed farms, 99.6 percent.

## Hacienda Vieja During the Nineteenth Century

By the time of the emancipation, four of Cañamelar's six sugar estates had been operating for at least twenty years. These all lay in the fertile southeastern portion of the municipality, in an area watered by several man-made irrigation canals and endowed with large stretches of fertile marshland.

Hacienda Vieja, which, as Colonia Vieja, is the subject of much of this part of the discussion, was founded as a cane plantation during the first half of the nineteenth century. Its founder was the son of a Spanish royalist, a captain of cavalry, who had come to Puerto Rico in flight from Bolívar's government in Venezuela. It was not possible to ascertain whether the founder of Vieja received the land in a grant from the *real hacienda* before the practice of making such grants was discontinued, but it is likely that he did. The founder is first mentioned in the available municipal records in 1860, when he and other plantation owners of Cañamelar appealed to a royal official for a reduction in taxes. The reduction was requested because the terrible local droughts had been killing cattle and necessitating expenditures for irrigation by the estate owners. Mention is also made of the lack of free labor (*"pocos brazos libres"*) in the municipality. The owner of Vieja plantation at that time resided in the city of Ponce, and not on his estate. As early as 1852, this man had brought the children of two of his slaves to the local parish for baptism, suggesting that his hacienda may have been operating at that time. In 1861, he wrote his will, which contains the earliest documented assignment of the hacienda lands that could be found.

In 1872, along with other plantation owners of Cañamelar, the owner of Vieja shared in a royal subsidy or tax exemption to agriculturists who had invested privately in irrigation works. An additional item in the record of the subsidy indicates that the laws providing for royal support were enacted some twenty years after the irrigation systems were constructed. This is further evidence that Vieja plantation was in operation by 1852. The amount of cane under cultivation or irrigation in 1872 is not given, but since only 1,328 cuerdas, much of which was unirrigated, were planted to cane as late as 1897, irrigation was probably not extensive.

In 1880, the agricultural wealth of the Vieja estate was assessed at nearly 14,000 pesos, while the cattle of the estate were worth 1,000 pesos. The estate was at that time the third most valuable enterprise in Cañamelar. The Registry of Property for 1881 describes Hacienda Vieja as a property of 1,796 cuerdas, partly in cane, with pasture, mangrove swamp, and forest. Grinding mill capacity. is not given, nor is any figure furnished for the amount of land planted to cane, so that informant information had to be used in the following reconstruction.

The hacienda had a grinding mill which was equipped with three evaporators and stood, together with a small distillery, on the hacienda plaza. A large house for the owner or administrator, barracks remaining from slavery days, an "orphans" home (which, according to aged informants, had been used for the quartering of orphaned slaves purchased before 1873), a small hospital or infirmary building, and storehouses of various kinds were among the other hacienda facilities. A small house was located at the *tala,* or workers' subsistence crop area. Woodland located on the hacienda supplied the starting fuel for the grinding mill (the fires were kept up with the dried cane pulp, or bagasse), and tinder for the agregado families. A plantain grove supplied some food, and plantain leaves were used to plug the perforations in the bottoms of the sugar barrels. (These were left open when the sugar crystals were coagulating, while the molasses was allowed to seep through.) There was also a grove of *malanga* (probably *Xanthosoma sagitti-*

*folium* Schott) on the hacienda which was used by the agregados. Substantial stretches of pasture were needed to graze the hacienda stock; pasture was also set aside for the livestock owned by the agregados and hacienda artisans. Clearly, Hacienda Vieja was a highly developed productive unit in 1881, staffed with its own resident laborers and with many facilities provided for their use.

By 1882, Hacienda Vieja had been incorporated. It continued to operate as a corporation until the turn of the century, when it was still owned and supervised by members of a single family. Its lands and buildings had remained substantially unchanged for many years, and its sugar production was based on the cultivation, grinding, and processing of 300–500 cuerdas of land, part of it irrigated, and part naturally watered lowland.

North of the hacienda itself lay the subsistence plots of the workers, some as large as five cuerdas. Here agregados could raise crops for their own use, and at no cost, on their own time. Nearby was the *pieza de los pobres;* this plot of cane was ground around Christmastime each year, and the molasses, sugar, and rum produced from it were given to the poor of the neighborhood.

About 100 to 125 workers lived on the land of Vieja as agregados in the 1880s. Most but not all of these resident workers were the descendants of the hacienda slaves. Many were "white," and many were of mixed ancestry. (Puerto Rico has never had a bipartite "racial" division which lumps into a single "black" category those with any perceived African ancestry.) The work on the hacienda and the social arrangements for its workers were not divided according to any racial criteria, nor did persons of differing ancestry live separately.

Even more important for the evolution of Puerto Rican race relations than the absence of a bipartite "racial" division is the fact that the ex-slaves were generally more skilled at sugar-producing techniques of all kinds than were the descendants of freemen, whatever their racial background. The association of "race" and technical skill was thus an important aspect of Puerto Rican labor history. This association is doubtless rooted in the traditional distribution of tasks on slave-run haciendas before emancipation; slaves, rather than agregados, had usually been given the mill jobs and artisans' responsibilities because there was no question as to the regularity or dependability of their labor. In a report by a British consular official in Puerto Rico, written in 1875, we read: "In fact, in the process of sugar-making, the more skilled 'liberto' is generally employed within the boiling-house, while the free labourer does the rougher tasks of cutting and carrying the cane" (Great Britain Foreign Office 1875: 2). Thus the pattern of work distribution, though not apparently based on race, did take account of the distribution of existing skills; and by virtue of the history of local labor, the libertos would have occupied certain preferential positions in the period following emancipation.

Work on Hacienda Vieja lasted nearly all year. Then, as now, there were three growths of cane, planted so as to provide the mill with a regular flow of cane for grinding. Generally speaking, these growths differ primarily in terms of their maturation periods. Ratoon (*retoño*) cane grows for up to fourteen months, and two or more successive crops may be cut from the same planting. "Spring" (*primavera*) cane is cropped only once, and is grown for ten months or more. The "big growth" (*gran cultura*) cane, also cropped once, grows up to fourteen months before cutting. Hacienda owners balanced out these three growing cycles in order to achieve a continuous harvest during the grinding seasons. There were two such grinding seasons, rather than the present single season, each year, the first from Christmas until June, the second from August until October. The productive process was geared to the limited capacity of the small steam-driven mill and the most efficient use of local low-paid labor. Daily wages in this period, according to aged informants, ran at about a thirty-cent daily maximum for men, except for artisans and those who performed one special type of field labor; women received eighteen to twenty-two cents per day, children still less. Unable and often unwilling to mobilize the capital needed to shift to large-scale production, local estate owners eked out a profit by leaning heavily on low labor costs, a minimum of capital reinvestment, and paternalistic labor arrangements. For most of his work, the agregado was paid in services rather than in cash. On many haciendas (though, as far as could be determined, not at Hacienda Vieja), agregados were paid half their wages in *vales,* or scrip, redeemable at the hacienda store. Nevertheless, the hacienda economy must be thought of as a wage economy, at least in part. None of the agregados owned land, though many were allowed to work subsistence plots on hacienda land.

On Hacienda Vieja, women worked alongside the men. They fed cane into the grinders, loaded it on the hammocks which carried it into the mill, spread manure, cleaned seed, weeded, cleaned the fields after harvesting, and emptied the evaporating caldrons into the purging barrels. Evaporator tending (later, centrifuge tending), barrelmaking, ropemaking, cane cutting, seed planting, ditching and draining, and other technical jobs were done by men.

The processing apparatus of the hacienda was not very modern. Three horizontal iron cylinders were used to crush the cane. Double extraction, although developed much earlier, was not practiced. The cane juices were boiled by the anachronistic Jamaica Train method. Thickening little by little, they were transferred from caldron to caldron, then poured into the purging barrels. Here the molasses would drain out, leaving the crude, brown moscovado sugar. Hacienda artisans supervised this process and the packing of the sugar for shipment. The sugar was shipped in the same barrels in which it drained. The barrelmakers worked on the hacienda itself, though other haciendas had their barrelmakers in the town of Cañamelar. From Hacienda Vieja, the barrels were carried by ox-cart to Ponce, an eight-day trip, or loaded on small launches at the hacienda docks on Poyal Bay and carried thence to larger vessels for export.

Except for the grinding mechanism itself, Hacienda Vieja was operated entirely by human and animal power. The workday began at five or six o'clock in the morning and continued until five or six o'clock in the evening. A ten- to twelve-hour day, with perhaps an hour for lunch, was maintained. Relatively long midday breaks seem to have been common, even in slavery times. The brief ten o'clock pause for breakfast, which is religiously observed by the cane workers of Cañamelar today, was also customary in the nineteenth century. Lunch was brought to field workers by their wives or children. Much of the food was grown locally, since workers had small subsistence plots and could keep animals, and in the 1880s the area produced a good deal of beef and work cattle.

Yet there is conflicting evidence about the kind and quantity of food available. Barring serious drought, the subsistence plots were able to supplement the imported polished rice, dried salt cod, and red beans. Chick-peas, plantains, malanga, taro, sweet potatoes, yams, cassava, and corn were among the locally grown subsistence crops. A variety of herbs (*blero, verdolaga,* etc.; cf. Mintz 1951b) were gathered and used, both as food and medicinally. While greater variety in diet seems to have been the rule in the earlier period, the rice–beans–salt cod pattern preferred in 1948–49 was apparently already established in the food choices of local people.

If measured in terms of the use or consumption of manufactured or imported items, the standard of living of the Vieja workers was much lower in the eighties than it is today. Most, if not all, of the Vieja workers were then agregados, living in the barracks, relics of slavery that stood about the hacienda plaza. The wives of the agregados prepared their food in the kitchen, a centrally located building, lined with crude hearths. It was then carried into the one-room shacks where whole families lived. Furniture was made locally and was very rough. Only one laborer on Hacienda Vieja had an iron bed in the eighties. Clothing was very simple; several local seamstresses and tailors made most of it by hand. Rope-soled sandals were the only shoes worn by working people. Utensils carved out of coconut shells and gourds served as dishes, with a glass or china plate or two set aside for special occasions.

There was no hacienda store on Vieja. When workers had some small purchase to make, they would visit the village of Oriente. *Quincalleros,* ambulant peddlers, visited the hacienda regularly, as they continued to do until well into this century.

Medical care came from the hacendado's shelf, or in the form of herbs, roots, and the like, which were used to make teas, infusions, compresses, and other medicines (Mintz 1951b). The nearest doctor was in Ponce, several days' journey by carriage. Aged informants recalled numerous cases in which death might have been avoided had a doctor been available. Hacienda workers also lacked schools and churches. Local chapels, which typified the Cuban plantation pattern, seemed to be completely absent in Puerto Rico, perhaps because of the relatively small average size of its sugar plantations. The only school was a private institution with one teacher, run for the sons of the middle class and inaccessible to workers' children.

The work of the hacienda was directed by an administrator who was a member of the landowning family. Three foremen, or *mayordomos,* directed the labor force. Local hacienda artisans included two barrelmakers, two carpenters, and a blacksmith and his assistant. These men earned more and had higher status than any of the field laborers. Intermediate in status and in income were the *paleros,* or ditchers, who were field laborers, but with special skills.

The paleros' work was associated with the maintenance of irrigation systems and the adjustments necessary to keep growing cane from rotting in the poyal swamp areas. Ditches had to be dug in thick, plastic mud, their level delicately altered, yard by yard, to match the slope of the land and the water table. The paleros were famous among field laborers, since they traditionally went to work in their Sunday best, changing into their work clothes in the fields, and washing and changing again before returning home. This practice was undoubtedly related to the nature of their work, which kept them knee-deep in mud and water for much of the day; but it was associated in the minds of elderly local informants with the special prestige attaching to the paleros' skills. The paleros used distinctive long-handled, straight-edged shovels, often studded with brass or copper rings, and made their own handles from local woods, the butt of the handle hand-carved from a wood reputedly "cold" to the touch. A special sandal, the *plantilla,* was used on the left foot for seating the *pala* (shovel), and surveyor's lines were skillfully thrown by the palero in determining the pitch of the land. All of these details suggest some of the special knowledge and adeptness associated with a job which, in other contexts, might be regarded as no more than brute labor. Yet it need hardly be added that all the famous paleros of the region were black men and, in all probability, libertos or the direct descendants of libertos.

The limited contact between Cañamelar and the rest of Puerto Rico and the world required the local economy to be a substantially self-sufficient one, even though the enterprise was fundamentally capitalistic in its organization, its use of free landless labor, its reckoning of profits, and its market orientation. Thus we are confronted with a capitalistic enterprise cloaked in a version of manorial tradition and isolation—a typical example of a remarkable nineteenth-century plantation form which existed in Puerto Rico and many other locales.

While sugar was the cash crop, the land of Cañamelar in the 1880s was not so fully dedicated to cane cultivation as it later came to be. Balancing cane agriculture was the locally contained and sustained processing of cane. Other industrial, agricultural, and handicraft activities were also important. A flourishing brick industry was located in the town. Tanbark was collected from the mangrove swamps for the tanneries of Ponce. Tailors and seamstresses worked in the town of Cañamelar. Enough artisans lived there to support a social club, after the custom of artisans in all Puerto Rican towns of the time—"a casino of the second [artisan's] class." The artisan listings for 1880–81 include: barrelmakers, masons, carpenters, coach repairmen, blacksmiths, ropemakers, and mechanics. While the absolute number of specialists in Cañamelar has increased since the turn of the century, proportionately far fewer workers are specialists today.

The hacienda was primarily a family-owned and family-operated enterprise. Usually, a member of the family would administer the property, as in the case of Hacienda Vieja. If no member of the family lived on the hacienda, then some executor or manager employed by the family would take up residence in the hacienda house, and assume the responsibility for the hacienda's operation. The hacienda was thus the seat of continuous face-to-face, reciprocal deference-respect relations between the owner or manager and his family on the one hand and the hacienda agregados on the other. The resulting attitudes were formalized, personal, and of long standing.

> When Don Jaime would come with his family to watch us dance the *bomba* [an African–Puerto Rican dance] on the plaza, what a good time we would have! The family wouldn't stay long, but they would joke with all the *negritas ancianas,* and Don Jaime would laugh every time a new verse was sung. Sometimes he would call over the children and tease them, never badly.
>
> Don José Sánchez always blessed the little Negro children who would gather around him when he walked from the house to the

boiling house. He was a hard man, but he was accustomed to joke with the children, and throw pennies for them to fight over.

There was never a problem in those times about money. One needed very little. People weren't so proud or always so ambitious then. And if you needed a few cents very badly, you would always be able to borrow it from the mayordomo, who would know you, and the kind of work you were able to do.

The conduct of the members of the different groupings on the hacienda—the owner or manager and his family, the assistant mayordomos, the artisans, the workers of the fields—was disciplined by law and custom. Hacienda agregados did not challenge the authority of the hacienda owner. He cared for them when they were ill; he provided them with employment; he was often godparent to their children. Life was lived very largely within the hacienda itself, the owner its ruler.

The barrio setting, toward the close of the century, was one of apparent internal stability and tranquillity. Actually, the situation was not stable because of the losing battle local operators were waging against the more cheaply produced sugar of their foreign competitors. In 1902, Hacienda Vieja added a centrifuge to its mechanical equipment and was thus able to produce finer sugar than the moscovado type. This kind of improvement was part of the patching and mending that typified most pre-occupation changes. But by 1902 great factory centrals were already going up both to the east and west of Cañamelar. The patchwork improvements of the small hacienda owners were in vain.

## From Hacienda to Colonia: 1905–29

By 1905, the owners of Hacienda Vieja had decided to sell their lands to one of the new American corporations. One of the members of the owning family became a land agent for the purchasing corporation. Vieja ground its last crop in 1905, and in the following harvest the raw cane was carried by boat to the new factory central of the corporation. Since the cane in subsequent harvests went to the American central, much of the processing no longer took place on the hacienda. An old-time cultivation chief for the new corporation reports that at least twelve haciendas stopped grinding in 1904 alone in only three municipalities on the south coast. "On the present area of the estate of one of the largest American companies," a Department of Commerce report states (1917: 248), "there were formerly thirty-one old mills. The cane now grown on this area is ground by one factory." Barrelmakers, hacienda mechanics, and technicians found themselves out of work. A railroad was constructed along the coast, and cane could be brought to the central more rapidly and efficiently. Working cattle lost some of their importance, and many ox tenders became cane cutters.

In areas adjoining Hacienda Vieja some landowners chose not to sell their lands to the new corporations, and rented them instead. One such owner would never sell, and in 1953 his land was still leased to a corporate organization by his descendants, who resided in the Canary Islands. Something of the quality of the hacienda way of life is revealed by this man's stipulations regarding the hacienda he owned. The machinery was to be oiled and kept in operating condition, and each year enough cane was to be ground and processed into sugar to test it. This was done until 1929. Several years later, the rusting machines were sold to Japan. In most cases, the high prices of cane and the opportunity to make a clean break with Cañamelar and the sugar industry were too tempting for local hacendados; one by one, they sold or leased their land and moved away from the municipality.

Shortly after the mill of Hacienda Vieja stopped grinding, engineers visited the area to see how irrigation might be used to expand the cultivated acreage. The hacienda artisans had been displaced occupationally. The center of the hacienda's activity now lay outside its grounds and, in fact, to a large extent outside Puerto Rico itself. By the dissolution of the local connection between hacienda mill and land tracts, the sale or lease of the lands, and the centralization of the productive process outside the hacienda community, a new axis of social organization was introduced. Vieja was no longer a largely self-sufficient community (though with production for market, of course) but a tributary farm and labor reservoir of the great central. Hacienda Vieja had become Colonia Vieja.

By 1912, the construction of Vieja's irrigation works was well under way. Both a public and a private system were being developed. In 1913 the workers' subsistence plots were put in cane.

Much of the land which formerly served as pasture or unexploited woodland was likewise converted to cane. Wood for fuel, formerly gathered freely by the hacienda workers, had now become a cash commodity. Charcoal making and retail selling developed as a business, as the coastal woodland was rapidly cleared, the logs being used as railroad ties.

Work opportunities increased enormously and wages rose as more and more dry range was converted into fertile cane land by irrigation. A one-dollar head tax was levied on cattle owned by agregados and pastured on the Colonia's land. The local subsistence pattern of home-grown vegetables, livestock, free sugar, molasses, and rum, and occasional gifts of fresh meat by the hacendado was largely upset in this transitional period. Before 1913, when the sugar harvest ended, hacienda workers had gone to the highlands to work in the coffee harvest. In the nineteenth century, coffee had been the more important crop. But as the area of land in cane increased sharply, the situation was reversed. Workers began to come from the highlands, and many stayed on after the cutting was over. The coastal wage scale became, and has remained, higher than that paid in the coffee harvest.

Although the conditions of life on south coast haciendas were exceedingly rough at the turn of the century, they were apparently much less so than those which prevailed in the highlands. It is not surprising, therefore, that highland workers came to the coast to fill the need for cheap labor engendered by the expansion of cane lands. There was rapid expansion on the coast—of population, economic production, land use—as the old family-type hacienda patterns crumpled under the impact of the centralization of the sugar industry. In the highlands, old hacienda patterns were passing too, but owing to lack of capital and markets, neglect, and hurricanes rather than to the expansion of or new adaptation in the zone.

The migrants from the highlands were mainly farmers and sharecroppers of Spanish ancestry. They had lost their lands because of the hurricanes, the exorbitant rates of interest, and the loss of the European coffee markets. Now they chose to compete in the wage-labor market. The coastal population had a long tradition of simultaneous slavery and forced wage labor. While a largely Caucasian labor force had always been plentiful in the sugar industry because of the forced labor laws, the new influx of highland workers, also mainly Caucasian, had a marked social effect on coastal life. At first the highlanders stayed apart as much as they could.

When I came here in 1907, the colored people lived on the Colonia. I got work with the woodcutting crew that was clearing the land here, and they let me put my house here near the beach. At first, I stayed mainly with my crew. But there was a group of white slaves [agregados] living on the Colonia, and I got to know some of them. They told me not to be bothered by the colored people. You know that in the highlands we say the colored folk are witches. I soon found out they are all right. The white slaves, some of them lived here their whole lives and they got along fine with the Negroes.

When we came here from the highland (*altura*), we settled near the Rillieux family [a large Oriente family descended from the slaves of a French hacendado]. There would be bomba dances each weekend, and I would go to watch and dance. Well, my father would get furious because I was dancing with Negroes, and he would blame my mother, who was not so white as he.

Because of the practice of training slaves as hacienda technicians while agregados were given the less specialized jobs, some of the Negro people of the coast were economically more secure, better educated, and more fully adapted to a wage-earning way of life than were the highland newcomers. The expansion of American influence in the zone had displaced many of the technicians and specialists of the coast, but these people had reintegrated themselves into the newly expanding pattern. Then, as today, the older coastal dwellers sought to disassociate themselves from the rougher and poorer-paying jobs in the cane: cutting, loading, and so on. The white agregados who had worked alongside black freemen on the coast before the North American occupation helped to cement relations between white highland newcomers and the local inhabitants. No distinctions were made in the giving out of jobs in the field phase of the industry; as had apparently always been the case, black and white worked together, often with the local experienced black worker the teacher and the lighter-skinned highlander the willing apprentice.

There is no doubt that this process of mutual accommodation involved some acculturation of the highlanders to local norms of life.

On Saturday and Sunday nights, the local dances were principally bomba. These dances involved drumming—the drum is also called bomba—with verses sung by a soloist and the answering refrain by a chorus. The local bomba dances—almost entirely extinct by the 1940s—included the Belé, Calenda, Holandés, Lero, and Punjáb. Of these names, only the second is unmistakably African in origin. The others may attest to the diffusion of peoples—or, more likely, musical styles—from elsewhere in the Antilles. Some of the local families sang *rosarios* in a French-based creole language, suggesting migration from either Haiti or the French and formerly French Antilles (Martinique, Guadeloupe, St. Lucia, Grenada, Dominica, etc.). Some family names, such as Godreaux and Godineaux, also suggest French Antillean origins. The local wake (*velorio*) pattern, which included "chasing the ghost" at dawn, differed from that of the highlands, and a few minor food usages may also indicate African origins.

A full description of the antecedent cultures of local people is not available, but there seems little doubt that the period 1900–1950 was one during which many highland migrants began to change culturally toward local community norms. It might be argued that these changes involved a certain amount of "africanization" of culture, but it needs to be remembered that the coastal population had been culturally (as well as physically) mixed for a century at least, and probably for much longer. Marriages between coastal people of differing appearance had been common since the eighteenth century, and the highland newcomers mixed freely. (As one old ex-slave remarked, "In affairs of the heart, no one gives orders.") Attempts to discover whether color alone was ever a ground for preventing a union between persons of differing appearance, but in the same class, turned up no useful information. In spite of this, there is a common belief among lighter-skinned persons that darker-skinned people seek marriage with persons whose skins are lighter than theirs. In the 1940s an elaborate terminology of physical description was still employed, including many euphemistic locutions, suggesting a strong consciousness of physical difference.

It was in 1905–7 that the lands of Hacienda (now Colonia) Vieja passed formally into the direct ownership of the American corporation. We have noted that, among other changes, subsistence-crop lands and pastures were put into cultivation, a tax was leveled on agregado livestock, woodlands were cleared, and family management was replaced with a managerial hierarchy composed mainly of outsiders. Shortly after the acquisition of the Vieja land, a company store was set up on the Colonia, and a system of token money introduced. Medical services were supplied by the corporation in the form of a small hospital located at the large central and a medical practitioner who would attend the sick of the corporation's neighborhood colonias.

A strong tendency developed to use piecework methods rather than set new production standards for field labor. This may have been due to the fact that the American corporation wanted to estimate the maximum efficiency of the labor force as a basis for later production standards or, more likely, that the corporation felt that maximum profits could be extracted by piecework payment. Until the corporation had worked out its own estimates on labor performance, it used labor recruiters to hire and supervise workers and make payment arrangements with them. Even the hardest and most skilled jobs in the field came to be done by incentive piecework. Piecework techniques doubtless played some part in destroying the distinctions among laborers based on skill and experience. Among those who suffered most were the paleros, whose work was immensely demanding physically and required great skill besides. Many aged paleros complained of having been ruptured by the terrible work pressures imposed on them during the first decades of the century. Moreover, the piecework system tended to dislodge men from the particular tasks they had done traditionally, and to homogenize the work force at the lowest common denominator of skill. The gradual introduction of machinery in the fields also broke down older patterns of work.

The company store on the Colonia Vieja offered commodities at prices equal to or below those of competitors at Oriente village and in Cañamelar. It carried a wide variety of stock and was conveniently located; consequently, it rapidly became entrenched in the local consumer buying patterns. The "ticket system" was employed in paying company store bills. Workers purchased goods on credit, and the purchases were charged against their pay slips at the end of the workweek. The store managers sat at the pay tables at each colonia having a company store, and the worker's debt was subtracted from his wages before they were paid out. A week's pay of a few cents after deductions was not unusual, according to older informants. Furthermore, informants maintain that cheating by managers and clerks was common, and that scales were kept behind a wire frame, making it difficult for the customer to see if he were being cheated.

Company credit and incentive piecework wages were tied neatly together by the managerial system. As cane land expanded and the need for labor grew, labor recruiters were employed. Some of these recruiters became labor contractors for a whole colonia; they were called *rematistas*. Others were crew bosses (*encabezados*). These recruiters, familiar with the time and labor needed for a given job, would come to an agreement with the manager of the colonia on the price for a particular job. On payday, after deductions for store purchases, the pay would be turned over to the rematista or encabezado, and he would set the pay for each man, according to his personal estimate of the man's ability. The cooperation between rematista and manager, the utter dependence on the rematista's judgment, the credit system at the company store, and the lack of any standardization of rates—all meant that unscrupulous managers and rematistas could cheat the worker of part of his wages and control his outside activities both through control of his credit and of his opportunities for work. Because so much of the land of Cañamelar had been consolidated under one corporate system, a "malcontent" or "agitator" who lost his job might search in vain throughout the municipality for another. Another aspect of this piecework system was the control exercised by the rematistas over highland immigrants seeking work. These men might be forced to buy their food and lodging at the rematistas' houses. This was frequently part of the stipulation on the basis of which they would be given work. When this was the case, rematistas would compete fiercely to get their crews the most work, often to the disadvantage of local workers.

The abuses of the work system during this period resulted from the lack of any revised standardization of rates after the corporate central system had replaced the family-type hacienda system in the area. The shift from thoroughgoing paternalism to an impersonal, pure wage-competition system took some time to accomplish, and it was throughout a disorganizing period. In the past, appeals could be made to the hacendado, who would listen to them, however condescendingly; but the hacendado was no longer available. Wages were relatively good, but still hardly enough to live on; and the downward ·pressure on wages grew day by day, as new migrants arrived. Local workers sought to establish personal relationships with the managers, store managers, and labor foremen, but this was difficult. The managerial hierarchy consisted of employees, not of proprietors; it could be shifted from place to place; its interest in the productive process was impersonal; its status with relation to the laborers was determined by salary and occupation rather than by a long personal history.

The sociopolitical atmosphere was menacing. Most of the workers were agregados, always at the beck and call of the mayordomos. The threat of losing one's house, one's job, one's credit at the company store, hung over everyone. Dependent on the corporation for credit, housing, and labor, workers could not organize easily. But a strong spirit was not·long in developing. An ex-slave talks proudly of having shaken the hand of Samuel Gompers when that labor leader visited Ponce in 1905. A union was created, intimately connected with the Socialist Party of that period. The managerial staff of the Colonia attended political rallies in order to check on the agregados. Political activity on the Colonia itself was unheard of.

The ripening of the land-and-factory combine system came during World War I. The violent and important sugar industry strikes of that period have never been forgotten in Cañamelar. One of the notorious company administrators remarked at the time that he hoped the wives of the strikers would end up walking the streets wrapped in dresses made of fertilizer sacks. *"No hay cuña mas mala que la de la misma madera,"* the older workers say, when they reminisce grimly about the harshness of this native Puerto Rican administrator.

### Maturation of the Rural Proletariat: 1929–48

The land-and-factory combine continued unchanged and, if anything, expanded until the time of the Great Depression. During the depression the combine sought to maintain its customary high rate of return in the face of plunging prices and contracting markets. This required cutting the costs of all operations and a significant curtailment of any lingering features of paternalism which did not contribute to profits.

The depression period was marked by a great increase in covert political activity on the part of the workers and the continuation of union organizational activities. Puerto Rican workers had seized eagerly the privilege of the franchise extended to them in 1917, and in the forty-year period between the establishment of American control and the later depression years these people acquired a political education.

Shortly before the end of the depression period, in 1938, the roots of a new political party were established. Up to that time, the Socialist Party, with the backing of the Free Federation of Labor (Federación Libre de Trabajadores), affiliated with the American Federation of Labor, had acquired some power, but only by jettisoning part of its program. It was precisely to the now disillusioned, and politically awakened workers of the south coast—and to sugar workers everywhere—that the new Popular Democratic Party (Partido Popular Democrático) made its appeal. This party, which won a slim but crucial control of the Puerto Rican legislature in 1940, followed its victory with a series of politically important reforms. Workers who were agregados could not be summarily deprived of their residence rights, and land purchases were begun to enable agregados to resettle on government-owned land. The right of workers to participate openly in political and union activity was reasserted, and workers could not be fired for such activities. The right to organize unions on the colonias was established. Token money was abolished; the labor recruiter (encabezado and rematista) patterns were weakened; and the company stores were ordered to dissolve their legal connection with the landholding and central-owning corporations. Large tracts of fertile cane land were purchased by the government, to be run as government farms.

Medical care, which had been meager and largely in the hands of the corporation, came more and more to be the responsibility of the central government, implemented through the municipal administration, and the municipality now spends much more on medical care than the corporation ever did.

Some of these reforms were successful; others were evaded by legal circumvention. The new freedom of political activity led to the establishment of a new union for workers, including an all-important sugarcane workers' branch. This union replaced the Federación Libre and allied itself unofficially with the new party in power.

Demographic movement in the barrio during the last ten or fifteen years before 1948 was away from the colonias, out to the beach and to the village of Oriente. In 1940, the municipality of Cañamelar bought a cuerda of land in Barrio Poyal for the use of squatter families. By 1949, the plots on this tract had been redivided; plots occupied by single families in 1940 held two (or three) in 1949. The beach of Barrio Poyal had only a scattering of houses in 1940, tenanted mainly by fishermen; in 1949 it was a growing community in its own right. Most of the newcomers were migrants from the highlands; some were ex-agregados from the colonias.

From this brief sketch it will be seen that the period from 1873 to 1948, just seventy-five years, was one of intense social change for Barrio Poyal. In the barrio and, in fact, on the whole coast, slave and bound laborers had been converted to free and competing workers in this short period. Landownership reached an unsurpassed degree of concentration. With this marked change in ownership came concomitant changes in the productive process. Capitalist, corporate agriculture took the place of the paternalistic family-type haciendas. The workers of Barrio Poyal came to be part of an insular "rural proletariat," with rights to union organization and the vote. Their way of life no longer rested on the locally based, tradition-bound, face-to-face social system of the hacienda. The people of Hacienda Vieja were much more members of a community than participants in the wider society; the people of Colonia Vieja are at least as much participants in the wider society as they are members of the colonia community. The culture of today is largely a synthesis of old hacienda patterns of thought and activity with newly developed ways of behaving, conceived under the pressures of rapid proletarianization.

### Conclusions

In this chapter, we have traced the changes in the relationship of several small Puerto Rican sugarcane estates to the wider world.

As these relationships changed, the lives of local inhabitants were also transformed, particularly in the direction of a deepened dependence on external forces, a sharper delineation of class identities, and an erosion of the class differentiation that had traditionally marked local estate communities. These processes have been described here as a "proletarianization" of rural workers, marking their entrance into a national working class, with the loss of many locally distinctive features.

But the materials have touched only tangentially upon the themes of slave and free, black and white, African and European, and it may be useful to reexamine the data briefly from these vantage points. In Puerto Rico, as elsewhere in the New World, physical type has always been associated with slavery, since Puerto Ricans of African descent have their origins in enslavement and transportation, over a period of nearly four centuries. Several features, however, distinguish the history of Puerto Ricans of African descent from, say, that of Africans in the United States. To begin with, soon after the first enslaved African reached Puerto Rico, a population of freemen of color began to form, and throughout the history of Puerto Rican slavery, the number of such freemen almost always exceeded the number of enslaved. This process of continuing manumission was linked not only to institutions created for the purpose, but also to the highly irregular economic development of Puerto Rico, which created circumstances that made it cheaper to allow slaves to buy their freedom than to keep them enslaved.

Second, in Puerto Rico the distinction between slave and free seems always to have been more important socially than the distinction between black and white; in other words, freemen of color did not suffer *to the same extent* as their opposite numbers in the United States from a stigma based on color alone. This is by no means to say that color prejudice was absent; but such prejudice was always tempered somewhat by other considerations— wealth, skill, and education were doubtless among the most significant mediating factors.

Third, there were not, after the earlier epochs of Puerto Rican history, effective barriers against socially approved unions between persons of dramatically different phenotype. Fourth, as we have noted, the crude simple division of persons into two categories, "black" and "white," did not typify the Puerto Rican code of social assortment. Given the possibility of approved unions across "color lines," this signified that a very substantial proportion of the people of Puerto Rico was of "mixed" ancestry, even soon after the Conquest. As a result, the drawing of color lines became less relevant to the island's social history—even though civil discrimination against darker fellow citizens, laws that singled out black freemen and slaves for special punishment, and racial prejudice against the darkest people all existed over the centuries.

Fifth, the peculiar history of forced-labor legislation, treated here and in the preceding chapter, noticeably affected the history of race relations, since by lowering the social status of "white" free men this legislation effectively elevated the relative status of "black" slaves. Finally, as we have seen, the sugar industry gave the freedmen special access to certain technical jobs in the period following emancipation, thus preserving some of the recognized sources of prestige which, before emancipation, had characterized the slave-and-agregado pattern.

Many of these features have their parallels in the rest of the Hispanic Caribbean and, to a certain extent, in certain other New World areas as well. In each case, however, local peculiarities must be documented in order to identify likenesses and differences. At the moment of the North American invasion, Puerto Rican libertos possessed sources of status and prestige that had been maintained in the face of local social prejudices and in spite of the history of slavery. The modernization of the sugar industry effectively eroded these sources, even though that may not have been the intent of the North American entrepreneurs. It is said that darker technicians were discriminated against during the transition to the corporate land-and-factory combine, but it has not been possible to document this assertion. It is indeed true that, impressionistically at least, the managerial and technical staffs of the massive south coast plantations rarely seem to include many very dark persons— and this may be a result of the more familiar brand of North American racism. But the picture, if correct, is in some curious ways less significant than the general erosion of traditional patterns, which turned highly differentiated, localized social hierarchies into simple reservoirs of unskilled labor, erasing distinctions that had been intricately linked to considerations of social history and of perceived color.

From the point of view of Africanisms and the preservation of an African heritage, the case described here reveals to some extent the ways in which a new cultural blend could emerge from the encounter of two traditions. The population of Cañamelar ranges in physical appearance from black to white, with every possible intergradation represented. But the culture of the people cannot be divided comparably. Instead, the norms of behavior of the local community do not vary in any noticeable way in terms of the ancestry, real or imputed, of any individuals in it. There are common-law unions of "whites" and of "blacks"; black Catholics and white Catholics; persons of similar phenotype and of dramatically different phenotype within one family; white people who dance the "African" bomba and black people who sing and play the "Hispanic *decimas;* and so on. When one seeks to identify features of social assortment, or of behavior, which permit the isolation or distinction of persons of differing phenotype, one is—happily— left with hardly anything at all.

And yet it would be incorrect to assume on this basis that either consciousness of color or assortative criteria based on color are lacking. There are children's songs that ridicule black people; black persons are sometimes referred to—usually, furtively—as *"feo"* ("ugly"); and a special euphemistic terminology exists for the description of persons whose appearance falls toward the black end of the scale. It is noted by some that the blacker people of Cañamelar are descended from slaves; the bomba, though danced by all, is considered an "African" dance; darker people are believed to be inherently more skilled mechanically, to have "different" voices, to drum more habitually than whites, to have big feet, and so on, and on.

What seems most important, however, is that in Puerto Rico, unlike the United States, the prime elements of prejudice cannot be marshaled to divide black from white to make "racial" differences the primum mobile of social relations. The fates of the Puerto Rican working poor are united in ways that the working poor of the United States might find difficulty in comprehending. Thus the history of one plantation, in the course of nearly a century and a half, offers a lesson very different from that afforded by any comparable situation in the American South. Indeed, the Puerto Rican instance contrasts with the American North as well, since darker Puerto Ricans in a city such as New York face the choice of not acculturating (in order to remain "foreigners") or of "becoming Negroes," in line with the United States perception of color.

Several other points deserve mention. First, the people of Cañamelar, at the time the fieldwork for this chapter was done, lived predominantly in common-law unions, approved and accepted (if deplored in ideal terms) by the community. It would be impossible to detect any difference in marriage patterns associated with color in the community; the norm was, in other words, a community norm. In the United States, on the contrary there has been a tendency to associate forms of mating with color as well as with class, and there are some statistical data to support this association.

Though Puerto Rican mating patterns did not differ by color, they may have differed by region. It might be contended that common-law unions had their origins in slavery; but Puerto Rican culture history also suggests that such unions were common in the remote highland regions of the country, and that we may be dealing here with two different (and possibly convergent) traditions rather than with a single tradition. In any case, no one in Cañamelar associates color with any distinctive mating pattern, nor is any such separate pattern identifiable.

A second, related point has to do with the ability of darker Puerto Ricans to match the success of their fellow citizens in the labor market. If anything, the data suggest that darker Puerto Ricans succeeded more often, at least in the period following emancipation. If the capacity of household heads to earn a living is not individually tilted against the darker segments of the population, then it becomes difficult to read into the social circumstances any necessary relationship between darkness and misery. Or, to put it more baldly, shared misery prevented the social isolation of Puerto Rico's darker-skinned citizens from its lighter-skinned citizens—and this has proved to be a key to the understanding of Puerto Rican "race relations." The contrast with the United States hardly needs to be delineated; the facts speak for themselves.

At the same time, it is historically correct to argue that in island-wide terms there has long been an association in Puerto Rico between darkness and economic disadvantagement. What distinguishes the Puerto Rican case is the presence of very large numbers of economically underprivileged "whites," and the absence of any tendency to make physical differences stigmata that transcend similarities of class position. While it is not true that a poor white man is "black," while a rich black man is "white," it is true that in Puerto Rico race hatred has never become a psychic consolation for the oppressed.

North Americans badly need to divest themselves of the illusion that Latin America is a racial paradise, and that color prejudice is nonexistent in its codes of social relations. But this is a very different matter from arguing that there are no differences between North America and the countries of Latin America or among the various social codes of different Latin American countries. Careful study of the sociology of all the societies of the Hemisphere should reveal much that is not yet known about such variations, thereby enhancing our understanding of the North American case and its mysterious distinctiveness.

# II

## CARIBBEAN PEASANTRIES

Up to this point, we have dealt with the deliberate shaping of Caribbean life by imperial force, beginning with Columbus's "discovery" nearly 500 years ago. That force has by no means been stilled; throughout the Caribbean one still sees the consequences of centuries of imperial rule, even where such control appears to have ended. But thus far we have only begun to develop the theme of response and resistance—the ways in which the peoples of the Caribbean have dealt with the pressures imposed on them by imperial agents.

European capitalism and its instruments—colonialism, the plantation system, slavery, forced labor, political and educational institutions—created Caribbean societies of a particular quality and character. In doing so, the European powers made the most of certain rather unusual advantages: the bewilderment of newcomers transplanted to a foreign setting; the smallness of Caribbean colonies that left "malcontents" few places to escape to or hide in; the destruction of the indigenous populations with which the newcomers might have allied themselves; the relative absence of alternative modes of subsistence and survival; and so on. These factors severely reduced the range of possible responses available to would-be resisters. But they could not eliminate all of those responses; and, as we have seen, "resistance" can take many different forms.

131

We need now to expand our view of such resistance by considering the most important structural alignments by which Caribbean peoples could establish their own perspectives, their own styles of life, vis-à-vis the world outside. Since the plantation system, both in slavery times and after, depended heavily on external power—military, political, economic—for its existence, the ideal antithesis to the plantation would be small-scale, self-sufficient agriculture (or better, horticulture), with a minimum dependence on either externally produced commodities or on market opportunities created by external demand. Such an antithesis did, in fact, arise on occasion in Caribbean history, as when palisaded runaway slave communities consolidated themselves around their own agriculture, with little trade, and relatively little dependence on outside institutions. But in the Caribbean region as elsewhere, the styles of life developed over time characteristically included acquired desires for at least a few goods and services that necessarily originated outside relatively self-sufficient communities. What is more, such communities, here as elsewhere, came to be subject to claims imposed by local and colonial governments, no matter how self-sufficient their inhabitants might be. In fact, over nearly five centuries, continuous involvement with forces emanating from other centers, particularly Western Europe, has probably been more pronounced in the Caribbean than in most of Asia, Africa, and even the balance of Latin America.

Nonetheless, patterns of substantial agrarian self-sufficiency did arise in the course of Caribbean history, and many such patterns persist in strength to this day. In most cases, they are associated with the formation of a peasantry—that is, of a class (or classes) of rural landowners producing a large part of the products they consume, but also selling to (and buying from) wider markets, and dependent in various ways upon wider political and economic spheres of control. Caribbean peasantries are, in this view, *reconstituted* peasantries, having begun other than as peasants—in slavery, as deserters or runaways, as plantation laborers, or whatever—and becoming peasants in some kind of resistant response to an externally imposed regimen.

Thus Caribbean peasantries represent *a mode of response* to the plantation system and its connotations, and *a mode of resistance* to imposed styles of life. Typically, the history of Caribbean peasantries is full of false starts, regressions, and struggles for power between plantation and peasant adaptations. Peasants need land, capital, and at least some markets, in addition to the skills and physical effort their work requires; their major resource is their own labor and that of their families. Plantations are typically rich in capital, in land, and in market access, but must have large quantities of relatively cheap labor. Often, Caribbean plantation systems have responded to the growth of a peasantry by importing more labor (sometimes, even at the peasantry's direct expense), rather than coerce peasants into plantation labor. However, as we have already seen, on many occasions coercion has proved an easier solution than increased migration. In any case, the plantation system typically defines its needs as if labor were already in oversupply—since, historically, plantation labor has always been miserably paid, relative to the wages for comparable work in temperate lands. To put it more accurately, the worst-paid work pays even worse in the colonies than in the mother countries—and migrations from the colonies to the mother countries continue to demonstrate this.

It would be misleading to suppose that the coexistence of plantations and peasantries is always marked by open conflict between these two very different modes of agricultural adaptation. In the contemporary Caribbean these modes are in fact often cooperant, and individuals or even whole communities may maintain a peasant adaptation while engaging in part-time work on the plantations. Plantations and peasant communities tend to exploit different ecological zones, not so much because peasants prefer highlands or cannot work savannas as because the lowland plantation adaptation has driven them out. Hence the "struggles" between plantations and peasant communities are likely to take the form of competition for scarce resources—such as agricultural extension assistance, government-supported irrigation, and highways. Such struggles are consistently won by the plantations.

But there continue to exist in many parts of the Caribbean local peasant adaptations that are not linked to the plantation economy. The best example is probably that of Haiti, where a sturdy peasantry emerged out of the ashes of the Haitian Revolution and has continued to exist—though often on the razor's edge of starvation —ever since. Effective peasant adaptations also exist in Jamaica, in Guadeloupe, on many of the smaller islands, and on portions of the surrounding mainland. Such peasantries do not by any means form a single undifferentiated category. They represent many variable modes of adaptation, each differing in some respects from the others.

The following chapters are concerned both with the contemporary peasantries of the Caribbean and with the historical origins of peasant ways of life. It is important to keep in mind that most people who came to the islands were dragged there, or came under substantial disadvantages. Hence the peasant adaptation is in one sense almost always evidence in these islands of the triumph of one pattern over another. In the following chapter, some of the main paths along which Caribbean peasantries have taken on their characteristic shape are described. This treatment is neither complete nor detailed; it serves mainly to point out how little is still known about the origins of the rural sectors of Caribbean societies. The principal point, perhaps, is that we cannot really understand the origins or nature of peasant adaptations in the Antilles by studying them in vacuo. Each such mode of adjustment began as—and remained—a means of coping with existing economic conditions, frequently regressive, to which the peasant style was a response.

Chapter 6 deals with the emergence of a particular type of peasant community in Jamaica shortly after Emancipation. In this case, we get rich evidence of the slaves' abilities to employ skills learned in slavery in their own defense as freedmen. Some critics may feel that the slaves are to be belittled for having absorbed the skills imposed upon them in slavery. Others may note, however, that these same skills gave the newly freed an opportunity to escape the tyranny of plantation life and to create a different style of life.

Since this adaptation involved the application of essentially horticultural skills to a peasant (as opposed to a plantation) holding, it offers an opportunity for comparison with the postbellum United States South, where an independent yeoman pattern for the ex-slaves was ostensibly to have been created. In the Jamaican case, the planters eventually surrendered local political power to the Crown, rather than see it pass into the hands of the freedmen.

But the planters were not able to destroy the Jamaican peasantry entirely, nor to deprive the people of their essential self-respect. Doubtless, the fact that Jamaica was a colony, subject to the Foreign Office, and that its population was overwhelmingly black, sometimes helped to protect the common people from their own ruling class. The relationship between the United States South and the rest of the country, while a colony-metropolis relationship in some regards, differed very significantly from that, say, between Jamaica and Britain or between Martinique and France. The existing power blocs in the United States South were able to maintain local control over the freedmen in ways that were simply unavailable to the Jamaican planters. In fact, only in concert with the national government were the Southern politicians able to maintain the forms of exploitation of black Americans that developed after the Civil War. In the islands, on the contrary, the economic interests of the planters were often opposed to those of the power blocs in the metropolises. Hence the differences between Jamaican and United States freedmen must be measured not in terms of their relative poverty—for example—but rather in terms of their access to a life-style that would allow them to retain both a sense of patrimony and a sense of self-respect.

Chapter 7 carries the argument somewhat further. Both as slaves and as freedmen, Jamaicans exercised considerable skill and initiative in growing and marketing agricultural crops. The relationship of the slaves to the marketplaces has been one of the most important features of Jamaican social history, and marketing remains an essential part of Jamaican rural life. In Chapter 7, the background to marketing practices in that country is sketched in, and the relationship between cultivation and marketing, during slavery and after, is suggested..

Though these three chapters do not take us any further into the Caribbean past than those which precede them, they move us away from the modernizing aspects and toward the more traditional aspects of Caribbean social history. The reasons for this lie in the essentially conservative quality of the peasant adaptation—by which is meant only the great extent to which it is forestalled from changing. We may at least speculate that those features of Haitian rural life which appear to be African in origin have not remained unchanged simply because those who incorporate them want to stay the same—but also because too few alternatives have been available. Nor is it altogether quite so simple; since more *vodoun* ceremonies can be observed in downtown Port-au-Prince than in any rural Haitian district, the peasant adaptation by itself can hardly be charged with heavier emphasis on African adaptations. Still, Haiti as a whole has remained less changed during the past century than perhaps any other Caribbean society; and this is surely related in part to its isolation. The Haitian peasantry is simply the most isolated segment of a country largely cut off by circumstance from the world outside, though still subject to its pressures.

The Jamaican case is somewhat different, since Jamaica became an independent country only a few years ago, and Jamaica's relationship with the outside world, including the English metropolis, remains cordial. Haiti, after all, defeated its colonial master in war, and was isolated thereafter almost as much for punishment as for profit. The Jamaican countryside retains a good deal that can be traced (or attributed) to Africa, but one needs to discuss the ways in which such traditional materials are used and viewed in order to do more than reify the content of a culture.

African (or putatively African) cultural materials have rarely had any political significance in Haiti, except in relation to the ways class membership is imputed. Vodoun instead of (or in addition to) Catholicism; the creole language instead of (rather than in addition to) French; rural life instead of urban life—such aspects of culture expressed as values separate the privileged from the poor rather than the "African" from the "non-African." Only during the period of the United States occupation of Haiti (1915–34) did the issue of African origins gain political significance—when Haitian scholars and intellectuals urged their colleagues to rediscover their own identity by acknowledging just how "African" their culture and their ancestors were.

The picture is otherwise in Jamaica. There, the genuine or putative African content of local culture is somewhat less pronounced than in Haiti. But the effects of British colonial rule have been far more profound in Jamaica than the effects of French colonial rule in Haiti. British lower-school educational methods and standards diffused throughout Jamaica—even while the Jamaican people received far too little educational assistance. Class standards—often best represented by the attitude and style of life of local teachers—posed conflicts for the Jamaican child that were rooted in class differences but were expressed in substantial measure as a rejection of what was (or was supposed to be) African in character. Thus there have always been substantial grounds for suspecting that any form of cultural resistance or protest (as in religious expression, dialect, and philosophy of life) would become involved somehow with the African past and its interpreted significance. In recent years, this imposed linkage between things African and modes of resistance to class and color prejudice has grown stronger—particularly as Jamaicans have gained a wider knowledge of outside events, a fuller understanding of the nature of colonialism, and a more disillusioning sense of a world from which they feel excluded.

For Jamaican peasants, as for Haitian peasants, the image of Africa is not in fact very significant. Ordinarily, a Haitian peasant spends no time reflecting on the origins of his religious beliefs, the way his food is cooked, or the language he uses—and, indeed, why should he? Much the same, it seems, holds for a Jamaican countryman. But in Haiti such matters have rarely been transformed into politically relevant considerations, whereas in Jamaica the occasions for such transformations have been frequent, and the process has in no sense stopped.

Hence it is not sufficient to talk about "more African" or "less African," or to catalog particular cultural elements accordingly. Instead, it is essential to view these elements in terms of their symbolic significance, both narrowly (in families, local communities, regionally, and among national classes) and widely (in relationship to external power, imperialist domination, and the bigger issues of colonialism and racism), for the ways people actually behave.

There is yet another, even more important dimension to the problem. The Caribbean peoples appreciate particular manifestations of modernity: transistor radios, improved roads, medical care, movies, mechanical tools, refrigerators, and much else. It would appear that none of these peoples are prepared to reject all such intrusions all of the time, either to defend the past or to maintain an "African" style of life. But since the past is, indeed, a past much

drawn from ancestral African cultures, modernizing change is often
"de-africanizing" change. However, non-African elements of the
Caribbean past may also be affected: the Puerto Rican people often
see modernization as involving the loss of Hispanic culture rather
than African culture, and their dilemma is no less real. But in societies such as Haiti, Jamaica, and Trinidad—in the last instance,
the political and symbolic issues are substantially complicated by
the presence of a large Indian population—much of the fabric of
daily life that is changed by modernization processes seems to involve the loss of "African" substance.

These issues need not be pursued here, though they will be taken
up in the last part of this book. They are raised now, partly because they may make the reading of the following chapters more
pointed, partly because they can throw light on "africanism" as a
political development in the United States. Until the twentieth century, black nationalism did not take on a firm africanist cast in
North America. Garvey was, of course, a Jamaican. Earlier black
militants in the United States, while often aware of Africa and its
significance, did not interest themselves quite so much in the culture and behavior of black North Americans. In fact, until the
twentieth century, Africa was not a welcome subject in most black
North American circles, and the white mythology about Africa was
very widely accepted by its black victims. In the now-famous exchange between the white anthropologist Herskovits and the black
sociologist Frazier, it was Frazier who took the position that the
African past had been expunged from United States life. Generally
speaking, Africa did not exist for North Americans of any color
until this century.

And yet the contemporary North American scene has been utterly transformed in this regard, mainly because of the "discovery"
of Africa by black North Americans. This discovery has involved
the symbolic incorporation of a real and imagined Africa into the
consciousness of millions of North American blacks. It would serve
no useful purpose to dwell on any built-in misconceptions that have
accompanied this symbolic incorporation. There is utility, however,
in trying to broaden the concept of Afro-America or "African
America" to include more than the United States—to view the
black experience in the New World in all its grandeur and tragedy,

and to develop a richer comprehension of the diversity and subtlety of its expressions. The first three chapters of this part seek to take note of one very important pathway taken by Afro-American cultures.

Moreover, the peasant adaptations perfected by Caribbean peoples, beginning with the first importations of African and European laborers in the sixteenth century, have survived—albeit in usually very modified fashion—into the present. Hence our concern is not only with the origin and growth of peasant adaptations, but also with the ways in which these adaptations have continued to survive in the modern world. In the two concluding chapters of Part II —Chapters 8 and 9—aspects of contemporary Caribbean peasant life are described and the rationale of current peasant adaptations is explored. Here the reader will discover that Caribbean peasantries have much in common with peasantries elsewhere—but also that they are, as a consequence of their peculiar historical experiences, in some ways particular and unique.

Caribbean history has been marked by a series of quite sharp discontinuities, the sharpest among them being the coming of the Europeans. As we have already seen, this event transformed aboriginal life in the islands, eventually eradicating Native American cultures and destroying or assimilating the peoples who "carried" them. Then, during the succeeding centuries, the Caribbean region was repopulated with newcomers from Europe, Africa, and Asia, and a whole new array of local cultures took shape in the islands.

But what does it mean, in terms of the everyday needs of people, to say that new local cultures developed? Daily life imposes a wide variety of continuous demands, which are normally satisfied according to established—so-called traditional—practice. The tools employed in agriculture, the crops grown and prepared as foods, arrangements for eating and sleeping, and all the other technical and material details of ordinary life are not invented on the spot, borrowed uncritically, or developed only as needed by some casual hit-or-miss procedure. Tastes in food are acquired; tools are fashioned and employed according to socially learned and standardized practices; choice, taste, and preference became organized around specifiable ranges of acceptable variation. In fact, the universal characteristics of the social life of peoples are order and regularity, predictability of performance, and standardization of behavior. In other words, the organized social life of human communities is, normally, an end product, with variation, alternation, and change built into the system itself.

Viewed in this way, the life-styles of Caribbean peasant communities are perhaps of special interest, since they are not ancient, and since their shaping was intimately associated with the movement of peoples into what were essentially "frontier" areas. This is by no means to deny the important Amerindian cultural component of Caribbean peasant life-styles, but to stress the diversity of traditions, of imported cultural influences, that played a part in the creation of the "new" peasantries, and the reconstituted nature of the new life-styles. We wish to discover how people drawn from many different ancestral pasts, and subjected in most cases to one or two centuries of very intense repression, could establish their own ways of life, synthesized from their varied pasts and from their learning experiences in their new homelands. We deal, in other words, with peoples whose social histories in situ are short; whose prior social relationships were colored by their subjection to naked force; and for whom the establishment of peasant life was in most instances a mode of escape or a mode of resistance, or both.

In view of this special social history, it is difficult to understand why any scholar of this portion of Latin America should have concluded that Caribbean peasantries closely resemble those of the European subcontinent. The peasantries of such societies as Jamaica, Puerto Rico, and Haiti differ dramatically from those of Europe, as well as from those of the Andes or the Central Plateau of Mexico, precisely because of their relatively shallow social history, their diverse cultural origins, and the special circumstances under which they assumed their peasant identity. The majority of Jamaican peasants, for instance, are descended from African slaves; they won their freedom principally by the Emancipation of 1834–38—though it was their own efforts that made freedom matter, and the Maroons had partially secured their autonomy in war and by treaty at an earlier time. In Haiti, the peasantry was formed principally after the Revolution (1791–1804)—though here, too, maroon bands had created viable communities even earlier. The relatively less numerous peasantry of Puerto Rico came into being somewhat differently, had a longer social history, and went through several stages of change, as we have already seen. That Puerto Rico was settled both by Spanish colonists and by African slaves (many of whom became freedmen at a relatively early point in Puerto Rico's colonial history), and that the plantation system never came to dominate Puerto Rico as it had British Jamaica (after 1655) and French Saint-Domingue (after 1697), helped to determine some of the social features that appear to differentiate the Puerto Rican peasantry from comparable Caribbean groups elsewhere.

The term *peasantry* is used here to refer in general to those small-scale cultivators who own or have access to land, who produce some commodities for sale, and who produce much of their own subsistence (Wolf 1955, 1966; Firth 1951). Though it is possible to specify the term far more precisely, this usage is adequate for present purposes. In Puerto Rico, Jamaica, and Haiti, we may say that the peasantries are clearly subject to political, economic, and social forces emanating from domestic urban centers of power —as well as from foreign societies, mediated through local power-holders—with particular reference to their productive capacity and their taxability (Wolf 1966; Redfield 1953: 31–32; Kroeber 1948: 284).

When we turn from a typological or structural characterization of peasantries to the content of their lives, we deal with a different aspect of their reconstitution—in some ways, a more modest aspect, related to the ways that the routines of daily life were worked out, diffused, and reconciled as standards of behavior, and passed on from generation to generation. The substance of daily life is, in each case, also a social product, but it has to do with the ways individuals see their world, deal with it in locally acceptable and understood terms, and maintain its continuities, even while change goes on. The best way to illustrate this, perhaps, is by example.

Any visitor to rural Haiti who is served coffee—or, when people are too poor to offer coffee, water—will note an almost invariable practice: the proffered beverage is always brought on a small wooden tray, and the top of the tray is covered with a small cloth, on which the cups or glasses rest. Only in a most extraordinary rural setting would a beverage be served without these modest amenities. The custom, in other words, is more than just a custom; while coffee is the preferred offering, and water a poor substitute, these acceptable alternatives are wholly different from the use of a tray, which is clearly *comme il faut*. Both the coffee and the tray are part of Haitian rural culture; but they differ in the value attached to them.

Another example may be drawn from butchering practice. In rural marketplaces, cows are butchered for local sale, and the technology of butchering is quite uniform. When the animal is slaughtered, one may observe a custom which has strong ritual overtones, but which is not practiced by all butchers. The custom involves smearing the eyes of the dying animal with its own blood, and some butchers practice this custom matter-of-factly whenever they kill a cow. Various explanations have been offered, most involving a symbolic concealment of the identity of the butcher. But it is important that not all butchers do this; and in the municipal abattoirs, where scores of cows are butchered daily, more systematically and swiftly, the custom is never followed. If one asks a rural butcher who does not follow the practice what he thinks about it, he will usually respond by saying that he doesn't "believe in it." Hence there are two perceived alternatives, both acceptable in local culture. It would be interesting to know whether there was once a time when all butchers smeared the eyes of dying animals with their own blood; but today, in any case, there are two alternative practices, and they seem to be mutually exclusive: any particular butcher either does or does not follow the ritual.

These three examples—the mandatory use of a tray for guests, the alternative offering of coffee or water, and the alternative use or nonuse of a butchering ritual—suggest the ways in which different elements in a culture are regarded by those who adopt them; the examples themselves are of little importance, but they do indicate something about the way cultures are constructed, informed by belief and value, and—though we do not here discuss the acquisition of such practices—perpetuated by learning. We could, of course, multiply the examples or draw them from wholly different areas of life: religion, marriage practices, technology, cuisine, and so on. The point here is to put the tremendous mass of behavior in any Caribbean peasant subculture into the perspective of its social history: to remind ourselves that all of these beliefs, customs, values, and practices were sifted down, standardized, and diffused among the peasantries during relatively short periods lasting several centuries at most.

Life in peasant communities everywhere is built around a number of fundamental life-events—birth, the definition of adulthood, conjugal union, and death—and around a series of calendrical markers, such as the seasons, the variation in rainfall and sunlight, the planting and harvesting of crops, and the attached ceremonial significances of these markers. All of these events and processes are intimately linked to the concrete, material world in which the peasantry lives, and which it perceives according to its own norms and understandings. How that concrete, material world impinges upon the peasantry's consciousness, how a Caribbean peasant perceives what is good and proper, evil and inappropriate, possible and impossible, constitutes a series of phenomena which Caribbean ethnology requires its students to describe and to analyze. Such an exercise may be concerned only with the present character and quality of peasant life. Ideally, however, one may wish to unite past and present in any description of how things are. Of course, the symbolic significance, the implicit and explicit meanings and values of behavior, are more easily studied as they are at present. Yet it is possible to conjecture, at times usefully, about the emergence and consolidation of such meanings and values.

This section of the book seeks to demonstrate some of the major ways in which Caribbean rural populations began to create distinctively Caribbean life-styles even before the end of slavery. Slavery, for all its horrors, was never able to eradicate the humanity of the slaves; and we have seen that certain built-in oppositions within slavery itself often enabled the slaves to do far more than merely survive. Nonetheless, the end of slavery in the islands completely changed the relationships among island populations, and Caribbean peasantries obtained their first genuine opportunity to develop their characteristic styles only after freedom.

This happened in different ways in different locales. Earlier, we saw how hacienda and plantation forms handled the transition from slavery to freedom in the Puerto Rican case, and how the growth of modern industrial plantations, toward the close of the nineteenth century, created a qualitatively different order of change among rural folk. The cases of the peasantries were different, first of all, because change was generally so much more hampered in the peasant settings. The prime instance is Haiti, where rural life became stabilized on a peasant base during the middle decades of the nineteenth century, and began to change drastically again only after the United States invasion beginning in 1915. In Puerto Rico and, even more, in Santo Domingo, it was the North Americans again, beginning soon after the start of the twentieth century, who created vast new pressures for change. Another way of saying this is to stress the importance of external forces, both in establishing new-style plantations and in changing the tempo and character of peasant life.

The two final chapters in this part are concerned with questions of culture persistence and culture change among Caribbean peasantries, each being a brief commentary on a particular aspect of peasant culture. Chapter 8 offers yet another view of Jamaican marketing, picking up where the preceding chapter left off. The historical background of the Jamaican internal marketing system gives us a basis for examining the way that system works today, and for noting certain characteristics of the system which have—or lack—noticeable continuities with the past.

This chapter also raises the question of what might be called the "rationality" of peasant economic life. The fact is that too few observers have analyzed the peasant life-style with the seriousness it deserves, while too many have assumed a certain poverty of economic skill on the part of the peasants. This view is particularly unfortunate when one notes that the plantation system has always battened upon the favoritism of governments, both local and metropolitan, while the peasantries have always been regarded as the "backward," "conservative," or "ignorant" sectors of Caribbean rural life. Thus, for instance, though some commentaries suggest that Caribbean marketers go to market mainly for the hell of it, we are now accumulating solid evidence that the economic life of the peasantries is neither so barren nor so idiotic as we have been led to believe. Chapter 8 tackles some of the related issues head-on, seeking to explain in what ways Jamaican internal marketing practices are rational, economically beneficial to Jamaica, and deserving of defence by policymakers.

The final chapter in this part, Chapter 9, takes yet another tack, this time more explicitly comparative. The frequent criticism that Caribbean history has always been written from the outside looking in is sometimes overdone; nonetheless it is true that few have sought carefully enough to write it from the inside looking out. That this has been the case for so long doubtless reflects the complex colonial experience of the region, its own students swiftly acculturated to the norms and perceptions of imperial scholarship, trained in metropolitan centers of learning, and suppressing many of their most original insights about the Caribbean past. Fortunately, the last thirty years have seen a magnificent reversal of this tendency, and young Jamaicans, Trinidadians, Martiniquans, Cubans, and others have begun to create a whole new tradition of historiography. This trend has meant a disciplined return to both primary and secondary historical sources that could reveal—even if frequently in distorted fashion—the quality of Caribbean life on the local level.

Chapter 9 is intended as a suggestion about supplementary techniques for historical research—a kind of reasoning backward from the contemporary features of rural Caribbean life, particularly among peasantries. Only one such theme is dealt with here: that of the peculiar significance of yard and house in the lives of rural Caribbean peoples. A little is said about the historical origins of rural practices in these regards, but the emphasis—as in the rest of the preceding chapters—is upon the creative and synthesizing character of culture growth in the islands. With this chapter, the discussion of rural and local modes of adaptation is concluded. But it should not be thought that the necessary research has already received the attention it truly deserves from historians and historical ethnologists. The chapters in this part only purport to indicate what might be done, and perhaps even a little about how the task might be tackled—nothing more.

# 5

# The Origins of
# Reconstituted Peasantries

The history of the Caribbean region begins in 1492, and its present character shows the effects of five centuries of complicated contact. This lengthy and complex past creates genuine analytic difficulties, when one seeks to classify the peasantries of the region in any orderly fashion. An attempt is made here to describe these peasantries as expressive of forms of resistance to European enterprise, as modes of escape or of contrary adaptation. But the origins of the peasantries have been diverse: some came into being only relatively recently; others flourished—and withered—at an earlier time. We lack anything like a complete account of the present distribution of peasant peoples in the islands, and even our criteria for defining a peasantry are open to serious question.

Nonetheless, there may be some utility in seeking to describe some of the main ways in which Caribbean peasantries came into being, if only to indicate what we know of the history of these groups. By and large, Caribbean peasantries have been "interstitial" groupings, living on the margins of Western enterprise. But reflection on these "interstices" tells us something about the direction and intent of imperial strategy in the islands, and allows us to discern more clearly how the peasantries responded to such strategy. If the emphasis seems to rest unduly on conflict, on resistance, this is because only rarely and briefly have European powers or even local governments viewed the peasantry as more than an "obstacle" to development; and the reasons for this negativism, as well as the negativism itself, still persist.

It is certainly not our intent to describe the peasantries of each and every island and mainland Caribbean society as they are now constituted, nor even to examine the full list of historical processes by which such groups came into being. Rather, we shall describe a few major modes of peasantry formation, each of which enables us to perceive, from a somewhat different viewpoint, the challenge of European or state power, and the reaction of local people. Each such instance is substantially independent of the others, though commonly one mode of formation might lead eventually to the appearance of a different adaptation at a later time.

## The Squatters

The first such adaptation is that which typified the early period of settlement in the Greater Antilles, in the period before Spain was seriously challenged by its North European rivals. The period begins soon after the Conquest, and continues until the rise of large-scale sugarcane plantations in Cuba and Puerto Rico and, to a much lesser extent in Spanish (that is, eastern) Hispaniola, near the start of the nineteenth century. In these large islands, held uninterruptedly by Spain until nearly the mid-nineteenth century in the case of Santo Domingo, and until 1899 in the cases of Cuba and Puerto Rico, peasantries of mixed cultural and physical origins seem to have come into being as a mode of escape from official power. The locus of settlement was invariably in the interior of the islands, and the settlers were often deserters, escaped slaves from other islands, freedmen of color, and Europeans seeking to detach themselves from government surveillance and control. Such settlers were often squatters on Crown land, engaged in what was, technically, illegal settlement. Their crop repertories and horticultural techniques are little known, but appear to have included elements originating in Amerindian (Arawak), African, and European cultural heritages. They produced most of their own needs and sold little to outsiders—most such trade, in fact, seems to have been based on smuggling through illegal ports.

Fray Iñigo Abbad y Lasierra, whose *Historia Geográfica . . . de
Puerto Rico* was published in 1782, gives us some idea of the life
and manners of this curious peasantry (Fernández Méndez 1969).
He is astonished, for instance, that they preferred their hammocks
(*hamacas*), an item of Amerindian origin, to regular beds; that
their meat consumption was low, and that they could be satisfied
with a bit of rice and land crab; that they used heavily sweetened
coffee to still their hunger pangs; that they loved cockfighting and
dancing; and that they were not given to long hours of hard work
in the fields. But it is clear that the people Abbad is describing
represent a local adaptation to nonplantation life—that they are,
in fact, quite happy to be barefoot, to sleep in hammocks, and to
limit their labor to their own notions of necessity.

As we have already seen, this was the group out of which the
Puerto Rican sugar industry was to fashion a work force of almost
50,000 for the new plantations of the nineteenth century. In so
doing, the sugar industry undercut badly the competitive position
of its interior frontiersmen, and the highland areas of the island
probably never fully recovered. Thus, this first category of peasants
—the term is only barely applicable—consisted of people whose
adaptation probably depended on the absence of a fully developed
sugar industry; and the growth of the industry constituted a major
element in its destruction. This is not to say, of course, that Puerto
Rico's peasantry disappeared in the early nineteenth century, but
rather that the balance was thereafter heavily weighted in favor of
plantation enterprise.

## The Early Yeomen

A second peasant category stems from the development of indentured labor systems in the islands of the Lesser Antilles, such
as Barbados and Martinique, under the influence of British and
French planters, in the mid-seventeenth century. Such indentured
laborers received a grant of land when their term of labor ended,
and it was common for them to settle down in the Lesser Antilles
as a peasantry. This category approaches much more closely one
part of the conventional definition of peasantries as landholders
who produce much or most of their own consumption, while also

producing items for sale; in most cases the former indentured servants of the Lesser Antilles produced tobacco, indigo, and other products for European markets. But the growth of the plantation system—a system which accounted in good measure for the original importation of indentured servants—was also to lead to the destruction of such peasantries. Not surprisingly, this process of destruction took on a clear racial character, since the original indentured servants were all Europeans, while those who supplanted them were African slaves. Merivale (1841: 75–76), referring to the British islands, states:

> The early settlers who occupied in such numbers the soil of the Antilles, seem to have been chiefly small proprietors, who lived on the produce of their estates. When the cultivation of sugar was introduced about 1670, the free white population rapidly diminished, and continued to do so for a century afterwards. The whites in Barbadoes are said to have increased until they amounted about 1670 to 70,000; but these early calculations must be received with doubt: in 1724, there were only 18,000, there are now [1841] 16,000. Antigua contained 5,000 in the reign of Charles II, now only 2500. The history of the other Windward Islands is precisely similar. Jamaica, from its extent of surface, and fitness for a variety of productions, did not present the same diminution; yet even there the number of whites remained stationary at about 8000 from 1670 to 1720. This declining condition of the white populations, showing how unsuited these islands were to become, what their first occupiers imagined they would, the scenes of extensive colonization from Europe, chiefly proceeded from the monopoly of land, consequent on the cultivation of sugar. As mentioned in a former lecture, it was found that the small proprietor could not compete with the large one, in raising this staple product. Coffee, and still more sugar, requires a number of hands, and the simultaneous application of much labour at particular seasons. Thus this species of agriculture resembles in some respects a manufacture; and, as in manufactures, the large capitalists have great advantages. . . . Hence all accounts of our West Indian colonies, in the first half of the last century, teem with complaints of the decay of small proprietors, and the consolidation of all classes of society into two, the wealthy planters and the slaves (Merivale 1841: 75–76).

The economic fundamentals which made the plantation more expeditious than the small farm as a medium of colonial development under mercantilism need not detain us. What matters is that the process was general in the New World area embraced by what Philip Curtin (1955: 4–7) has aptly called "The South Atlantic System." The slave plantation was, in general, an expansive agro-social enterprise, land being regarded as the expendable factor in production. Improper land utilization led swiftly to exhaustion, whereupon new land, rather than improved agriculture, became the solution. Eric Williams quotes Merivale: "It is more profitable to cultivate a fresh soil by the dear labour of slaves, than an exhausted one by the cheap labour of freemen." And Williams continues: "From Virginia and Maryland to Carolina, Georgia, Texas and the Middle West; from Barbados to Jamaica to Saint Domingue and then to Cuba; the logic was inexorable and the same. It was a relay race; the first to start passed the baton, unwillingly we may be sure, to another and then limped sadly behind" (1944: 7).

The accompaniment of this relay race was the persistent and successive extirpation or degradation of yeoman cultivators. L. C. Gray (1941) has documented part of the process in the United States South. Merivale, as cited, did much to reveal the underlying dynamics of the process for the British West Indies. Ortiz, in his *Contrapunteo Cubano* (1940), and Guerra y Sánchez in his *Sugar and Society in the Caribbean* (1964) touch on the parallel theme for Cuba. Though much work remains to be done in order to clarify how yeomen and free squatters were driven out of other parts of the Caribbean by the plantation system, everything we know makes clear that this was not a racial but an economic matter, intimately connected with the plantation system, and the support it consistently received in the metropolis, whether in London, Paris, Madrid, or elsewhere.

However, since the plantation system depended so heavily on slavery, and since slavery fell most cruelly upon African peoples, an assumed relationship has been posited between slavery and race, which conceals a significant part of Caribbean historical reality. All that we know about the social history of the Caribbean plantation system convinces us that the planters were, in one important respect, quite without prejudice: they were willing to employ any kind of labor, and under any institutional arrangements, as long as the labor force was politically defenseless enough for the work to be done cheaply and under discipline. Hence it is a serious error of interpretation to posit any necessary relationship between slavery and race, ignoring all of those instances where non-Africans were enslaved, or otherwise coerced, by the plantation system. This is by no means to say that slavery in the Caribbean region was the same as slavery in other places and at other times; throughout Afro-America, the slavery institution assumed a highly distinctive character, probably never duplicated anywhere else. But just as Caribbean slaves were sometimes Indian, so Caribbean peasants have often been African; the key to the processes by which plantations and peasantries arose or declined is fundamentally economic and political, not racial.

## The Proto-Peasantry

A third category of peasantry I have referred to elsewhere as a "proto-peasantry" (Mintz 1961a), by which I meant simply that the subsequent adaptation to a peasant style of life was worked out by people while they were still enslaved. The full story of life on Caribbean plantations has by no means been written. But we may be sure of a number of general characteristics of Caribbean slave systems: the formal slave codes never represented, other than very superficially, the actual character of life in each society; each island society differed in certain important ways from every other, with regard to its treatment of the slave population; and in each and every system, the slaves were able to work out certain creative adaptations, in spite of the profoundly repressive conditions under which they were forced to live. "There is something in human history like retribution," wrote Karl Marx (1857), "and it is a rule of historical retribution that its instrument be forged not by the offended, but by the offender himself." The chronicle of Caribbean proto-peasantries seems to confirm this ringing assertion.

Repeatedly, activities which the slaves were compelled to carry out in order to benefit the planters also enabled them to demonstrate their intelligence, resourcefulness, and creativity. Repeatedly, the planters were struck by the slaves' capacities to function very differently in new contexts—when producing their own foods or going to market, for instance—from the way they functioned under the whip. The planters, of course, explained the difference in terms of the slaves' contrariety; but the slaves—and occasional foreign visitors—knew better. Often these selfsame skills turned out to be basic in establishing the freedmen's independence from the plantation after emancipation; and Part III deals with just this development.

The proto-peasantry, then, are slaves who later became peasant freedmen, either through emancipation (as in the case of Jamaica) or revolution (as in the case of Haiti), and whose particular repertories of agricultural skills, craft techniques, crops, and all else represent important "blendings" of traditional and new materials. Commonly, among such peasantries today, one finds both African religious elements and European religious elements; African crops and European, Asian, and Amerindian crops; African food-processing techniques and food-processing techniques from many other areas; and so on. Those of a proto-peasant past form the largest Caribbean peasant category, both numerically and in terms of historical origins. But this category has remained rather poorly defined, in contradistinction to other categories of rural agrarian people in the region.

### The Runaway Peasantries

A fourth category shares much with the preceding categories but also differs in important ways and deserves separate treatment. These are the "runaway peasantries," which were formed by escaping slavery rather than by submitting to it. Throughout the Caribbean region—in Mexico, Colombia, Puerto Rico, Cuba, Saint-Domingue and Jamaica, as well as in Brazil and the Guianas—the creation of maroon communities in defiance of slavery and the plantation system was a common occurrence. Such communities must be separated, for some purposes, from individual escapees—who could attach themselves to the maroon communities only when they were accepted into the maroon bands—and from instances of resistance or rebellion in situ, in which slaves attacked their masters locally. The rationale of the maroon pattern was to create a new and free kind of community outside of, and in opposition to, the slave plantocracy and, where possible, to establish diplomatic relations with the plantocracy on the basis of some kind of recip-rocal treaty. The best-known instances are probably those of Ja-maica and Surinam (Dutch Guiana); but maroon communities elsewhere also established treaty accords with the slave society, as in Mexico (Davidson 1966) and Cuba (Pérez de la Riva 1952), and sometimes became runaway-slave hunters themselves as part of their compact.

Since the slaveowners and the metropolitan governments carried out frequent attempts to destroy the maroon settlements, their in-habitants often lived under the threat of war, and their economic integration with the outside world was correspondingly impaired. To the extent that they were compelled to maintain complete iso-lation, such settlements were not, typologically speaking, "peasant communities." But the history of such groups, in general, has been one of extermination or of transformation into peasantries. Thus, to take the Haitian case, we know that substantial maroon bands survived for generations in the borderlands of Spanish Santo Do-mingo. We do not know whether such bands had formal contact of any kind with the Haitian revolutionary movement after it be-came a movement of the slaves themselves; but we are inclined to assume that the maroon bands, like the revolutionaries, became settled peasantries after the Revolution. Debbasch, in his mono-graph on *marronage* (1961, 1962), has indicated what evidence we have that the maroon groups of prerevolutionary Haiti main-tained their previous contacts and amities after the Revolution; but it is likely that they became part of the Haitian peasantry in general in the postrevolutionary period. The relationships between proto-peasantries and maroon bands, though hardly known at all, could prove of immense significance for our understanding of slave resistance. For the moment, what we know is largely surmise.

These attempts to define certain historical trajectories in regard to peasant subcultures do not take the place of serious studies, either in the form of fieldwork or documentary research; in fact, fieldwork and research should test and refine (and, if necessary, discard) such formulations. Nor should a typological category as wide and as loose as that of "the peasantry" disguise in any way the immense cultural variety that typifies peasant societies every-where. Certain features of the Caribbean peasant adaptation origi-

nate in the general conditions—ecological, economic, political—
under which the emergence of peasant groups occurred. We are
able to trace the particular effects of these conditions in single
cases, as is done in some of the following chapters. Thus, for instance, in both Haiti (French Saint-Domingue) and Jamaica, the
slavery regime produced two highly variant responses among the
slave population: escape and struggle on the one hand, accommodation and the learning of specific skills on the other. But the general
sociological conditions under which the slaves had to respond to
the immense pressures put upon them do not in any way explain
the contemporary differences between, for example, Haitian and
Jamaican peasants, nor even, necessarily, their contemporary similarities. The heavy commitment of the Jamaican peasantry to
market-oriented production of pimento (allspice: *Pimenta officin-
alis* Lindl.) and bananas, when contrasted with that of the Haitian
peasantry's production of coffee, implicates significant differences
in seasonal activity, the use of family labor, attitudes toward the
land, and much else, that are dependent on the nature of the crops
themselves and on the marketing arrangements imposed from outside on the peasantry. Such differences cannot be "explained" by
reference to history as such, nor do they hinge on any shared characteristics of the peasantry, except in the most general sense. In
other words, the delineation of a "developmental path" along which
the peasantry has evolved in any particular Caribbean case is little
more than a highly abstract exercise, until the necessary historical
and ethnological research to confirm or disprove such postulations
is carried out.

### Caribbean Peasantries as a
### Social Science Problem

The assertion that it is useful to study Caribbean peasantries
as cases of resistance to the plantation regime is likewise open to
attack—though a number of young scholars (e.g., Marshall 1968)
have begun to make very good use of this perspective. A core feature of the argument rests on the assumption that Caribbean populations, whether slaves, indentured laborers, or contract laborers,
have consistently struggled to define themselves either within cul-

turally distinctive *communities* or as members of family *lines*—
that is, they have not *generally* responded to the plantation regimen
in terms of their class identity but along other dimensions of social
affiliation. A key to this assertion is the significance of land for
Caribbean rural folk—a significance that far exceeds any obvious
economic considerations. The slaves sought desperately to express
their individuality through the acquisition of material wealth, and
some of the following selections indicate the ways in which this
might be done. Torn from societies that had not yet entered into
the capitalist world, and thrust into settings that were profoundly
capitalistic in character on the one hand, yet rooted in the need for
unfree labor on the other, the slaves saw liquid capital not only
as a means to secure freedom, but also as a means to attach their
paternity—and hence, their identity as persons—to something even
the masters would have to respect. In these terms, the creation of
peasantries was simultaneously an act of westernization and an act
of resistance.

Such responses were not limited to the formation of peasantries
alone, however. All kinds of skills could be pressed into use to
achieve the same results: craftsmanship, fishing, trade, veterinary
science, hunting, and much else. In all such cases, the slaves—and
at a later time, the contract laborers who succeeded them—sought
to *become persons,* to define themselves, in terms of what they knew
and could do. We have already seen how, on the Puerto Rican plantations, special skills were a source of prestige, wealth, and self-
respect for black freedmen. This was even truer for the peasantries,
and for all those who managed to escape the plantation regimen in
order to define their lives outside its iron order.

This may very well be one of the most important ways in which
a contrast may be drawn between the North American and the Caribbean instances. If one were asked to specify the single feature
of the Caribbean past that might best account for the differences
in circumstance facing the North American freedman and the freedmen of the Antilles, this—in the view of the present writer—would
be the feature to explore. By what processes of disfranchisement,
terror, and psychological pressure were the black freedmen of North
America deprived of the means to define themselves *economically*
as men? I would say that the answer to this question would explain,

at least on some very general level, all of the derivative destructions of individuality, dignity, and self that white North America has sought—ultimately, in vain—to impose upon its black victims. Such an assertion remains surmise, for the most part. But the endless controversies about "culture deprivation," the supposedly non-existent black nuclear family, and much else that now typify the North American politico-intellectual scene, cannot be resolved only by revalidating the cultural norms of black Americans; it is essential to revert at some point to lower-order explanations of a more molar kind.

All of this takes us far from the task of formulating a typology of Caribbean peasantries. But it does suggest one way in which these peasantries must be evaluated historically: namely, by assessing the means used by the Caribbean masses to resist a system designed to destroy their identity as human beings.

# 6

## The Historical Sociology of Jamaican Villages

Much of this book has been devoted to the social history of slavery and the plantation system, since these twin institutions played so vital a role in the development of Afro-Caribbean societies. But on many of the islands, inland from the plantations that stretch along their coasts and especially in their rugged interiors, there are large numbers of peasant farms, usually small in size and often very traditional in the character of their agriculture, but important for their economic and cultural role in Caribbean life. With the exception of those islands lost by Spain in 1899, and those too small or too lately occupied ever to have developed a full-scale plantation system, however, the peasantry everywhere in the Antilles is a relatively recent social product, a population reconstituted into a new economic form during the decline and fall of the slave-based estate system.

That is, Caribbean peasants are everywhere a secondary development within the islands. In the case of Jamaica, Sherlock has referred to the "strange and absorbing story of how, out of the social rubble inherited in 1837 a resilient people began to create its own New World" (Sherlock n.d.: 3). This goes too far, perhaps; the peoples of the Caribbean had begun creating (and re-creating) their own New World even before they were debarked in chains; and the rubble they inherited was sometimes—and proudly so, as in the case of Haiti!—of their own violent making. Yet it is perfectly true that Caribbean peasantries represent a transformation of one kind of laboring population into another, by historical processes which varied somewhat in character from one case to the next; and the study of those processes has barely begun.

Final and complete emancipation within the British colonies in the New World, declared effective on August 1, 1838, freed approximately 311,000 persons in Jamaica alone (Cumper 1954b). It was assumed by most observers, though not by the planters themselves, that these new freedmen, over 218,000 of whom had been "praedial" (that is, field) slaves (Cumper 1954a: 39), would continue to serve as the labor base for the plantation system. Joseph Sturge, the famous English Quaker abolitionist, predicted:

> In a state of freedom it may be expected that the conditions and resources of an agricultural labourer, working for regulated wages, will be, as they are in England, superior to those of a paltry agriculturist, cultivating his little plot of land with his own hands; and it is evident therefore that the negroes will generally prefer working on the estates. Their strong attachment to the place of their birth, to their houses and gardens, to the graves of their parents and kindred, exceeding what has been recorded of any other people, is another circumstance which favours their continuance as labourers on the estates to which they are now respectively attached (quoted in Olivier 1936: 109).

But Sturge did not take sufficient account of the vindictiveness and relatively desperate economic situation of the planters, or of the legitimate and very intense desire of the freedman to establish himself as a yeoman farmer.

In Jamaica, the independent peasantry came into being almost entirely after Emancipation. Under the leadership of Baptist, Methodist, and other missionaries—who had worked fearlessly for Emancipation once they realized that their missionary labors with the slaves had become impossible in the face of planter resistance—the Jamaican freedman got his clearest opportunity to become a peasant cultivator. At first, the process had a curiously unpremeditated and undeliberate character. Punitive laws passed by the Jamaica Assembly, which was dominated in the post-Emancipation period by the planters, were leading to a powerful movement of ex-slaves off the estates. The pull of the independent homestead predated Emancipation, and some settlement of freedmen had already occurred (Cumper 1954b: 135). But the trend became much stronger after freedom for all was enacted.

In order for new freedmen to become independent farmers, certain conditions were necessary. First, they would have to be able to grow subsistence crops successfully. The essential skills for subsistence agriculture had been mastered by the slaves under slavery itself in Jamaica, since it was customary to compel the field slave to grow his own foodstuffs on unused estate land (Lopez 1948; Hall 1954). Second, the freedmen would require outlets for surpluses which could be exchanged for cash to buy the things which were not within the individual's capacity to produce for himself but were already part of his consumption patterns. Here, too, success had also been partly assured by Jamaican slavery itself, since slaves had been permitted, even encouraged, to market their surplus at island markets. These markets continued in strength after Emancipation, even increasing in number. Moreover, there grew up a brisk export trade in agricultural staples, many items formerly produced on estates becoming peasant products. Pre-Emancipation agricultural and marketing practices of the slaves were the major means by which they could accumulate liquid capital, and this capital formed the basis for the third condition required for the formation of a free peasantry: money with which to buy land. The availability of the land itself was the fourth essential condition for the growth of a peasant class.

Land might be acquired simply by squatting on Crown property, and this occurred, though its importance in the total picture may have been exaggerated (Olivier 1936: 133, 141–42). Or the land could be bought up by individual freedmen from ruined estates or the surpluses of economically viable estates. Much buying of this kind took place, but it was not the most efficient or successful means for resettling freedmen as peasants. It was in this immediate post-Emancipation period that the leaders of the Baptist and Methodist missionary churches hit upon a third means for the acquisition of land: buying up in toto ruined estates upon which they might resettle parishioners as independent peasants in *church communities*.

The idea, which caught hold swiftly and had an almost revolutionary effect upon Jamaican society, can be attributed mostly to the Baptist ministers William Knibb and James Phillippo. Reverend Phillippo had in fact founded a village for freedmen during the period of the Apprenticeship (1834–38), and may be considered the originator of this scheme (Payne 1933: 60). But it was after Emancipation, when the pressures, both positive and negative, to get off the estates became irresistible, that the church-founded free village system flowered. Paget (n.d.) has provided the best brief summary of this movement. Between 1838 and 1844, 19,000 freedmen and their families removed themselves from the estates, bought land, and settled in free villages. In terms of the total population affected, this figure may represent an aggregate of as many as 100,-000 persons. The initial transformation of ex-slaves into independent yeoman farmers on a grand scale was accomplished in less than a decade. Its social and economic importance for the subsequent character of Jamaican society cannot be overestimated.

The ministers Phillippo and Knibb, who initiated the free village movement, were followed by many others. The Reverends Burchell, Abbott, and John Clark were among these. Of particular interest here is Rev. John Clark. Clark came to Jamaica in 1835 to assist Rev. James Coultart at the Baptist Church at St. Ann's Bay, on the north coast of Jamaica, in the Parish of St. Ann. Reverend Coultart died in 1836, and Reverend Clark moved thereupon to Brown's Town, in the highlands—called the Dry Harbour Mountain district—of the same parish. The St. Ann's Bay Church was delegated to another minister, and Reverend Clark was charged with the church at Brown's Town and with ministering to the needs of the Baptists in the surrounding district. The Apprenticeship system, instituted in 1834, was operative in those years. Reverend Clark, like many of his fellow ministers, noted and protested against abuses in this alleged gradual transition from slavery to freedom and played a role in the fight against its continuance. Emancipation was enacted in 1838, two years before the Apprenticeship was originally to have been terminated.

During the Apprenticeship period, Reverend Clark was in correspondence with Joseph Sturge, who had emerged as the leading abolitionist in Great Britain, since Clarkson was of advanced age and Wilberforce was dead. Once Emancipation was enacted, it was with the help of Sturge—who, it will be remembered, had mistakenly believed that the slaves would remain resident on the estates after freedom—that Reverend Clark undertook to establish free villages under church sponsorship. Clark's influence in creating a peasantry in the Dry Harbour Mountains region of St. Ann was considerable. In the course of his work, he established or helped to establish a large number of free villages. From the impetus provided by church sponsorship, other free villages grew without the deliberate patronage of the missionary churches.

Clark's report to Joseph Sturge (Clark 1852) states that over twenty free villages were founded in the Dry Harbour Mountains of St. Ann alone in the years immediately following Emancipation. They held fifteen or sixteen hundred families, about three-fourths of the enfranchised population of the district (Olivier 1936: 115). In the first three years of freedom, the peasantry connected with the Baptist churches of St. Ann Parish spent 10,000 pounds for the purchase of land (Underhill 1861: 328), and Knibb claimed that up to 1845, forty-three free villages had been founded in that parish alone (cited in Underhill 1861).

## The Free Village of Sturge Town

According to Reverend Clark's testimony, the first free village founded under his sponsorship was Sturge Town. Reverend Clark (cited in Olivier 1936: 113–14) describes that village specifically in his report to Joseph Sturge:

The first property I bought contained 120 acres of good land, about eight miles from Brown's Town. The cost, with expenses of conveyance and surveying was about 700 pounds sterling. Of this amount rather more than 400 pounds sterling was paid down by about eighty or ninety of the people, and the remainder by instalments and by additional purchasers. Nearly 100 building lots, and an equal number of acres for provision grounds, were surveyed. Small neat cottages were speedily built, and the land brought into good cultivation. There was a house and two or three acres of land left clear after the whole cost was paid. The house was converted into a schoolroom, and placed in trust for the benefit of the villagers, who erected a large booth, as a temporary place of worship, capable of containing 400 or 500 people. A chapel and mission house have subsequently been built. The settlement was called Sturge Town (now Birmingham).

The present writer spent part of the summer of 1952 engaged in fieldwork in Sturge Town. The fieldwork was too brief and too often interrupted by other obligations to permit more than sporadic collection of data, but some of the information gathered will be reported here. Of particular interest was the later discovery by the writer, in the map collection of the Jamaica Institute, of an original map which appears to be that made by or for Reverend John Clark after he purchased the property, previously named Angwin Crawl, upon which Sturge Town came to stand (Fig. 1). (The term *crawl*, cognate with Portuguese *curral*, Afrikaans *kraal*, etc., was the Jamaican planters' designation for a pen for swine or slaves.)

In an examination of some hundreds of maps in the collection, this was the only one of its kind found, and it was the purest stroke of luck to have found it, since it was discovered *after* the fieldwork period in Sturge Town. It is certain that this is indeed a map of the same property; though no name appears on the map, it corresponds in shape to the original property pictured on Jamaica cadastral maps of the area (Fig. 2), and the names of the contiguous properties correspond as well. The cadastral section carries both the names Angwin Crawl and Sturge Town on the holding; and old Sturge Towners reported that the former name of the village had been Angwin Crawl. According to Reverend Clark, the Sturge Town property contained "120 acres of good land"; according to the cadastral section and the deed of transfer, it contains 126 acres. The difference may be concealed in Reverend Clark's phrasing; it is not a significant difference in any case.

To judge from the appearance of the Clark map, it was drawn up at some point after the property had been purchased and surveyed, and some, but not all, of the holdings had been taken up by settlers. The arrangement of the house plots, the varying character of the agricultural plots, and certain other features of settlement as indicated on the map, raise questions concerning the original nature of this church-founded free village. By tabulation, there are seventy-four individual agricultural holdings (of which seventy-

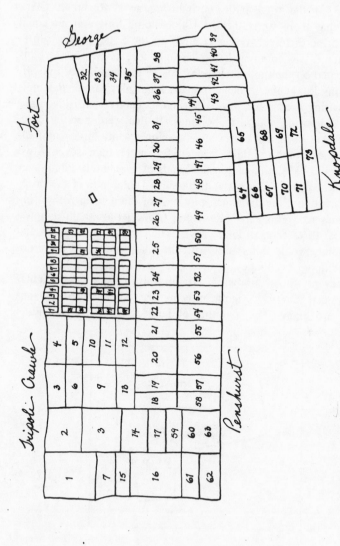

Figure 1. Tracing of what appears to be the original Clark map of the Angwin Crawl property, St. Ann, Jamaica.

three are numbered); seventy-two house plots (of which twenty-seven are numbered); and a large, undefined plot greater in size than that of the total indicated housing area. Reverend Clark claimed that there were "nearly 100 building lots, and an equal number of acres for provision ground" in the Sturge Town settlement when it was completed; though only seventy-two house plots are indicated on the map, later reference to the number of individuals buying lots makes it clear that the large plot east of the indicated housing area must have been subsequently subdivided into additional housing and farm holdings. If this were not the case, then the land in excess of seventy-two (or seventy-three) agricultural holdings and the land needed for more than seventy-two houses would have remained in the hands of the church. Planimeter calculations, using 126 acres as the assumed total area of the property, indicate that the undefined plot east of the delineated housing area comes to 16.66 acres. Reverend Clark writes that "a house and two or three acres of land" were left clear after settlement, and this certainly would not square with the Clark map, had there not been additional occupancy of the undefined northeast lots.

The seventy-three numbered agricultural plots are of particular interest since they vary significantly in size. The possible reasons for this are many. The amounts of land acquired by individual

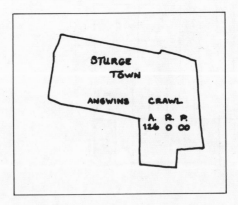

*Figure 2. Copy of the cadastral section showing the Angwin Crawl–*
*Sturge Town property, St. Ann, Jamaica.*

settlers may have varied in accordance with their variable capacity to pay, with some maximum perhaps being set by the church. Again, the size of the purchasable landholding may have been based on the size of the purchaser's family. Or the holdings may have been staked out with regard for variations in soil quality, topography, and the like—though this last seems unlikely, given the small overall size of the property. Lastly, some favoritism may have been shown. It is at least possible, in any case, that the original settlers varied in their economic status from the first, and this could be a sociological datum of primary importance.

From Reverend Clark's description of the founding of Sturge Town, and from descriptions of the community provided by later writers, we may say something relatively specific concerning the sociology of this one church-founded free village. For instance, Clark's comments indicate that the majority of the original settlers were known to him personally, and that they were members of his church. He thus describes "eighty or ninety of the people" paying for their land, stating that some land was paid for "by additional purchasers." This strongly suggests that Sturge Town was a solidly Baptist community from its very beginning. We can also assume with fair assurance that all of the settlers in such a village were churchgoers. The same sentence indicates, of course, that the land was bought, not given to the settlers, and goes on to say that some of it was paid off in installments. Since Clark specifies that the land, together with the conveyance and survey expenses, cost "about 700 pounds sterling," we may assume that settlers could purchase their holdings for approximately seven pounds per acre. Clark (cited in Olivier 1936: 113) indicates that current prices for settlers' land in St. Ann ranged from three to twelve pounds per acre. If the 1,000 pounds purchase price in the Records of Land Purchases (Spanish Town, Jamaica) is for land alone, this would have raised the price per acre for settlers to approximately eight pounds. Though this price was not excessive at the time, the fact that some people paid off their obligations in installments indicates some degree of continuing financial control by the church, and of continuing financial obligation on the part of the settlers.

From the subsequent description we learn that a school and a church were added to the community immediately upon its establishment. The school was run by the church. The church itself, according to Clark's letter, was staffed by a local minister, Samuel Hodges, who, at the time of Clark's writing, had been living in Sturge Town for "the last seven or eight years" (Clark 1852: 8), that is, from about 1843 or 1844 until 1851 or 1852. Thus, not only did Sturge Town consist of a religiously homogeneous or near-homogeneous group, but it had a church-run school and its own chapel and resident minister. That minister, or another, was there at the time of the visit of Candler and Alexander, who passed through Sturge Town in 1850. The report of these visitors contains the following brief on Sturge Town:

> Population 541; houses, wattled and shingled, 103; wattled and thatched, 2; huts, 6; total of houses, 111; floor of apartments, boarded, 45; terraced, 163. Families, 113, parents, 228; children and unmarried persons, 313. Children who attend the day school, 112; Sabbath school, 200. Copies of the Scriptures, 187. Each house has its separate acre of land, where, in addition to provisions, pimento is frequently cultivated, and in some instances sugar-cane. There are also in the village some small wooden mills for grinding the cane, and on almost all the little properties some simple contrivance for expressing its juice. Such villages, built on the summit or slope of some fine hill, interspersed with bananas and plantains, and shaded by mangoes and breadfruit trees, have a very pleasing appearance, and greatly enliven the face of nature. The moral condition of Sturge Town is, we believe, superior to most that have not the advantage of a resident missionary (cited in Olivier 1936: 114).

This description provides a little new information, some directly, and some inferrable. There has been a slight growth in population and an increase in the number of houses. Neolocal residence predominates (113 families, 111 houses). Crop diversification seems strong, but the quotation is naive in this regard. Pimento, a tree crop, is not normally "cultivated" but spread through the agency of nature. It is a traditional export crop in Jamaica, and was probably sold for export by Sturge Town people. Other tree crops mentioned are mangoes and breadfruit. Surpluses of these foods were probably also sold for distribution in the island markets, as they are today. Cultivation of sugarcane in an area wholly unfitted for it is a common persistence in the Caribbean, and rural people often prefer the crude brown "moscovado" sugar to refined white sugar. The presence of small wooden mills is certain evidence of production for sale. We have noted that the internal marketing system grew rapidly in Jamaica after Emancipation; so did peasant production of export crops and products, such as pimento, beeswax, annatto, fustic, logwood, and honey. Production for sale was a major means of acquiring money for the purchase of land, after the Emancipation as well as before.

The family-parent figures indicate family stability. The differences in house type and flooring do not suggest significant economic dif- ferentiation, but the description is too thin to permit definitive judgments in this regard.

Reverend Clark's letter, cited earlier, must have been written some time after the visit of Candler and Alexander. While stressing the success of the free village movement, Reverend Clark indicates that the fervency and piety of the people were waning at the time he wrote. The villagers, he says,

> should be aided for a few years to maintain their religious and educational institutions . . . [because] at the present time they are unable, in consequence of the reduction of wages, frequent want of employment, distress arising from the ravages of cholera and smallpox, and heavy taxation, to contribute more than one third of the amount they once cheerfully gave towards building chapels and school houses and supporting their pastors and teachers. There are also not a few who do not sufficiently value religious and educational advantages to make sacrifices to obtain them (Clark 1852: 11).

Reverend Clark's concern for the villagers in church-founded settlements was realistic. In spite of the influence the missionary churches might wield over the free settlements, there might be tendencies toward either a decline of religiosity on the one hand or the growth of a "folk" variety of Christianity on the other. Curtin has assembled evidence that a folk version of Christianity, with emphasis on leading of the spirit, possession, and ideological synthesis with elements of African religions, even predated the development of organized missionary churches in Jamaica (1955: 28–41; cf. also Hogg 1964). In some instances, organized churches were subtly changed in character to bring their doctrines and prac-

tices more into the line with obeahism and myalism, religious forms
originating at least in part in the African tradition. The final firsthand report the present writer was able to locate, in the form of ab-
breviated notes made by Underhill, makes mention of just such a
change in Sturge Town:

STURGE TOWN TABERNACLE. Rev. John Clark, pastor. Number
of members, 107. (It is necessary to mention that this church is a
secession from the church under the native minister, Mr. McLaggan,
and arose out of certain occurrences connected with Obeahism, in
which the minister and some of the members were involved). 'We
are a handful of corn'. Have no fault to find as to attendance; attendance 'most beautiful', except it be wet and sloppy in the town. The
classes in the town are pretty well attended. There are about 700
persons in Sturge Town; all attend either the Tabernacle or Mr.
McLaggan's. The Sunday School is very good; but some of the
teachers come late. Very few backsliders; but they attend chapel
regularly. The leaders are very attentive to their duty and look after
the 'slack'. If you scold the people, you make them worse. There are
many complaints about the estates. People are not getting rid of
religion, though it is not as it was twenty years ago. A little before
and after freedom there was more piety, everybody 'was going to
chapel'. All felt the yoke of Satan, and looked to religion for comfort
then. Young people 'feel no lash'; yet they are coming to chapel; but
do not exhibit such great piety. There is not so much religion now as
before the cholera. People do not feel so much now as at the time
when 'free come'. There was not so much trouble in admitting members then as now, piety was more apparent, there was no need to
examine so strictly. Some deacons and leaders hesitate now to
recommend for membership any who are not married people. Young
people can earn money for themselves, and are not so dependent on
the old people; they do not listen as formerly to the old people 'to
tick to de gospel' (1861: 312–13).

This final description comes about 20 years after the founding of
Sturge Town—though, curiously, the exact date of the founding of
the village (probably 1839) is nowhere given. (Henderson 1931
indicates that the school and church were opened in 1840.) It
suggests that, while the Baptist church still wielded considerable
influence in the village, .new forces had arisen which were causing
change in various ways—by providing competing faiths; by enabling

the young to earn money independently of their families; by hampering any careful or exact perpetuation of the original ideology of the free village through the children of the settlers. Yet even Underhill's rather pessimistic picture still conveys the idea of a largely homogeneous church community. People still attend church regularly; the outbreak of obeahism (which Sturge Towners in 1952 knew about from hearsay but could not detail, since it had occurred over a century before) had been quelled and services were back to normal; the "leaders are attentive to their duty and look after 'the slack.' "

No written reports on Sturge Town after 1861 are known to the writer. But in 1952, when it was possible to spend a brief time in that community, certain continuities from the past were still visible. There were still two churches, both non-Established, and the Baptist church was the larger and its congregation bigger. The Baptist church still held some land, operated for its own support. The school was still operated by this church. The lay leaders of the Baptist church included most of the richer landholders in the community—though none of these men would be considered wealthy by United States standards. (The biggest landholder in Sturge Town in 1952, so far as could be determined, held sixteen acres of land.) The Baptist church was still the center of social and recreational activities, as well as the leading religious organization. When a new teacher moved to the community, he immediately became involved in Baptist church activities, though not himself a Baptist. One young local girl, upon beginning her practice teaching in the village, shifted her membership from the competing church to the Baptist church. Opportunities for technical education and higher education generally seemed to be most accessible through the Baptist church, though it must be emphasized that membership in a different church did not prevent the Baptist minister from giving all possible help to a young person. The community had produced several outstanding Jamaican leaders during its history, in the fields of education and religion. In short, though the writer's data are much too limited to allow any elaborate conclusions, it is apparent that the founding church was still playing a central role in the life of the village and its residents in 1952. Further fieldwork in this village is necessary to evaluate much more precisely the importance of the founding institution, over a hundred years after Sturge Town became a peasant community.

## The Sociology of Free Villages

If the church-founded free villages initially shared so many general sociological characteristics that they might be considered to form a "community type," the question is immediately raised whether these villages today are more like each other in their sociology than they are like other Jamaican villages with differing histories. A definitive answer is impossible, but it might be useful to attempt an enumeration of the characteristics which may have been common to these villages when they were founded.

Cumper (1954b) was the first recent writer to call particular attention to the need for determining whether church-founded villages might indeed be regarded as representing a distinctive community type, and the present chapters owe much to his analysis. In brief, we can no longer afford to view Jamaican rural communities as homogeneous or undifferentiated. Particular ecologies, particular traditions of land use, special historical circumstances, and other local peculiarities have surely affected the special social composition and organization of these communities; in all likelihood, there are abstractable classes or types of settlement. In the case of the church-founded villages, we can say nothing of much use about the character of the land upon which they were formed. Though we know that such estates were often described as "ruinate" (which helps to explain why the land was up for sale), this must be interpreted from the perspective of large-scale sugarcane production, not peasant cultivation. So far as land use is concerned, we have already seen how the original disposition of the land may have created a "baseline" for subsequent practice. Even more importantly from our point of view, the social organization of the church-founded village was at the outset very much under the control of the church itself. We must seek to make clear in what ways, if any, this control was manifested in later developments and continues to be manifested at the present time—keeping in mind always that we are dealing with only one community "on the ground."

A summation of the expectable sociological characteristics of the church-founded free village, related to the role of the church in maintaining a historically distinctive type of community subculture, might read as follows:

1. It was a geographically definable community;
2. It was a socially definable community;
3. It was wholly or largely a religiously homogeneous community, at least initially;
4. Its population was differentiated in certain sociological regards from the freedman population as a whole in being:
   *a*) more literate;
   *b*) more closely tied to organized Christian churches;
   *c*) more thrifty;
   *d*) composed of stable monogamous families;
   *e*) dependent on and indebted to the missionary church;
5. It was isolated:
   *a*) geographically in many cases;
   *b*) ideologically, initially and perhaps for some time afterward;
6. It was under relatively strong church control due to:
   *a*) financial obligations;
   *b*) pressures exerted by coreligionist neighbors;
   c) the influence and power of church leaders;
   *d*) difficulties in securing land outside the community;
   *e*) direction of schools by the church;
7. This church influence had good chances of perpetuation due to:
   *a*) continued geographical isolation, in many cases;
   *b*) the church's role as a funnel for outside opportunities (missionary training, opportunities based on preliminary education, local restriction of economic opportunities);
   *c*) likelihood of village, or at least intrafaith, endogamy, due to geographical isolation, church-sponsored recreation, parental and neighborly influence, etc.

The geographically definable character of the original church-founded free villages is of great importance for the nature of their later development. Cohen (1953) has described his difficulties in delimiting the rural community which he studied in Jamaica; and in a later paper, M. G. Smith (1956b) makes the point that the contemporary rural Jamaican community must be defined according to a set of variables, such as topography and patterns of mating and visiting, rather than by equating "community" and "village." The need for sophisticated techniques to delineate the social boundaries of modern Jamaican communities arises because of the way such communities were established or the way they have grown up over time. Particularly where these communities bordered large towns, or developed in areas within which they might expand by successive small-scale purchases of land, their borders have become difficult to specify. But the *original* free villages, unless they were founded near or within the confines of existing towns, were indeed geographically definable as communities. We know this because of the way they were established: that is, through the purchase of a whole large estate, in the midst of other such estates, which was then subdivided among settlers.

To this day, Sturge Town is geographically definable in these terms. It has indeed extended itself through purchases of adjacent land by some residents and through the creation of a Land Settlement community (Thatchfield) on another estate bordering it. But it does not present the helter-skelter picture of continuous and extended settlement in many directions and, seemingly, according to no preconceived order, that is so characteristic of many other Jamaican communities. Free villages like Sturge Town, then, were not congeries of scattered homesteads but artificially created nuclei of population, with a particular internal social structure.

Every such free village—at least every such village founded under church sponsorship—was composed at the start of practicing coreligionists in good standing. While every single newly settled freedman in a given village might not have been of the same faith, Reverend Clark's testimony and that of other contemporary missionary leaders make it clear that church-founded free villages were religiously homogeneous as well as geographically and socially definable communities.

It seems fair to argue that the populations of the church-founded free villages differed to some degree from the remainder of the freedman population. In all likelihood they were more literate,

Bible-reading having been an important practice and educational objective of missionary congregations. Moreover, the village inhabitants were probably more uniform in their attachment to an organized religion than was the population as a whole. The people of the church-founded villages doubtless varied in their sincerity and fervency, and surely the missionaries must have been deceived at times by parishioners whose motives were not wholly pious. Yet the descriptions provided us make it likely that for the most part these villagers took their religious affiliation seriously.

Probably—one might better say possibly—the settlers as a group were more thrifty and industrious than other freedmen. This may be an unsupportable speculation. Yet those who acquired land first in the church-founded free villages were the savers, who had managed to lay something by during the Apprenticeship or before, and they were the church members in good standing. Thrift in itself may be of little importance in the present context. What is important is the degree to which we may be allowed to speculate that the settlers of the church-founded free villages shared an ideology based on church membership and acceptance of its Christian tenets, particularly thrift, industry, and other doctrinal precepts associated with "uprightness" and humility. Lay church leaders in Sturge Town in 1952 were exemplary in these regards; most of them were relatively well-to-do peasants and extremely hard workers. Significantly, the village itself enjoys a reputation among the middle class of the whole parish as a place where the best-mannered rural people and the best domestic workers come from!

Cumper (1954b: 137) has pointed out that church-founded free villages would consist at first of populations composed of monogamous families. This point is of primary importance, since monogamy would distinguish the people of such villages from the freedman population as a whole. The writer's 1952 census data for Sturge Town are not complete enough to indicate whether the village differs significantly in this regard from its parish or from Jamaica as a whole; but the incomplete data give the impression that it does.

The people of the church-founded free villages entered into a relationship of obligation to their churches when they were first settled. This circumstance emerges as perhaps the most important of all in its effect on the present-day character of such villages, and will be treated in detail at a later point.

These villages were usually isolated geographically at the time of their founding, as pointed out earlier. In St. Ann, this is true for many such villages besides Sturge Town. Geographical isolation can serve as a powerful bar to culture change, of course. But isolation is not a function of geography alone. M. G. Smith writes (1956b: 298):

> Plantation economies and social systems have persisted on the plains, while peasant type economies and societies were developed among the population which settled the hills as squatters, freeholders, or with Mission assistance. One often finds today a general denominational attachment in some of these hill communities, and to some extent this attachment reflects the historical conditions in which Missions assisted their establishment. But today, church influence is probably dominant and integrating only where the community is considerably isolated.

The writer grants that this may be the case. Sturge Town is indeed an example of a community whose geographical isolation has persisted. But ideological or social isolation may persist even where geographical isolation has declined. And certain kinds of contacts with the outside may serve to strengthen existing patterns rather than to weaken them. The sociological and anthropological literature is full of descriptions of part-societies which have retained cultural distinctiveness and social isolation even in strongly urban contexts or in situations of repeated and intense contact. The marketing pattern of many Sturge Town women, which takes them regularly out of the community and even to Kingston, has probably served to maintain cultural stability rather than to provoke change, since it allows villagers to conserve culturally approved standards of consumption which are very old and not rapidly expanding. The regular visits of Baptist ministers for Sunday services, wherein the community is "penetrated," are not sources of change so much as a powerful force for conservatism and the retention of old habits. Accessibility to change, therefore, cannot be viewed simply along an isolation-contact continuum, but must be seen rather in terms of the character of contact and its effect on people,

and in terms of the strength of existing forces for cohesion and conservatism within the community.

At the time of their establishment, the church-founded free villages were under relatively strong missionary control. Individuals
were surrounded by neighbors who were also coreligionists and
probably often kinfolk as well. This suggests that internal pressures
for conformity were present. Lay church leaders could exert influence in maintaining such conformity; they continue to do so in
Sturge Town today. The way this control may operate can be
illustrated by reference to the problem of accessibility to land. It
was usually difficult to get access to additional land outside but
conveniently near the free villages, and growing population meant
that pressures for land would inevitably arise unless people emi-
grated. In the case of Sturge Town, additional holdings were
gradually acquired by rental or, rarely, purchase from adjoining
estates. But the scarcity of smallholder land in general came to
mean that those short of land would either have to walk great
distances to their fields or leave the community entirely. In one
case recorded in 1952, a Sturge Towner walked twenty-two miles
each time he went to his fields, which he rented. He was anxious
to acquire the right to work a piece of church property in Sturge
Town. But he was not a faithful member of the local church and
did not get the use of the land. This is by no means to claim that
church membership was a condition for economic or social assistance; but it seems likely that churchgoing improves one's community standing and, accordingly, one's local economic opportunities. To what extent such incidents may have been important in
earlier Sturge Town history cannot be established.

The lack of economic alternatives in such communities may have
confronted the land-hungry villager with three choices: leave the
community entirely; invest an unusual effort in obtaining a source
of income far from the community while maintaining residence in
it; or conform carefully to all the community's social rules in the
hope of finding an economic niche within it. It is not our intention
to suggest that the church exercised any deliberate policy of exact-
ing conformity from villagers through special economic controls.
Even if this had been its intent, the church's village resources were
much too limited to have made this possible. Rather, conformity

on the part of villagers was to be expected regardless of local social and economic lines of power.

Control of local schools is also relevant for an estimate of the church's total influence. Schooling in a country such as Jamaica is the sine qua non of economic and social advancement. While the non-Established church schools are not, in the writer's opinion, used as instruments of indoctrination villagers tend almost naturally to think of the school and church as a unit. A student's future success is bound up with his early education, and the impression he makes on his superiors in school. The fact that the schools in the church-founded free villages are usually under church supervision even today is therefore of great importance in understanding the social structure of such villages.

These various circumstances, related to the sociology of the villages at the time of their founding, were perpetuated in varying strength in the following century. We begin with a picture of geographical isolation; a definable community social structure; a religiously homogeneous community; a village population sociologically distinguishable from the free population as a whole; financial and moral indebtedness to the founder church; church control of education; internal pressures for conformity exerted by lay leaders and neighbors; external pressure for conformity exerted incidentally by the church itself; and an absence of alternative economic opportunities of all kinds for local people. To the extent that such initial characteristics were perpetuated, we may assume that the local community tended to maintain its original character. This is, of course, a circular statement because much more needs to be known about the degree to which Sturge Town and communities like it have indeed remained as they were. The schools continue to be church-supervised in many cases. The lay leaders of the church continue to be community leaders—the larger landholders, the teachers, and the political workers.

In the beginning, the missionary churches added to the social landscape of Jamaica a large number of religiously homogeneous communities, many of which were isolated physically from the larger society and provided settings for their own perpetuation. The missionary-created peasant villages had a population which might be viewed as a distinctive subculture; to some extent, they may still have it. The villages were clearly under the sway of the churches responsible for founding them. They were administered, insofar as there were community problems, by the ministers who founded them, or their successors. They were single-church and single-school communities which owed their existence to the church, and were morally and economically in debt to it. Cumper (1954b: 156) has even collected evidence that the churches played an important judicial role in the villages they founded. It is no wonder, then, as Cumper has pointed out, that while the planters referred derisively to Reverend Knibb, the outstanding leader of the Baptist missionary movement in Jamaica and a founder of many free villages, as "King Knibb," his followers used the same designation with pride.

Inevitably, discussion of the history or present-day status of villages such as Sturge Town must lead to some reflection on their character as Afro-American or Afro-Caribbean communities. The missionary movement in pre-Emancipation Jamaica, though reviled and even menaced by the planter class, was undoubtedly a strong force for the Europeanization or westernization of the slaves. The theme of salvation, acceptance of the Gospel, acceptance of the condition of slavery on ideological grounds, literacy, regular prayer, acceptance of the authority of ordained ministers (all of them, at least at first, English and white), and much else clearly conditioned the "de-africanization" of the believer, at least in significant areas of belief and value.

This process, however, cannot be assumed to have occurred in all aspects of the slaves' or freedmen's lives. If anything, one would expect that the establishment of peasant freedman villages, while consolidating the control of the missionaries in some areas, might also have provided an opportunity for the perpetuation of independent patterns established under slavery, for example, in such spheres as agriculture and marketing and expressive media (proverbs, folktales, myths). Pressure against the perpetuation of older patterns would presumably have been strongest in the area of religion, since conversion to a Christian ideology would have predated the establishment of the freedman village system. Nonetheless, as we have noted, "backsliding" sometimes took the form of religious innovation, innovation that involved in some ways the restoration of the more traditional (or "African") religious forms that had been supplanted by Christianity. Such restorations of earlier stages in the evolution of Afro-Caribbean religion are not reducible to any simple formula; the present chapter has referred to this aspect of Sturge Town history only very tangentially. But the extent to which freedman villages encapsulated in their cultural forms aspects of slave life that might survive less intact otherwise is a matter well worth considering.

In effect, the creation of free villages in the Jamaican countryside provided a distinctive setting for the elaboration of a new kind of rural society. Though many institutional features of these villages were predetermined by church control, and by the preparation of the peasantry for their life as freemen before Emancipation, other features of local life persisting from slavery may also have been conserved or "protected" by the sociology of missionary administration. It was, to a remarkable extent, within the confines of church-founded villages that the broad outlines of contemporary Jamaican rural life were filled in. Yet we still do not know to what extent such villages actually provided a different context from that afforded by "informal" settlement. A satisfactory answer would have to hinge on further field research.

## Conclusions

The peasantry of Jamaica in its majority came into being in the period immediately following Emancipation. Though the basic requirements for attaining the status of peasants were in the hands of the Jamaican freedmen themselves, executive leadership and, to some extent, capital, were provided through the missionary churches in a great number of cases. Under the stimulus of church leadership, large numbers of church-founded free villages arose in the mountainous interior of the island. The sociology of these villages may have distinguished them from other free villages in Jamaica, and the fact that they were established by missionary churches signified that their populations could likewise be distinct from the freedman population as a whole.

Given the character of the church-founded free village, it may be justifiable to suppose that the Baptist peasant had a lifeway at least initially differentiated from that of peasants not intimately associated with a church group. The characteristics of this imputed distinctiveness might be inferred from the sociological features already attributed to the church-founded free village as a community type. They would include a greater responsiveness to community pressure; a heightened concern with respectability; a stronger interest in literacy, social and economic advancement, and "toeing the line"; and, it might be supposed, a greater respect for "law and order," duly constituted authority, and persons having high ascribed status. To some extent, as Cumper has suggested, it was in this context that the minister became a substitute—an altogether preferable substitute—for the estate owner, the overseer, the slave driver, the judge, and the custos. This shift in authority and leadership was of crucial importance in the establishment of a free peasantry in Jamaica; stress has been laid in this chapter on the significance of the missionary leaders in creating and perpetuating peasant communities.

Yet there is a real possibility that due to their special social and religious character the free villages are to this day characterized by a special sociology, and perhaps by a distinctive channeling of locally developed initiative along idiosyncratic lines of endeavor. It is suggested here that the history of local communities in a country such as Jamaica can still be reconstructed, at times in considerable detail, and that such reconstructions can prove valuable in understanding the present-day social organization of these communities. For both practical and intellectual reasons, the teasing out of the history of particular Caribbean peasantries is a useful task for the problem-oriented social scientist.

# 7

# The Origins
# of the
# Jamaican Market System

This chapter deals with the origins and growth of the Jamaican internal market system and the local small-scale agriculture which is served by that system. The Jamaican census of 1943 indicated that out of an agricultural labor force of 221,376, there were 49,200 peasants who operated holdings of ten acres or less, while 16,972 peasants had larger holdings. In addition, a significant proportion of the agricultural labor force listed as wage earners was simultaneously engaged in cultivating owned land in plots of less than one acre or in cultivating rented land (Cumper n.d.).

The Jamaican peasantry of today originated two centuries ago within the physical boundaries of the slave-worked sugar estates and within the normal pattern of slave-estate administration. Since the slave plantation elsewhere in much of the Caribbean region—in Puerto Rico for example—served to destroy rather than to create the peasantry (Mintz 1951a, 1959), the forces at work in the Jamaican case are of particular interest. Jamaican internal marketing is closely intermeshed with the rise of that country's peasant class.

Under slavery, the owners and managers of estates in the British Caribbean faced the problem of feeding their slaves. The alternative extremes were either to have the slaves produce as much as possible of the food they ate or to import all of their food. Of these two courses the first, though not always practicable, was the more desirable. If the slaves could feed themselves, the estates would save the cost of imported foods and avoid the risks contingent upon importation. When warfare disturbed merchant shipping, a frequent occurrence in the eighteenth century, and shortages of imported food resulted, food prices rose (Ragatz 1928). Moreover, when import shortages existed, the slaves could not be adequately fed even if the planter could afford high food prices. Prolonged interference with the importation of food introduced a vicious circle of high prices, malnutrition, and reduced production and profits.

Yet there were often difficulties in the way of local food production, and it is no accident that today in the British Caribbean, the peasantry and food production sites are found chiefly in mountain areas or in areas otherwise unsuitable, by reason of location, or of soil or weather conditions, for sugar production. Until the 1830s land and slave labor were the essential factors of sugar production. Capital equipment and technical know-how became important only after the Emancipation and the opening of the British sugar market to foreign competition in the second half of the nineteenth century (Goveia 1959).

The sugar planters wanted to plant sugar wherever it could be planted profitably but at the same time had either to provide land on which food could be raised for the labor force or risk the uncertainties of importing food. Generally speaking, where land was flat and fertile, the cane was planted; where it was not, food was grown for the slaves and dependence on food imports was considerably reduced. Thus, throughout the archipelago, the flat or gently sloping islands (e.g., Barbados, Antigua, St. Kitts) were almost entirely planted to sugar, whereas on the mountainous islands (e.g., Grenada, St. Vincent, Jamaica), where sugar cultivation was limited by topography planters had at their disposal relatively extensive areas on which food crops might be grown.

Jamaica, the largest of the British islands, contains distinctive coastal plains and interior valleys as well as mountain areas. On this island, therefore, both patterns developed (Beckford 1790, 1: 154–70). On the few estates which lay quite apart from steep mountain slopes the use of food imports tended to prevail; but on those estates (the majority by far) which included rough hills or slopes or other

poor-quality sugar land within their boundaries, the tendency was
to produce food. Clearly, whatever the individual planter's preference as between importing and producing food for his slaves, his
actual practice was much influenced by sugar prices, the lay of his
land, and the condition of the soil.

Where food production was undertaken, the planter had to decide
whether to include the work in the regular supervised agricultural
program of the estate or to offer the slaves inducements to undertake
it voluntarily. As will be demonstrated, a thoroughgoing dependence
on the regulated production of food was never achieved; in large
measure, food crops were raised by the slaves in the absence of
compulsion, and under conditions which implicitly acknowledged
their responsiveness to the same incentives as those which operated
for the free Jamaican.

In short, there was no generally accepted policy for supplying
the slaves with food. Where an estate had land not wanted for cane,
the slaves were usually allowed to cultivate food crops on it in their
spare time. When war threatened or when for other reasons food
imports were insufficient to meet the demand for them, laws were
usually passed requiring estate owners to undertake the cultivation of a stipulated quantity of land in foodstuffs as an estate operation (Leslie 1739: 233; Edwards 1793, 2: 132). Since in years of
warfare the prices offered for sugar tended to rise, thus encouraging
the expansion of cane fields, in Jamaica the laws requiring local
food production were customarily honored only in the breach. In all
the islands, and especially in those in which the food-import system
prevailed, the provident planter attempted to time his purchases of
imported foods judiciously in order to keep his costs down and his
stocks ready in case of shortage (Pares 1950: 126–27, 136). At the
same time, the unsupervised cultivation of food stocks by the slaves
themselves grew steadily more important whenever the estate contained land to support this activity.

The slaves used such land to produce a variety of foods, such as
tree crops, vegetables, and edible herbs and roots, as well as craft
materials. These foods and materials were raised primarily for their
own use. But eventually—and the details of the process are regret-
tably dim—surpluses came to be taken to local markets and exchanged for other commodities or sold for cash. The proceeds of

these transactions accrued entirely to the slaves, apparently from the very first. Market day, customarily held on Sunday so as not to interfere with estate cultivation, became an important social and economic institution.

Consideration of the system of agricultural production and marketing by slaves briefly noted above raises questions which are a prime concern of this chapter. It is not at first apparent, for instance, why food production should have been left to the slaves' initiative and not have been more commonly regulated as a part of the estate's program of cultivation. It is even less apparent why the slaves were permitted to go to market, sell or exchange surplus produce, and retain the goods or money received. Further, there is the question of the origins of the markets themselves. Also, we may ask precisely what crops the slaves chose to cultivate, why these were chosen, and with what skill and proficiency the enterprises of production and marketing were executed.

Exact and wholly satisfying answers to these questions are not yet possible. For most of them, however, we have been able to formulate reasonable answers based on the available data, and it is convenient to begin with the subjects of crops and agricultural skills.

There had been a background for cultivation and its associated processes before the English conquest of Jamaica and the rise of plantation agriculture, and even before the Spanish discovery and conquest of the island. To some extent at least, later patterns of subsistence were derived from these older adjustments.

Jamaica was occupied by Arawak Indian cultivators at the time of its discovery and early colonization by Spain. Parry writes that the native Arawak cultivated cassava (manioc) and perhaps a soft variety of maize, and gathered shellfish, roots, and berries (Parry n.d.: 30). Further information suggests that the Jamaican aboriginal crop repertory included "tannier" (*Xanthosoma* sp.), sweet potatoes, beans, capsicum, and a variety of uncultivated fruits (cf. Sturtevant 1961, 1969; Taylor 1962). The diet was apparently sufficient and well-balanced (Sauer 1950: 487–543; 1954: 20–21).

The Spanish settlement of Jamaica substantially eliminated the Arawak, but not their crops. Las Casas and others note the continued cultivation of the foods mentioned above, and the only important innovations mentioned are the raising of livestock and the curing of pork and bacon (Cundall and Pietersz 1919: 15). Nonetheless, some of the earliest references to cultivated plants after the English occupation in 1655 make it clear that new crops had been added during the Spanish period or introduced soon after the English landed. The Spaniards certainly were responsible for the introduction of the banana, nearly all the then known varieties of citrus, the sugarcane, and probably arrowroot. The English may, perhaps, be accredited with the introduction of the potato (Blome 1672: 25; Hickeringill 1661: 20; Parry n.d.: 31), as well as bread-fruit, dasheen (*Colocasia esculenta*), and the mango.

Some of the root crops so important in later peasant agriculture and diet spanned the three periods. Cassava and sweet potatoes, as we have noted, were cultivated aboriginally. The "yampee," or "cush cush," a true New World cultivated yam (*Dioscorea trifida*), is popular to this day in Jamaica. Sloane did not mention it in his exhaustive botanical work (1707), and Parry thinks it fair to assume that it was introduced from the American mainland after that time. Sloane did mention *Dioscorea cayenensis,* the "yellow Guinea yam," which Parry believes came to Jamaica from Oceania, probably via West Africa, in the eighteenth century. By the start of the nineteenth century, there were at least six cultivated yam varieties in Jamaica, as well as the taros—the so-called "eddoes, dasheens, and cocoes or cocoyams"—which are of Oceanian origin and probably became established in Jamaican peasant cultivation and cuisine in the eighteenth century. Finally, there are several important plants whose dates of entry can be precisely fixed. Parry (1955) refers to the akee (from West Africa, 1778), the mango (from Oceania, 1782), and the breadfruit (from Oceania, 1793, carried by Bligh on his second voyage).

## The Slaves as a Proto-Peasantry

From these enumerations, it will be seen that the crop possibilities open to Jamaican cultivators were considerable indeed. But very little, unfortunately, is ever afforded in the early reports concerning the agricultural methods themselves. Beckford, writing in 1790, probably provides the fullest description, and that all too sketchy and vague:

When a tract of negro-provisions is regularly planted, is well cultivated, and kept clean, it makes a very husbandlike and a beautiful appearance; and it is astonishing of the common necessaries of life it will produce. A quarter of an acre of this description will be fully sufficient for the supply of a moderate family, and may enable the proprietor [read "cultivator"] to carry some to market besides; but then the land must be of a productive quality, be in a situation that cannot fail of seasons, be sheltered from the wind, and protected from the trespass of cattle, and the theft of negroes.

If a small portion of land of this description will give such returns, a very considerable number of acres, if not attended to, will on the contrary, yield but little; and those negroes will hardly ever have good grounds, and of consequence plenty of provisions, who are not allowed to make for themselves a choice of situation, and who are not well assured that it will be well guarded and protected (Beckford 1790, 1: 356–57).

At a later point, Beckford states:

All kinds of ground provisions and corn are, as well as the plantain, successfully cultivated in the mountains; but as this is done by the negroes in their own grounds [i.e., provided individually by the owner or overseer] and on those days which are given to them for this particular purpose, it does not enter into the mass of plantation-labor (Beckford 1790, 2: 129–30).

And further:

The manner in which the negroes occupy themselves in their grounds is rather an employment than a toil, particularly if the wood be felled, and the land be cleared; but if they have heavy timber to cut down, the labour will be much, and the danger will be great; for they often get maimed or killed in this precarious operation, in which are required not only strength but likewise foresight.

They generally make choice of such sorts of land for their ground as are encompassed by lofty mountains; and I think that they commonly prefer the sides of hills, which are covered with loose stones, to the bottoms upon which they are not so abundant. Some will have a mixture of both, and will cultivate the plantain-tree upon the flat, and their provisions upon the rising ground; and some will pursue a contrary method; for in the choice as well as change of situation, they seem to be directed more by novelty and caprice, than by convenience or expediency.

They prepare their land, and put in their crops on the Saturdays that are given to them, and they bring home their provisions at night; and if their grounds be at a considerable distance from the plantation, as they often are to the amount of five or seven miles, or more, the journey backwards and forwards makes this rather a day of labour and fatigue, than of enjoyment and rest; but if, on the contrary, they be within any tolerable reach, it may be said to partake of both.

The negroes, when working in their grounds, exhibit a picture of which it will be difficult to give a minute description. They scatter themselves over the face, and form themselves into distinct parties at the bottom of the mountains; and being consequently much divided, their general exertions can only be observed from a distance.

If the land be hilly, it is generally broken by rocks, or encumbered by stones; the first they cannot displace, but the last they gently remove as they proceed in their work, and thus make a bed for the deposit of the plantain-sucker and the coco, or of the corn and yam.

Upon these occasions they move, with all their family, into the place of cultivation; the children of different ages are loaded with baskets, which are burdened in proportion to their strength and age; and it is pleasing to observe under what considerable weights they will bear themselves up, without either murmur or fatigue. The infants are flung at the backs of the mothers, and very little incommode them in their walks or labour.

The provision-grounds in the mountains, or polinks as they are called in the Island, admit of not much picturesque variety. Upon these are cultivated, and particularly upon those in Liguanea (a fertile tract of ground in the neighborhood of Kingston), all kinds of fruit and garden stuff, or coffee, coco, ginger and other minor productions of the country (Beckford 1790, 2: 151–87, passim).

It is known that the slave cultivators burned off the land they were preparing to plant. This technique, contemptuously referred to as "fire-stick cultivation" in Jamaica, is of doubtful origin. It may have been continuous with aboriginal practice, but this cannot be easily proved.

The provision grounds, which normally lay at some distance from the huts of the slaves grouped near the center of the estate, were set apart agriculturally from the tiny house plots, or "yards." On the patches of land around their huts, the slaves cultivated fruit trees, garden herbs, and crops which were very easily stolen or very delicate. The distinction between house plot and provision ground persists to the present and is characteristic of Jamaican peasant agriculture. Stewart, writing in the first quarter of the nineteenth century, makes clear reference to the distinction between house plot and "polink":

> Adjoining to the house is usually a small spot of ground, laid out into a sort of garden, and shaded by various fruit-trees. Here the family deposit their dead, to whose memory they invariably, if they can afford it, erect a rude tomb. Each slave has, besides this spot, a piece of ground (about half an acre) allotted to him as a provision ground. This is the principal means of his support; and so productive is the soil, where it is good and the seasons regular, that this spot will not only furnish him with sufficient food for his own consumption, but an overplus to carry to market. By means of this ground, and of the hogs and poultry which he may raise (most of which he sells), an industrious negro may not only support himself comfortably, but save something. If he has a family, an additional proportion of ground is allowed him, and all his children from five years upward assist him in his labours in some way or other (Stewart 1823: 267).

This use of the term *polink,* which H. P. Jacobs (personal correspondence) believes to be related to the Spanish *palenque* (a palisade or palisaded village, cf. Friederici 1960: 469–70; later, a fortified runaway slave village, as in Cuba or Colombia), is interesting in itself, symbolizing the link between independent cultivation and the status of the slaves. In any case, the major local sources of food appear to have been the provision grounds, or polinks. That these normally lay upon the slopes where cane was not grown suggests that the particular techniques of cultivation were adjusted to the terrain, a pattern which persisted long after Emancipation and still largely characterizes peasant agriculture in Jamaica. This is of more than passing importance. Peasant agriculture in Jamaica has been repeatedly criticized for its erosive effects. It is true that failure to make long-range investments of labor and materials on such land is destructive. But it ought to be borne in mind that it is not necessarily the cultivation methods as such, or even the crops, which are destructive.

The "choice" of hilly land for such cultivation followed from the monopolization of coastal plains and interior valleys by the plantations. It has never been conclusively proved, in fact, that the small-scale production of the Jamaican peasantry is in itself inherently less productive or more destructive than other systems of production *on the same land*. (This does not contradict the justifiable claim that productivity would be increased and erosion slowed by proper terracing, crop rotation, manuring, the building of retainer structures, and so on.)

Sauer has written very explicitly of the *conuco,* or garden plot of the Antilles:

> When Indians gave way to Negro slaves, the latter took over for themselves, rather than for their masters, the cultivation of the Indian crops, and added thereto such African things as the greater yam, the pigeon pea or *guandul* [*sic*], okra, and the keeping of fowls.

> The food potential of the traditional *conuco* planting, or provision ground, is hardly appreciated by ourselves, be we agricultural scientists, economists, or planners, because its tradition as well as content are so different from what we know and practice. Yields are much higher than from grains, production is continuous the year round, storage is hardly needed, individual kinds are not grown separately in fields but are assembled together in one planted ground, to which our habits of order would apply neither the name of field or garden. And so we are likely to miss the merits of the system.

> The proper *conuco* is, in fact an imitation by man of tropical nature, a many-storied cultural vegetation, producing at all levels, from tubers underground through the understory of pigeon peas and coffee, a second story of cacao and bananas, to a canopy of fruit trees and palms. Such an assemblage makes full use of light, moisture, and soil—its messy appearance to our eyes meaning really that all of the niches are filled. A proper planting of this sort is about as protective of the soil as is the wild vegetation. The *conuco* system can make intensive use of steep slopes and thereby may encounter erosion hazards that should not be blamed on the system itself, as commonly they have been (Sauer 1954: 21–22).

Sauer's contentions, while unproved, certainly demand reflection. In fact, the adjustment of Caribbean peasantries to the aftermath of slavery, to the circumstances of a ruined economy, and to freedom deserves more study than it has yet received. Such study can profitably examine the view that the patterns of human and horticultural occupancy, the system of cultivation, the paths of distribution of products, and the economic relationships of the peasantry to other classes form one interwoven system. We contend that this system had begun to evolve long before the Emancipation.

Information on the agricultural implements used by the slaves is discouragingly scanty. The most important were the bush knife, or cutlass, and the short-handled hoe. We have been unable to ascribe an origin to these tools; a case might be made for either England or Africa. It is likely that at first they were provided by the plantation, and this might argue against an African origin (Great Britain Public Record Office 1836).

With regard to the crops generally preferred for cultivation and cuisine, our information is again less than satisfactory. Several early authors suggest that the slaves preferred to cultivate plantains (and bananas?), corn, and vegetables rather than root crops, attributing this preference to either imprudence or laziness. The planters themselves preferred to see root crops planted since these would better survive hurricanes (Edwards 1793, 2: 132). Renny (1807: 87) believed it was the slaves' preference for plantains and corn that led them to neglect the root crops. And yet yams, sweet potatoes, dasheen, tanniers, cassava, and the like could hardly have become established as preferred peasant foods only after the start of the nineteenth century. It seems fair to suppose, therefore, that any favoritism the slave cultivators may have shown for plantain, corn, and vegetables over root crops could have arisen as much from the market situation as from anything else, and it is possible that these items were supplied in significant quantities to naval and merchant vessels. That the planters never actively interfered with the slave cultivators' crop choices is in any case of great interest, and seems to underline the mutual respect for customary arrangements which held between the estate owners or managers and the slaves. It also explains the vagueness of the accounts of the provision grounds given by Beckford and others. The only points which these commentators make with clarity are the distinction between house plots and polinks, the "high" productivity of the latter if conscientiously cultivated, and the fact that the slaves were allowed to take surpluses to market, dispose of them, and keep the proceeds.

The first of these points is of interest because it indicates that even where estates were limited in size and did not contain slave provision grounds, the slaves were not absolutely dependent on imports. Even in Barbados and St. Kitts, for example, there were house plots (Coleridge 1826: 132). But it was upon the polinks that the foundations of the free peasantry were established, and here we turn to the local trading of the slaves and the origins and early growth of the marketplaces.

Extracts from the writings of two West Indian proprietors of the late eighteenth century will serve to give the planter's view of the relative advantages of food production as against food importation and to suggest one very powerful motive for the reluctance of masters to supervise production on the polinks.

> *Friday Feb. 10th, 1792.* My voyage to Antigua has put me in full possession of the question concerning the best mode of feeding the negroes. I am speaking of the difference in this situation in regard to plenty and comfort, when fed by allowance by the master, as in Antigua; or when by provision grounds of their own, as in St. Vincent. In the first case, oppression may, and certainly in some instances and in different degrees doth actually exist, either as to quantity or quality of food; besides the circumstances of food for himself, the negro too suffers in his poultry and little stock, which are his wealth. The maintenance of his pigs, turkeys, or chickens must often subtract from his own dinner, and that perhaps a scanty one, or he cannot keep stock at all; and a negro without stock, and means to purchase tobacco, and other little conveniences, and some finery too for his wife, is miserable.
>
> In the second case, of the negro feeding himself with his own provisions, assisted only with salt provisions from his master (three pounds of salt-fish, or an adequate quantity of herrings, per week as in St. Vincent's) the situation of the negro is in proportion to his industry; but generally speaking, it affords him with a plenty that amounts to comparative wealth, viewing any peasantry in Europe (Young 1801: 287–88).

Bryan Edwards, a contemporary observer whose main experience was of Jamaica, wrote on the same subject:

> The practice which prevails in Jamaica of giving the Negroes lands to cultivate, from the produce of which they are expected to main-

tain themselves (except in times of scarcity, arising from hurricanes and droughts, when assistance is never denied them) is universally allowed to be judicious and beneficial; producing a happy coalition of interests between the master and the slave. The negro who has acquired by his own labour a property in his master's land, has much to lose, and is therefore less inclined to desert his work. He earns a little money, by which he is enabled to indulge himself in fine clothes on holidays, and gratify his palate with salted meats and other provisions that otherwise he could not obtain; and the proprietor is eased, in a great measure, of the expense of feeding him (Edwards 1793, 2: 131).

Both these observers mention the advantage of having the slaves produce their own food, but it is interesting that Edwards, the Jamaican planter, is more explicit about the consequent savings enjoyed by the master. In the small, relatively flat, arable islands, such as Barbados or Antigua, the planter could allot land to food cultivation only by impinging on areas which, generally, could be more profitably planted in cane. He tended therefore to restrict the land at the disposal of the slaves to small house plots, to depend heavily on imports of food, and, when the food trade was disturbed, to include, however reluctantly, some food production in the general estate program.

In St. Vincent and the other mountainous islands of the Windwards, the planter's decision was affected by the relative unsuitability of his land for sugar production. The "sacrifice" of allotting land to food cultivation was not so strong a deterrent, and the advantages of having a comparatively well-fed slave force and of reduced dependence on food imports were clear.

In Jamaica, the largest of the British islands, with the largest estates and the greatest variety of soil, topography, and climate, the planter usually had land on his estate which, except in periods of unusually high sugar prices, he would never consider using for cane. There is much evidence that in Jamaica the area in sugar cultivation expanded and contracted under the influence of rising and falling sugar prices (Hall 1959: 13). As prices fell, marginal sugar areas became submarginal and were, at least temporarily, thrown out of cane cultivation. But even when the process worked the other way, and cane fields were extended in responses to the promise of higher prices, there was generally a significant area which, because of its high unsuitability, would remain beyond the sugar line.

It is worth noting that in Barbados and the Leewards (except mountainous Montserrat) there is still a heavy reliance on food imports; that in the Windward Islands and Montserrat the sugar industry declined under the competitive conditions of nineteenth-century free trade in sugar and that these islands now export food-stuffs to Barbados and the Leewards; and that only in Jamaica have both food production and sugar production managed to survive.

But from the two extracts quoted above, it appears that deciding whether or not to allow the slaves to cultivate foodstuffs was affected by more than "classical" economic considerations of diminishing returns to land. We have shown that even where polinks were not usually allowed, house plots were, and many of the contemporary explanations account for the system by a sort of medievalism modified by the realities of colonial slave-plantation life in the eighteenth century. There is the implied concept of the estate community, of the advantages to be gained from "a happy coalition of interests between the master and the slave"; and indeed, the eighteenth-century sugar estate, with its great house and surrounding fields, its "village" of workshops and slave quarters, its unfree agricultural population, and its complement of skilled craftsmen, was, superficially, not unlike the medieval manor. Even further, although sugar cultivation was the basic occupation, the workers had access to estate "waste" land (the polinks), where they labored on their own behalf, not only growing food but also grazing small livestock and collecting the raw materials for their handicraft products.

But superficialities apart, there was a very important reason why masters should be concerned with securing this happy coalition of interest. It was simply that, since there was neither an ethical nor an economic basis for any such coalition (and here we diverge from the ostensible medieval pattern), they must try to introduce and stimulate it. At any rate, the wiser masters would because, as our two writers argued, the slave with a better diet, a small source of income, and a feeling of proprietorship in land was less discontented, less likely to run away, and less dangerous as a potential rebel. It would be of interest to test this opinion by comparing data on slave desertions, riots, and other indices of disaffection in, for example, Antigua and St. Vincent. But such a comparison would have to take into account the disincentives to desertion and other forms of slave resistance in flat, fully occupied, and small islands, and the greater chances for successful resistance in the larger, mountainous, and less fully occupied islands (Patterson 1967; cf. also Patterson 1970).

The slave was not supervised in his food cultivation, and this activity was never included, except in brief periods of shortage or threatening shortage of food, in "the mass of plantation-labor." Supervised field labor was repugnant to the slaves, and in the social hierarchy of the slave population the field slaves occupied the lowest rung (Smith 1953). Supervised cultivation of food would have necessitated either a reduction of the time spent in cane cultivation, which the masters would not have willingly conceded, or an increase in the daily hours of compulsory estate labor, which would have encouraged disaffection and rebellious sentiments among the slaves.

But the accounts quoted above were written more than a century after the practice of allowing slaves to cultivate estate backlands, or polinks, had been established. The writers, therefore, might simply have been trying to explain, in the light of their own experience, the reasons for a custom whose beginning and original intention were unknown to them. They tell us not how the practice began but only why it was still favored in the late eighteenth century.

Blome, writing in 1672 from the notes of Governor Sir Thomas Lynch, in Jamaica, gives detailed instructions for the setting up of a "Cocao [sic] Walk" or plantation, and his advice includes careful explanations of the need for provision grounds for servants and slaves (Blome 1672: 15–21). Sloane's introductory notes to his great work on the flora of Jamaica, published 1707–25, say of the slaves:

> They have *Saturdays* in the Afternoon, and *Sundays,* with *Christmas* Holidays, *Easter* call'd little or Piganniny Christmas, and some other great Feasts allow'd them for the Culture of their own Plantations to feed themselves from Potatoes, Yams and Plantains, etc., which they plant in Ground allow'd them by their Masters, beside a small Plantain-Walk they have by themselves (Sloane 1707, 1: 52).

Leslie, writing in 1739, states:

> Their owners set aside for each a small Ground, and allow them the
> Sundays to manure it: In it they generally plant Maiz, Guiney Corn,
> Plantanes, Yams, Cocoes, Potatoes, Etc. This is the food which sup-
> ports them (Leslie 1739: 322).

Though we have not been able to establish a precise date for the
beginning of this practice, Blome's statements, coming but 17 years
after the English occupation, make it clear that it was generally
adopted even on the earliest estates.

We do not know, however, whether it became the practice to
provide slaves with provision grounds immediately upon the establishment of a new plantation. Conceivably, the managers of a new
estate might have attempted to institute food production as a matter
of course at the time the estate was set up. But this is not likely to
have been the case. When a new estate was being established, when
slaves were being bought, land cleared, buildings erected, and factory machinery installed, managerial attention would probably have
been directed almost exclusively toward the main objective of
getting the first sugar off to market. Imported foods probably bulked
large in an estate's first years. If food production by the estate
slaves was undertaken in those years, it was presumably in the
slaves' free time. Much of this is surmise, but thus far we have
found no contrary evidence. Estate-supervised production of provisions never seems to have been undertaken without pressure from
the island legislature and, as we have stressed, unsupervised cultivation by the slaves goes back to the early years of the occupation and
may have been conjoined with the start of the estates. By the late
eighteenth century what might have begun as a conveniently casual
system of industrial feeding had become a tradition with which it
would have been profitless and dangerous to interfere.

### The Slaves as Marketers

In these circumstances the emergence of local marketing arrangements is not surprising. The unsupervised production of food crops
by slaves provided the very basis of an open market system. Each
slave cultivated as, and what, he wanted to cultivate. His primary

concern, originally, might well have been his own household needs. But because his neighbors also had free choice of whether to plant, what to plant, and how much to plant, the range of small transactions which might take place even among the slaves of a single estate must have been considerable. For instance, the volume of exchange would have been increased by the fact that some slaves would prefer to produce minor handicrafts, some to raise small livestock, some to grow food, and some to act as intermediaries among these diverse producers. The Jamaican higgler, or middleman, also finds his prototype in the slave society (Lewis 1861: 41). Under a system of estate-organized food production this specialization could never have emerged. It would have been choked off by the routine and the compulsory conformity of estate agriculture.

Exactly how the first slave producers came to market their surplus stock is not known; nor can we pin down with assurance the founding date of the first market in Jamaica. The first legally established marketplace, however, was created in Spanish Town (Santiago de la Vega) in the year 1662, seven years after the English occupation, at the request of English settlers.

> Whereas the settlement of our Island of Jamaica is much hindered or obstructed for want of a Faire or Markett for the sale and buying of Horses, Mares, Mules, Assinegoes, Cowes, Bulls and other Cattle and many other necessaries for the use of our subjects there and whereas our Towne of Snt. Jago de la Vega in our said Island is commodiously situated for the keeping of such a Faire or Markett therein . . . [we] by this our present Charter doe grant and confirm that . . . [the] inhabitants of our said Town of Snt. Jago de la Vega for ever have a Faire or Markett in our said Towne . . . four times in every year . . . for the sail of horses, mares, mules, assinegoes, cows, bulls, and all or any other cattle and all or any other goods and commodities whatsoever of the groweth or produce of our said Island and all or any goods, wares and merchandizes whatsoever with all liberties . . . according to the usage and customs of our kingdome of England (Institute of Jamaica 1895: 146).

The emphasis in this statement is on the establishment of a market for livestock. Furthermore, this is a quarterly market only, and one may judge that its original intent was to serve the free population of Jamaica. Yet we learn that the need for a market-

place had been recognized and acted upon less than a decade after
the occupation; it is also worth noting that the market here described was set up quite matter-of-factly according to English law.
Though the slaves came to play a central role in Jamaican internal
marketing, it is clear that this first legal market was English, not
African, in conception and form.

Edward Long, describing events in the 1660s, tells of large numbers of small cultivators who produced food for the markets of
Spanish Town (the capital) and of Port Royal, then a headquarters
of the buccaneers where

> the great consumption of provisions of all sorts in that town, and
> for the outfit of so many privateers, created a very large demand for
> cattle, sheep, hogs, poultry, corn, and every other similar supply
> furnished by planters and settlers. And it is owing to this cause that
> we find such a prodigious number of these little settlements grouped
> together in all the environs of St. Jago de la Vega [Spanish Town],
> and in the maritime parts not far from Port Royal harbour, which
> were then full of people, all subsisting well by their traffic with that
> town.

But, he continues, the suppression of the buccaneers and the founding of the sugar industry led to "the declension of Port Royal, and
the dissipation of the petty settlers, who from that period began to
spread themselves more into the inland parts," while the establishment of large estates led to the buying out of many of these small
settlers "by the more opulent planters or merchants" (Long 1774,
1: 282–83).

But as settlement and the sugar industry and trade increased,
activity in the capital town and in the ports of the island would also
have grown. New demands for food supplies would have been met,
not by those early European small-scale farmers whom Long described, and in whose interest this first market had been officially
established, but by their successors in the business of food production. The great majority of these successors, we believe, were slaves
who sold in officially designated and other marketplaces the produce they raised in their spare time on estate lands.

Since it was the individual slaves or slave households who produced provisions on the estate backlands, then clearly they would

be the sellers of surplus produce. Either individual slaves would go marketing, or else they would make voluntary agreements among themselves for marketing one another's produce. Certainly no sane estate manager would ever have conceived the idea of collecting and selling produce from separate slave provision grounds. The effort would have been pointless. If the estate kept all or even a share of the proceeds, voluntary food production by the slaves would have fallen off. In any case, the prevention of transactions between slaves of the same estate, or even of adjacent estates, would have been physically impossible for the limited and generally inefficient subordinate managerial staff.

Undoubtedly, the earliest transactions between slave producers were not conducted in markets. What seems probable is that the establishment of markets on the English model afforded a setting in which the slave producer could most readily buy and sell what he wished. The slave's part in market activity probably grew swiftly in importance, but the details are nearly all obscure. Hickeringill (1661) and Blome (1672), two of the earliest observers, do not refer directly to markets, though Blome did state that provisions were "very dear" in Kingston, and the reference seems to have been to locally produced foodstuffs (Blome 1672: 32). Cundall makes a revealing reference to a market for the year 1685, less than a quarter of a century after the first legally recognized market was established; asserting "In May, the negroes at a usual Saturday market at Passage Fort having made some little disturbance, the market was suppressed by the Council" (Cundall 1936: 99). Note that this market was "usual" and that Negroes participated in it.

Leslie (1739) provides an abstract of laws in force under the second government of Sir Thomas Lynch (1671–74), and these laws make plain that a number of markets were established, formalized, and maintained under government provision even in this early period. Laws regarding the weighing of meats, occasions of sale, market days, and so on were put into effect in the seventeenth century (Leslie 1739: 170–78).

Formal legal acknowledgment of the slaves' rights to market had been given, in negative form at least, as early as 1711: "Hawking about and selling goods (except provisions, fruits, and other enumerated articles) to be punished, on conviction before a magistrate, by whipping, not exceeding *thirty-one lashes*" (Long 1774, 2: 486–87). The exception is more important than the law, since it read: "This restraint is construed to extend only to beef, veal, mutton and saltfish; and to manufactures, except baskets, ropes of bark, earthen pots and such like" (Long 1774, 2: 486). In 1735, the law is stated in positive terms: "Slaves may carry about, and sell, all manner of provisions, fruits, fresh milk, poultry, and other small stock of all kinds, having a ticket from their owner or employer" (Long 1774, 2: 492).

It is interesting to compare the lists of goods in which slaves were allowed to trade. The purpose of restriction was, of course, to prevent them from dealing in stolen goods. A slave with a carcass of beef was, prima facie, guilty of having slaughtered his owner's cattle. A slave offering metalware or saltfish, neither of which was produced on the island, was clearly suspect of having raided the estate stores. But clearly, between 1711 and 1735 there was some change. In the former year, slaves are forbidden to sell "beef, veal, mutton and saltfish"; in 1735, they are permitted to trade "fresh fish, milk, poultry, and other small stock of all kinds." This suggests either a belated legal acknowledgment of the range of slave production or—more likely, since the laws were generally permissive and not restrictive in this matter—a fairly rapid extension of productive activities by the slaves in response to a growing market for their produce. Accounts of the late eighteenth century and after almost invariably list pigs, goats, fish, poultry, eggs, and milk as products sold by the slaves. This last item may have been goats' milk or perhaps cows' milk bought by the slaves from the estate owners for retail trading. Yet the cattle may have been owned by the slaves themselves. In his journal entry for March 2, 1816, Lewis (1861: 102–3) writes that he purchased from his slaves, at fifteen pounds per head, cattle which they owned and grazed on the estate's pasture. As will be discussed further, later laws restricting the free movement of slaves always excepted their marketing operations.

The importance of slaves to the Jamaican domestic economy in the third quarter of the eighteenth century, is revealed at length in the intelligent and thorough discussions provided by Long, one of the most careful and thoughtful writers of the eighteenth century.

In 1774, by Long's estimate, of the 50,000 pounds in currency circulating in the island at least 10,000 pounds, or 20 percent, was in the hands of the slaves, most of it in the form of small coins (Mintz 1964). Money was scarce, and this scarcity adversely affected daily commerce and interfered with transactions. The island had serious need of small silver to

> enable the housekeepers and Negroes to carry on their marketing for butchers meat, poultry, hogs, fish, corn, eggs, plantain and the like. (Long 1774, 2: 562).

> A small copper coin might be found extremely convenient here, as enabling the lower class of inhabitants not only to exchange their silver without a drawback, but likewise to keep down the prices of the small necessaries of life: which is a matter that has been thought of great importance to every trading community; and is especially of moment to this island, where the Negroes, who supply the market with small stock, and other necessaries, as well as the white families supplied from those markets, must be very much distressed, if they should ever be wholly deprived of a minor currency accommodated to their dealings with each other (Long 1774 2: 570).

Long describes a number of markets, but his description of Kingston market is particularly revealing:

> At the bottom of the town, near the water side, is the market place, which is plentifully supplied with butchers meat, poultry, fish, fruits, and vegetables of all sorts. Here are found not only a great variety of American, but also of European, vegetables: such as pease, beans, cabbage, lettuce, cucumbers, French beans, artichokes, potatoes, carrots, turnips, radishes, celery, onions, etc. These are brought from the Liguanea mountains, and are all excellent in their kind. Here are likewise strawberries, not inferior to the productions of our English gardens; grapes and melons in the utmost perfection; mulberries, figs, and apples exceedingly good, but in general gathered before they are thoroughly ripe. In short, the most luxurious epicure cannot fail of meeting here with sufficient in quantity, variety, and excellence, for the gratification of his appetite the whole year round. The prices are but little different from those of Spanish Town; but where they disagree, they are more reasonable at Kingston, the supplies being more regular, and the market superintended by the magistracy. The beef is chiefly from the pastures of Pedro's, in St.

Ann's; the mutton, from the salt-pan lands, in St. Catherine's: what they draw from the penns in St. Andrew's parish being very indifferent meat (Long 1774, 2: 105).

Long did not criticize the virtual monopoly which the slaves had come to exercise in internal marketing; rather, he repeatedly suggested means to broaden and extend it. He objected to the pay system in country barracks of the Army, where the officers disbursed the pay. It would have been better, he argued, had the common soldiers received their pay directly:

> With the money in their hands, the men might purchase much better in quality, and more in quantity, of fresh meat and wholesome victuals . . . every country-barrack would attract a market for the sale of hogs, poultry, fresh fish, fruits, and roots, which are articles produced and vended by almost all the Negroes (Long 1774, 2: 303–4).

Indeed, by the time Long was writing, the slaves were not only central to the economy, as the producers of the cash export commodities, principally sugar, but had also become the most important suppliers of foodstuffs and utilitarian craft items to all Jamaicans.

The customs of slave-based subsistence farming and marketing clearly provided the slaves with their best opportunities to accumulate liquid capital, as Hall (1954: 161–63) and others have demonstrated. Long, too, writes:

> Even among these slaves, as they are called, the black grandfather, or father, directs in what manner his money, his hogs, poultry, furniture, cloaths, and other effects and acquisition, shall descend, or be disposed of, after his decease. He nominates a sort of trustees, or executors, from the nearest of kin, who distribute them among the legatees, according to the will of the testator, without any molestation or interruption, most often without the enquiry, of their master; though some of these Negroes have been known to possess from £50 to £200 at their death; and few among them, that are at all industrious and frugal, lay up less than £20 or £30. For in this island they have the greatest part of the small silver circulating among them, which they gain by sale of their hogs, poultry, fish, corn, fruits, and other commodities, at the markets in town and country (Long 1774, 2: 410–11).

Thus, one century after the first legal Jamaican market was created, the slaves had made a place for themselves in the free economic activity of the country which would never thereafter be challenged.

Our continuing emphasis on the slaves' role in supplying and maintaining the internal markets, however, should not obscure another aspect of the economy as it was constituted under slavery. At the end of the eighteenth century, Jamaica's major exports, measured either in bulk or in value, were typically plantation products: cotton, coffee, ginger, and pimento to a lesser extent and, most important, sugar and rum. But other items also reached foreign markets, and quantities of these were derived from slave holdings; that is, they were produced on estate backlands by the slaves. Here may be mentioned gums, arrowroot, castor oil, turmeric, hides, supplejacks, oil nuts, cows' horns, goatskins, and wood products. These items were exported through a growing class of small merchants who lived in towns and did their business in conjunction with local markets. There is scarcely any descriptive information on these traders and their commercial relationships with slave producers; yet such relationships, well reported in the years after Emancipation (Sewell 1861: 219–20, 248–51), must have taken on their characteristic form under slavery. Large quantities of imported goods consumed by the slaves passed through the hands of local importers, the largest traffic being in clothes, household wares, and other items of comfort and convenience not provided by the estate owners.

By the start of the nineteenth century, reports by observers on slave production of provisions and slave buying power had become quite matter-of-fact in character. Dallas, writing in 1803, reports:

> Every proprietor is compelled by law, to cultivate in ground provisions (of course indestructible by hurricanes) one acre for every ten negroes; besides the allotment of negro territory. To cultivate this allotment, one day in every fortnight, belongs to the slaves, exclusive of Sundays and holidays. Thus they raise vegetables, poultry, pigs, or goats, which they consume, bestow, or sell. While some raise provisions, others fabricate coarse chairs, baskets, or common tables. These are bartered for salted meat, or pickled fish, utensils, or gaudy dresses; of which they are very fond. Their right of property in what

they thus acquire, is never questioned; but seems completely established by custom (Dallas 1803, 1: cviii).

It will be seen that certain customary arrangements had been secured, and these appear to have been observed by master and slave alike. The marketing arrangements, the increasing dependence of townspeople and free people on slave production, the customary system of slave inheritance, and the slave's attitudes concerning his property rights in the fruits of his labors, all must have grown up gradually and to some extent at least outside the law. They were maintained and accepted by the small group which wielded overwhelming power in the society because they were economically and socially convenient, even necessary, once they had begun to take shape.

By the time the nineteenth-century observers had begun to write of the markets and the slaves' role in them, the pattern had well over a century of traditional practice behind it. No really important new crops entered into the slaves' cultivation, diet, or marketing after 1800; and the slave code which guaranteed rights to market had long been in force. After Emancipation, many new markets would appear, and the scope of economic activity open to the freedmen would be much increased. But Emancipation, insofar as marketing and cultivation practices were concerned, only widened opportunities and increased alternatives; apparently it did not change their nature substantially.

Mathew Gregory ("Monk") Lewis, an estate owner, reported on his 1815–17 visit to his Jamaica estates:

In my evening's drive I met the negroes returning from the mountains, with baskets of provisions sufficient to last them for the week. By law they are only allowed every other Saturday for the purpose of cultivating their own grounds, which, indeed, is sufficient; but by giving them every alternate Saturday into the bargain, it enables them to perform their task with so much ease as almost converts it into an amusement; and the frequent visiting their grounds makes them grow habitually as much attached to them as they are to their houses and gardens. It is also advisable for them to bring home only a week's provisions at a time, rather than a fortnight's; for they are so thoughtless and improvident that, when they find themselves in possession of a larger supply than is requisite for their immediate occasions, they will sell half to the wandering higglers, or at Savannah la Mar, in exchange for spirits; and then, at the end of the week, they find themselves entirely unprovided with food, and come to beg a supply from the master's storehouse (Lewis 1861: 41).

Lewis's comments indicate that the slaves were inclined to make much of their provision grounds. Certainly they must have found it a relief to escape from the regimen of labor in the cane fields and to work on "their own" cultivations. Lewis's observations on their attachment to these far-off fields are even shrewder than he realized. The assumption some observers had made that the slave, once free, would be unable to give up his residence at the center of the estate because of his emotional attachment to his house and garden there, proved to be very mistaken. The slaves must also have responded well to the feeling of autonomy which work on their provision grounds afforded. As Emancipation approached, other observers, particularly missionaries intent on establishing the slaves' capacity for freedom, tried to confirm this:

> If the vices of the slave belong then to his condition, that condition should be changed before the nature of the negro is deemed incapable of elevation, or susceptible of improvement. That his defects are redeemed by no good qualities would be a bold assertion; that they are mingled with so many good ones as they are, is to me a matter of the greatest wonder.
>
> To say that he is not industrious without reference to the object for which his exertions are employed would be an absurd remark; to say he is indolent, where his labour is exacted without reward, is to prove nothing.
>
> But where the negro labours on his own ground, for his own advantage,—where his wife and children have the price of his own commodities to fetch him from the market-town, no matter how many miles they have to trudge, or how heavy the load they have to bear,—where the wages he received for his services are at his own disposal,—where his own time is duly paid for, not in shads and herrings, but in money a little more than equivalent to the advantages he deprives his own ground of, by transferring his extra time to the estate he is employed on—the negro is not the indolent slothful being he is everywhere considered, both at home and in the colonies (Madden 1835, 1: 136–37).

In fact, the marketing system in which the slave had been long involved not only prepared him for freedom but demonstrated his capacity to live as a freedman.

At the same time that the missionaries were working courageously for Emancipation, they deplored the Sunday markets. Their mournful pronouncements provide some useful information on the markets themselves. Bickell describes a market in Kingston on the day of his arrival in August 1819:

> It was on a Sunday, and I had to pass by the Negro Market, where several thousands of human beings, of various nations and colours, but principally Negroes, instead of worshipping their Maker on His Holy Days, were busily employed in all kinds of traffick in the open streets. Here were Jews with shops and standings as at a fair, selling old and new clothes, trinkets and small wares at cent. per cent. to adorn the Negro person; there were some low Frenchmen and Spaniards, and people of colour, in petty shops and with stalls; some selling their bad rum, gin, tobacco, etc.; others, salt provisions, and small articles of dress; and many of them bartering with the Slave or purchasing his surplus provisions to retail again; poor free people and servants also, from all parts of the city to purchase vegetables, etc., for the following week (Bickell 1836: 66).

Concern that the slave did his marketing on Sunday was not restricted to the missionaries, however. The shopkeepers who kept the Sabbath were effectively cut off from sharing in the consumer market the slave represented. Long, in 1774, had sought to demonstrate that there was more to the profaning of the Sabbath than met the eye. He noted the comment of a contemporary:

> It is certain that the sabbath-day, as at present it is passed, is by no means a respite from labour: on the contrary, the Negroes, either employing it on their grounds, or in travelling a great distance to some market, fatigue themselves much more on that day, than on any other in the week. The forenoon of that day, at least, might be given to religious duties; but I think it rather desirable than otherwise, that the after-part of it should be spent on their grounds, instead of being uselessly dissipated in idleness and lounging, or (what is worse) in riot, drunkenness, and wickedness. If such an alteration should take place, Thursday might be assigned for the market day, instead of the sabbath, and prove of great advantage to all Christian

shop-keepers and retailers; the Jews now grossing the whole business of trafficking with the Negroes every Sunday, at which time there is a prodigious resort of them to the towns, and a vast sum expended for drams, necessaries, and manufactures. This alteration would therefore place the Christian dealers upon an equal footing, which they do not at present enjoy (Long 1774, 2: 492).

"No Sunday markets" was probably the only issue in Jamaican history on which missionaries and proslavery writers were able to agree, though their reasons were wholly different.

The significance of this concern is the proof it offers that the marketing activities of the slaves were in fact very important to the Jamaican economy. The economy itself rested on the plantation system and slave labor; but the circumstances were such that the slaves could make a second valuable capital-building contribution through their individual efforts. And the same observers who debated whether the slaves were capable of learning even the fundamentals of Christian teaching were surely aware of their very human capacity for creating and employing wealth by cultivation and commerce. Had it not been for the slaves' skills as producers and distributors and their needs as consumers, there could scarcely have appeared in the Jamaican economy a numerous class of middlemen, import and export dealers, and retailers. The importance of slave marketing was legally recognized in the laws which regulated the behavior of the slave population. Renny cites a law revelatory of this:

And whereas it is absolutely necessary, that the slaves in this island should be kept in due obedience to their owners, and in due subordination to the white people in general, and, as much as in the power of the legislature, all means and opportunities of slaves committing rebellious conspiracies, and other crimes, to the ruin and destruction of the white people, and others in this island, prevented, and that proper punishments should be appointed for all crimes to be by them committed; be it further enacted by the authority aforesaid, that no slave, *such only excepted as are going with firewood, grass, fruit, provisions, or small stock and other goods, which they may lawfully sell, to market, and returning therefrom,* shall here after be suffered or permitted to go out of his or her master or owner's plantation or settlement, or to travel from one town or place to another, unless such slave shall have a ticket from his master, owner, employer, or overseer (Renny 1807: 255 [italics added]).

Thus even the sharpest vigilance was relaxed to facilitate the marketing practices of the slaves, and the exceptions cry for explanation. It would be hard to explain them completely and with certainty. But it may be fair to contend that the growth of town populations and the increased demand for the products of the slaves' spare time labor encouraged the participation of slaves as sellers and suppliers; that the growth of the market and the emergence of new demands enlarged the quantity and variety of items which reached the markets; that the activity of the markets increased the slaves' buying power, and that this led in turn to increases in the number of local merchants, retailers, moneylenders, etc., who became dependent on the slaves' surpluses and buying needs for their income; that the free people in the towns gradually came to depend on the slaves' marketing activities for the satisfaction of their daily needs; and that long before Emancipation, the markets and all of the related institutions which maintained them had become core features of Jamaican society and economy. Such seems to have been the situation in Jamaica in 1834, when slavery ended and the Apprenticeship system began.

### Freedom and Constraint

In most of the British West Indian colonies, an attempt was made to bridge the gap between slavery and freedom by an intervening number of years of Apprenticeship during which masters and slaves were to condition themselves for the new order of a free society. But the Apprenticeship system asked too much of mere mortals. It allowed the masters the labor of their slaves for a stated number of hours per week. Beyond this limit, the slaves (or "apprentices") had the right either to refuse to work for their masters or to demand wages for the work they did. The Apprenticeship system failed to serve its purpose, however, and was curtailed. It was too much to ask that a man should be a slave on weekdays and a wage earner over the weekend. The Apprenticeship system ended at midnight, July 31, 1838, exactly four years after it was inaugurated. At its conclusion, the expected disagreements between ex-masters and ex-slaves began.

The great variety of those disagreements need not detain us. They have been fully described elsewhere (Burn 1937; Hall 1953), and our present concern is with only one of the sources of discontent. Estate slaves had been housed in huts or tenements provided by their owners, and they had been allowed to cultivate estate backlands. Now, as free wage workers, they were asked to pay rents for huts and land, and ex-masters and ex-slaves faced each other as landlord employers and tenant employees.

A vast potential for misunderstanding and conflict was created by the new situation. Under slavery, the Jamaican planters had made much of the freedom which they allowed the slaves in the cultivation of the backlands.

> I do not believe that an instance can be produced of a master's interference with his Negroes in their peculium thus acquired. They are permitted also to dispose at their deaths of what little property they possess; and even to bequeath their grounds or gardens to such of their fellow-slaves as they think proper. These principles are so well established, that whenever it is found convenient for the owner to exchange the negro-grounds for other lands, the Negroes must be satisfied, in money or otherwise, before the exchange takes place. It is universally the practice (Edwards 1793, 2: 133).

There, precisely stated, are three points of immediate and important relevance to the post-Emancipation squabbles over rents and wages. The first is that slaves were allowed to acquire and bequeath property of various kinds; the second, that they were even allowed to bequeath their provision grounds, or gardens; and the third, that planters so fully recognized the slaves' rights to these grounds that they offered compensation whenever it became necessary to convert an area of slave cultivation to estate purposes.

There is no need to discuss further the reasons why the slaves were allowed to keep the money and goods they received in their marketing transactions, but since they were allowed to keep them it was only logical to allow bequests. The alternative would have been an unworkable estate tax system of one hundred percent death duties on the "property" of deceased slaves. And without the full cooperation of the slaves themselves, it would have been impossible to assess the property of any individual slave, given the crowded living conditions of the slave quarters and the circumstances of a lifetime of unaccounted small purchases and transactions.

The fact that planters usually compensated slaves who were made to give up provision grounds to estate uses is reasonable enough. If the slaves were required to provide most of their own food, they clearly had to have the necessary resources at their disposal. If they were deprived of certain plots of provision grounds, they would have to be given other grounds yielding crops, or a supply of food, or money with which to fulfill their needs until other land was allowed them and they could collect their first harvest. From the planter's point of view—unless he were disposed to see his slaves starve—the need would be obvious.

It is the fact that slaves were allowed to bequeath provision grounds which is most difficult to explain. At first glance, this would seem to imply that for each estate a time would come when, all of the backlands having been appropriated, there would be no marginal areas left free for cultivation by newly arrived slaves. Yet this could never happen, in part because of the high rate of slave mortality, and more so because of the way in which newly imported slaves were absorbed into the estate organization. "The practice is that of distributing the newly-imported Africans among the old Negroes, as pensioners (with some little assistance occasionally given) on their little *peculium,* and provision-grounds" (Edwards 1793, 2: 126). Thus, new arrivals were simply taken into the existing pattern of provision ground production, and slave importation did not necessitate the setting aside of more land for spare-time cultivation.

The system appears to have been favored by all concerned. From our point of view, it is of interest because it was the course of action least likely to encourage continued introduction of West African methods into Jamaican slave estate agriculture. Admittedly, the newly arrived slaves would, by their language and behavior, revive memories of Africa among a few of the longer enslaved, but in their new households they were the newcomers, the trainees, and the minority voice. Edwards claims that the new slaves were in fact pleased with the arrangement, and ever afterwards considered themselves as the adopted children of those by whom they were thus protected, calling them parents, and venerating them as such; and I never knew an instance of the violation of a trust thus solicited and bestowed. In the course of eight or ten months, provided they are mildly used and kept free of disease, new people, under these circumstances, become reconciled to the country; begin to get well established in their families, their houses and provision-grounds; and prove in all respects as valuable as the native or Creole negroes (Edwards 1793, 2: 127).

The new slaves thus became operators on the household's provision grounds, and later, perhaps, as heads of the households in a succeeding generation, inherited the right of use of the land. And this is where the emphasis must be placed, for as Edwards himself showed, no slaves held provision grounds by legal right of property in land (1793, 2: 147). The land belonged to the estate owner. The use of it was allowed to the slaves. What slaves were permitted to bequeath was certainly not a plot of land, but rather the right to continue to cultivate a certain piece of land for as long as the owner or estate manager permitted that land to be cultivated in provisions. The slaves, never disillusioned in the matter, may well have considered a certain piece of land as their "property"; the master, under no illusions, recognized the arrangement for what it was, namely, a free letting of land in return for which he hoped to have a well-fed and contented slave-labor force. After Emancipation, of course, employers were no longer directly concerned with the condition of their workers' minds and stomachs, the *peculium* was quickly forgotten, and money rents were imposed.

The Emancipation was the most important event in Jamaican history after the English conquest of the island. The Jamaican freedman of 1838 had to work out his style of life anew. The material needs of daily living would be met by personal effort and because of personal motivation; the hated compulsion of the planter was no longer a spur to effort, and the freedman easily learned to live without it.

The freedman's most important means for establishing his independence was by repudiating his previous status as an estate laborer and becoming a peasant, that is, an agriculturist who produced, wholly or mainly on his own land, the bulk of his own food needs and a surplus for sale. The inspiring transformation of the Jamaican people into a free and independent peasantry has been described at length many times; but our concern here is with the freedman's preparation for this transformation. Aside from funds for the acquisition of land and housing, the freedman had to have skills and knowledge which would enable him to live independently. In this he had been prepared for independence by certain conditions of slavery, notably the initial insistence or concession that he provide his own food (Mintz 1955, 1958). At the same time, it must be made clear that newly enslaved Africans carried to Jamaica and absorbed into the estate system and the slave household did not have to learn everything anew. Some of native America's most important foods, such as maize and cassava, were carried to West Africa as early as the sixteenth century and were adopted there with incredible rapidity and success. Later, food-bearing plants had been brought from West Africa to the West Indies. In certain major crops, therefore, and perhaps in the technology and equipment of cultivation, there was much that was already familiar to newly arrived slaves.

Nevertheless, we have largely avoided dealing with the important question of Africanisms, either in agriculture or in marketing. In the case of Jamaican agriculture, the available historical data have not yet been totally and thoroughly analyzed, while sufficient data simply are not available to assess the degree to which Jamaican marketing might have been derived directly from West African practices. Such common West African features as separate royal and commoner markets, royal monopolies in certain products, and price fixing by the court (Herskovits 1938) were of course absent and could not have been expected to occur. The first formally established marketplace, with its schedules and regulations, appears to have been a wholly English innovation.

This is neither to argue that prior marketing activities by slaves (or, for that matter, English colonists) did not occur, or that African traditions played no part in the conduct of marketing activity. Especially interesting, perhaps, is the fact that women carry on most marketing activity today in Jamaica, as they did, and do, in much of West Africa. But specification of the role of the African past in shaping the Afro-Caribbean present will require much careful historical research, to free the argument from simple comparisons of trait similarities, and to deal with complex functional relationships between modes of behavior and the attached values and attitudes of those who carry out such behavior. There is no evidence that women outnumbered men among the slaves trafficking in Jamaican marketplaces in the eighteenth century; during the first part of the nineteenth century, most of the descriptions cite male marketers or whole families in the marketplaces, as they cite whole slave families at work on the provision grounds. Women may have become predominant as the freedmen acquired land of their own and became independent peasant cultivators. Hence, the resulting division of labor might parallel African patterns in some cases, without necessarily being derived from them in any simple, invariant fashion (Mintz and Price 1973).

Enslavement, and slavery itself, meant removal from familiar landscapes, the breakdown of institutions dependent on specific groups of personnel (a priesthood, a court and king, a legal profession), and the forced separation of the members of kin groups of all kinds. It meant sudden and forcible introduction into an estate system and a social order with economic objectives entirely foreign to the newly arrived slaves (Hall 1954: 153–54). And because among each shipload of new arrivals the men usually far outnumbered the women, slavery demanded a total reconsideration of the place and roles of men and women in society, beginning with fundamental questions about new patterns of mating and domestic organization, which the slaves themselves had to resolve under what were often viciously repressive conditions.

Within the plantation, life was supposed to be lived as the master ordered; and to a large extent, this was the case. But we have amassed evidence to demonstrate that the patterns of cultivation and marketing developed largely outside the formal demands of the plantation regimen, either with the overt and explicit cooperation of the planter class or, in some cases, without it. Most interesting, perhaps, the remarkable economic performance of Jamaican slaves made their society dependent on the slave group in ways that no early planter could have predicted—or might have been willing to concede. We see here, then, a clear instance in which the internal contradictions of the plantation system made possible the development of adaptive patterns by the slaves themselves, patterns which might be said to have contributed both to the effective operation of the system on the one hand and to its progressive weakening on the other.

In all this, we still remain uncertain as to the role of the African heritage. Neither slaves nor masters—and it is too often forgotten that the difference in this respect was one of degree—could retain their entire past under the new conditions of plantation life. For the slaves, of course, the difficulties were multiplied by the oppressiveness of slavery itself, as well as by the diversity of their ethnic and cultural origins. Yet slavery made the slaves alike—it inevitably lent a commonality to their suffering; and we have sought to show how the resourcefulness and creativity of the slaves were employed to make their situation somewhat less intolerable. In spite of important recent work (e.g., Patterson 1967; Brathwaite 1971), the unraveling of the ways in which the Caribbean's diverse cultural origins were reworked into new patterns remains largely unfinished. Instead of a simple search for like elements in isolation, or the assertion of rather vague generalizations of a philosophical order, what is needed is more thorough historical research on both sides of the Atlantic, to discover what was, and thereupon to determine how the present came to be.

We shall attempt to carry the description of Jamaican markets and marketing further forward in time in the next chapter. Here we have sought to outline some of the fundamental features of the market system in the early period of Jamaica's history as a British possession. We think that both the peasant economy and its marketing pattern originated within the slave plantation. We feel that a tendency to overattribute features of Jamaican peasant culture to the African culture stream may have slighted the role of European culture and culture history. This is not at all to diminish or undervalue what must have been a very substantial African contribution, nor is it to argue that the African past was irrelevant to life on the plantation—within which these patterns probably took on their new forms. But the real question is not one of fractions or proportions; it is, rather, one of documenting precisely the ways in which new cultural patterns are actually created out of older substances, as an aspect of the development of a general theory of culture.

Adequate study of the Jamaican peasantry, both in its historical roots and its ethnographic present, has only begun. As the grand lay historian of Jamaica, the late Ansell Hart, has written:

Plantation economy, absentee proprietorship and the overlordship of the British combined to produce Jamaican traits of delegation, dependence, and 'tek a chance,' above which however, tower the Jamaican's humor, sentiment, physique, capacity for hard work and generosity. There are of course many strands to the story of the undesirable traits which emerges from the plantation economy: neglect, economic insufficiency, malnutrition, disease, etc. Subsistence economy on the other hand developed into the main source of supply of staple food; and besides giving the slave a 'bellyful,' produced directly by himself for himself, also gave him access to the Sunday market, a money economy, important social contacts in field and market and some degree of self-reliance and independence. The cultural and economic effect of what began as subsistence production was immense (Hart 1955: 1).

# 8

# The Contemporary
# Jamaican Market System

As the preceding chapter demonstrates, the Jamaican marketing system by which almost all perishable vegetable foods and many other products are conveyed from the primary producer to the ultimate consumer is very old. The original determinant of this system was the plantation practice of compelling the slaves to produce the bulk of their own food; but compulsion seems to have become less and less necessary, since the slaves were able to benefit in various ways from independent production. This development hinged on yet another basic feature of Jamaican society: the creation of public marketplaces throughout the island, beginning toward the end of the seventeenth century. But, as we have seen, it was the accomplishments of the slaves themselves that made the marketing system work: the slaves produced substantial surpluses beyond their own consumption needs, which they were allowed to sell, and they were given some freedom—which they exercised well—in disposing of the economic rewards of their marketing activities. The growth of this pattern expresses certain contradictions within the plantation system, and it is within the play provided by such contradictions that the accomplishments of the slaves—while still slaves—are most dramatically revealed.

The production of food surpluses by slaves, and the transmission of such surpluses to open markets within which free men, as well as slaves, could buy and sell, brought the slave sector of Jamaican society into interdependent relationships with the free sectors in ways that militated against the repressive ideal of the plantation system. The marketing system enabled some slaves to use their free time for craft specialization rather than agricultural production. They, too, were able to sell their products in the marketplaces. Basketmakers, pannier makers, leatherworkers, woodworkers, and other artisans, for instance, who worked at their crafts or at other jobs for their masters during the week, were enabled to exchange their products for foods and other needed commodities. Other slaves, on other islands, were able to engage in fishing (Price 1966), food processing (Handler 1971), potting (Handler 1963), and other such activities. Though these activities probably originated, for the most part, as services for the master class, the marketing system facilitated the flow of products to other consumers. Hence a wider division of labor among the slaves emerged as a consequence of market opportunities; even more, for the access to liquid capital enabled the slaves to exercise consumer choices, to change their standard of living, and to function—in this regard, at least—more like free men than the controllers of the Jamaican plantation system had ever intended at the outset.

Marketing also enabled the slaves to congregate somewhat more freely in centers where news as well as goods could be exchanged, and where a brief respite from the plantation regimen might be enjoyed. Although the missionaries objected vigorously to the fact that the markets were traditionally held on Sundays (e.g., Bickell 1835: 66, 204), it was there that many slaves received their first direct exposure to Christian teaching. The marketplaces were undoubtedly also venues for courtship, education, and—inevitably—the plotting of rebellions. It is important in these connections to keep in mind how repressive the daily routine of plantation life could be.

It was out of these background features, discussed at greater length in the preceding chapter, that the modern system of Jamaican internal marketing arose. We are dealing, of course, with a timespan of more than a century. But in much of daily life, the present character of the Jamaican peasantry is not radically different from what it has been, more or less continuously, for the past 140 years.

Food preferences, the use of animal and human energy in agriculture, agricultural practices, and many other contemporary features show surprising continuity with descriptions of Jamaican rural life a century ago.

## Features of the System

In order to describe the present pattern of marketing, seven features of that pattern will be discussed briefly. The first is the predominance of women in marketing. This characteristic is certainly of long standing, though we lack convincing evidence that it predated Emancipation. Such writers as Sturge and Harvey (1838), Bigelow (1851), and Livingstone (1900) remarked on the predominance of women, and Livingstone in particular showed an awareness of the special significance of this phenomenon: "They appear unconscious of any hardship in the arrangement which transfers to them so large a part of the burden of life. It gives to them a certain power, apart from sex, over the men, which in the circumstances is perhaps essential" (Livingstone 1900: 220). But there is as yet no thoroughly convincing evidence that the present-day disproportion of female marketers obtained before Emancipation in Jamaica—if anything, male marketers may have been more common. Patterson, who has done some research on Jamaican marketing history (1967: 224–30), has nothing to say on differing proportions of male and female slaves in the marketplaces; and Goveia's magnificent historical study of British Leeward Islands slavery, though it contains frequent references to the local markets, also gives no indication that women were predominant before freedom.

Hence there may be grounds for supposing that male marketers were as important as female marketers before 1838—or, as is the writer's opinion, that male marketers may have been more important. The puzzle is complicated by our ignorance of the extent, if any, to which land-use privileges were granted to female slaves on the Jamaican plantations. This, too, is a question to which Patterson (1967) failed to address himself; and the writer has no evidence that land use was ever afforded other than to male slaves—though their families (and it does bear noting that their families are referred to with surprising matter-of-factness in the literature) commonly helped them on the provision grounds. The significance of land-use privileges for marketing practices is clear, if one supposes that the pattern of female marketing arose as a consequence of the rise of the Jamaican peasantry. The slaves could, at most, work their provision grounds a little more than one day a week; with the acquisition of their own land after Emancipation, the cultivation system which had arisen during slavery could be extended, becoming the major pursuit of the peasant freedmen. Accordingly, there may be grounds for believing that female marketing—at least to the overwhelming extent that it prevails in modern Jamaica—grew in conjunction with the spread of peasant agriculture. This remains surmise, however. The one piece of information known to the writer that argues against such an interpretation is symbolic in nature. During slavery, divorce among the slaves was consummated by tearing in two the *cotta,* or headcloth (Gardner 1874: 182; Phillippo 1843: 218–19; Long 1774: 2, 413; cf. Cassidy and Le Page 1967: 123; according to Beckwith [1929: 63], a handkerchief was later used for this purpose). One can guess that this practice signified the breaking in two of a symmetrical economic relationship between male cultivator and female marketer.

A second characteristic of Jamaican marketing is the use of money, rather than barter, for exchange. Though Edwards (in a letter) reports that Portland higglers barter such tree crops as coconuts and breakfruit for such ground crops as scallions in a highland marketplace in the Upper Yallahs Valley, cases of this kind are certainly rare (cf. Katzin 1959, 1960). The evidence for the historical continuity of cash media seems extremely strong. The importance of money in market trade was stressed, for example, in the very well-documented testimony of Edward Long (1774). Long believed that one-fifth of the cash circulating in Jamaica in his time was in the hands of slaves, largely as a result of their marketing activities (Mintz 1964), and he testified to their dominance of market trade in general.

The availability of a standardized medium of exchange, which serves for nearly all marketing transactions, makes it possible for today's marketer to exchange her stock for cash entirely and even to repeat the process several times in the course of a single week, or during a particularly busy two- or three-day period. Moreover,

the goods may pass through the hands of a whole chain of intermediaries before they reach the ultimate consumer. This process is
of considerable importance in economies of the Jamaican kind;
here, capital is very dear, labor very cheap. Profit margins are usually small, and the individual trader has no guarantee that she will
gain in any particular series of transactions. From the consumer's
point of view, a long chain of intermediation may seem inefficient
and sometimes costly, since it may increase the final selling price of
the goods in question. But it bears remarking that the opposite situation may also occur, as when a glut in the retail market causes
prices to fall sharply; then, it is the intermediaries who lose, and
the consumers who profit accordingly. In other words, the multiplicity of traders does not automatically increase prices, and the
competition among traders usually keeps prices in line.

This, then, is the third characteristic of modern Jamaican marketing on the local level: the large number of small-scale traders
engaged in it. Not only is the number of such traders very large,
relative to the quantity and value of the goods conveyed from small
farms to final consumers, but each trader commonly participates in
only a segment of the intermediation process. Some traders sell only
at small, local marketplaces; others in cities, particularly Kingston
and Montego Bay; some are retailers, some wholesalers; some trade
only part of the time, others are full-time professionals; and so on.
Thus, a highly complex network of individuals is engaged in the
operation of the market system, and myriad series of interpersonal
relationships link traders with each other, and with the farmers and
consumers who stand at each end of the chains of intermediation.

A fourth characteristic of the system is that goods carried in
internal marketing are usually delivered by those who deal in them.
In other words, the truckers of produce are also carriers of market
women, and the bulking and bulk-breaking of produce are carried
on through a series of intermediate steps. Accordingly, the amounts
of human energy and talent invested in the system are very considerable, and the competition which typifies this system, and others
like it, involves large numbers of independent, small-scale traders.

Most such traders operate on the basis of very small quantities
of accumulated capital. This capital is usually borrowed, at least

initially, either from the marketer's husband or, more commonly perhaps, from a small businessman who is likely to charge high rates of interest, particularly since the loans are for very short periods. Though many market women are successful enough to truck more substantial quantities of produce to market each week, the majority are very modest dealers, who may carry a single basket-load—perhaps forty to sixty pounds—on each trip. Thus, a general smallness of scale is a fifth characteristic of Jamaican marketing.

The calculation of profit margins is very difficult (Mintz 1957). Katzin's important papers (1959, 1960) tell us something; but much of what we know is deducible from the general circumstances under which trade takes place. The major background factors are the presence of large numbers of intermediaries who compete on the one hand for the stock they buy from the peasantry and on the other for the custom of retail buyers; the tendency of most Jamaican consumers, even urban housewives, to buy in very small quantities; and the perishability of most of the commodities, particularly in a context of subtropical climate and few refrigeration facilities. The most important of these factors, however, is the competition among sellers; and Bauer's assertion (1954: 26–27) that producers and consumers would circumvent the intermediaries if they found the price of their services unreasonable is entirely convincing. The sixth characteristic to be noted, then, is the general determination of profit margins by the background features noted above. It is probably quite safe to assert that in most cases the profit margins of small-scale intermediaries are in no sense out of line with profit margins in other sectors of the Jamaican economy.

Finally, a seventh general characteristic of the system is the tendency for intermediaries to carry a diversified stock, partly in accordance with the productive patterns of Jamaican small-scale farms, partly in order to distribute risk. Since gluts in particular products are unpredictable; since some products are more perishable or more fragile than others; since customers buy a variety of items, usually in small quantities, the small-scale intermediary probably derives some long-range benefit from carrying a diversified load of items for sale, particularly if she is a local retailer, or buys from peasant producers.

## Higgler Operations

These characteristics may now be viewed against the backdrop of Jamaican peasant farming, with which they are intricately interwoven. First of all, it is hypothesized here that the Jamaican marketing system, as described above, and the Jamaican pattern of small-farm cultivation are wedded not only historically, but functionally and psychologically as well, and that changes in either of these institutional segments of Jamaican culture would result in changes in the other. Had it not been for the pattern of subsistence-plot cultivation under slavery, and the perpetuation of subsistence cultivation by the growth of a rural peasantry after emancipation (Paget n.d.; Lopez 1948), the Jamaican economy would have taken on a very different character. The production of a per capita agricultural surplus within the internal economy under slavery facilitated and made advantageous the development of a strong marketing pattern which, as we have seen, may have rested in some measure upon the African cultural heritage of the slaves. After Emancipation, the market system proved of great value to the small-scale cultivator who, by its means, was provided with the cash he needed to supply himself with items that could not be produced locally.

This situation still obtains. In fact, the interdependence between higglers and small-scale cultivators, between marketing and small-scale agriculture, may be even stronger today than it was a century ago. The small-scale cultivator's capital fund—like the higgler's—is minimal, his production very small, and his margin of profit narrow. He depends heavily on the higgler, who helps him to transform part of his products into cash. The owners of the numerous small farms still operating in Jamaica depend on the sale of at least some items for money. And while the owner-cultivator of half an acre may be unwilling to invest the time and energy necessary to go to market to sell his handful of yams and cocos, he is quite happy to sell them to the market woman who scours the neighborhood to buy just such odd handfuls of resalable goods.

The small-scale farmer also is unwilling to put half of his half-acre into corn or scallions or any other single crop for fear of a seasonal glut, when all he has produced may have to be sold at a loss, if, that is, it can be sold at all. He prefers to diversify his crops in order to reduce the risk involved in the production of any one item. Thus, just as the higgler distributes risk in marketing by carrying a selection of items, the small-scale farmer distributes risk in production by crop diversification. The market woman who buys from the small-scale farmer is subject to the very same dangers her supplier faces.

However, the diversification which reduces risk in production and distribution increases their complexity. Some have argued that if the Jamaican small-scale farmer were willing to put his entire half-acre into a single crop and then sell the harvest to a wholesaler, the agricultural and marketing processes would be made much more efficient. But to this argument both small-scale farmer and higgler are likely to respond: "Efficient for whom?" On a number of occasions when small-scale farmers have put all their land into a single crop, they have lost everything. The small-scale farmer cannot afford to put all his resources into the production of a single item, the market for which is not guaranteed. Given the uncertainty of demand, and the marketing system by which all internally consumed crops are handled, the man who farms on a small scale in Jamaica must diversify; given diversified farming on a minuscule scale, the marketing system will tend to remain unchanged.

The higgler provides the essential link between producer and consumer in the whole process of local distribution because no one, at least in present-day Jamaica, is willing to take her place. So long as farmers sell their surplus in the form of several hands of bananas, a handful of akees, a few breadfruits, half a dozen eggs, and so forth, truckers who, in some countries, serve the consumers' needs by buying wholesale in the countryside and selling wholesale to retail stores or jobbers cannot supplant the higgler in Jamaica. No trucker can profitably tour the Jamaican countryside buying on the scale of higgler operations. It would take him several days to acquire a load of often highly perishable goods, since he would have to purchase these goods in tiny quantities. Moreover, since there are no wholesale outlets for these goods, he would have to unload his stock through the resale to individuals of similarly tiny quantities. The higgler, on the other hand, is able to carry on her business profitably on a small scale because her capital outlay is very small and she is willing to work on an extremely low margin of profit. She is willing to do this because higgling is one of the very few ways in which she can obtain a cash reward, however small, for her labor.

In the course of her transactions, the higgler makes a significant contribution, not usually recognized, to the functioning of Jamaican society. In the process of providing the consumer with needed produce and the small-scale producer with an access to market, she pays a very high rate for services. Thus, she contributes up to a third or more of her gross income to the trucker. (The number of trucks engaged in carrying higglers and their goods to and from markets is considerable: it is not unusual to see twenty trucks at one of the busy country markets, and there are eighty-seven such markets in Jamaica.) She frequently pays as much as 5 percent or more interest for *three days' use* of capital borrowed from the butcher or shopkeeper who finances her business. Finally, in return for letting her sell, the market itself may collect 5 percent of the estimated selling value of her load in addition to other fees.

At this point it may be useful to consider briefly the nature of consumer demand on the island, since Jamaican production and distribution, whose interrelationships we have been considering, are linked to the kinds of demand situations which Jamaican consumers create. Certain sectors of consumer demand seem to be relatively stable, for instance that of the suburban buyers of Cross Roads, St. Andrew, or of the staff of the University College at Mona, St. Andrew. But these are relatively circumscribed consumer groups, composed of buyers with assured incomes and fairly fixed buying habits. The broad base of Jamaican consumers consists of individuals with irregular incomes who, because of this, the writer would hypothesize, manifest irregular demand for goods. Among the consumer sectors whose demand is regular and assured, it may be possible to eliminate the market woman (and, to some extent, the markets as well), and to establish greengrocers on the American or British model, because in these sectors consumer demand is sufficiently stable to encourage businessmen to risk investment at every stage of the production and distribution process—cultivation, trucking, wholesaling, and retailing. But the irregularity of demand among the majority of Jamaican consumers probably precludes any overall replacement of the present marketing system.

## Conclusions

Thus it would appear that small-scale agricultural production, the prevailing marketing arrangements, and the character of consumer demand are functionally interrelated. The writer has restricted himself mainly to the first two components of the total system—production and marketing—because the connection between them is fairly clear. In Jamaica they are interdependent and reinforce each other. Yet it is conceivable that a market system like Jamaica's might be viable in society where peasant farms are much larger in size; contrariwise, a small-scale farming pattern like Jamaica's might go hand in hand with a very different marketing system. The writer does not hold that the two adaptations are inseparable, or that any change in one is certain to destroy the other; he would suggest, however, that before any substantial changes are made in either pattern, serious thought be given to the possible consequences for the other.

From the point of view of the small-scale cultivator, there are good reasons for keeping an "uneconomic" farm. Owning land has a very special meaning in Jamaica, and being independent on the land is a value of deep significance to the Jamaican peasant. One can reason that the very small farms are frequently wasteful from the agronomic, conservation, and economic points of view. Much the same may be said of the market woman and her scale of operations. She, too, operates an "uneconomic" and "wasteful" business. But she, too, is maintaining her independence. In describing their fellows, many market women have told the writer that "one week she gains and the next she loses, but she'd rather be a higgler and make a shilling than work in someone's house." In a country where over 70,000 adults, most of them women, are employed as domestics (Cumper n.d.), where labor is relatively plentiful, where average incomes are low, where no social barrier prevents lower-class women from working, and where the only economic alternative to marketing is domestic labor, it is easy to see why many women choose to be higglers.

Mention has been made of the division of labor between men and women which, historically and functionally, seems to parallel that between cultivation and marketing, although by no means strictly so. This division of labor characterizes thousands of individual rural lower-class peasant families. The higgler wife, or "partner," provides an outlet for some of her cultivator husband's foodstuffs. At the same time, higgling provides the wife with a largely separate economic activity in which the husband does not exert a great deal of control. The marketing pattern probably has a considerable effect on the husband-wife relationship in thousands of Jamaican families. How the wife's independent or quasi-independent role as marketer and contributor to the total family income influences conceptions of authority, equality, dignity, and other basic value-concepts within the family seems to be virtually unexplored. The writer would hold that an intimate functional relationship obtains between the marketing system and the patterned sexual roles that Jamaican peasants consider permissible and desirable.

That basic Jamaican peasant values are involved in being a higgler, and hence "independent," in having a source of income largely separate from that of one's mate—these are as yet unsubstantiated hypotheses. The more basic hypothesis that small-scale farming and the present system of Jamaican internal marketing neatly sustain one another also requires substantiation, and can be proved or disproved only by careful field studies. Such studies would throw additional light on one of the most fundamental institutions of Jamaican culture.

# 9

## Houses and Yards among Caribbean Peasantries

Throughout this book, the point has been made repeatedly that the parallel social histories of the Caribbean islands have produced numerous similarities among the rural peoples who inhabit them today. These similarities originated in good measure from a common history of slavery and forced labor, the domination of the plantation system, and the narrow range of economic alternatives available to those who resisted that system by developing life-styles outside it.

Today's rural Caribbean folk may be divided roughly into rural proletarians, who work on and for plantations; peasants, who have access to land and produce their own food and market commodities; and people who fall somewhere between the rural proletariat and the peasantry, and generally both work their own (rented or shared) land and engage in wage labor (Cumper n.d.; Comitas 1964; Frucht 1967; Handler 1965, 1966).

Many of the social characteristics of rural Caribbean populations are shared by persons in all of these categories. Others are largely limited to persons in one or another category, for reasons having to do with their particular style of life. Thus, to take one obvious example, control over the labor of one's family members is much more typical of peasants than of rural proletarians, while the purchase of a large proportion of the family's food is obviously more typical of rural proletarians than of peasants. Hence any discussion of similarities and differences among rural Caribbean peoples must take account of major differences in the activities associated with making a living.

But there are of course other reasons why Caribbean rural peoples are culturally homogeneous or heterogeneous. We have seen that the origins of these peoples are very diverse, and that the populations of different Caribbean societies have been subject to many different cultural influences. We do not seek to "explain" the presence of African religious elements in Haiti and Trinidad, for instance, in terms of the economic history of these two societies, but in terms of the strength of the particular cultural traditions or heritages borne by those who settled them. Again, that the Jamaican people speak one language, the Haitian people another, and the Puerto Ricans a third is plainly due to the respective metropolitan cultures to which their peoples were subject, rather than to any general feature of economic history, or to any contemporary difference in rural life-style.

Any comparative study of the rural subculture of the Caribbean region plainly requires some plotting of similarities and differences. The historically oriented scholar will want to know how a particular cultural feature became part of contemporary life, and to examine its distribution in the region as a whole. He will recognize that both similarities and differences may be attributable to traditions that have persisted or that have been differentially discarded since newcomers from other parts of the world came to inhabit the islands; or to influences that shaped the life of local peoples during or after the slavery epoch; or to particular local conditions—economic, demographic, ecological—that affected the creation of living patterns over the centuries.

Scholars interested in the Caribbean region in the past have often been preoccupied with the survival of one or another particular cultural tradition. Herskovits, for instance, a pioneering anthropological student of the African tradition in the New World, was especially concerned with the tracing of African elements in Caribbean life (cf., for instance, 1930, 1937, 1945, 1947), while other scholars have been more interested in documenting the importance of various European traditions (cf., for instance, Greenfield 1966). Amerindian elements have attracted the attention of still other observers (cf., for instance, Taylor 1951; Sturtevant 1969). All of these research workers have been aware that there was no single, unified European or African or Amerindian tradition, and each has made contributions to our understanding of the processes by which one or another cultural element or complex has been modified, synthesized, and reworked, in terms both of its particular form and content and of its symbolic meanings, values, and associations for those who perpetuated it. Haitian religion, for instance, is rich in features that can be traced, more or less precisely, to the African past, but these features have rarely survived in any unmodified, or "pure," form. The processes of change are in some ways even more interesting than the particular origins of one or another trait, since these processes exemplify a general characteristic of human cultures: their complex capacity simultaneously to change and to remain the same.

But for reasons unconnected with the intellectual quest itself, retentions are sometimes perceived as more interesting than losses or replacements in culture, and some cross-cultural similarities are thought to be more interesting than others. This may be illustrated with a few Caribbean examples. Almost everywhere in the Caribbean, rice and beans (or "peas," as they are sometimes called) are a key item in local cuisine. Puerto Rican rural proletarians call the combination *"el matrimonio"* (the married couple), and clearly prefer the dish to cornmeal, another common food, which is somewhat disdained. Haitian peasants eat rice and beans every day, if they can afford it, and prefer the combination to millet which, like cornmeal in Puerto Rico, is a less acceptable common food. Just as Puerto Rican folk are reluctant to serve *funche* (boiled cornmeal) to a foreign visitor or an honored guest, so Haitians dislike to serve their guests *piti-mi* (millet). Much the same is true in Jamaica, where rice and peas are a preferred item, not replaceable by "food" (which here means root crops such as yams and taro, or green bananas, or breadfruit). These taste preferences are probably all traceable to the period of slavery, when rice and beans constituted a luxury dish, as compared to the other foods mentioned. People do not describe their preferences this way, of course; but rice and beans were not a traditional dish in the original homelands of any

Caribbean population, and the taste was probably acquired in the islands.

But the interest of scholars in this cross-cultural uniformity seems slight. They seem to display far more interest in an item such as akee (*Blighia sapida* Koen.), a tree crop of particular importance in Jamaica, the origin and name of which is clearly African (Cassidy and Le Page 1967). Akee is usually eaten with what the Jamaicans call "salt fish," which is dried cod, and which, probably like rice and beans, became standardized in Caribbean cuisine under slavery. Yet akee is unknown in the Eastern Caribbean (where a wholly different fruit, the guinep or *quinepa* or *kénèp, Melicocca bijuga,* is called "akee"), and it is hardly known in Haiti or the other Greater Antilles. We can specify easily the date the akee arrived in Jamaica; apparently it reached Haiti considerably later. In Jamaica, the akee remains a comfortably specific African retention; in Haiti, it is not eaten.

Both the Jamaican and the Haitian rural subcultures exhibit numerous features of African provenience; the differential distribution of akee is one way in which these societies are unlike; but the "retention" of akee in Jamaica is somehow regarded as "more interesting" than its absence in Haiti. In contrast, the "retention" of *akansan,* a cornmeal mush of African provenience (though corn itself is American in origin) in Haiti seems to be considered more interesting than its absence in Jamaica. And the presence of such foods as *akra* and *doukounou* in both islands, both African foods, both with African names, is even more "interesting," it seems, because here we have two parallel "retentions," surviving the holocaust of slavery in both societies.

Why some of these facts should seem more exciting than others is, indeed, not difficult to determine. Features of Caribbean life that can be traced to the preslavery African past appear as testaments to the toughness and pride of the human spirit—which, indeed, they are. But survivals from slavery seem to be viewed merely as testimony to cultural defeats and losses. The use of words from African languages, the cooking of foods originating in Africa, the worship of gods of African provenience all appear to document the will to endure, to resist; but the significance of survivals from the slavery epoch is apparently diminished by the circumstances of their origin.

However such a view risks belittling the accomplishments of Caribbean peoples during their period of sorest trial. The slavery experience tested to the limit the strength and resourcefulness of millions of newcomers from other lands. The significance of that experience is expressed in the contemporary cultures of Caribbean peoples, just as are both the preslavery and postslavery pasts. The task of historians of these cultures is to disentangle the origins and growth of the life-styles of the Caribbean region, and to seek to analyze the very complex processes by which cultural forms changed and were consolidated. This is not a different task from documenting the capacity and will of people to resist oppression. To survive at all under slavery was a mode of resistance; the cultures of contemporary Caribbean peoples are in their entirety a testament to such resistance.

Cultures lack pedigrees, and it is not surprising that the Caribbean peasantries of today expend little effort in disentangling the varied sources of their beliefs and practices. Haitian peasants apparently see no contradiction in a religion that contains elements drawn from the African, European, and Amerindian pasts; Jamaican peasants draw no distinctions among words of African origin and words of English origin. Puerto Rican peasant singers worry little that their *aguinaldos* are of substantially European derivation, while their *plenas* are much more "African." This is by no means to say that consciousness of such differences is entirely lacking. But rural folk in these societies are much more likely to perceive differences of these kinds in terms of differences between rural and urban life-styles, or between one class and another, than in terms of particular historical origins.

Implicit in the above argument is the need to bear in mind certain general points about the nature of similarities and differences in the rural subcultures of the Caribbean region. First, economic, ecological, or demographic similarities and differences unite or divide different rural populations in the same society. Second, there are similarities, either within one society or between comparable peasant sectors in two or more societies, that are traceable to a common cultural heritage predating slavery, as in the case of important features of African origin, including lexicon, cuisine, religion, language, folklore, and music. Third, there are commonalities that may be traced to the experience of slavery itself, as well as to the parallel impact of European domination—as in the case of the common use of Spanish in both Cuba and Puerto Rico, or the parallel proto-peasant adaptation in both Jamaica and Haiti. Finally, there are similarities and differences arising from the conditions of life following the slavery epoch and intermingled with the influences cited in the first point. Thus, for instance, Puerto Rican peasants and rural proletarians share many features of life, but also differ in significant ways. Their similarities are traceable in large measure to common historical experiences; their differences are due in good part to differences in their economic style of life, stabilized during their earlier development, and still operative.

From a systematic or analytic point of view, similarities traceable to the colonial period are as significant as those that hark back to an earlier past. Both similarities and differences are useful and important means for reconstructing the past, be it the recent past, the period of slavery, or the ancient pasts of the homelands—including, in the case of Amerindian cultures, the pre-Columbian pasts of the islands as well.

Though the volume of historical research on the Caribbean region is vast, relatively few books and papers have dealt with the origins and history of peasant subcultures and the similarities and differences among them. Even rarer are historical studies which deal in a detailed fashion with one or another aspect of rural life in the region as a whole. Marshall's research on the origins of (British) West Indian peasantries (1968) is promising. Wolf's study of the peasant subculture of Puerto Rico (1956) provides a useful introduction to the structural attributes of one Caribbean peasant society. Several precisely focused and detailed papers, such as Sturtevant's (1969) on the processing of root starches, and Handler's on arrowroot (1971), indicate both what is possible and what remains to be done in documenting fully the development of peasant technology in the region. Not only must such research provide a full picture of this development for any one island or peasant subculture, but the studies of comparable phenomena among different island populations must be combined to pinpoint similarities and differences in the processes of development.

Here we need to remember that the peasant subcultures evolved in most cases in the face of metropolitan or insular government opposition, and that observers, both contemporary and in the past, have paid very little attention to the life-styles of rural Caribbean peoples. Only a few historically minded scholars have sought to get behind the so-called imperial tradition of historiography sufficiently to document what peasant life-styles are really like. Price's (1966) paper on Caribbean fishing and the history of Caribbean fishermen and fishing techniques, stresses the growth of a fishing subculture in the margins of Caribbean societies and documents its importance as a way in which local people could escape the tyranny of plantation life. Much the same sort of treatment should be given the peasantries, and the work is only now beginning.

### Characteristics of the House-and-Yard Pattern

In the present chapter, a tentative first attempt is made to organize a little of what is known about one aspect of Caribbean peasant life, the house and yard, and the meaning of these for rural people. The importance of the house and yard as a setting for daily activity is obvious: here decisions are made, food is prepared and eaten, the household group—whatever its composition—sleeps and socializes, children are conceived and born, death is ceremonialized. To speak in terms of some common house-and-yard pattern, without taking account of the many factors that produce variation and difference within the pattern, would be entirely unjustified. Yet there are certain very general similarities, even cross-cultural—that is, occurring across the boundaries of different Caribbean societies —that require description and explanation, and it is principally around such similarities that the chapter is built.

But it is also intended to relate the concrete, material character of the house and the yard to the activities which go on in and around them, to suggest the ways that things and ideas are fitted together, made into (and learned as) patterns, as systems and subsystems of culture, and passed on to the next generation. Too often "material culture," the term by which anthropologists refer to the concrete expression of culture in tangible objects, is seen as divorced from the world of values, ideas, beliefs, and behavior. But it is through such material representations of culture that people relate to each other, express themselves and their values, interact, and carry out their activities. Hence the house is far more than a fabrication of wood and thatch, the yard far more than a locale for the house. Together, house and yard form a nucleus within which the culture expresses itself, is perpetuated, changed, and reintegrated.

A number of writers, some geographers, some ethnologists or historians, have examined the houses of Caribbean rural folk from the vantage point of their history as architectural forms. Doran, a geographer, has interested himself in what is technically known as the "hip-roofed" cottage, a distinctive house-type widely distributed through the British and Dutch Antilles; found less commonly in Haiti, the French Antilles, and Trinidad; rare in the Dominican Republic; and almost entirely absent from Cuba and Puerto Rico (1962). Doran weighs four possible historical sources for the hip-roofed cottage: aboriginal America, Spain, Africa, and Western Europe. He concludes that aboriginal America and Spain may be discounted as possible places of origin, holds in abeyance the possibility of African influences, and opts for a "circum-English-Channel" hearth of origin. His analysis is based both on the contemporary distribution of the form, and on what can be learned about its historical spread during the seventeenth and later centuries. Métraux, an ethnologist, has concentrated narrowly upon Haitian house-types (1949–1951), but has dealt more exactly with details of construction and type variants; though he stresses the importance of European architectural influences, he leaves open the question of African traditions. Métraux expressed the hope that Africanist colleagues would evaluate his Haitian materials in the light of what was known about West African house-types, past and present, but such comparative treatment remains unrealized. Moral, a geographer, has also concentrated on Haitian house-types (1957), but discounts African influences; Revert, also a geographer, reaches similar conclusions for the rural homesteads of the French Antilles (1955). Pérez de la Riva imputes African origins to the rural houses in Cuba (1952), but his argument is poorly developed, particularly since he seems to accept the notion of a single African architectural prototype. All of these authors deal, on one level or another, with the question of origins; all admit that the information is insufficient for any firm conclusions.

The question of architectural origins is, in one sense, fairly straightforward; if we had enough information about African and

Caribbean house-types, past and present, we would at least be able to chart similarities and differences, and perhaps to indicate the evidence that argues clearly for one or another place of origin, even if firm and definite answers were not forthcoming. Houses are a useful unit of comparison, precisely because they consist of a limited number of different materials (wood, stone, thatch, mortar, mud, cement, metal, etc.) and elements (roofs, doors, lintels, frames, window openings floors, stoops, etc.), which may or may not be diffused as interrelated assemblages. Studies of such forms are consonant with North American ethnology's traditional concern with the origins and diffusion of elements and complexes of culture, and with the way such forms change in space and in time, as they are adapted to new uses or new environments.

In seeking African origins for Caribbean house-types, however, the historical ethnologist or geographer faces certain clear-cut difficulties. For instance, we have no certain evidence that newly arrived Africans were ever able to build their houses according to their own traditions. If African elements are present, we must assume that the migrants were able to retain their architectural knowledge until they became free and could build their own houses, or that some variants of the original types were constructed and the techniques preserved by runaway slaves, by early generations of freedmen, or in some other way. Patterson, who has amassed considerable evidence on the daily life of Jamaican slaves (1967), is silent on this point; Brathwaite (1971) tells us what he can. Research workers on other islands have done little more. The comparable task is probably no easier when we deal with such features of culture as folklore, religion, musicianship, ethnobotany, crop uses, and the like, though the attribution of features, particularly lexical features, can sometimes be more certain.

But the cultural forms of a people are not only historically derived—products or consequences of the past, so to speak—but must also fit in with the needs and beliefs of those who employ and preserve them today. Such needs and beliefs are reflected in use, in behavior, and in the values people maintain. The houses of Caribbean peasantries are more than historical aggregates of past tradition; as the settings for many of the most important contemporary rural activities, they must be studied as behavioral contexts and not merely as historical products. The questions this pursuit raises are concerned more with similarities and differences arising from the differential adaptations of newcomer populations to the pressures imposed upon them by the Caribbean experience, and less with the specific historical origins of particular traits or complexes.

Such an exercise requires that some attention be given to the background conditions of peasant life in the region, the customary or usual distribution of population, and the forms of settlement and land use that peasant populations employ. Though peasant settlement and land-use patterns vary not only from one Caribbean country to another, but also from one region to another within the same island society, certain general characteristics provide a context within which to examine house uses and the attached values and attitudes of the peasantries. Seven such features are enumerated here, each of which will be dealt with in turn: (1) the peasant adaptation is primarily to the highlands and to sloping terrain, rather than to coastal floodplains and alluvial fans or to intermontane valley floors; (2) main cultivation grounds do not usually adjoin the houses of their owners; (3) house plots are often dispersed rather than clustered and are sometimes scattered along a slope or strung out upon a mountain spur; (4) usually, only one sexually cohabitant couple occupies a house, though several houses (and several couples) may share a yard; (5) each homestead, whether consisting of one house or more, is usually surrounded by at least a small quantity of land, and set off from the outside by a fence, clumps of vegetation, or a hedge or living fence; (6) the yard may be associated intimately with the house, and its land may have important ritual or kinship significance; (7) house and yard often have particular symbolic meaning for local people, though this may be implicit and little noticed by outsiders.

## The Highland Adaptation

These seven features may now be discussed at greater length, in order to clarify the place of house and yard in the daily life of Caribbean peasantries, and to indicate something of the history of the features. We have seen that peasant agriculture is predominantly a highland adaptation on the major islands because the coastal plains and interior valleys were frequently taken over for plantation cultivation at an early stage. In general, this division between coastal estates and highland small-scale farming on the larger islands has not varied significantly, except in the case of Haiti. There, the plantation system was largely destroyed by the Revolution, reappeared briefly thereafter, withered away once more, and was then reinstituted in certain narrow coastal regions of the north and around Port-au-Prince in the twentieth century. By and large, the countryside remains a peasant domain. In Jamaica, the plantation adaptation is ancient and has, if anything, expanded since the nineteenth century; coastal areas, except in the south, are largely monopolized by plantations. Much the same is true of Puerto Rico, where the expansion has been very intensive since 1900.

In all three countries, however, the peasant adaptation is paramount in the highlands of the interior. Peasant holdings are prevailingly small—one to ten acres, and more commonly one than ten—and owners often cultivate several plots, which may be held by various arrangements, including leaseholding, sharecropping of various kinds, and renting. In some regions, both within these three countries and elsewhere in the Caribbean, the peasant adaptation may rest heavily upon a tradition of rented land; but access to land to permit small-scale cultivation with family labor is very common, even when land is not owned. The agriculture itself is typically very diversified. Such diversification is a means of distributing risk, as we have seen in the case of Jamaican peasant farming; it also provides a perennial trickle of food crops, both for subsistence and for sale; maximizes the utility of the land, relative to the availability of labor; and may even serve to maintain fertility, as by intercropping, the use of catch crops, and the like. Sauer (1954) has suggested that the reputation of Caribbean peasant agriculture as a "land-killer" may be undeserved, arising from the need to cultivate on hilly slopes with sharp runoffs and shallow topsoils, rather than from the agricultural techniques themselves. However, it is true that the failure to use fallowing, fertilizer, rotation, terracing, and other land-protective practices typifies such agriculture; it is also true that the farming of widely scattered plots greatly increases the necessary investment of time and energy—though this difficulty is hardly the fault of the peasants, unless one wishes to hold them responsible for traditional systems of inheritance that often lead to the progressive fragmentation of holdings.

## Kitchen-Gardens vs. Provision-Grounds

Normally, agricultural holdings are separate from the houses of their owners, and may even be located some distance away—as much as ten miles, in many cases. Both in Haiti and in Jamaica there is a clear historical precedent for this separation which does not, however, completely explain it today. We have already seen that estate slaves commonly grew their own subsistence on plantation uplands, using lands judged unsuitable for the major plantation crops. It was on such lands that the slaves acquired or perfected their horticultural skills, developed their own standardized agricultural practices, learned the characteristics of Caribbean soils, mastered the cultivation of new crops, and otherwise prepared themselves for their reconstitution as peasantries. A wholly distinctive crop repertory, adapted to the new settings, was created by combining familiar African crops, such as "guinea yams" (*Dioscorea sativa*) and okra, with native American crops, including corn, sweet potatoes, potatoes, tomatoes, and species of *Xanthosoma;* European vegetables, such as cabbage and carrots; and Southeast Asian cultigens, including the breadfruit. Such agricultural tools as the short-handled hoe, the mattock, and the bush knife were adjusted to new conditions—though we are still uncertain about the provenience of these items. Citrus, avocado, mango, coconut palm, papaya, soursop and akee trees were cultivated, to provide cover, fruit, and wood—together they illustrate well the intersection of different agricultural and orchard traditions. Techniques of land-clearing—by burning, tree-girdling, and the removal of stones for walls and shelters—were developed, again probably by combining different traditions of land use. Moreover, techniques associated with food processing, storage, preservation, and seed selection were perfected, though the origins of these techniques have never been wholly disentangled.

But these myriad skills and usages took shape during slavery for the most part, either on the plantation uplands where slaves grew their own food, as in Jamaica and Haiti, or in the maroon communities of the interior. We have seen how frontiersmen developed a pattern of casual cultivation in the interior of Puerto Rico—again, outside the normal routine of plantation cultivation, or even in open opposition to it. Pérez de la Riva has developed the theme of the Cuban maroon community, or *palenque,* as a by-product of the concealed cultivation plots of runaway slaves (1952)—though the role of such communities in Cuba has been overshadowed by the better-known exploits of the maroons of Jamaica, Dutch Guiana, and Brazil. According to Pérez de la Riva, so developed was the palenque adaptation in Cuba that one famous community—Bumba —was able to carry on agricultural trade not only with neighboring haciendas in Cuba itself, but also with Santo Domingo and Jamaica, by means of small craft!

All this, however, is a far remove from the more common pattern of "proto-peasant" adaptation, developed within the confines of the plantation. There, the separation between house plot and provision ground was a clear function of the control wielded by the plantation system over the slaves. The "garden," or provision ground, was always located in portions of the plantation that were not used for the major crop, and in which it was not normally intended to plant that crop—as we have seen, plantation owners tried to avoid taking up for sugarcane any of the land they habitually provided the slaves for growing their own provisions.

But the huts of the slaves, unlike the provision grounds, were regularly located near the center of the plantation itself, on or near the "plaza" and below the "great house," where the slaves could be guarded and watched. "Adjoining to the [slave's] house is usually a small spot of ground," wrote one Jamaican observer in 1823, "laid out into a sort of garden, and shaded by various fruit-trees. Here the family deposit their dead, to whose memory they invariably, if they can afford it, erect a rude tomb. Each slave has, besides this spot, a piece of ground (about half an acre) allotted to him as a provision ground." (Stewart 1823: 267).

This separation of subsistence plot from house plot, and the use of the house plot for fruit trees (as well as spices, etc.) and as a family cemetery, is typical of Jamaica and Haiti to this day, though probably not at all of Puerto Rico. There is little evidence that the division into house plot and provision ground, so ubiquitous in Jamaica and Haiti, was ever pronounced in Puerto Rico, nor is there evidence in Puerto Rico of familial house-plot burial grounds.

## Dispersal of Houses

In many parts of these three island societies, it is difficult to define community boundaries in terms of settlement, particularly in the highland interiors. Admittedly, the coastal plantation areas exhibit nucleated settlement patterns, with rows or clusters of houses formed into company towns, *colonias,* or line villages. Such aggregates are also common along principal roadways, near major towns and cities, and around special enterprises, such as the bauxite mines of Jamaica and Haiti. But the highland countrysides show little comparable nucleation, even though national populations may be quite dense, as in Puerto Rico and Haiti. In Jamaica, the missionary-founded free villages still show coherent patterning and form, as we have seen in the case of Sturge Town; but in general, all three of these societies display scattered highland settlement. This dispersion is revealed in the actual distribution of households: in a straggling row along a ridge; scattered around a central water supply in the form of a spring, well, or standpipe; set unevenly into the side of a hill; or, often, substantially isolated from one another. This is by no means to say either that such settlement is incoherent and random or that people entirely lack a sense of community—but all three societies contain substantial numbers of rural folk who have chosen to remain dispersed in terms of household occupancy.

## Household Composition

As yet, we have said nothing about the composition of groups within households. This is obviously a question of very considerable importance in any study of marriage, family, and kinship in Caribbean rural society, and it has received much attention in the literature (cf. particularly Solien 1960, Greenfield 1961). To begin with, one of the most striking characteristics of Caribbean peasant subcultures in these regards is the fact that the domestic unit or kin group housed under one roof only rarely includes more than one sexually cohabiting couple (Mintz 1956, 1960; Davenport 1961).

In fact, the rule of independent residence for cohabiting couples appears to hold for almost all rural Caribbean folk, proletarians as well as peasants—as in the case of Cañamelar, the Puerto Rican plantation community discussed earlier (Mintz 1951b, 1953b, 1956). In effect, this signifies that the establishment of new conjugal associations depends on access to an unoccupied house plot and, commonly, to possession of the means to build a house.

Though the point may sometimes be given exaggerated importance (cf., for instance, Otterbein 1965, and Price's 1970 critique), the linkage between most forms of domestic union and the availability of a house plot or house is nonetheless very significant in Caribbean rural life. In Haiti, Métraux (1951: 116) writes, "the peasant builds his hut when he intends getting married or taking up employment. It represents a young man's first effort and action to free himself. An offer of marriage is out of the question unless the man proves he is in earnest by laying the foundations of the future family home." Davenport (1961: 446), writing of Jamaica, describes the invariable rule by which young men set up a separate household when they take wives: "As long as their father remains fully active, they will move out and establish their own households with their spouses, even though this might only be across the yard. . . . The rule of household formation, then, is that no single household will contain more than one active conjugal pair." Cumper (1961: 398–99) points out that in Barbados, where the definition of a peasantry is open to some question, the establishment of an independent household—usually on rented land, at first—is a customary precondition for the establishment of a family by those who approximate a peasant status. While it is indeed true that some kinds of conjugal union and the fathering of families can and do occur in these societies *without* the prior establishment of an independent household for the cohabiting pair, the relationship between independent domicile and cohabitation is the basis of certain important types of conjugal union.

But a significant exception should be noted. In fieldwork carried out among Puerto Rican peasants in 1948–49, Wolf found that newly married couples sometimes moved in with the wife's family: "This ideal form of residence removes the young husband from the circle of his own father's family and avoids conflicts between the young wife and her mother-in-law" (1956: 206). Apparently, under certain circumstances neolocal residence near the home of the wife's parents is also a possible choice; but Wolf gives no figures on the percentages of different modes of residence in the community he studied.

The importance of this exception is twofold. On the one hand, it runs counter to what is otherwise usual in domestic settlement, both peasant and proletarian, in the Caribbean. On the other, it suggests the possibility of the presence of an extended kinship group under one roof: a phenomenon as common in West Africa as it is rare in the peasant subcultures of the West Indies. In fact, the insistence on separate residence for cohabiting couples in Caribbean peasant life stands in stark contrast to what is known of the African past. It is all the more interesting, then, that this exceptional form is reported for highland Puerto Rico, which, in terms of its culture history, is probably the least "African" rural sector of the three societies.

The point, of course, is that a mode of residence, a pattern of settlement, a form of marriage shared by peoples in differing cultures may be traced either to a common origin on the one hand or to parallel or convergent experiences or present-day needs on the other. If Puerto Rican highland peasants do, indeed, display characteristics reminiscent of an African past, such features may be attributable either to that past or—as is in this case much more likely —to local historical (economic, ecological, demographic) factors producing an analogous form.

Contrariwise, the general absence of more than one cohabiting couple within a single household cannot be regarded as an aping of "European" residence patterns. If anything, it more closely resembles the domestic life-style of European urban proletarians than that of the European middle classes; and this resemblance is not likely to be wholly fortuitous, given the historical experience of Caribbean peoples in past centuries.

The value placed on separate residence is expressed neatly in the Puerto Rican pun-proverb, "Que se casa pa' su casa"—"Let those who marry go to their own house." But separate residence does not necessarily mean a separate yard, as we have already seen. Often, more than one house occupies a yard, though the occupants of two or more such houses are usually related consanguineally. For instance, the traditional Haitian house-and-yard unit, the *lakou,* often included several households (Bastien 1951: 29–36; 1961: 481; Métraux 1951: 10). The unit was headed by a senior male, usually with his wife and unmarried children in one house, his married sons and their families, and perhaps other relatives, in other houses. Though this kind of multihouse homestead has declined swiftly in Haiti, losing its organizing influence as an economic, social, and religious unit, Bastien describes a lakou as follows:

> In 1948 one was found which still included ten households with a total of twenty-seven members, all related, and belonging to three generations. A father and his four sons held about two-thirds of the whole estate, while the rest was divided between the father's sister, two nephews, half-brother, and the concubine of one of the sons and her infant (Bastien 1961: 481).

There may appear to be certain superficial similarities between such a group and the residence group living on indefinitely indivisible family land in Jamaica (Clarke 1957), but analogies of this kind are risky, not only because the actual compositions of such groups are different, but also because their social functions differ as well. The Jamaican residence group normally consists of both the male and female children of the deceased progenitor, who are supposed to share equally in the land, though the land is to be held undivided. But the group cannot be viewed as a corporate group—engaged in common activities as a group—and it is rarely coresidential (in the sense that several homesteads occupy the same plot, as is true of the traditional Haitian lakou). "Family land, in the process of transmission and use has in the main long ceased to have agricultural value," Clarke (1957: 44–45) tells us, "apart from the economic trees with which it is usually well stocked. It represents security in the sense that any member 'in need' can erect a hut on it and live rent free. . . . On the other hand it runs counter to the ambition to own land [individually] and the dislike of usufructuary communal rights only." In Haiti, a somewhat comparable situation is described by Comhaire-Sylvain (1952). Though Haitian law holds that no inheriting individual need accept a share in undivided property, actually such property may be held unchanged by a group of inheritors for one generation or more (Métraux 1951). Such holdings can come into being on the death of a land-owner, since it is customary in Haiti not to divide up such land for some time.

In Jamaica, a man can create family land simply by leaving his property to his children undivided (Clarke 1957). Unless they are willing to undergo litigation for division, the property will continue to be held by several persons, or some inheritors will sell their shares to others. Indeed, there may have been a time when the landowning, land-use, and inheritance practices of the Jamaican peasantry very closely resembled those of their Haitian counter-parts. In both Jamaica and Haiti—and far more swiftly in Jamaica than in Haiti—the trend has been toward individualization of land-holdings, more scattered residence, emigration of at least some of the inheritors-to-be (though often retaining continuing rights in undivided land), and the sale of some shared land to other co-inheritors.

The problems of land tenure and the transmission of land rights among Caribbean peasantries remain largely unsolved, in spite of interesting and careful work by such scholars as Clarke (1953, 1957), Comhaire-Sylvain (1952), and M. G. Smith (1956a). The distinction between house plots and agricultural land has be-come more and more widely recognized, but cross-cultural varia-tions among Caribbean peasantries have still been only very in-completely analyzed. Nor is it possible at present to evaluate either general patterns or local distinctions with regard to possible African influences. We can perceive certain systematic contrasts between official legal systems affecting land and its inheritance, and the locally accepted and traditional practices of the peasantries (Clarke 1957; M. G. Smith 1956a), but much more work is needed before such differences can be traced convincingly to one or another tradition.

Hence, the relationship of local forms of kinship organization and family structure to the physical expression of the local group's character, as embodied in house form, homestead, and yard, in these three societies, requires further study. Scholars such as Clarke (1957), M. G. Smith (1962), Davenport (1956) and R. Smith (1956) have demonstrated that the forms of family organization extant in much of the Caribbean are stable in character, and adaptive to the contemporary social and economic circumstances of the societies in which they are found. The analyses of these family forms suggest that domestic organizations go through cycles of development, and that the "family types" to be found in the Caribbean area are probably developmental stages in one or more sequences of domestic organization. Such sequences are intimately associated with particular forms of household. Studies by R. Smith and others have illuminated the earlier period in the study of Caribbean kinship, when it was assumed that family "types" were to be explained in general historical terms, either as the products of North European and African traditions of social organization, or as the results of centuries of slavery. In fact, the importance of specific historical circumstances for particular forms of domestic organization has not yet been properly assessed for Caribbean societies. But the functionalist studies of recent years have put the weight of analysis on the relationships between domestic organization and characteristics of the wider contemporary society.

## The House and the Yard

The homestead is a place, a setting: yard and house together define the sphere within which much daily life is lived. They also define (or express) the ways that the personnel of the household are divided up—by age, sex, role, and otherwise. Of Jamaica's lower-class people in general, Davenport writes:

> In physical layout the lower-class household consists of a house, a detached kitchen or cookhouse, and a yard area. Each of these areas is the location of important activities which make up the domestic routine. The house is usually used mainly for sleeping and for storing clothing and other articles of personal value. The poorer the household, the more the use of the house is restricted to just these activities, while the houses of the more well-to-do will have space and furnishings for additional activities such as relaxing, entertaining, and eating. Houses vary from simple one-room structures made of wattle and thatch and with earth floors to multi-room buildings of frame or concrete construction, metal or shingle roofs, and plank or cement floors. . . . The cook house is usually a temporary structure

and has less care lavished upon it than on the living house. It is used
for preparing and storing food, and in most poor households, the
family eats here in bad weather. It can also serve as a general
utility shed and working space when other special structures have
not been erected in the yard for these purposes. The yard is the
scene of great miscellany of activities. On this swept ground between
house and kitchen, the children play, the washing is done, the family
relaxes, and friends are entertained. In it and surrounding it a few
food-producing trees are grown, the small animals are tethered, and
space is given over to a small vegetable garden. The yard is frequently
fenced to keep animals in, and neighbors pay respect to this boundary
by never entering without being asked. Far more respect, however, is
paid to the house, for this cramped space affords the only real sanc-
tum of privacy for the household against the rest of the neighborhood.

The house, yard, and kitchen are dominated by the adult women
of the household, for most of the perennial work which goes on in
them is in their charge. Women prepare the food, do the washing and
mending, tend the kitchen garden, look after small animals, and
most important, look after the children. . . .

The adult men and older boys of the household assist in heavier
tasks, such as looking after the larger and more valuable animals (if
there are any), repairing the house and cook-house, chopping logs,
spading a new kitchen garden, and even assisting with the processing
of food products which are to be sold. But men's work is not nearly
so confined to the round of domestic duties as is the women's. To
them falls the major responsibility of the cultivation plot, or 'ground,'
as it is called. In many instances this is removed some distance from
the house site, and the men go to and from it daily, leaving the
women in charge of the household activities and children. Men, of
course, do most of the wage work which takes them away from the
domestic scene. They alone congregate in one another's yards or at
the local shops to socialize. . . .

Although the division of adult labour is not rigidly fixed by sex,
it is the context of the household group which makes it clear. The
rule, as in many European societies, is that women dominate the
services of the domestic scene, while the men are concerned with
productive working outside. Each sex may assist the other in some
of his or her work, but this assistance is supplementary to the major
responsibilities in each sphere. . . . It is this general but flexible plan
which enables the household group to adjust and maintain itself in a

variety of situations and with a variety of difference compositions (Davenport 1961: 435–37).

This careful description, quoted only in part, reveals well how the house and yard express the division of labor within the household, the flexible character of the household group in dealing with the round of daily and yearly activities, and the different activities for which house and yard are a common setting.

## The Yard: Material Uses

The integrity of house and yard as a unit, and its degree of intactness and separation from the outside varies greatly, and cannot be judged solely in terms of its physical form. But usually the peasant homestead is set off from the outside by some physical barrier. Often in highland areas, a visitor is not even aware of the presence of a house until he reaches the barrier which shields it. This barrier may consist of scattered clumps of vegetation, walls, living fences, ditches, picket fences, trees and groves of bamboo, or even the slopes of gullies (Métraux 1951; Mintz 1962; Street 1960). When living fences are used to separate the yard from the outside, they may serve several purposes at once. In Haiti, for example (Mintz 1962), living bamboo is sometimes used for fencing; it can be used to make an important musical instrument (*vaksin*), for rain gutters, to make carrying baskets for chickens, etc. Sisal (*Agave rigida,* var. *sisalana*), commonly grown alongside a living fence, can be cut for sale as fiber, and can be used to make rope, bridle headstalls, and croupiers, and as a reinforcement for baskets. Other plants used as living fences or to supplement such fences have comparable uses; a few are grown largely for their decorative effect, including varieties of croton.

Some plants are commonly grown within the yard, on the house plot. Such plants are to be distinguished in several ways from those grown on provision grounds. Thus, in Haiti, in terms of their eventual use, at least three sorts of plants are grown on house plots: (1) minor vegetables, which may also be decorative, such as eggplants, hot peppers, and tomatoes; (2) items which may enter into commerce but which also have domestic uses, such as cotton (for lamp wicks), sisal (for rope), and vetiver (for thatch, and to keep out insects); and (3) trees which provide fruit, shade, or craft materials, such as avocados, guavas, coconut palms, and lataniers. Plantains and bananas, which can be stolen easily, are also sometimes planted inside the yard. In Haiti, the minor foods, especially spices, grown near the house are called *"diab diab"* and often serve as small presents to visitors. The distinction between these kinds of cultivation and the cultivation of provision grounds, principally by men, is quite clear.

## The Yard: Symbolic Meaning

But the yard is far more than a site for occasional cultivation. We have seen that the land on which the house stands often links groups of kinsmen. The significance of such links is far greater when the plot has been used as a family cemetery, as is commonly the case in Haiti and as was once the case in Jamaica. The organization of affective and ceremonial life around the yard as a repository of tradition, and as expressing the continuity of a kin group, is one of the most promising subjects of research for those interested in the role of the African past. This is perhaps particularly the case in Haiti, where the yard often served both as a burying ground and as the locus of the *oûmfo,* or *vodoun* temple, which expressed the religious continuity of the family group with its ancestors (Métraux 1959: 59–60). Métraux (1954) also points out that the burying group is considered indivisible and inalienable by Haitian peasants, and that even when the house plot is sold, its burying ground remains accessible to the original owners, even to the right of burying kinsmen there. Some of the same reverence for the yard, especially as a repository of ancestors, is observable in Jamaica as well.

What is more, the yard may express continuity at the beginning of life, as well as at its end. In Jamaica, if a fruit-bearing tree is "given" to a newborn child by burying his umbilicus at its foot, the tree is usually within the yard. The placenta is often buried beneath the door stoop, as are other effluvia of birth, and the protective intent of these procedures is clear in what people say when describing them. The yard thus protects the continuity of the kin group, as well as the individual; the links between dead ancestors and newborn children are represented in the yard, expressed and maintained by the generation which stands between them.

But the wider symbolic meaning of house and yard goes even beyond these quite specific details. What might be called the ritual significance of the yard and house is revealed in behavior. One approaches the yard circumspectly in all three societies, indicating one's presence in some way before entering the yard, and usually a-waiting acknowledgment. In Haiti, the guest shouts "hònò!" (honor) before entering, and does not cross the threshold until he hears the reply "réspè!" (respect). In Puerto Rico, the peasant's words for house and yard, *bohío* and *batey,* are Arawakan (Taino) terms having a certain emotional significance. The batey, or yard, is where men normally congregate to talk, and the overtones of the word are revealed in various ways. The name of the Popular Party newspaper was *El Batey;* and Governor Muñoz Marín greeted his party cohorts at the insular convention of 1948 with the words: "How large is our batey." In Jamaica, the word *yard* is sometimes used to define one's total span of activities. When one is told by another person to keep out of his yard, this means essentially to stay out of his way, out of his life. Cassidy and Le Page (1967) point out that yard often means both house and yard in Jamaican speech and thought: /nómbari nó da a yáad nou/ means "no one is at home now"; /wi kyan go a mis mieri yáad/ means "we can go to Miss Mary's place."

## Conclusions

We have argued that the seven features of the house-and-yard complex stem from the histories of Caribbean rural peoples, particularly the experience of slavery and the plantation system, and the usefulness of the peasant adaptation as a response to regimentation and oppression. It remains to consider some of these features in the light of this general assertion. The earliest post-Columbian settlement of the highland interiors of these societies by independent cultivators was uncontrolled, irregular, and often secretive. The Puerto Rican highlander, the *jíbaro*—a word which, to this day, means "shy"—has remained a symbol of the half-wild, the cimarron or feral, the withdrawn peasantry. Though such a peasantry has now almost disappeared in Puerto Rico, and was in any case much overdrawn in the political propaganda of recent decades, this image of the peasantry and the stereotypes attributed to it still persist (Steward 1956). In Jamaica, the reconstruction of the peasantry began in 1838, but we have seen that many of the basic skills of the freedmen were learned before Emancipation, within the confines of the plantation. Much the same was true in Haiti, though slavery was ended there by revolution. In all three cases, there is substantial evidence of the role of runaway slaves in creating the beginnings of a peasant adaptation while slavery was still in its heyday; and in all such cases, there are good grounds for supposing that many continuities with the African (and, particularly in Puerto Rico, the Amerindian) past might be best preserved. These are histories, then, of disengagement and of resistance; and the characteristic features of the peasant adaptation are bound up with an escape from various modes of regimentation. We have seen that the reconstituted peasantry of Jamaica received strong support from the missionary churches, and such communities still manifest, in some instances, the institutional sponsorship they enjoyed. But peasant settlement otherwise has always been, for the most part, unorganized, unofficial, and sporadic.

This is the basis, then, for supposing that such characteristics as scattered settlement, the intactness of yard and house as a unit, the insistence on separate households for each cohabiting couple, and the circumspection with which the yard of another is approached, are all derivable to some degree from the historic conditions under which the peasantry was formed. The thought that a man's freedom begins inside his own fence has other origins besides the Caribbean experience; but it may have taken on additional significance in terms of that experience. Given the very special circumstances by which the ancestors of today's Caribbean peoples were "modernized," and the extremely early development of capitalist modes of production in the islands, it may be more apposite than it seems to recall Luther's insistence that "good fences make good neighbors."

For much of rural Caribbean life, as we have seen, the house-and-yard complex is much more the domain of women than of men. Cooking, garden care, washing, and especially the care of children are largely in the hands of women; the "lap-baby," "knee-baby" and "yard-baby"[1] stages of childhood typical of the United States South find their ready parallel in the Caribbean rural setting. But the activities of males may also be centered in the yard, even if men frequently gather elsewhere. If the yard contains fighting cocks, beehives, a burying ground, a ceremonial temple; if it is what the Jamaicans call a "balm-yard" (where healing is done; cf. Hogg 1964); if food or liquor is sold as part of the household's activities; if fishing boats are beached or stored there—in all such cases the yard's uses are divided and complementary, sometimes overlapping but more commonly separate. The relationship between yard and house may thus be viewed partly in terms of the conjoined activities of males and females, partly in terms of the different uses to which each, yard and house, is put by members of one or both sexes. The house, particularly among poorer peasants, is not important in it-self as a material representation of the domestic group or family; houses are often moved from one site to another. But the yard is an extension of the house, and land remains immensely important for Caribbean peasants. The yard is an extension of the house, just as the house is the living core of the yard; the outer limits of the yard come to represent the outer "walls" of the house itself, as it were.

None of the similarities among Caribbean peasantries with regard to the house-and-yard pattern should be allowed to conceal impor-tant exceptions, however, or the very considerable variation within a common pattern. Both the exceptions and variations cannot be written off as deviant or idiosyncratic, but require equal attention as variants. Thus, for instance, the use of the yard for minor sub-sistence items is clearly correlated with some particular tradition; but the practice does not—indeed, cannot—persist under circum-

1. In Jamaica, however, the term *yard-child* has a special meaning. A yard-child is the illegitimate child who lives at the house of its father, rather than with its unmarried mother. Those who live with the mother may be called "illegitimate" (Cassidy and Le Page 1967). This curious usage—which may be extremely rare—strikes a different note, for it calls our attention to those children born of cohabiting couples that do not coreside, an ex-tremely important aspect of familial and domestic organization in rural Jamaica, though far less so in Haiti and Puerto Rico. This subject is relevant to present considerations, but cannot be dealt with in this chapter.

stances of intense crowding of houses, aridity, saline soil, etc. The movement of highland migrants to the sugarcane region of the south coast of Puerto Rico was marked by the transfer of the kitchen-garden habit to the new setting, a setting wholly unsuited for it. Over time the pattern was eroded, and it has largely disappeared. But highland migrants to the coast—most of them of peasant origin —share the coastal pattern of separate (neolocal) residence on marriage, a pattern that seems to typify the proletarian population as well as substantial portions of the peasantry. And whereas fences do not typify all coastal proletarian dwellings in Puerto Rico, migrants from the highlands are accustomed to put them up when they can, and to retain them, even if old-time coastal proletarians do not. Thus the picture is in fact complex, and requires more study.

Under the circumstances, is it possible or useful to attribute a common characteristic of the life-styles of three Caribbean peasant peoples to some general aspect of the past, in view of the many differences among them? The answer must be as tentative as the propositions advanced here. There is need for much more careful study of the intimate life-patterns of Caribbean peasantries; the expressed values and attitudes of the people themselves must be recorded. Until that time, such propositions simply enable us to ask more and, it is hoped, better questions. Because the three peasant subcultures discussed here may differ dramatically from those with which other observers are familiar, and because they often appear to differ in some common direction, there is a strong temptation to generalize about them, and about the Caribbean region as a whole. Only careful functional and historical studies, carried out on a comparative basis, afford the means of assessing the forces that have given these peasantries their form, and of weighing the effects of particular forces over time.

# III

# CARIBBEAN
# NATIONHOOD

The fifty or more separate territorial units that make up the Caribbean region—here defined more extensively than before—stand at various points along a continuum from formal political dependency on a foreign power to total political sovereignty, and in various degrees of economic, social, even psychological dependency on their present or former colonial masters. In formal terms, Haiti has been independent since 1804, Santo Domingo (the Dominican Republic) since 1844; other formally sovereign Caribbean insular states and Guyana only achieved their independence since the beginning of the twentieth century. Two of the three Guianas and British Honduras (Belize) remain formally dependent (former British Guiana became independent Guyana in 1966); French Guiana (Cayenne) is a Département of France. Of the Greater Antilles, Cuba has been formally independent since the turn of the century, Jamaica since 1962. Puerto Rico is a "free associated state" of the United States; whatever the debates about its status, it is a North American dependency, though it exercises certain privileges that distinguish it from the United States Virgin Islands, say, or American Samoa.

Within the Lesser Antilles, Trinidad and Tobago (1962) and Barbados (1966) have become independent in recent years; Martinique and Guadeloupe, like French Guiana, are French overseas

Départements. The remainder of the smaller islands, including both the British and North American Virgin Islands, are in one or another sort of colonial relationship to metropolitan powers: the United States, Great Britain, France, and the Netherlands. The details of dependency—and even certain major features—vary, however. Thus, for instance, certain of the British West Indies, such as Dominica and St. Vincent, are classed as "associated states," technically enabling them to sever their ties with the United Kingdom without its approval; and Grenada is now independent.

As a result of the Spanish-American War, the United States became a public colonial power in the Caribbean, and Spain's last possessions in the New World, Cuba and Puerto Rico, were wrested from it by force. Other European powers with Caribbean colonies —Sweden and Denmark—surrendered their possessions at different points in time. Saint Barthélémy was ceded to the French by the Swedes in 1878; Denmark sold its Virgin Islands to the North Americans in 1915, consummating an intention that it had expressed nearly half a century earlier.

Nonetheless, it bears careful notice that the firm presence of three major European colonial powers in the Caribbean persists, and that the United States has never seriously disputed a distribution of power that predated the so-called Monroe Doctrine. Unquestionably, the United States has persistently increased its influence in the region, not least by the armed seizure of Cuba and Puerto Rico and repeated invasions of many supposedly sovereign states. In the case of Cuba and Puerto Rico, North American economic influence had penetrated deeply long before the Spanish-American War, and the United States had recognized that it would dominate these territories eventually, as Spanish power waned; the North Americans were far more concerned to keep Britain out than to get Spain out. The colonial claims of other powers in the region were not disputed, as long as these were not enlarged, and as long as they constituted no threat to what the United States regarded as "stability"—according to its own conceptions—in supposedly sovereign states.

The obverse side of this coin is equally etched. Europe knew that the Caribbean was bound to become a North American sea; the geopolitical facts made this inevitable, as long as the United States continued to flourish. From time to time—for instance, in

1812, and again during the Civil War—some glimmering of an alternative possibility may have been discerned; but the spread of North American influence after 1865 was as certain as anything in world politics could be.

We start, then, with the most obvious of geopolitical facts: the presence of North American power. Most certainly, events since 1959 have again called that power into question; yet Guantánamo is still a North American naval base, and the resolution of the "missile crisis" strongly suggests that some geopolitical facts are more widely accepted than others. The history of the North American presence has been one of repeated intervention in the affairs of sovereign Caribbean states—for instance, Haiti, Cuba, and Santo Domingo—and a careful expansion of economic influence in the colonies of European powers. The touching regard shown by the United States for the claims of other powers has always rested on the implicit assurance that there would be "no trouble"—and whenever "trouble" has appeared likely, the United States has been prepared to act. This is but one of many reasons why the existing position of the United States on Cuba is of such tremendous interest, suggesting as it does at least some change in the philosophy of American policy in the region. One can—indeed, one must—discuss Caribbean political life in terms of the internal character of Caribbean societies; but one may not do so as if the United States did not exist, or as if it existed on the other side of the world.

The second obvious geopolitical fact is, of course, the continuing European presence in the region. Curaçao, Surinam (Dutch Guiana), and several other Caribbean colonies are Dutch; most of the islands in the chain from Puerto Rico to Trinidad are Dutch, English, and French; independent Trinidad and Tobago, Barbados, and Jamaica are part of the British Commonwealth; Martinique and Guadeloupe (and their dependencies) are closely linked with France. The significance of such continuing associations—"dependencies" is more accurate—is many-sided, often subtle; but in the simplest terms, these Caribbean societies stand in intimate relationships of all sorts to specific European countries, and those relationships neither are, nor can be, readily eradicated.

We have already seen that some of the distinctiveness of the Caribbean region as a whole inheres in its lengthy colonial career, its subjection to particular kinds of European domination, its role in the early development of overseas European capitalism—especially as plantation colonies—and its corollary function, within these terms, as an entrepot of people, as well as of ideas and of capital.

Throughout this treatment, stress has been laid on the importance of the past, for the Caribbean past lives so fully—in many cases, so depressingly—in the present. This is the case not only because the islands and the nearby mainland became colonial so very early, but also because they remained so. One need only contrast Ghana and Barbados, to take two random examples, to get some sense of the distinctiveness of the Caribbean region. Ghana, like most of East and West Africa, became a British colony toward the close of the nineteenth century, and won its political independence in the middle of the twentieth. Barbados, like much of the eastern Caribbean, was colonized by Britain in the early seventeenth century, yet remained colonial a decade later than Ghana. Of course, the Greater Antilles had been colonial for nearly 150 years before Barbados was even settled, so that Caribbean colonialism now has nearly five centuries behind it—and much of the region is still colonial, even in formal political terms. In fact, it would be fair to argue that, except for certain "ports of trade" or imperial enclaves—a Macao, a Pondicherry, a Goa, the slave stations along the Guinea Coast, etc.—most European colonialism from the fifteenth to the eighteenth centuries was an American phenomenon. By the time that much of Africa and Asia had become truly colonial—in the sense of *belonging* to the European powers—the Caribbean had been colonial in this very sense for periods of up to 400 years. The only important exception, of course, was Haiti; and this case deserves (and will receive) special attention.

Thus we treat a region that not only knows well the colonial ambiance, and that lives within it in many cases to this day, but that also experienced very early some of the specific effects of being colonial. Those effects accompanied European imperial incursions in the region, beginning on the eve of the "discovery," and they have given to the Caribbean much of its distinctive and particular character. It needs emphasizing that certain kinds of "modernization," "westernization," or "development" can and do occur within the colonial framework; but we must specify what varieties of these processes actually typified the Caribbean case. Though it would be difficult to establish the following assertion in any firmly convincing manner, it appears that the special character of Caribbean societies flows from a series of imperial impositions which, once set in motion, were maintained with remarkable fidelity. That is, the Caribbean tends to be homogeneous and different from much of the rest of the world because processes begun centuries ago have continued to function with little intervening modification, and it is precisely this long-term "social ossification" that makes the region distinctive. This is by no means to say that no changes have occurred—there have, in fact, been numerous and important changes. Nor is it to say that other world regions do not resemble the Caribbean, often because of parallel processes. But the world was not the same in the seventeenth century as it was in the nineteenth, and the effects of certain colonial undertakings on local life were accordingly different. Populations react to new developments in good measure according to what they already are, and perceive; the Caribbean brings to our understanding some harbingers of the future of Africa, say, or Asia, and it can do so precisely because its past has been so consistent with its present.

The objective of the North European conquerors of the Antilles —first in the lesser islands and later in the Greater Antilles—was to create wealth for the metropolises within a mercantilist framework. Spain, which had begun the process in the large islands in 1492, was just as fully committed to this objective, but due to certain internal differences or contradictions within its metropolitan system, and to the lack of an evolved private capitalist sector at the time of the Conquest, it could not achieve this aim; moreover, Spain became obsessed with the American mainlands after 1519, and thereafter its economic interest in the Caribbean region declined sharply. But Spain again came to share this objective after about 1760, as demonstrated by developments in Cuba and Puerto Rico, and by the special legislation of the period, designed to free certain economic forces that had hitherto been held in check. Thus the processes which Spain initiated at the outset—the extirpation of native populations, the importation of slaves, the introduction of export crops and the plantation system, the establishment of closed economic circuits between colony and metropolis, etc.—were again set in motion by it, at a later time. In terms of the processes that concern us here, it is reasonable to say that Spain began and ended Europe's hopes for a New World Mediterranean, since it colonized the islands of the Caribbean almost 300 years before the United States even existed, then surrendered its last possessions there to the upstart offspring of an ancient enemy.

These differences in timing have profoundly affected the character of the Caribbean region, and mark its internal differentiation. The Caribbean is as homogeneous as it is because of the twin forces of imperial imposition and popular response; it is as differentiated as it is because that imposition was multiplex, diffuse, and conflictual, and because each responding population differed in significant degree from every other. Hence it is not surprising that Cuba, which developed in the shadow of North American empire, was viewed by the North Americans as a "ripe fruit" that would fall into their hands once they were in a solid enough position to beat back the Spanish without risking war with the British. The very shape of Cuban political (and economic) development between 1768 and 1899 clearly reflects the presence of North American power—just as events immediately before and after 1959 reflect the specific application of that power. Again, the independence of Haiti in 1804 represents an unexpected (and, in the view of both Europe and the United States, an unforgivable) development. A comparison of these two countries today, other than in terms of climate, geology, the material content of their rural cultures, ethnobotany, etc., would reveal hardly any similarities at all. And yet both of these societies are invincibly Caribbean.

Under the aegis of the plantation system, certain processes were set in motion that deserve special notice, from the point of view of their effects upon the peoples subject to them. We keep in mind that these processes began at different times in different islands; that the metropolitan powers were themselves culturally different, and exercised their imperial prerogatives in different ways; that the ecologies and particular characteristics of the islands varied; that the peoples upon whom these undertakings were imposed were often ethnically diverse; and that the interactions with these peoples occurred at different stages of colonial development. Allowing for these many qualifications, however, certain general points may be made.

We have seen that island populations formed part of a pioneering overseas expansion: generally speaking, it was European capital (at least at first), non-European labor, and Caribbean land that were combined to create new enterprise. Yet the migrant laborers—indentured, contracted, enslaved, or technically free—were generally subjected to considerable restriction of movement; the adaptations of migrant groups to the situations in which they found themselves in the Caribbean region usually had to be worked out under very basic constraints, imposed by the European mode of settlement and colonial administration.

The plantation system itself, as we have seen, dictated in good measure the form that those constraints took. On the whole, plantations were big enterprises for their time, and demanded large quantities of unskilled labor; their work schedules reduced jobs to a simple common denominator, and tended to treat the laborers as interchangeable; capital investment (though highly variable) was usually heavy, and cost accounting commonly made the plantation enterprise a business, its owner a businessman more than a planter.

The effects of the domination of such enterprises were felt throughout the region, wherever men were brought together in large numbers, with more coercion or less, to plant, harvest, and process; such "factories in the field" go back to the sixteenth century in the islands, and have continuously affected not only the economy of the region, but also the character of its communities and of the people in them. To some important degree, it can be hazarded that Caribbean social history gave to its peoples a life-style adapted to the anonymity, depersonalization, and individualization of modern life, but did so when such phenomena were by no means yet recognized for what they were.

Here may well lie some of the important ways in which Caribbean peoples differ from other so-called Third World populations, where rooted identity in village communities, "tribes," extended kinship groupings, religious and ceremonial affiliations, and other preexisting bases of group organization and group stability militate against the individualization of local people. This is by no means to say that comparable processes of individualization and deindividualization are not occurring elsewhere in the "underdeveloped world"; but it does suggest that the experiences of Caribbean people may reveal in substantial measure what may occur in the future elsewhere—though, of course, with significant differences.

It is perhaps in some degree due to these processes, occurring as they did in a colonial, depressed, and rigid context, that the Caribbean region has proved so rich a fount of political leadership. Put another way, the remarkable production of Third World leaders in the Antilles may well be an indication of the maturation of certain processes there that have begun elsewhere only more recently. Active colonialism—the effective conquest of sovereign peoples, or the seizure of the colonies of others—provokes a variety of insights among its victims. Nationalism may take on a wholly new form when a congeries of similar peoples is homogenized by conquest; a colonialism based on active mass production for a world market creates an awareness different from that created by a colonialism based on peasant production of the same commodities; peoples subjected to external domination but neither enslaved nor transplanted will have a consciousness different from that of peoples who have endured all three features of Antillean colonialism. The production of numerous outstanding political thinkers, leaders, and revolutionaries in Caribbean societies is in large part a consequence of the specific forces that have engulfed those societies for so long a period—not only that the Caribbean became colonial at an early time, but also that it has so long remained colonial; not only that its labor force was transplanted, but also that, having been transplanted, it could hardly alter its fate thereafter; not only that the industrial mode was introduced within agriculture, but also that the industrialization of agriculture has persisted and become intensified.

But political leaders in the Caribbean have only rarely worked seriously toward any kind of pan-Caribbean consciousness or identity. Men such as Williams of Trinidad, Castro of Cuba, and the late Norman W. Manley of Jamaica have envisioned such an identity, but it remains in good part a dream of the future. To begin with, it is wholly expectable that the identity of Caribbean peoples should emerge in good part out of the linkage, real or symbolic, between colony or erstwhile colony and metropolis. The lack of commonality among Puerto Ricans, Haitians, and Jamaicans—say

—may be somewhat startling, yet it is completely understandable. In terms of language, metropolitan culture, economic and social ties, and much else, these societies are as different from each other as if they lay in three different seas. The lines of power and of consciousness run from each insular society to the world outside, even in terms of such everyday matters as where imported foods come from, where young people go away to college, where vacations are spent. For ordinary folk in these three societies, the same is true— or even truer. A rural Puerto Rican has little time to worry whether the refrigerator or television set he hopes someday to own is made in the United States, Spain, or Czechoslovakia—his primary concern is to own it. The Puerto Rican slum dweller who migrates in search of a "better" life goes to New York—not to Havana or Madrid. And the Jamaican who migrates would go to London if he could—and now goes to Ottawa or to New York if he can.

Hence the unification of the Caribbean as a region has largely been an intellectual pursuit—or a pursuit of intellectuals—and its unification with the rest of the Third World has occurred in good measure through the specific experiences of its professionals and intellectuals in other colonial regions or in the very capitals of the metropolises. The experiences of the Trinidadian George Padmore in West Africa, of the Martiniquan Frantz Fanon in Algeria, of the Trinidadian Chinese Eugene Chen in China—these underlie the new consciousness of Caribbean intellectuals, as do the experiences of successive generations of British colonial elites in the universities of Great Britain, of French colonial elites in the universities of France, and so on. Involved in such experiences is a secondary recreation of the homeland, based on different removes from the realities of colonial life. It would not be too much to say that some measure of the African nationalism created in the wartime years in Europe's capitals was percolated through a Caribbean vision which, however sophisticated, had never really experienced the Africa it conjured up. And the agonies of such processes are suggested by the return of the Trinidadian novelist V. S. Naipaul to the India of his forebears—revealed as even more foreign to him than the island from which he had come, or the Britain in which he chooses to live.

But at the same time that the various societies of the Caribbean region are economically and psychologically enfeoffed by the imperial powers—even now, when many of them have become politically sovereign—the character and quality of that involvement is highly variable, and it is accompanied to an equally variable extent by feelings of local identity. The peoples of the former (and present) British West Indies do not find a commonality in their British cultural origins, and the struggle to create an alternative identity out of the African past promises to be a long (and perhaps vain) one. The peoples of Martinique and Guadeloupe do not feel that they come from the "same place" (and, of course, they do not). They may equally accept or reject the Gallic portion of their pasts; but they do not find unity in such acceptance or rejection, nor do they yet consider themselves "African" in any significant way. The Haitian people are, again, wholly different; what they may have in common with the peoples of Martinique and Guadeloupe—whether it lie in French civilization or in African civilizations—gives them no deep sense of commonality. If anything, Haitian intellectuals sometimes betray a certain refined pity for their colonial colleagues from the French Antilles; while French Antilleans may unguardedly remark the backwardness and isolation of Haiti. These highly impressionistic assertions do not mean that some common Caribbean identity is entirely lacking, or that it will not grow—quite the contrary. The metropolitan domination of the region has done all that it can to prevent the growth of just such a commonality of spirit and will, and the task of maintaining disunity will certainly become more difficult for the imperial powers, not less. Yet there is no reason to believe that political independence for every component unit in the region will lead automatically to a new kind of regional unity; much more likely is the crystallization—perhaps temporary— of local distinctiveness, and the deeper recognition that nearly five centuries of differentiated colonialism has, indeed, produced as many differences as similarities.

The case of the Hispanic Caribbean is somewhat different. It is worth recalling that the Greater Antilles were entirely Spanish until the British seizure of Jamaica in 1655, and the cession of western Hispaniola to France in 1697. Haiti won its independence in 1804. Cuba and Puerto Rico remained Spanish colonies until the Spanish-American War, whereupon they became North American colonies. Santo Domingo achieved its independence in 1844, and has lain within the sphere of North American power ever since—

and is of course more so today than ever before. Thus the three major territorial units of Spanish background—Santo Domingo, Cuba, and Puerto Rico—substantially traded one master for another at the close of the last century. All have felt the massive effects of North American influence—economic, cultural, political—yet all remain in very significant ways triumphantly Spanish. Together with Haiti, these three countries exhibit characters noticeably different from those of the rest of the Antilles, and this difference deserves comment.

Though it is not possible to substantiate the assertion firmly, it can be argued that the emergence of a national (that is, Caribbean) identity—as opposed to a metropolitan identity—proceeded further in the Hispanic Caribbean than elsewhere in the region. This stabilization of local nationhood arose, in the writer's view, in somewhat different ways in each case; while the Haitian case is again rather different. Spanish colonial administration was probably the most rigid of all the systems imposed on the Caribbean region, and the distinction between islander and European became explicit very early in the colonial career of each Spanish-dominated society. Moreover, the settlement and development of the Spanish possessions in the Greater Antilles took a very different form from that which typified other colonies in the same region. We have seen that Spanish economic interest in the Antilles declined sharply after the conquest of the mainland. In good measure, the Spanish Antilles remained forgotten during the period between the Conquest and the late eighteenth century, and their societies developed with relatively little external pressure from the metropolis. The combination of rigid but somewhat forgetful colonial control, the distinction between homelander and pioneer, the lack of intense economic development, and the presence of empty mountainous interiors all contributed to the growth of cultures in Cuba, eastern (Spanish) Santo Domingo, and Puerto Rico that were not only different from those of the other islands, but also quite similar to each other. In all three cases—but primarily in Cuba and Puerto Rico—it was upon these cultures that Spanish (and later, North American) interests undertook to erect a plantation economy, in the late eighteenth century and thereafter. In the process, all three societies changed, and a resistant response developed—strong in Cuba, much weaker in the other two societies. The commonality of the three cases, as well as the important differences among them, past and present, requires fuller treatment than I can provide here.

The case of Haiti is, in many ways, unique. France's richest colony before the Revolution—and quite possibly the most lucrative colony in modern world history—Saint-Domingue was transformed into a classic plantation society by the French in a period of less than fifty years. But Saint-Domingue's colonial career under France was short-lived (in effect, 1697–1791), and its internal character was different from that of other large Caribbean plantation colonies in one all-important way: the rapid emergence of a prosperous intermediate social category during slavery. The *gens de couleur,* or *affranchis,* of Saint-Domingue were intermediate in physical appearance, civil status, and all else—except their psychological commitment to French civilization and culture. They played an important role in making the Haitian Revolution possible—though they played it wholly unwittingly—since that Revolution was a servile revolt, a slave revolution, made possible by the unwillingness of the French imperium to give up slavery on the one hand, or to meet the demands of the *affranchis* for civil equality on the other.

Herein, we turn seriously for the first time in this portion of the book to the issue of slavery, and to the issue of color. Not that these issues have no relevance to the rest of the Caribbean! But the case of French Saint-Domingue is perhaps of special interest because it can be argued with considerable force that, had it not been for the *affranchis,* the Haitian Revolution might have been delayed long enough to assimilate the colony to the kind of status eventually achieved by the colonial master in Martinique and Guadeloupe. The appearance of a creole population of intermediate physical character is, in the case of Saint-Domingue, less significant than the rapidity with which the *affranchis* rose to positions of power and wealth in that society. This remarkable achievement was possible even though the colonial system in that colony, by its very nature, was counterpoised against the readiness of some French colonials to acknowledge, to free, to educate, and to protect their illegitimate children by slave mothers. Comparable processes occurred everywhere in the region, but they were never so massive or so accelerated. In Saint-Domingue these processes sustained powerful contradictory forces, turned free men of color into important slaveholders and defenders of slavery, and completely undercut the original plantation system ideal, as described in earlier portions of this book.

The revolution destroyed the French planter class, and most of the *affranchis* as well. Haiti was launched upon its independence with what might well have been the most pessimistic prognosis in modern world history: ravaged, hated, and feared by the slaveholding powers (including the United States); chained by economic indemnities to its former colonial master; and almost totally lacking in the skills, diplomatic contacts, and means necessary to build a modern nation. Surely the wonder of the second republic of the Hemisphere is not that it has fared badly, but that it has fared at all. The experience of the Soviet Union yesterday, or of China and Cuba today, are as nothing compared with the hostility, hate, and meanness faced by the Haitian people after 1804. In effect, the world's punishment was near-complete isolation, and the price was paid by the Haitian people rather than its rulers. It is in this sense, *and in this sense only,* that one dares to call the Haitian Revolution premature. It was not premature for the 450,000 slaves who had suffered under one of the most repressive regimes in Caribbean history; and for their ancestors, the Revolution had come far too late.

But there is another side to the Haitian saga, and it has to do with the sense of Haitian identity, of nationhood. We have not yet begun to discuss the internal character of Caribbean societies from the point of view of nation-formation, and that task remains. For the moment, it is worth remarking that Haiti, as indicated earlier, is the one nation outside the Hispanic Caribbean where a sense of national identity, separate from the attachment to an imperial power, grew at an early time. What Haiti lacked was a sufficient engagement with the outside world, and a sufficient development (in economic, political, and other terms) to nourish the feelings born of struggle against the European oppressors. Not until the United States invasion of 1915 were the Haitians compelled to reconsider who, and what, they were, and to begin to escape from the blinding pride that had marked their becoming France's first successfully rebellious colony. Thus the United States invasion of 1915 marked a turning point in the growth of Haitian identity, just as the Haitian Revolution had marked the beginnings of that identity.

In the following chapter on Haiti, the emphasis is not so much on identifying the roots of national identity in any exhaustive way, but on dramatizing some cf the particularities of this case. A final chapter attempts to put the question of Caribbean nationhood in somewhat wider perspective—but, again, very tentatively. Before going on to these chapters an additional general point may be worth making.

Many attempts to describe the character of Caribbean societies have been limited to particular cases, making generalizations very difficult. Other efforts, by treating the region as homogeneous and undifferentiated, have created an image of sameness that reflects poorly the extent to which these societies differ from one another. The chapters which follow doubtless suffer from both of these faults; but some attempt is made in each to move back and forth from the general to the specific, in search of certain shared or distinctive characteristics which may help us to grasp the complexity, if not all of its significance. In doing so, it is necessary to attempt to avoid several common errors of interpretation that have typified much writing of this kind; and one may remark these errors, even if one then proceeds to repeat them:

1. The error of treating the Caribbean region as an undifferentiated sector of what is now popularly called "the Third World." It is a mistake to view Cuba as another Guatemala (or Bolivia as another Cuba), whether the mote is in the eye of the C.I.A. or of North American socialists.

2. The error of treating the rural sectors of these heavily rural and agrarian societies as if they were internally undifferentiated, without attending to differences in wealth, landholding, scale of operations, the presence or absence of wage earning, etc.

3. The error of treating color as some sort of constant in Caribbean societies, without noticing both its different significance in different sectors of the same society, and its even greater differential significance in different Caribbean societies. To treat a man of a certain physical appearance as if that appearance had the same sig-

nificance in Cuba, say, as in Jamaica, is to misperceive one of the most subtle and complex social aspects of Caribbean life.

4. The error of treating class—whether defined by economic or by social criteria—as a unilateral index of the internal composition of Caribbean societies. This is perhaps particularly confusing when imputations about class consciousness are based on the indices alone, without serious fieldwork.

5. The error of treating culture—in the sense of socially acquired patterns of behavior, and their attached symbolic values—in a similarly undifferentiated fashion, as if the culture of some single Caribbean society, such as Cuba or Haiti, were homogeneous.

6. The error of treating the colonial impact as simplex, ignoring as inconsequential the immense time-span, the national imperial differences, the local variety, and the significance of *response* by local peoples. No thinking Caribbean intellectual makes the mistake of supposing that the effects of the colonial period were the same in Cuba and Haiti—or even, for that matter, in Jamaica and Trinidad, both erstwhile colonies of the same power.

These errors are difficult to avoid, and, accordingly, the following chapters may fail more than they succeed. But it is sometimes useful to serve notice on oneself, at least to facilitate more fundamental kinds of criticism by others. The study of Caribbean nationhood is in so early a stage of development that one hopes an outsider can still say something useful. The real work will undoubtedly be done by Caribbean scholars; and that work has already begun.

One final point. In the last chapter of this part of the book, an attempt is made to fit the discussion of nationhood into the theme of the Afro-Caribbean tradition. In order to do so, it is necessary to discuss, among other things, the place of consciousness in the political ideology of Caribbean peoples. Commonality of origin, commonality of social form or of belief, commonality of fate, and a common territory may be thought by some to underlie nationhood —but they emphatically do not equal it. If the test of government is war, as a famous Marxist once remarked, then the test of nationhood is government. Caribbean peoples sail among rocky reefs, and their struggles for independence have often ended in the exchange of one master for another. The place of consciousness is hence immensely important; a genuine Caribbean nationality will demand of its people that they know who they are and accept that knowledge—not that they be alike. But they must think themselves enough alike in fundamental ways so that they are prepared to define themselves and to defend themselves in opposition to others. That likeness, in the Caribbean instance, is consciousness. That it is still largely lacking in many Caribbean societies should hardly surprise us; far more surprising is the extent to which these societies have contributed to the study and exercise of nationalism (sometimes within a Marxist framework), in the face of so dreadful a colonial history.

# 10

## The Case of Haiti

Few countries in modern times have received so bad a press from foreign observers as Haiti. A small, rugged nation, born of an exhausting and destructive revolution, its people poor, disease-ridden, illiterate, and erratically led, independent Haiti gives the impression of having drifted aimlessly (and painfully) for more than a century. Observers from "more developed" lands have had a field day —and still have—bemoaning the evil consequences of a mass of African slaves having turned upon their masters to destroy them and their works. It is still fashionable to allude to Haiti in deploring independence movements, racial desegregation, indigenous political leadership, and economic sovereignty. Yet far too little scholarship has been invested in delineating the national and international forces that have operated to keep Haiti poor and backward; nor has contemporary research led to sufficiently revealing comparisons between the social history of Haiti and that of its neighbors in the region.

Though the societies of the Caribbean Sea differ significantly from one another, many of them share certain general historical experiences. Unlike the colonial areas of the Old World, these islands were largely populated from abroad, and in this regard they resemble the Atlantic lowland areas of mainland America. However, the colonial history of the islands meant that they would long remain the instruments of policy formulated in foreign capitals. Jamaica, Puerto Rico, and other islands were, during most of their postconquest history, the outposts of far-flung colonial empires, and the design of their societies was conditioned by this dependence and subjugation. As "plantation islands," their agriculture, demography, mode of settlement, and social structure were attuned to metropolitan needs and objectives. Unlike most of Africa and Asia, as we have seen, the Antilles lost their native populations almost entirely, owing to enslavement, overwork, disease, and war, early in the era of conquest and settlement. There remained vestiges of native traditions, assimilated into the new, growing cultures of the postconquest period. Native Americans, where they were able to survive, were largely assimilated through interbreeding with Old World migrants.

The newcomers from Europe, Africa, and Asia, bringing with them what they could of their ancestral traditions, were never able to transfer their social heritages as intact bodies of belief and behavior. Hence the cultures of the new Caribbean societies were built up out of elements originating in many different places, while their social forms took shape under conditions of colonial control. The peoples of the islands were able to maintain some continuities with the past, even while the new setting and changing conditions led to the development of certain innovations in society and culture. In a few Caribbean societies, Haiti included, freedom brought with it the opportunity to create a reconstituted peasantry whose ways of life combined elements from the African and American Indian past, as well as considerable European and Asian influence, in new cultural constellations.

Haitian country folk are a particularly good example of such historical processes. The crops Haitian peasants cultivate include the maize, sweet potato, and manioc of the indigenous native American (Taino) people, and other cultigens which had been domesticated in mainland aboriginal America, such as papaya and the avocado; items from Oceania, such as taro and mangoes; sesame and sugarcane, which originated in the Middle East and India; and vegetables from Europe. Their domestic animals, including cattle, swine, and fowls, are nearly all from the Old World. The chief agricultural tools—hoe, billhook, and dibble, which are well adapted to Haiti's shallow topsoil and hilly terrain—may be European or African in origin; the practice of burning off weeds before planting may be African or Native American. Each trait—crop, tool, practice—confronts one with the diverse and entangled culture history of the Haitian people. What is true of agriculture is true of all else. The religion of Haiti is at once two religions: Catholicism *and* vodoun. Yet these two belief systems form a single ideology for most Haitians, particularly in the rural areas and among those of the urban lower classes. The creole language is similarly complex in origin. While its lexicon is predominantly derived from French, parts of its syntax are not of Romance origin. For instance, the use of postpositive nominalizing particles and the absence of gender typify Haitian Creole, and are decidedly not Romance in character. Much the same is true of creole terminology; for example, animal names and anatomical terms are mainly French in origin, but some cooked foods carry names of African provenience.

The "mixing" of various elements of culture from different traditions is, of course, neither uniquely Caribbean nor uniquely Haitian. All cultures are growths, and change by losing and gaining traits and by combining and recombining their substance in new ways. The virtual extirpation of indigenous culture, however, occurred in few areas outside the New World; it was particularly characteristic of the coastal and lowland areas of this hemisphere. Hence, Caribbean culture is almost entirely transplanted and has only recently been synthesized. An additional distinction of the Caribbean area derives from the persistently colonial character of the islands and the effects of this colonialism on local life. Wherever the plantation flourished, large populations of African origin grew out of the original importations of slaves. This was true from the southern United States to Brazil, but was especially marked in the Caribbean islands, where local populations of European extraction were either absent or reduced by the spread of the plantation. Only in Puerto Rico, Cuba, and Santo Domingo, and in some of the smaller islands that developed no plantation system, were substantial proportions of Europeans to be found. In Haiti, the early cultural admixture of Colonial Spanish and Native American was soon swamped by the cultures of Africa. The European cultural component became predominantly French after 1697, when the western third of Hispaniola—today's Haiti—was ceded to France.

But Haitian society did not come to be purely African, in any sense, nor is it more than broadly similar to the other societies of the Caribbean. The kind of society in which the French masters and their African slaves met and mixed, and the subtropical, colonial environment in which they lived, imposed their own conditions for culture growth. What part of the African past the Haitian people could keep alive was limited by the regimen of slave plantation life; what they could borrow or copy from their masters was affected by the social relationships between those who held power and those who had to submit to it. Ultimately, independence meant that the Haitian people could employ what they already knew and practiced under slavery, but in a wholly new social setting.

The substantial isolation that followed independence led to slowed change, both social and cultural, and to the gradual spread of the peasant way of life throughout rural Haiti. From 1804 until the United States occupation in 1915, Haiti was probably less affected by external developments than any other country in the Hemisphere. (In this regard, its social history is noticeably different from that of the other Caribbean islands, some of which, like Puerto Rico and Cuba, were forcibly brought back into the mainstream of world developments in the same century in which Haiti withdrew from it.) The peasantry of Haiti in the nineteenth century was therefore able to develop a traditionalism of unusual firmness and persistence.

However, a high price has been paid for this traditionalism. The economic productivity of the rural cultivator has not risen; it can be argued convincingly that poor land use, erosion, and population growth have meant lower levels of consumption for the common people today than obtained a hundred years earlier. The rural masses, though consisting overwhelmingly of landholders, have been unable to break out of a stagnation that is economic as well as cultural. Such stasis has been based to some extent on the limited responsiveness of the rural folk to outside stimuli. But also important in hampering economic growth is the national institutional system, which took on its characteristic shape after 1804, and under which the rural masses still live. The system is controlled by a numerically small segment of the national population that is markedly distinct from the peasantry itself.

The nature and internal differentiation of this elite needs much more study, though from the information already available it seems clear that the elite is by no means a single, solidary class embracing all but the peasantry. Whatever its structure, however, the relationship between the peasants on the one hand and the real holders of power on the other must be understood if one is to understand Haiti. The peasant is defined in terms of the elite; he is dependent on it and subject to it. This is what is meant when it is said that the peasantry, like the elite, forms only a part-society. Yet without the peasantry, there would be no elite. The elite live by controlling and taxing the rural masses, and find their sustenance and their power in rural productivity. Elite and peasantry, then, are bound together in unequal but interdependent relationships in Haiti, as they are in other less developed societies of a similar kind. In such cases, the political role of the peasantry is usually minor, and few opportunities may arise for the expansion of its political strength. If the peasantry fails to increase its productivity in ways that enable it to control more of its own surpluses, its effect on national political decisions may narrow rather than widen, and this ominous possibility has become a worldwide phenomenon. It becomes more intensified wherever the growth of industry and trade is unaccompanied by parallel growth in peasant productivity or in new and more widely representative national institutions.

That the separateness of peasantry and elite had visible and sociologically important expression in physical type in Haiti was a clear consequence of that nation's history. But the traditional preponderance of light skins at the top of the structure and of dark skins at the base is less important than the domination of the entire structure, and of the institutional means for changing it, by a mere fraction of the national population. It is the *power* of the elite which has mattered; its physical appearance has been a historically derived expression of that power. A balance of politically weak masses against numerically sparse powerholders is common, perhaps particularly so in the "less developed world"; but each such case has certain distinctive characteristics. Thus Haiti's special nature is not simply a consequence of its being a peasant society in which a small group dominates the masses. As a rural, agrarian, unindustrialized, politically sovereign, and quasi-capitalistic country, Haiti shares much with other lands; but in each of these regards its particularity needs to be asserted.

## The Rural Sector

The rurality of Haiti is extreme, not simply because there are no concentrations of population in excess of 25,000, except for the capital, Port-au-Prince, and Cap Haïtien, but also because towns of intermediate size are few in number, and the urban concentrations in the country's two cities are in large part of relatively recent rural origin. Port-au-Prince dominates all the economic, political, and social activities of the Republic. Furthermore, the rural towns have been losing to the capital, not gaining from it. Until the United States occupation, the larger coastal towns, such as Jérémie, Jacmel, and St. Marc, were united economically with one another (and to some extent with the capital) by a lively coastwise shipping system, and the inland towns were tributary to those of the coast. During the occupation, the growth of inland transport strengthened the interior towns while coastwise shipping declined, but the capital grew even more important as the sole economic center of the Republic. Since the 1940s, the rapid deterioration of the road system has enfeebled both the inland and the coastal towns; only Port-au-Prince has remained strong.

The dominion of Port-au-Prince is firm, and there is no focus of power in the countryside that can counteract it. The few foreign enterprises in Haiti that base themselves outside the capital city use local port facilities (e.g., Miragoâne for Reynolds Aluminum, Cap Haïtien for the sisal plantations of the north) and do not affect the development of interior transport. The only passable roads in the Republic run from Les Cayes in the south to the capital, and from Cap Haïtien in the north to the capital. Transport simply symbolizes the power that Port-au-Prince wields, since the same circumstances characterize all other national institutional arrangements. Thus Haiti is an extreme example of urban domination, even though its urban population is a small fraction of the national total. The consequence has been to cut off most of the rural folk from the apparatus that effects national decisions and shapes national policy. Haiti's national legislature, never important in limiting presidential power, is less so today than ever; at best, it only represented the interests of the provincial towns as opposed to the capital, never the interests of the mass of country people.

The local military and judicial officials possess the formal authority vested in them by the state, and their power is very considerable. Few local people would dare challenge their decisions, and the devices for appeal against arbitrary exercises of authority are few. Admittedly, at the lowest local level the *chef de section*—who is traditionally appointed by the captain of the military in the *commune* center and is himself a peasant—is subject to some restraint by local inhabitants. Jean Comhaire (1955: 620–24) has argued that the people of a community are capable of insisting on democratic procedure in matters requiring decision by local authorities; more recent writers (Lahav 1973) are less persuaded. In any case, such decisions have little or nothing to do with larger issues. The peasantry cannot directly make its wishes felt in national politics; and national politics are conducted almost without reference to the aspirations of the rural masses. It is precisely the separateness of local life from the mainstream of national decision-making that demonstrates the political impotence of the peasantry.

### Haitian Agriculture

Haiti's agrarian nature cannot be expressed simply by characterizing it as a rural and peasant country. Haiti does not have a "land problem," as that term is conventionally applied to Latin America. It does, it is true, suffer from a land shortage, inasmuch as too little land worked at too low a level of productivity must feed too many mouths. But a very substantial proportion of the rural masses owns land, or has regular access to it. Although most land is held in small plots and without clear title, persons who own no land or who lack land to work are proportionally fewer in Haiti than in any other Caribbean country, and perhaps fewer than in any country in Latin America.

Haitian agriculture, with the exception of a very few large-scale plantations in sisal and sugarcane, is adapted to small plots on hilly land which are worked with intensive labor and few tools.

Compared with agricultural production, especially of cash crops, in most mainland Latin American countries, productivity is low. The peasantry is conservative in its agricultural practices, and not ready to make changes unless these entail minimal risk and the gains to be realized from them are clearly demonstrable (Erasmus 1952: 20–26). Peasants cultivate with three goals in mind: cash income from world-market commodities (for instance, coffee, sisal, vetiver); cash income from items produced for local sale and consumption; and subsistence. While they are heavily involved in production for sale, their crop choices and land-use patterns rest fundamentally on a subsistence orientation. All grow a substantial part of their own food, especially sorghum, maize, sweet potatoes, taro, manioc, malanga (*Xanthosoma sagittifolium* Schott), plantains and bananas, fruits and vegetables, and rice where possible.

The land is invested with considerable affect: gods live in it; it is the ultimate security against privation; family members are buried in it; food and wealth come from it; and it is good in itself, even if not cultivated. While such attitudes are common in peasant societies, Haiti's history of slavery, and the acquisition of access to land through revolution, has perhaps given a special symbolic significance to landowning. Land is valued above all else and is sometimes held "uneconomically"—that is, even when the capital and labor power to work it are lacking.

The history of land acquisition by the peasants after 1804 is particularly striking. The French plantations lay in ruins, never to recover, while early authoritarian attempts to restore the prerevolutionary economy under native Haitian leadership soon failed. In the course of a century, the Haitian people laid claim to their own soil, while population growth and the adoption of the French tradition of equal inheritance progressively reduced the average size of holdings. In spite of some plantation development after the United States occupation, most agricultural land in Haiti is still in small holdings, and "land reform" in the conventional sense—the breakup of large estates and the creation of a class of small landholders—is practically irrelevant to Haiti's needs.

As today's peasantry cultivates, so its womenfolk market. Nearly three hundred marketplaces serve the towns and countryside, some of them patronized by thousands of buyers and sellers on market days. By participating in active small-scale trade, the wives of the peasants contribute in a limited way to national economic efficiency and growth. As in all heavily agrarian economies marked by poor storage facilities, inferior transportation, and low consumer incomes, there is considerable substitution of labor for capital, and there are high losses through spoilage. Except in the marketing of export commodities, much time is consumed in bargaining, in carrying, and in hand-processing of various sorts. But these activities are the accompaniments, not causes, of the general low level of development of the Haitian economy.

The economic challenges posed by agriculture on the one hand, and by marketing on the other, differ significantly. Since these activities are carried out predominantly along the lines of a sexual division of labor, the Haitian countryman farmers and their marketing wives apparently differ to some extent even in their attitudes. Foreign observers of the nineteenth century commented regularly on the industry and energy of Haitian rural women, stressing their predominance in trade. Some writers have attributed this division of labor to the West African tradition, since women are the marketers, men the farmers, in many African societies. Leyburn has pointed out (1941) that the militarism and political unrest that have marked Haiti during so much of its history were serious impediments to peaceful trade. Women came to predominate in marketing, he theorizes, because men did what they could to avoid the towns, since they were often impressed into roving army bands if they traveled far from home. Whatever the historical causes may be, it has been established that the women of Haiti's countryside carry on most of the internal trade, while their husbands do most of the farming. These women, on the whole, know more about the towns, mix more easily with outsiders, and show more intrepidity in trade than the men do in agriculture. Yet it has been demonstrated that their energy and daring can do little to increase the level of productive activity since, for most of them, the scale of enterprise is so modest and the available economic opportunities so restricted.

## Craft Technology

Haiti's lack of large factories, mechanized production, and a skilled industrial labor force means that the country is underindustrialized by any of the usual measures. But Haitians do produce by traditional craft methods a surprisingly large number of the articles they need for daily life. In the countryside many persons are engaged, mostly on a part-time basis, in craft activities and home industries that have their roots in the prerevolutionary era. Leatherworkers operating small, crude tanneries still flourish. Charcoalburners and operators of small lime kilns that produce building material are found in every village. Smiths make and repair simple tools, working with forges of archaic design. Combs are made from cows' horns and tortoiseshell, buttons from bone; carrying-bags, fish traps, and a wide variety of baskets from withes, bamboo strips, and grasses; wooden bowls, mortars and pestles, tool handles, and spoons from local woods; dippers, pots, and candelabras from tin cans; and sandals from tires and inner tubes. Sawyers cut and dress timber; cabinetmakers still manufacture simple furniture of traditional design from the fast-disappearing tropical woods; many women, working either with the simplest sorts of sewing machines or by hand, make clothing for domestic use and for sale. Along the coasts there are dugout makers, shipbuilders, and sail- and seine-makers. Simple mattresses, fabricated from local grasses, are sold in every large marketplace, as are crude ceramic wares made by local potters. At the start of the twentieth century, Italian immigrants brought a sturdy tradition of cobbling to Haiti, which has been destroyed only recently by the flood of American imported shoes; until recently, *vitièlo,* derived from the name of the most famous of those Italian cobblers, was a colloquial term for shoe.

One of the striking features of Haiti's craft tradition has been its relative stability since the Revolution. It was under slavery that Haitian crafts first became "westernized," employing what were then standard French practices, adjusted to local colonial conditions, probably with some modifying features from the African past. It was before the Revolution that the Haitian people stabilized their consumer tastes, agricultural and craft standards, and work procedures. Such preferences and standards were worked out primarily in terms of the demands of the plantation regime itself; but even the most repressive social system leaves some opportunity for acculturation. Today's sugar-making shops and rural rum distilleries employ techniques centuries old and little modified. Housebuilding and woodworking techniques in the countryside have remained substantially unchanged from an earlier era. The prevailing quality of Haitian rural and craft industry, then, is one of great stability and conservatism.

At the same time, however, major events since the Revolution have left their imprint on Haiti's crafts. Hardly a roadside village in Haiti, for instance, lacks an automobile mechanic, even though these men are mostly self-educated and work with hardly any tools. Their skills became part of Haitian culture in this century and are often of a simple order no longer typical of more developed areas. Tire tubes, for instance, are "vulcanized" by the use of an ingenious device made from a board and an oil piston, kerosene providing the heat to make the seal; this technique, along with the sewing of damaged truck tires, was almost certainly introduced and diffused by the United States Marines.

But these quaint additions do not alter the fact that shop and factory industry are nearly absent, and extractive industry virtually nonexistent. Haiti's one alumina extraction enterprise, foreign-owned, operates irregularly. There is but one flour mill, and that is also foreign-owned. One or two textile mills and sugar factories, established with foreign capital, still function, as do a modern cement factory and a few other small plants established during and after the 1950s. These industries, scanty as they are, are of great importance to Haiti, since they represent substantial investment, hold out the promise of reduced dependence on imports in significant categories, and contribute to the beginnings of an industrial proletariat. However, they involve only a tiny fraction of the national labor force, and they have not proved entirely successful. As a result, Haiti lacks any reserve of labor acquainted with modern industry, even though many of its people, both urban and rural, work at tasks that might be considered more industrial than agricultural.

## Haitian Sovereignty

More important for the present discussion, the minor developments in Haitian industry have not led to an expanded market and have not resulted in any firm increase in productivity. Industrial growth of the kind that has occurred in the nations of Western

Europe—or for that matter in Mexico or Argentina—is entirely lacking. The exceptional nature of its absence becomes, perhaps, especially clear if Haiti is compared with such neighbors as Jamaica or Puerto Rico. These countries—one now independent, the other a North American dependency—have both gained substantial increments from the investment activities of outsiders; Haiti has experienced few such increments, even as a result of the United States occupation. Its citizens cannot readily migrate anywhere (though very many have, indeed, migrated since the late 1950s, especially to New York City); its educational system cannot prepare its people adequately for the modern world; its civil service has proved neither stable nor reliable; its labor force has had limited experience with the factory system; and even two decades of active North American intervention did nothing to remake the economic and political structure of the nation. Some of the "development projects" foisted in more recent years on the people of a presumably sovereign Haiti by foreigners working with Haitian officials would not have been tolerated by the colonial representatives of any foreign power obligated to report its activities before the United Nations Trusteeship Council. In view of these things, one is tempted to maintain that Haiti has suffered from all the disadvantages of political sovereignty while enjoying none of its advantages.

Unlike those colonial dependencies that were able, over time, to develop internal political ideologies through which to face the pressures imposed by the colonial powers, Haiti was tested by hardly any challenge but its own lack of development. In this sense only can it be said that the freedom Haiti won in an incredible revolution against powerful enemies came to be a punishment. The struggle brought the Haitian people justified admiration in many quarters, but its price was isolation and virtual abandonment.

It was the United States occupation that gave the lie to Haitian sovereignty, and to the invincibility of its people. The Haitian "bandits," variously estimated to have numbered from 2,000 to 6,000, who died in what is probably best described as a war of resistance against the North Americans, were barely able to maintain even a brief local conflict against several well-armed companies of United States Marines.

The occupation gave Haiti little in return for its denial of the claim of national sovereignty. The public works and reform programs instituted by the United States, designed to give the country roads, schools, hospitals, a disciplined army, a "legitimate" government, and a schooled civil service, hardly endured longer than the occupation itself, since nothing was done to transform the social and economic base of the society. Within a decade of the North American withdrawal, the gleaming superstructure created by the occupation had begun to decay. The major effect of North American tenure seems to have been to make possible a more effective centralization of political control than had been operative in Haiti at any time since the fall of the Christophe regime; and the consequences of this change are still being felt.

## Haiti's Quasi-Capitalism

Small-scale rural cultivators are famous for their tendency to confine their consumption to culturally conventionalized levels— that is, to live as their predecessors lived before them. Though they may be involved in commercial activities that go beyond the limits of the communities in which they live, they seek to limit that involvement and to maintain their cash expenditures at a low level. It is in this sense that Haiti might be called a "quasi-capitalistic" society. To put it another way, small-scale peasants of the Haitian sort do not seek to change or expand their production, so much as to conserve a way of life set by tradition. This ideology of resistance to social and cultural change is a major obstacle to development; yet it would be rash to damn it without reflection. In Haiti, for instance, there has long been pressure on the rural masses to expand their production of coffee, the major export crop. However, this pressure has not been accompanied by any serious grass-roots attempt to improve coffee production or to offer genuine incentives to the cultivators. The peasantry has been given no assurance that an intensified effort will lead to gains *for them;* and they are unprepared to make such an effort merely because they are told that it will be good for Haiti. In fact, it is likely that the production of subsistence crops has expanded in recent years at the expense of coffee production, for the peasant knows that he can at least be sure of eating and selling locally such crops as maize, sorghum, and yams, regardless of what may happen in Port-au-Prince or to the world coffee market. This view, combined with the yeoman's painfully acquired distrust of those who prate at length concerning his welfare, has meant a virtual stagnation of agricultural export production, even though the entire nation quite literally depends on such production in order to progress.

The effect of this rural resistance is to create an apparent very sharp difference in goals between countryman and bureaucrat. It is perfectly understandable that the countryman should fail to see the connection between heightened coffee production and a higher level of public welfare and social services. His experiences hardly persuade him that it is his surplus-producing capacity that underlies the kind and quality of public institutions with which the state provides him. Nor do his efforts to produce more and better cash crops translate themselves directly into higher consumption, since he has no say in setting their price. Under the circumstances, it is naive to suppose that "education" alone can make the peasant's role in economic or political development a more active one. The disposition of rural people to maintain a habitual level of consumption, rather than to believe that an increase in productivity will result in an expansion of goods and services, is difficult to change; and the quasi-capitalistic quality of Haitian agricultural production is merely one example of that disposition. Consequently, economic change depends partly on changes in attitudes toward production. Until an agricultural extension service worth of the name is able to make a massive attack on the shortcomings of peasant cultivation in Haiti, rural economic conservatism will perpetuate itself. And agricultural extension will not be able to wage a battle for change— even when its services become adequate in quality and quantity —unless the promises of greater economic rewards or of improved social services for the rural masses are occasionally honored.

The term *quasi-capitalistic* has much less force, of course, when applied to urban enterprise. But there, too, economic activity has a curiously static quality as compared to enterprise in more developed countries. The Port-au-Prince capitalist is famous for "playing it safe." Import-export trade, tourist hotels, guided tours, gas stations, and urban slum real estate are more rewarding spheres of investment than shops or commercial farms. A small but economically important Syrian-Lebanese-Italian group limits its local investment accordingly, as do most of those "native" Haitians who carry on their businesses in the towns and cities. Traditionally, elite families have consisted largely of siblings who interlock their economic activities with government, the military, agricultural processing and exporting, the importation of consumer goods, tourist-connected services, and the professions. A slum block, a post in the ministry of tourism, a colonelcy, or a tour agency are likely to be lucrative investments; but few indeed are the Haitians who will take the risks needed to develop highly productive farms, to produce improved strains of poultry, or to introduce industrial skills through a modern machine shop. And the reasons for this lack of verve and daring are easy to find. Governmental instability, excessive taxation, lack of access to markets, and the absence of adequate roads, communications facilities, small-scale credit facilities, and the like mean that exceptional intrepidity is required to establish such enterprises. In striking contrast, foreign captains of industry—mainly from the United States—who invest in Haiti expect (and often get) governmental guarantees of a sort they could not dream of in their own countries; in this regard, they merely conform to Haitian expectations and exploit Haitian defenselessness.

## Background to the Present

Haiti's problems, then, are not simply those that face any less developed country, vast though such problems may be. Nor is it reasonable to lay Haiti's problems at the feet of the nation's present rulers. The structure of the national economy has not changed significantly during the past twenty-five years—except that boom years provided a temporary aura of prosperity—regardless of the philosophy or popularity of the regime in power. If nothing else, recent Haitian history demonstrates that United States aid—which averaged 12½ million dollars yearly over more than a decade—has produced no enduring improvements of any kind. It further demonstrates that, shockingly poor as the country is, Haiti emphatically does not depend on such aid. As of 1964, for instance, the regime in power was operating on a monthly budget of $1,800,000, only $400,000 of which went for purposes other than salaries. In other words, the ministries do little more than perpetuate themselves. The peasantry, living at a near-subsistence level, continues to produce most of what it needs, while restricting its cash expenditures even more severely than in the past. The risks—in terms, say, of public health—of running a society under these circumstances are great—but there is as yet no reason to suppose that a regime of the Haitian sort will be destroyed (or improved) by a show of popular unrest originating in the countryside. Difficult as life is for the Haitian countryman—and no people in Latin America lives more poorly—the real pinch is probably being experienced more acutely among the city folk than among their rural fellow citizens. It matters politically, therefore, who these city folk are and what they do.

To begin with, it bears noting that the Duvalier regime precipitated a massive exodus of middle-class, elite, and professional people to Africa, Canada, the United States, and Europe, and that this outward flow has continued for more than fifteen years. Moreover, it seems quite certain that the overwhelming majority of these emigrants do not have (or no longer have) any intention of returning to Haiti. The accession of Jean-Claude Duvalier to the presidency, accompanied by declarations of welcome to potential returnees, has as yet produced no substantial change in disposition on the part of the thousands of doctors, dentists, army officers, journalists, businessmen, and functionaries who left Haiti, and who still see little advantage in reestablishing themselves there, homesick though they may be. The new regime has undoubtedly opened up some "room at the top," though doubtless less than that represented by the exodus of the emigrants.

Second, it is significant that we lack any truly persuasive study or report on the replacement of lighter-skinned by darker-skinned Haitians in the upper sectors, even though many observers seem convinced that such a process was an important feature of the Duvalier epoch. On the one hand, it may be possible to argue that Duvalierist politics led to a significant average "darkening" of the upper sectors. But on the other, such an assertion does not rule out the very good possibility that mulatto and near-white members of the elite are still very important in the Haitian social system. That this may, indeed, be the case can seem more persuasive when it is remembered that North Americans inevitably interpret any event relating to "race" in Haiti in North American terms. Thus, for instance, a recent monograph on Haiti repeatedly refers to the late President Duvalier and his politics in terms of black power—terminology which wholly misrepresents the Haitian situation. To suppose that Duvalierism sought or achieved a gross elimination of persons of one shade in order to replace them with persons of another shade is to turn on its head the whole apparatus of power that has typified Haitian society since the Revolution. The linkage between color and power in Haitian history is real and specific; but color means *perceived* color, and perception of "race" in a society such as Haiti's is profoundly influenced by factors (such as class, education, one's own perceived color, and speech) that do not logically precede the perception of color but accompany it. Color, in other words, is not salient in Haiti in the way it is in a truly racist society like the United States. So important is this difference that we must set aside for the moment our discussion of the present character of the elite in order to note how some of Haiti's most intelligent observers have viewed its past.

In 1941, James Leyburn's immensely influential *The Haitian People* set forth in considerable detail the separation of masses and elite in Haiti. The book's central thesis was that Haitian society was sharply divided into two segments, and that the national institutional structure had maintained that division without significant alteration throughout the entire course of Haiti's history as a sovereign nation. At the base of the society was the rural agricultural sector, making up as much as 95 percent of the population; at the top was the elite, which dominated the governmental apparatus and all national institutions. These two segments of the society differed, in Leyburn's view, in all important regards: level of income, source of income, education, language, religion, social forms, values, attitudes, and so on. By carefully describing the history of Haitian society from the eve of the Revolution until the midst of the United States occupation, Leyburn revealed both the origin of this vast social cleavage and the various means employed to perpetuate it. Leyburn was so impressed by the gap which separated peasantry and elite that he chose to label these social segments castes rather than classes. Members of the elite earned their livings as rentiers, merchants, professionals, and in government, and never engaged in manual labor of any sort. They were predominantly urban in residence; their sons attended private lower schools, and then went on to higher education, usually abroad. The elite were French-speaking, although they also spoke Creole, Haiti's national language. Their religion was Catholicism; their forms of marriage and domestic organization were "legitimate" and "Western." The members of the elite viewed themselves as a kind of aristocracy, and felt little commonality with the yeomen.

In sharp contrast, the peasantry was rural, poor, worked the land, was illiterate, spoke Creole only, believed in *vodoun* rather than in orthodox Catholicism, usually practiced common-law marriages and was sometimes polygamous, and remained substantially isolated from the outer world. Finally, and importantly—though the significance of this factor was already changing—the elite differed from the rural sector in that the countryman was predominantly negroid in phenotype, while members of the elite were prevailingly lighter-skinned.

Leyburn noted that the United States occupation affected the nature and rigidity of the barriers separating the peasantry from the elite. For instance, he called attention to the fact that the presidents elected during the United States occupation were light-skinned members of the elite. It seemed almost inevitable that, when the North Americans sought men through whom to prosecute their plans for "stabilizing" Haiti, they would settle on educated and worldly politicians, men who were sufficiently trained and sufficiently pliant for the task. That these men were predominantly light-skinned was a corollary aspect of Haitian social history. In this way, Washington played some part in reinforcing and expanding elite power; and herein lies a paradox with which the author of *The Haitian People* had to deal. While the elite had been able to maintain their wealth and power in Haiti for nearly a century, the presidential succession before the United States occupation had largely been one of military chieftains, principally dark-skinned men from the north of the Republic. From the last quarter of the nineteenth century until the occupation, Haiti's presidents were almost all dark-skinned northern provincial leaders who seized power by invading Port-au-Prince and deposing their predecessors. Michel Oreste, who ruled for nine months in 1913–14, was the first civilian president in Haiti's history; and Sudre Dartiguenave (1915–22), the North Americans' choice, was the first president since 1879 who was both a southerner and light-skinned.

Hence, in describing the separation between the elite and the yeomanry, Leyburn found it essential to take note of the traditional special role of the military, with its particular overtones of color. Here was one institutional feature of Haitian society which was not directly dominated by the elite, and through which nonelite folk were able to attain special power. But in Haiti's case it is significant that the army itself was not firmly institutionalized; regional warlords, rather than a centralized officer corps, made the decisions. Leyburn cites Auguste Magloire, who enumerated *sixty-nine* "important" revolutions between 1806 and 1879; had this enumeration been extended, it would have been considerably larger. Of Haiti's twenty-four chief executives between 1807 and 1915, only eight were in office for a period equal to their elected terms, and seventeen were deposed by revolution. Before the United States occupation, then, the continuing power of the elite could be seen as somewhat distinct from the succession of nonelite generals who seized office over the years.

The financing of the many revolutions was usually provided by foreign merchants, bent upon installing a government that would grant them special concessions (Munro 1964: 326–31). The United States occupation ended this doleful succession of regimes, and by throwing its weight to the elite, by suppressing military activity in the countryside, and by reforming the army, the United States gave a new meaning to the separation of the elite from the yeomanry. Leyburn's interpretation was consistent with these events; yet some Haitian scholars have differed with his analysis.

In a lengthy review article, the dean of Haitian historians, Dr. Jean Price-Mars (1942: 1–50), questioned the applicability of the term *caste* to the social groupings of Haitian society. He noted that Haitian law after the Revolution never legitimized any distinction on grounds of physical type, unlike such societies as that of the United States—that, in fact, the very basis of Haitian polity was the absence of such distinctions. Furthermore, Leyburn's interpretation was vitiated by the fact that the elite and the rural masses were not entirely distinctive physically. In some parts of rural Haiti, particularly in the southern peninsula, there were many light-skinned people; and many individuals who qualified as members of the elite on all other counts were very dark in appearance. The fact that being "Negro" or "white" in Haiti was viewed as a matter of degree, rather than of kind, complicated by other criteria of social position employed in drawing distinctions, had important implications for the way social barriers had operated in that country.

In this regard, Haiti is aligned with most of Latin America, in contradistinction to the United States, where many persons believe that "one drop of Negro blood" (*sic*) makes a person a "Negro." The failure of North Americans to distinguish between sociological and genetic categories of physical type has led to considerable confusion in their dealings with Latin America and in their understanding of Latin American societies. North American race prejudice at its most extreme sees color as the primary basis for social ranking, and no individual accomplishment (for instance, in terms of economic or intellectual success) can overshadow the inferior status unalterably bestowed by certain physical traits. Haitian—and generally all Latin American—social distinctions do not rest solely on considerations of physical type; a black skin does not "doom" an individual if his attainments make him otherwise the equal of his lighter-skinned fellow citizens. Hence, it might be argued that the term *caste* would be more appropriate when applied to the Negro people of the United States (regardless of phenotype, and including those "Negroes" who are *sociologically* identified with the Negro people, even if their physical appearance is dramatically Caucasian) than to the peoples of Latin America. This distinction is, of course, particularly important in assessing the Duvalierist political philosophy and its impact on present-day Haitian society, if one is to avoid a simplistic racist explanation of a phenomenon far more subtle and complex than it seems.

Leyburn did not contend that all the effects of the United States occupation were in the direction of increasing the gap between the elite and the peasantry. For instance, he called attention to one unanticipated (but inevitable) result of the occupation: the large number of children whose fathers were United States Marines and whose mothers were members of the Haitian rural masses. In contributing to the growth of the physically intermediate population of Haiti, especially among rural folk, the occupation may have resulted in some bridging of the gap between peasantry and elite. Much more important, by its contributions to a broadening of the educational system, the occupation enabled talented black-skinned youths to improve themselves and to acquire new aspirations.

Economic and political developments in Haiti through the period 1941–57 contributed grounds for the modification of Leyburn's interpretation. Though Leyburn predicted that "for the present and near future it is safe to say that there will be no more black non-elite presidents" (1941: 101), subsequent events soon proved him wrong. In January 1946, the government of elite member Élie Lescot fell under military pressure; a junta facilitated the installation of Dumarsais Estimé as president. Estimé was a dark-skinned man from the countryside (the village of Verrettes, near St. Marc, in west-central Haiti) who had received a good education, served as a minister in the Vincent cabinet, and, as a deputy, married a lighter-skinned woman whose family's membership in the elite was secure. Estimé might well be considered a self-made member of the elite, but he was not born into it, and his accession to power was the political expression of new possibilities in Haitian life.

The changes Estimé's regime symbolized were rooted in the intellectual resistance to the United States occupation and in the search for a Haitian identity in the face of that occupation. The strangely easy domination that the United States wielded over Haitian society for several decades, and the relatively unexploitative but patronizing administration it provided, ended forever a fantasy that had gripped Haitian intellectuals for more than a century. The world of 1804, when a bloodied but defiant Haiti could bar by force of arms Napoleon's dreams of a New World empire (and thereby assist indirectly the territorial expansion of a still weak United States), had vanished. The time when a Pétion could aid, protect, and politically influence a sick and tired Simon Bolívar was long gone. The world had changed, while Haiti, the Haitians learned under their North American masters, had nearly stood still. For almost a century, Haiti's elite had taken justifiable pride in their ancestors' triumph over Napoleonic France, while remaining enthralled by French culture. This strange ambivalence would no longer do. In effect, the United States occupation compelled Haiti's scholars to rediscover what it meant to be Haitian.

As the writing of Jean Price-Mars (1928) expressed that identity culturally, so the regime of Dumarsais Estimé began to express it politically. For the first time, Africa, and not simply France, became an important part of the nationalist dialogue. The creole language began to be studied in its own right, and a program was launched to end illiteracy through education in Creole. Folkloristic studies, emphasizing the African component of Haitian rural life, especially as expressed in religion, came into vogue. Haitians began to explore their own society as a synthesis that was as much African as it was French—and as a synthesis, rather than as a mechanical alignment of two distinct traditions. The term *authentique* was employed to express what was "truly Haitian," and Haiti itself was viewed as a unique and original blending of two pasts. Under Estimé, rural folk of promise—and they were, in the nature of things, predominantly dark-skinned—were given greater opportunities, especially to be educated and to enter government service. These developments took place at a time when Haiti's economic situation was relatively good, and Estimé enjoyed a measure of popular support rare in Haiti's history.

Furthermore, it was during the Estimé regime that Haitian cultural life reached some sort of climax. In the 1920s, young Haitian intellectuals had been deeply shaken by the United States occupation and had begun to formulate their own answers to the questions it raised. Not only did Africa come into view as the wellspring of much that was Haitian, but Haiti's status as an occupied though once-sovereign power dramatized the need for a social and political philosophy that dovetailed with hemispheric and international realities. At that time, French intellectual currents also figured importantly in Haitian political thinking, both because the intellectuals of the French Antilles were inspired by Haitian history and interested in Haiti, and because those islands and Haiti shared a curious affinity in their "Gallo-African" cultures. Anticolonial and Marxist points of view were espoused by a few Haitians, but these perspectives were complicated by changing attitudes toward French culture in all of its expressions, and by a new feeling of kinship for the peoples and cultures of Africa.

The variety of views expressed by Haitian intellectuals was colored by differences no more subtle than those characteristic of the intellectuals of any other country in the Caribbean region—even though North American observers unfortunately persist in treating such differences as politically irrelevant. Some continued to embrace French culture and to reject "Africanism," deploring only the North American presence in Haiti. Others embodied their views in a staunchly Haitian nationalism and, as they began to view their country in a new light, invested the Haitian folk with an unrealistically romantic picturesqueness. Still others fastened upon the African theme with special intensity, and thereby gave a strong racist tinge to their nationalism.

Not surprisingly, perhaps, anthropology came to be seen as an important means for giving Haitians an accurate—that is, an "inside"—picture of their own society; a number of young ethnologists, mainly self-trained, began to publish works on Haitian culture. Soon anthropology was pressed into a political mold, anticipating similar developments in other "colonial" countries. The first novels purporting to deal with the common people, though sometimes tinged with idealized preconceptions of rural society, were published; and an impressive number of competent young poets devoted themselves to aesthetic explorations of the Haitian spirit. Haitian cultural and intellectual life, in short, was taken up with the rediscovery of Haiti and its peoples.

But the Estimé regime did not produce changes in the economic structure of Haitian society of an importance proportionate to the national cultural renascence. Even those modifications in the class structure for which Estimé is sometimes given credit might not have occurred, were it not for educational reforms that had begun in the 1920s and the beneficial effects of Haiti's prosperity in the mid-1940s. What Estimé could do was to open the ranks of an inefficiently large bureaucracy to able, if sometimes inadequately trained, newcomers of poor rural antecedents.

At the same time, as the Comhaire-Sylvains have suggested (1959: 179–89), a qualitatively different class group was beginning to emerge in Port-au-Prince during Estimé's presidency, and the presence of this group suggests that new economic forces were feebly stirring. The members of this new group enjoyed regular urban employment, were mostly literate and legally married, and harbored strong ambitions for the education of their children. Such persons certainly did not belong to the elite, and their behavior (as, for instance, their preference for speaking Creole rather than French) showed it; yet they were not part of the rural masses, nor merely the urban poor. The significance of this new group for the Leyburn "caste" theory of the elite is considerable. Even today, if such persons were to lapse into poverty, their ideology would continue to matter politically. Estimé's regime also loosed new political trends, since it gave some encouragement to labor unions at first, and it undertook the construction of urban low-cost housing. We are unable to measure the long-term effects of these changes, but their reality raises some questions about the rigidity that, according to Leyburn's analysis, characterized the Haitian social structure.

In May 1950, after an unsuccessful bid to extend his term of office illegally, Estimé's regime was toppled, again by a military junta. Paul Magloire came to power, the first military figure to become chief executive since the start of the United States occupation. Magloire moderated considerably the intensity of Haitian politics, and his administration was not marked by so sharp an ideological concern with the relative roles of elite and countryman. Times were good, and levels of life, both in the countryside and in the capital, were probably as high as they had been at any time in Haitian history. Certain economic gains were made in the tourist industry, in the processing of essential oils, in extractive operations (bauxite, copper), and in the manufacture of a few essential commodities. The official attitude toward private investment, even by foreigners, was unusually benign; and coffee, the big export crop, enjoyed a boom. Again, however, little effect could be seen in the basic economic structure. By 1956–57, when the Magloire regime was toppled, the era of apparent prosperity had come to an end.

## The Rise of Duvalier

Magloire's tenure ended as had his predecessor's; after a vain attempt to prolong his regime by forcing through new laws, he was brought down by the army. Magloire was succeeded by a series of juntas. The politics of the brief interregnum preceding the accession of François Duvalier were complicated by the rival claims of four presidential aspirants. These four men represented significantly different trends in Haitian thinking and were supported by different social groups. Duvalier, trained as a doctor of medicine and for long an enthusiastic amateur ethnologist, had been a political enemy of the Magloire regime and, as a former minister in the Estimé cabinet, saw himself as Estimé's ideological descendant. Duvalier appears to have become the army's choice, ostensibly because he was considered "manageable"; at any rate, it was Duvalier who finally emerged as president, ending the uneasy interim which followed Magloire's ejection.

The Duvalier regime, which endured until the president's death and has been perpetuated in the person of his son, added something qualitatively different to the Haitian political scene. North American interpretations of the regime's character and significance have probably exaggerated and misread the significance of the factor of color, as we suggested earlier, and have tended to reflect the sharp shifts in official North American policy toward Duvalier that have marked the past fifteen years. Thus, for instance, it was fashionable—particularly during the period of official North American disenchantment between the withdrawal of the United States Marine Corps mission and the death of Duvalier *père*—to assume that there was no popular support for the regime in Haiti. Yet such an assumption is probably wrong or, at best, unproved.

In an admittedly unrepresentative "survey" conducted secretly in Haiti around 1969–70, sixteen informants out of fifty claimed to be better-off than they had been five or ten years before; when asked how they would react if outside invaders of Haiti came near their communities, twenty-one said they would do nothing, twenty-seven said they would oppose the invaders, and no one said he would support them (Rotberg and Clague 1971). Though the authors honestly admit the extreme tentativeness of their survey, conducted under very difficult conditions, they do not seem to grasp that the results, however qualified, in no sense constitute an indictment of the Duvalier regime. In fact, one can at best only argue that Haiti's peasantry has been largely *irrelevant* to national political decisions (which has almost always been true since the Revolution) —but this is not the same as arguing that the Duvalier regime is unpopular with most of the peasantry. For many Haitians, Duvalier's political philosophy—or at least its expression in public state-ments—shared much with that of Dumarsais Estimé. That opposi-tion groups were united in their dislike of the regime and in their attacks upon its excesses does not prove that it was unpopular with the Haitian masses.

At the same time, the readiness of the Duvalierists to use force probably exceeds that of any Haitian government in a century. Such excesses, moreover, run counter to certain local traditions of po-litical behavior—for instance, the willingness to take familial con-nections into account when political revenge is carried out, the distaste for violence committed against women and adolescents re-garded as political enemies, and so on. The most important break with tradition, however, was the gradual undermining of the army as a political force—a force created in the first instance during the United States occupation.

In carrying out its plans, the Duvalier government played more creatively on inconsistencies in United States policy than had any preceding regime. While using United States military and economic power to consolidate itself, it employed a posture of anti–North American hostility in its search for internal sources of political support. It capitalized most strikingly on the deterioration of the United States design in the Caribbean region, both to exact con-cessions and to enhance an international image of itself as a stal-wart "democratic" regime. That Duvalier was able to stay in power in spite of internal disaffection, sometimes hostile United States propaganda, a dire economic situation, personal ill-health, and other woes indicates that he made certain correct assessments, not only of Haiti's potentialities for domination, but also of the contradictori-ness of United States policy, a contradictoriness that had been re-vealed with special clarity during the occupation.

The United States occupation had brought about no lasting changes in Haitian society in spite of nineteen years of continuous and autocratic rule. Many rather small-scale benefits were provided, particularly in the areas of health and health services, communica-tions, government administration, education, and transport (though the use of corvée labor on the roads led to serious abuses and stimu-lated sanguinary guerrilla warfare). But most significant, the United States institutionalized the army and the police. It dissolved the ragged bands of political mercenaries and transformed the officer-ridden army into a small, well-trained, and well-organized force. This force's eventual firm control of weaponry, communications, and transport ended the era of presidential succession by invasion, turned the army into the major locus of nonelectoral, president-making power, and may have ended forever the possibility of an agrarian revolt against the central authority. Another political effect of the occupation was the importance it imparted to the United States ambassador, whose political opinions thereafter would affect significantly the transmission of power at the top of the Haitian governmental system. The Duvalier regime took full account of the consequences of United States interest; and its leaders were able to observe the operation of that interest in the political events occurring between the fall of the Lescot government and the present, including the period following Duvalier's demise.

In the view of one acute observer, President Duvalier had to cope with three other loci of political strength in addition to the army and the United States ambassador in order to consolidate his power. The business community, located for the most part in Port-au-Prince, had strongly supported Déjoie's candidacy during the interregnum; its leaders were mainly members of the elite, and many had strong business and personal ties with North Americans and other foreign groups. Among the families of these leaders were Swiss, German, and French nationals, and some Syrians and Lebanese who held United States citizenship. The business community had played a part in the downfall of the Magloire regime, and business strikes were a typical political instrument for putting pressure on presidential incumbents. The clergy—particularly the Catholic clergy—also exerted political influence. Duvalier, while well aware of this, also attended to the importance of vodoun (or, as it is more commonly called, "voodoo") and to the influence wielded by its cult leaders, particularly in the countryside and among the urban poor. Finally, the president understood the strength of such groups as the university students, the small but politically aware labor unions, and certain professional associations, whose political effectiveness could be felt particularly in times of crisis. The Duvalier regime displayed intelligence as well as ruthlessness in dealing with these diverse centers of political strength and potential opposition.

The official request for a United States Marine Corps mission to "train" the Haitian Army was a brilliant political move by Duvalier, apparently designed to serve several objectives simultaneously. It is entirely correct that the renewed presence of the Marines in Haiti created considerable rancor in some circles, but it also strengthened Duvalier's hand in his dealings with all sources of internal opposition. To some extent it seems to have reassured the business community; and it reduced, rather than increased, the maneuverability of the United States in developing a "corrective" or "restraining" policy toward the Duvalier regime. Perhaps most important, it helped Duvalier to build a praetorian guard to counterbalance the power of the army.

Members of the Duvalier security police wore no official uniform (though blue denim pants and felt hats were affected). They carried out acts of terrorism against groups and individuals, and seriously weakened the policing function and prestige of the regular army. Some calculations put their operating costs at as high as one-third of the governmental budget. Though small groups of the security police were distributed throughout the country, the central administration stayed in the capital; urban units were dispatched to the countryside if any show of internal political resistance was sensed. This paramilitary, secret-police organization proved particularly useful for carrying out the murders of outspoken political opponents and for crushing draconically any threat of strikes in the Port-au-Prince business community.

Little is known of the antecedents of its members. While it was customary among the elite to describe these myrmidons as "trash," some of them were literate, had some education, vaunted a political ideology—a kind of nationalist-negritude mystique, with strong fascistic elements—and differed dramatically from the ragged, illiterate followers of the warlords of pre-1915 Haiti. In fact, the lieutenants of the security police were a direct, if somewhat deformed, product of the Estimé regime, a decade of structurally unsound prosperity, a culturally nationalistic ideology, and, more remotely, of the United States occupation itself. Since the 1960s this paramilitary force has begun to lose its importance.

With regard to the army, Duvalier followed a policy of careful attrition. While the United States Marine Corps "mission" was (probably unwittingly) serving to immobilize opposition, Duvalier began to change the character of the army general staff. In the course of less than seven years, he completely revamped the leadership of the army five times; this process not only kept the colonels off-balance but allowed the president to reward loyal younger followers—principally those with dark skins, it is said—with rapid promotions.

The relationship between the Duvalier regime and the Catholic clergy was one of increasing antagonism. At times, members of the clergy stood high in the regime, two having even served as members of the cabinet; but not the slightest church resistance was tolerated. The low point in Duvalier-church relations was the interruption of a Mass by an armed TTM (Tonton Macoute—literally, "Uncle [with the] Basket"—i.e., the bogeyman, in folktales) unit in downtown Port-au-Prince; later, leading members of the hierarchy were summarily ejected from the country, and the Jesuit order was banned. As the regime consolidated itself, church power waned significantly, both in the capital and in the countryside. Duvalier was not so unwise as to aim at the complete elimination of the church, but sought instead to "nationalize" the clergy on some mutually agreeable basis. He succeeded admirably.

Except among the elite, Catholicism in Haiti has always been colored by vodoun elements. The Haitian people as a whole do not differentiate what is "really Catholic" from what is not Catholic in their religious practices; in this regard Haitian countrymen resemble folk practitioners of Catholicism anywhere. By its misreading of the piety of the Haitian masses, and its unceasing hostility to vodoun—quite different from the church's policy in the so-called Indian countries of Latin America—the church failed to secure its influence over the Haitian people. In contrast, Duvalier's understanding of Haitian religious sociology proved superior, and was consistent with the *authentique* ideology of the 1940s, though doubtless much more extreme in its implications.

Finally, the Duvalier regime invaded such institutions as the National University and the trade unions, and maintains close surveillance over any individuals it regards as politically suspicious. Loyalty oaths are required at the university; a public press no longer exists; the unions, never strong, are now entirely powerless. But it should be clear from our description of the Duvalier regime that repression is not so much the key to Duvalier power as the means for perpetuating that power under Haitian conditions. The key to Duvalier power is to be found in the structure of Haitian society, in the social history of the past two decades, and in the policy of the United States, weakened by its inescapable preference for "stability" over "radicalism." In his own way, President Duvalier was as radical as he could be; but he was no Castro. It is now an open secret that Haiti's support for the sanctions against Cuba approved at Punta del Este was matched by economic concessions from the United States; that the Marines, knowingly or not, immobilized anti-Duvalier opposition in a period when its supporters could be picked off, driven into exile, or jailed; that the official Duvalier offer of Môle of St. Nicholas to the United States as a substitute for Guantánamo, though irrelevant, was warmly reassuring to some North American political thinkers; and that Duvalier, while he employed considerable "blackmail diplomacy" in his dealings with the United States and fell out of favor was still considered "reliable" at the time of his death.

Labeling Duvalierism "pathological" or "paranoid" contributes nothing to our understanding. The roots of this ideology are to be found in Haiti, not elsewhere; its supporters are the product of Haitian times and ideas; and their social identity, while not entirely clear, would probably pose few enigmas if enough data were available. In fact, the tendency to employ a complex theoretical terminology in describing societies of the Haitian sort, and to interpret political events in such societies as pathological variants upon an otherwise humdrum theme, has become a substitute for serious research into the history, economy, and social structure of such societies. Haiti is not, in fact, enigmatic; but our ignorance—concealed by the reference to "enigmas"—is not reduced by speaking of a black Honduras, a New World Liberia, a Caribbean Madagascar, or an Emperor Jones writ large. Haiti's enigmas, if any, will be solved by those who patiently acquire enough knowledge of its past and present to make sense of what has been happening there, not by those who substitute neologisms and bad imagery for research.

## The "Enigma" of the Peasantry

We have stressed throughout that our present inability to "explain" Haiti originates in good measure in our ignorance of the character and attitudes of the Haitian peasantry, who make up perhaps eight-tenths or more of the national population. Seemingly mute and invisible, apparently powerless, the peasantry of Haiti remind one of Marx's famous dictum that peasants possess organization only in the sense that the potatoes in a sack of potatoes are organized. Clearly, the Haitian peasantry plays little, if any, role in contemporary Haitian politics—though it is also clear that a century ago the national government was responsive to the peasantry in ways that it has not been since, and that peasant political resistance did, in fact, once manifest itself, even though it no longer does.

We are not in a position to explain fully how, and why, peasant political activity ended; but we are able to hypothesize that the North American occupation precluded, perhaps forever, the possibility of armed revolt in the countryside. It was, in fact, a series of such revolts, the fear of foreign (German) intervention, the defaulting on loans to North American banks, and "excesses" of violence in Port-au-Prince that led to United States intervention in 1915. The reform of the army, the weakening of port cities, the growth of the national bureaucracy, and the improvement of internal transportation during the occupation probably contributed to a reduction of peasant potential for political action. At the same time, the failure of the North Americans to develop industry or enterprise along modern (in this case, imperialistic) lines limited the growth of a proletariat, either urban or rural, and slowed political developments of the sort that followed United States meddling in other Caribbean islands, such as Cuba. Thus North American hegemony, typified by imperialistic maneuvers that were carried out almost absentmindedly, may have played a bigger role than has generally been recognized in the isolation of the Haitian peasantry from national decision-making.

The relationship between the peasantry and the national government is, in any case, mediated through only the skimpiest of institutional arrangements. The peasantry is economically under the thumb of large-scale export merchants, many of them foreign, as well as subordinate to the lowest-level politico-military officials, the *chefs de section*. But the main source of peasant "apathy"—a word which conceals more than it describes—is the lack within the peasant substructure itself of institutional development around which political response could be organized. It would not be justified to assume that this has always been the case in Haiti; on at least three important occasions in the last century, peasant unrest produced serious political repercussions (Moral 1961), and the national government seems to have become more rather than less remote from such unrest since North American influence began to be directly expressed in Haitian politics. In this connection, it bears noting that the North Americans provided what was probably the first truly effective and complete military occupation at rifle-point in Haitian history, an occupation which lasted nearly two decades. The shoring up of elite power in the capital, the strengthening of bureaucratic control, the establishment of effective communications and transportation, and the institutionalization of the army under the occupation—all easily justified as positive developmental undertakings—may have had as their corollary effect the final decline of peasant political expression, even on the level of jacqueries. At any rate, we have no evidence that the peasantry has made its voice heard in any significant fashion since the start of the North American occupation in 1915.

And yet the occupation did too little to create other kinds of social groupings that might have played a role in Haitian political development. We have seen that it changed the urban class structure in some ways. But the very limited plantation and industrial development that accompanied North American influence has not led to the appearance of either a rural (plantation) proletariat or of other socioeconomic groups that might have supplied political leadership. The class structure of Haiti reflects the country's history—perhaps too well. Even North American imperialism has failed to produce response groupings that could effect structural changes in the society, which remains very much a rural peasant world, overseen by city bureaucrats. Assertions that the Haitian people are not politically reactive because their child training ill-fits them to resist; because they are "accustomed to adjusting their expectations downward as their capabilities decline" (Rotberg and Clague 1971); or because they are "so inured to misery that even prolonged decline across the subsistence threshold does not usually occasion the violence inherent in a society with stable or improving conditions" (ibid.) reflect our ignorance of what Haitians actually feel and think. Such pessimistic assertions also reflect a lack of knowledge of the Haitian past. In fact, all assertions, pessimistic and otherwise, about peasant inclinations and capacities in Haiti make little sense in view of the paucity of serious studies of the Haitian masses. Until such studies can be made, Haiti's apparent enigmas will remain just that, no matter how many terms are invented to "explain" them.

Since we are seeking here to describe an Afro-Caribbean *nation,* at least a brief final word on race and culture is called for. Throughout this work, we have argued that the Afro-Caribbean world must be defined in terms of culture, rather than physical type—since physical type, like all else, has always been interpreted according to culturally defined modes of perception. Nowhere in the Caribbean do the categories "white" and "nonwhite" exist with the same rigidity of definition as in North America, not even in those Caribbean societies in which "race" is still psychologically and politically significant, and in which its perception is accompanied by considerable consciousness of difference. Rather, each Afro-Caribbean society has its own conceptions of where lines should be (or can be) drawn, its own code of social relations, its own system of group assortment—each derived from the distinctive social history of the society in question. Haiti is assuredly no exception; North American ideas about what "color" someone is are far more hindrance than help in understanding Haiti. Moreover, Haiti is not—and cannot be—racist in the United States fashion, in part because its genetic composition requires a very different drawing of lines.

Culturally, we know, Haiti has drawn heavily on the African past, as it has on the European (particularly the French) past. The dividedness of its traditions was dramatized during the American occupation, and we have seen how this conflict was expressed in the social, aesthetic, and intellectual life of the Haitian upper classes. The fact that the North American occupying forces reflected accurately (and perhaps exaggeratedly) the racist tone of North

American life (Schmidt 1971) only intensified the intellectual polarization of Haitian intellectuals. Herskovits (1937) and, following him, Bourguignon (1952, 1969) and Bastide (1969) conceptualized this conflict as "socialized ambivalence," the expression in some very fundamental fashion of the schism of origin that is said to have typified Haitian social history. Their formulation, however, can be useful only if its differential expression in different segments of Haitian society is clearly understood.

Though it can be argued that there is a high degree of cultural homogeneity *of some kind* throughout the class structure of Haitian society (expressed, it seems to this observer, in such cultural items as the universal use of Creole, certain foods, and dance forms, and in a number of common values, often subtly disguised), the cultural differences that divide the society are at least as important as its common cultural qualities. It is simply not possible at this time to establish scientifically the degree of coherence or noncoherence of a total society along these lines—though one may hazard the assertion that Haiti is, in many ways, a more integrated society *culturally* than is, say, Jamaica or Trinidad. If one makes reference to the social structure rather than to cultural forms, then Haiti reveals itself to be deeply divided—though doubtless not so sharply as Leyburn contended thirty-five years ago. The dividedness of Haiti expresses itself, we have argued here, more in the lack of any institutional framework uniting the peasantry with other social sectors than in the importance of perceived differences in color or culture. At its most extreme, the Haitian variant on Africanism in culture, represented by the Price-Mars and Roumain "movements" of three decades ago, neither sought to deny nor ignored the European, Amerindian, and other civilizational components in the Haitian past. One might even argue to the contrary—for the problem of Haitian cultural identity was far more one of reassessing the European contributions to Haitian civilization than of replacing them with African contributions which were commonly recognized to have functioned at least as importantly in Haitian life.

The role of the African past in Haiti's culture remains highly significant, but that past is rarely perceived consciously as such. That is, unlike most Afro-Caribbean peoples, Haitians are *at home with their own culture;* the ideological overtones that accompany being black, of African origin, with a glorious revolutionary past and a rather somber present, only reveal themselves fully in Haiti to those who are *not* Haitian. On some highly significant ideological and symbolic level, every Haitian—sired by the New World's second and bloodiest revolution, specter of a world to come long before Marx put pen to paper—has a special meaning for nonwhite peoples everywhere. But it is immensely important to keep in mind that few Haitians are likely to perceive themselves in this way. Everyday life has a way of becoming prosaic, no matter how glorious the historic past. Surely it is this difference in perspective which explains some of the rather surrealistic discussions that have taken place between Haitians and Afro-American militants in recent years. It is difficult to explain effectively, to those who have not enjoyed the experience, how *relaxing* it is to be black in your own country, when your own country has been (at least nominally) free for a century, and when your own country is yours, largely because hardly anyone in it is white. However much weight one assigns color differences within Haiti, the fact remains that those differences express themselves primarily in terms of class, and do not normally transcend class considerations. In other words, the line that divides Haitians most is *not* a color line.

Thus, Haiti, the New World's second nation and the world's first "black republic" (as many observers delight in calling it), is far more saliently black in the eyes of outsiders (of any complexion) than in its own. Its lack of national coherence, moreover, cannot fairly be attributed to matters of color, important though these are. Instead, as we have suggested here, Haiti still lacks—or has come to lack—the unifying institutional forms through which class and other conflicts could be mediated, settled, or fought out; and this lack is related both to the nation's isolation during the first century of its existence and to the effects of North American colonial rule not long thereafter. It is not enough to bemoan the feebleness of institutional forms, or to indulge in sanctimonious discussions of the dreary succession of petty tyrannies that have plagued the Haitian people. The will of the people is not heard and, given Haiti's present structure, need not be heard by those who are content to rule. This is the real problem of Haiti.

# 11

# Caribbean Nationhood: An Anthropological Perspective

The Caribbean islands and, to a lesser extent, the mainland colonies nearby, constitute the oldest sphere of Western overseas colonial enterprise. One both begins and ends a characterization of the Afro-Caribbean element in these lands by noting this; whereas most of Africa became colonial only well into the nineteenth century, the Caribbean had by that time been colonial for several hundred years. Moreover, the colonialism of the Caribbean differed significantly from all the other early adventures of the West in the world outside Europe. The exploitation of the Caribbean area involved the earliest experiments in transoceanic capitalism and "development" undertaken by the Western powers. These experiments entailed, among other things, the virtual extirpation of native populations through war, disease, and maltreatment; within a scant half-century after initial contact, many of the islands had been scourged of their aboriginal peoples. Those who were not killed off, or who had not died off, were assimilated genetically (and, in good part, culturally) by their conquerors.

Thus the Caribbean area was "modernized" and "westernized"—the terms are used advisedly—before any other major geographical region outside continental Europe, both by the elimination of indigenous populations and by the introduction of advanced forms of large-scale capitalistic agricultural undertakings. Since these processes required the substitution of new labor forces for those destroyed by conquest, it followed that Caribbean development, even before 1550, would depend very heavily upon the importation of migrant peoples. As is well known, the major source of such migrants was Africa; but Europe contributed a significant (if varying) proportion of the Caribbean colonizing stream; and, at a later point, Asia, too, was to add its share to the peopling, and to the cultural diversity, of Caribbean societies.

European colonialism has taken many forms since 1492. These forms have varied according to the objectives of the colonizing powers, the stages of development of the European societies at the helm, the responses of subjugated peoples to the European thrust, and the interrelations—political, economic, and military—among competing metropolises. In portions of Southeast Asia, for instance, the Europeans were often satisfied initially with the creation of ports of trade—beachheads on the peripheries of declining archaic states —through which prized commodities and some measure of political influence might be funneled. French and Portuguese footholds in India, and British claims in South China and Malaya, are illustrative. By contrast, in the highlands of Latin America, the Spaniards conquered massive populations of sedentary agriculturalists, decapitating the monolithic political structures superimposed upon thousands of villages and substituting themselves for their royal predecessors. Again, in societies such as Australia, the Europeans came as conquerors *and* settlers, effectively creating new Western societal transplants. In the United States north and west, and in Canada, yet another pattern developed—gradual expansion, concomitant with a steady herding of native populations into human corrals. These examples of variant modes of conquest, destruction, administration, and "development" varied also according to the stage of national growth of the colonial power itself; no one would seriously suppose that Leopold's Belgium, the Spain of Charles V, the Britain of Clive, Rhodes, or Raffles, or the United States of Teddy Roosevelt were engaged in structurally homologous colonial adventures, merely because all were colonial powers bending other lands and peoples to their will.

The modes of development likewise varied, and vary. In the Congo, quasi-military supervision of the gathering of forest products was a central mode of "development." In mineral-rich areas, mines were developed early; in Peru, for instance, perhaps as many as 40,000 semiproletarianized Quechua-speaking Native Americans were engaged in full-time mining by the 1600s. In West Africa, British colonialism led to a relatively late burgeoning of prosperous peasant producer groups who retained their land in freehold and entered vigorously into world currents of trade and economic growth. Thus, just as one may contrast time-periods, the reactions of colonial peoples, and the differing national policies of the colonial powers, so also may one contrast the particular forms of colonial undertakings.

In the case of the Caribbean area, the early growth of the plantation system defined in remarkably persistent ways the major means for integrating the colonies with their metropolises. By combining forced labor with "free" enterprise, this system created a new economic blend, which Eric Williams once described as combining the vices of both feudalism and capitalism with the virtues of neither. The plantation economy depended on the subtropical lowland ecology of the Caribbean islands and the littorals of their sea, an ecology admirably fitted to the mass production of food staples for the exploding urban consumer markets of Western Europe. Plantation business was, from the outset, big business, and a type of undertaking often strongly supported by the monarchs of Europe. It fitted well with the mercantilist thesis that colonies existed solely to benefit their metropolises, and ought not to compete productively with their "motherlands." As a form of organization, the plantation was a political and social institution, and not merely an economic one. As a system, it has dominated the Caribbean area for centuries, though changing its scale and its form in line with other developments.

Hence the primary defining features of Caribbean colonial history are ancientness; the rapid and thorough elimination of native peoples and their replacement with migrant stocks; the early inauguration of a curiously industrial and "modern" system of agricultural capitalism based on forced labor; and the "fit" of these features with the particular physiographic characteristics of the area itself. The islands were to become a major sphere of European interest and a principal center of investment and capital accumulation. Politically, militarily, and economically, they would remain important for centuries before relinquishing their primacy to other colonial areas.

But these facts say little concerning the internal organization of the Caribbean colonies, or their social and cultural characteristics. Here, at least five points may be touched on. To begin with, it is essential to recognize the differences in culture distinguishing British, French, Dutch, Spanish, and other colonial traditions. Among these traditions we must notice particularly that of the North Americans who, despite their late entry into the area as an active, occupying colonial power, have played a disproportionate role in Caribbean life in the last century. In the peopling and administration of the Caribbean, as elsewhere, these differences among the colonial powers affected the nature and spread of imperial cultural and social forms in new settings. Second, we must note that the host or newcomer populations also differed in each case, and that the development of local cultures hinged importantly on the nature of the encounter and interaction of colonial populations of differing origins and heritages with their colonial masters. Third, we must take account of important differences in scale, ecology, and resources in various Caribbean locales, and the effects of these differences on the growth through time of distinctiveness and similarity among different island societies. Fourth, we must recognize that colonial economic and political objectives differed not only from metropolis to metropolis, but also for the same metropolis in different colonies and at different time-periods. Thus, for instance, Spanish policy toward the plantation system in Cuba was very different in the seventeenth century from what it became in the late eighteenth century; while French policy toward the plantation system in its colonies differed markedly from that of the British. Finally, it must be remembered that, despite significant variations, the basic requirements of the plantation system produced certain uniformities among all Caribbean plantation colonies. These uniformities inhered primarily in the need to create and to maintain a large, disciplined labor force to carry out plantation tasks. Since the availability of land during early settlement in the islands made it impossible to create an agricultural wage-earning population, slavery, rather than wages, served to gear men to production.

Throughout the Caribbean, the planter groups were predominantly European in origin, and in many Caribbean colonies they remained European in identity and ideology as well. Relationships between a minority of European owners and a majority of African slaves were mediated through social structures marked by considerable rigidity. Typically, the class groupings of a colonial society such as seventeenth-century Jamaica or eighteenth-century Saint-Domingue began in the form of a bipolar structure, as broad at the base as it was narrow at the top. Planter-slave relationships—and later, owner-worker relationships—functioned locally in terms of plantation organization itself.

Caribbean societies waxed and waned in terms of the plantation economy, and the history of the area is replete with cases demonstrating that smallholders and yeoman farmers were driven out by large estates and slave labor wherever and whenever the plantation spread. Hence, plantation areas were characteristically denuded of yeoman settlements; while small farms and slave plantations might indeed coexist, as was the case during certain periods in Puerto Rico and Jamaica, they typically occupied different ecological zones, participated in different market relationships, and, for the most part, did not interdigitate socially. However, this separation of the peasant and plantation sectors was only one of numerous factors contributing to the lack of integral community growth in plantation regions. Slave populations, subject to an arbitrary discipline that included coercive limitation of opportunities of all kinds, were constantly cut off from institutional affiliations on the local (i.e., the community) level. Lacking purchasing power or freedom of economic choice, they could not attract traders or service-purveyors. Barred from educational facilities, frequently excluded from religious training, powerless politically, the slave populations were effectively isolated from most of the institutional forces that might have articulated plantation settlements as *communities*. In effect, then—and with the qualification that local conditions did, in fact, vary greatly—the plantation settlement was like a manorial estate in its isolation, though its population was enslaved rather than enfeoffed, and transplanted rather than native, and production was directed toward capitalist-market, rather than feudal, objectives.

Though slaves sometimes were enabled to acquire special skills, these were mostly of the sorts required primarily for plantation operation. There was only minimal opportunity for the local growth of artisan groups or intermediate classes of skilled workers, and little or no opportunity for the in-migration of craftsmen, doctors, ministers, storekeepers, teachers, and all of those other specialists and service-renderers associated with the growth of differentiated and articulated rural communities. Hence, the plantation system itself served to limit sharply the development of community institutions or social groups other than those minimally required for the effective economic operation of the plantations. Viewed from the vantage point of Western European history, then, the plantation system was a species of sociological blight, because of its extreme rigidity of operation, the deep chasm it created and sought to maintain between its major population components, and the enforced feebleness of secondary institutions within its sphere.

In general, neither the masters nor the slaves were able to transplant to the New World intact ancestral cultures or social forms. The cultural heritages of the migrants were not composed of lists of particular traits, and what survived in the New World expectably changed in form and function in the new settings. But most important, neither masters nor slaves could transfer more than certain elements of their preexistent organization to the plantation. Expectably, much of the transferred cultural content lost its former symbolic meaning, in the absence of a traditional social-structural framework.

## The Plantation System and Social Organization

The plantation system, then, as it evolved in the New World colonies, did not help to create either a replica of the European societies that gave rise to it or of the African societies from which its laboring masses were drawn. Lacking the social structure and the continuity of the European and African settings, the inhabitants of the plantation colonies were compelled to modify, to innovate, and to synthesize both social forms and cultural content in order to function. The masters and the slaves differed in culture, in physical type, and in access to power, and relationships between the two groups were of stringently limited and highly specific sorts. Among these were ties based on economic and sexual interdependence. The economic relationships were created within the context of plantation organization—though affected in each case by the diverse laws of colonial administration and by the differences between legal codes and actual practices. The sexual relationships were an outgrowth of, among other things, the monopoly of power wielded by the planters and the powerlessness of the slaves. Only rarely was a migrant group composed of equal numbers of men and women, and the relative scarcity of women under the traditional plantation system in most Caribbean settings, combined with the sharp difference in access to power between planters and slaves, led to special sexual and domestic conditions. Characteristically, the planter groups were able to regard slave populations as sexual reservoirs, and to recruit sexual partners from the slave groups almost at will. Though the actual practices varied widely from colony to colony—and even, to some extent, from plantation to plantation—three such patterns of sexual recruitment can be discerned.

The masters might acquire temporary sexual partners of slave status and different culture, while aspiring eventually to return to Europe and marry legitimately there; or they might maintain mistresses though married to European wives who accompanied them in their Caribbean exile; or, finally, they might marry wives who were originally of slave status and different culture, and legitimize their children (if legally permitted), as part of their settling down to stay in the Caribbean colony. All three patterns occurred in the Caribbean area; each suggests a somewhat different answer to the problems of creolization, and of the emergence of national cultures in the area. First (and, admittedly, in very simplistic terms), where women of almost inalterable inferior status were in effect the transient sexual objects of men who had neither wives nor any intention of settling in the Caribbean, creole culture had to take on its character in the virtual absence of any European culture model, however distorted. Second, where women of inferior status became the mistresses of Europeans living in legitimized unions with wives of European background, the beginnings of creole culture might create an invidious contrast to the European past, seen as the inaccessible patrimony of fathers who refused to acknowledge their social roles as models for their own sons. Third, where the masters came to stay, legitimized their unions with women of inferior status, and recognized their *own* alienation from the European past, creole culture in the most genuine, innovative sense could really begin to take shape.

These three statements of organizational alternatives are, of course, mere caricatures of historical reality; they do not represent any total underlying differences between particular colonies or colonial traditions, nor were they equally available alternatives for the planters in any given colony. Yet it may be hypothesized that the social histories of different plantation colonies were affected by the presence or absence of these patterns at different times and in different degrees, and that such patterns in turn influenced the establishment and consolidation of local creole cultures. If the slave and planter groups had remained genetically separated, social groupings intermediate in physical type and with status identities potentially different from those of either the masters or the slaves could not have appeared, and the original bipolar social structures could have been maintained indefinitely and in relative purity. But genetic intermixture did in fact occur in all of the plantation colonies, and problems of status assignment and allocation for the newly arising social groups inevitably followed. Members of such intermediate groupings might be systematically defined as slave in status if they were the offspring of slave mothers, particularly if the relationships between the planters and female slaves could not or would not be legitimized in any way. Under such conditions, the intermediate groupings might be assigned a status qualitatively different from that of either the slaves or the planters. Yet at times such intermediate groupings might be able to achieve statuses much closer to those of the planter groups than to those of the slaves, as happened in French Saint-Domingue. Especially important in this connection would be the presence or absence of institutional arrangements permitting the legitimation of sexual unions between masters and slaves and, perhaps, the accompanying legitimation of children born of such unions.

The changing status and identity of intermediate groupings in the plantation colonies is an extremely important aspect of the rise of Caribbean creole societies. Research on the history of such groupings does not yet enable us to make orderly comparisons between, say, such societies as French Saint-Domingue (until 1791), Cuba (until 1886), and Jamaica (until 1838), in order to analyze in detail the relationship between the nature of creole societies with plantations and slavery, and the position of intermediate groupings within them. But even the little we know suggests that the history of patterns of mating and domestic organization, and of the legal arrangements accompanying the growth of intermediate social segments, may bear significant implications for the understanding of the growth of nationhood in the Caribbean area. Of course, the differences between the legal frameworks for dealing with slaves and freedmen, on the one hand, and the actual, de facto patterns of behavior, on the other, must be specified very carefully. What we already know certainly demonstrates that, in some cases, institutional protections were sometimes honored only in the breach, while in other cases, the treatment of slaves and of freedmen might be milder in some regards than the laws themselves.

The subordinate social groups in the Caribbean colonies might view the metropolis as the guarantor of their rights, as was true of the *affranchis* of French Saint-Domingue, or as the ultimate source of their oppression, as was true of the slaves of Cuba. The superordinate social groups in these colonies might view the metropolis as the homeland, as was true of the planters of Jamaica, or as the creator of invidious distinctions between nationals and Creoles, as was true of the planters of Cuba. In other words, we are dealing with several sets of simultaneous variables: the civil codes affecting slaves and freedmen; the real social relationships among these groups and the planters; and the position of the metropolis, vis-à-vis the civil rights of Creoles of differing group membership within each colony. In order to see the consequences of these intersecting variables in any particular colony, we need to know the extent to which the planter group there could develop a genuine sense of identification with the colony itself, rather than remaining essentially in exile. On admittedly very impressionistic grounds, it seems probable that the planters of the Hispanic colonies were outstanding in the degree to which they developed insular—that is, creole, as opposed to metropolitan or Spanish—identities. These also seem to have been the colonies in which genetic intermixture proceeded most rapidly, and in which the rise of intermediate groups of free-men was rapid and more or less continuous. In the French colonies, such as Saint-Domingue, the French planters maintained a much warmer connection with metropolitan culture and society than was true in the Spanish colonies, though the rise of a powerful inter-mediate free group was swift and, in French Saint-Domingue, even-tually disturbing, socially and politically. In the British colonies, continuing identification with the mother country seems to have been strongest, intermediate groupings seem to have risen least rap-idly, and the legal circumscription of the rights of freemen seems to have been most effective.

The gross implications of these points are clear. Where freemen were able to achieve civil statuses approximating those of the Eu-ropean planters, and where the planter groups thought of them-selves as Creoles rather than as Europeans, the growth of national insular identities should have been most substantial. Where free-men were able to achieve civil statuses approximating those of the European planters, but where the planters themselves continued to view themselves essentially as Europeans in exile, national insular identity would hinge partly on the extent to which the freemen per-ceived themselves as allied with their former masters. In cases where freemen were kept in civil statuses that did not allow them to iden-tify freely with their former masters, and where those masters con-tinued to view themselves as European, the growth of national, cre-ole identity would presumably have been most retarded.

It will be understood that these assertions are almost entirely hypothetical in character. But perhaps they suggest a way of look-ing at the social history of the Caribbean region that will link con-temporary problems of nationhood with the workings of the past. It is at least likely that the presence of a group of powerholders who continued to see themselves as European rather than creole could hamper the growth of a spirit of insular or national identity among newly emerging freeman groups. In fact, the more such freemen might identify with their former masters, the more they would be alienated, willy-nilly, from *insular* society. Contrariwise, the more the planter groups thought of themselves as islanders rather than as Europeans, the more the freemen could share po-tentially in the creation of an insular identity. Obviously, this formulation leaves a great deal unexplained. In Saint-Domingue, for instance, the identification with France, French culture, and the *grands blancs* by *affranchi* slaveholders neither nourished a Haitian national identity nor consoled the slaves—who were doubtless as maltreated by *affranchi* masters as they were by French masters. Yet the relationships between slaves and freemen in Saint-Domingue were significantly different from what they were in, say, Jamaica, where a wealthy, powerful, and politically assertive class of mulatto planters never emerged. In Cuba, too, the growth of a massive free colored group greatly influenced the extent and character of creolization. Since the emergence of legal protections for the intermediate social groupings was tied to the institutional system operative in particular colonies, and since mating practices and domestic organization reveal in the first instance how such protections were secured or denied, it seems fair to contend that questions of national identity may be more closely linked than one might have supposed with the effects of the plantation mode on the kinship basis for group continuity.

The argument thus far suggests that the plantation system partially interdicted societal coherence at two levels of local group formation in Caribbean colonial societies: the community level, on the one hand, and the familial or domestic level, on the other. It also implies that these effects in turn limited the modes of integration of family groups and of communities with larger social groupings—the total insular society, or "nation"—and with national institutional frameworks, such as the educational system, the political system, and national religions. The workings of these negative effects are perhaps most clearly revealed by the extent to which the bipolar structures of traditional plantation societies have persisted into the present, expressed today in highly differentiated modes of mating and domestic organization, the relative paucity of local community organization, the limited participation of citizen masses in national political decision-making, the strong division into rural and urban sectors, and the lack of effective communication among different social strata. It is not only the presence or absence of intermediate social groupings that matters in weighing the importance of these aftereffects, but also the ideologies of identity of such groupings.

## Newcomer Populations

This picture is additionally complicated by the post-emancipation movement of new populations to the Caribbean region, primarily in answer to heightened demands by the plantation system for more labor. After emancipation, the planters stimulated the introduction of contract laborers to "normalize" wage levels in many colonies, and these migrations had marked demographic and cultural effects, as well as economic and political effects. While many contracted laborers came from Europe and Africa, the bulk of the new migrants came from Asia; in all, over 135,000 Chinese, nearly half a million Indians, and more than 33,000 Javanese reached the Caribbean area. Intraregional migrations also contributed to increasing complexity, as labor needs rose or declined in particular cases; thus Cuba, for instance, received nearly a quarter of a million Jamaicans and Haitians in little more than a decade (1912–24), with the expansion of North American sugar interests there.

These migrations signified the addition, in many societies, of massive groupings differing from antecedent populations in culture, language, and physical type. Moreover, these groupings were moving into situations of limited access to economic improvement, such that they could be confined for the most part to lives of unchanging plantation labor. Adequate comparative studies of the assimilation and adjustment of these newcomers to different Caribbean societies still need to be done; but it is clear that the degree and character of such assimilation has varied significantly, and in response to factors that are not yet altogether understood. One such factor may well have been the degree to which the receiving society already possessed an established population that considered itself native—that is, creole—on more than purely statistical grounds. The progressive assimilation of newcomers, in other words, was doubtless affected not only by the availability of economic and political opportunities to change their identification as outsiders, but also by the presence of what might be called an assimilation model, embodied in the social structure and values of the host society. The question, then, is: To what extent did the people of the receiving society consciously regard themselves as a national citizenry, and the island or colony within which they resided as their native land?

Put in these terms, it may be suggested—admittedly again, on impressionistic grounds only—that such societies as Cuba, Puerto Rico, and Haiti appear to have a more defined national identity than do such societies as Jamaica, Trinidad, and Guyana. If this assertion seems correct, one may at least speculate as to the reasons.

In the first place, Cuba and Haiti are sovereign nations, and part of the explanation may hinge on this obvious political fact. But Puerto Rico is not sovereign, and never has been—yet the people of Puerto Rico appear to be divided by fewer fundamental barriers than would seem to be the case in, say, Guyana. In the second place, it may be argued that the people of Cuba, Puerto Rico, and Haiti are less divided by ethnic differences than are those of Jamaica, Trinidad, and Guyana. Puerto Rico and Haiti, one colonial and the other long independent, have not had to assimilate large ethnically or physically distinctive populations, at least not since the eighteenth century. Jamaica, Trinidad, and Guyana have of course, been colonial for almost their entire history, and each has been required to assimilate large "stranger" populations in recent times. And yet Cuba apparently proved capable of assimilating its Chinese, Haitian, and Jamaican populations—not to mention the massive African slave importations of the nineteenth century—at least well enough to maintain its ideological identity as a nation.

It may be suggested again, then, that one possibly significant factor in the differentiation of national identity postulated here could be the early emergence of a stable creole culture, carried by a population that had come to identify itself with the island society within which it resided. In the Hispanic Caribbean, there were substantial populations that regarded themselves as Cuban, Puerto Rican, and Dominican, respectively, before British, French, and Dutch colonization in the islands had got seriously under way. Probable important factors in this "creolization" were the very uneven development of the plantation system in the Hispanic Caribbean, the early growth of peasant or yeoman sectors, and the attenuated influence of the metropolis in the rural areas during the seventeenth and eighteenth centuries. In the case of Haiti, a sentimental attachment to France paralleled political reality; after 1804, a Haitian national identity only very slowly emerged. The United States occupation, 1915–34, doubtless did much to reawaken Haitian national consciousness, however, since Haiti's isolation during the nineteenth century had been extreme. Most Haitians did not know they were Haitian, in any ideological sense, while the Haitian elite had continued to think of themselves as "colored Frenchmen." In Haiti today, as in the Hispanic Caribbean, a citizen may regard the erstwhile European colonizing power as the primary source of his "culture," without supposing at the same time that he is a Frenchman or a Spaniard, rather than a Haitian or a Cuban.

## Nationhood and "Race"

These various assertions, however, do not attack the matter of Afro-Caribbean influences on Caribbean nationhood. Here we recall that physical identity or appearance, as such, do not underlie the social relationships among Caribbean people, since such differences in each case are merely the reservoir of contrast upon which historically derived codes of social assortment have been built. It is a commonplace in Caribbean life that an individual's "racial identity" depends on a large number of intersecting nonbiological variables; and Hoetink, among others, has been careful to point out that "one and the same person may be considered white in the Dominican Republic or Puerto Rico . . . 'coloured' in Jamaica, Martinique, or Curaçao . . . [and] may be called a 'Negro' in Georgia" (1967: xii). "Color" or "race," in other words, is a function of existing modes of perception that are themselves a historical and cultural product, *not* a genetic actuality. This is not to say, of course, that Caribbean individuals do not vary in their physical appearance, but simply that such variation cannot be analyzed sociologically according to some abstract formula—and certainly not according to the culturally conventionalized perceptions of the outsider, regardless of his own physical appearance or self-perception.

Whatever local perceptions there may be of "race," the Caribbean sphere must be, first of all, set sharply apart from race-relations situations in the United States. Though many factors played a part in giving the North American situation its distinctive character, only several will be noted here, primarily in order to throw a contrasting light on the Caribbean region. First and foremost, North Americans defined as nonwhite have always been a minority

—albeit an immensely important one—in North American life. This fact alone distinguishes *most* Caribbean societies from the United States. Second, with the exception only of Haiti, the struggle against slavery in the Caribbean eventuated as a fundamentally economic and legislative struggle, settled definitively in each case in the imperial homeland; while that struggle in the United States divided a young nation against itself militarily, nonetheless failing to resolve a core contradiction in North American life. Third, the plantation society, of which we have said so much, grew as a subsidiary part of the North American economy, and never came to dominate that economy, as it did the economies of many Caribbean societies. Finally, North American society, unlike the societies of the Caribbean, began politically as a revolutionary society, within which opportunity was—at least in theory—not to be differentially distributed. These four ways in which Caribbean societies differ from the United States say much about the potential significance of Afro-Caribbean factors in future national Caribbean development.

The demographic dominance of nonwhites in Caribbean societies —with important exceptions, such as Cuba and Puerto Rico—has meant a significantly different perceptual setting for Caribbean people. This perceptual setting is further conditioned by the presence, in many of these societies, of a color continuum—one might better say, a distribution of phenotypic variety—paralleling the economic and social structures of the societies themselves. It is not surprising to discover in any Caribbean society that darker persons are overrepresented in the working classes and underrepresented in the governing and privileged classes; nor is it startling to find that the middle sectors of wealth and power are often commanded by persons whose physical appearance falls between those who are considered "white" and those who are considered "black." In the United States, of course, the distinctions among those perceived as nonwhite are fully appreciated within the nonwhite sectors but matter far less to the majority society; in the Caribbean, such distinctions—however they may be drawn locally—necessarily matter to everyone.

Accordingly, it is matter-of-factly recognized in many Caribbean societies that the nonwhite sector is itself commonly subdivided along various lines, and nonwhiteness alone lacks the significance it has in North America as a social, economic, or political category.

This does not mean, of course, that members of nonwhite groups are always unable or unwilling to ally themselves with one another for particular objectives. But such alliances have usually been specific and limited in the Antilles, and often appear to be difficult to maintain. Some might be tempted to argue that the political process in the Caribbean region—in those societies where nonwhites predominate—will simply lead to a supplantation of intermediately complexioned persons by those darker than themselves, as an earlier process might have led to the supplantation of whites by "coloureds." But it would be very simplistic to argue this, since lighter-skinned nonwhites have demonstrated an unusual capacity to retain power in the face of a "blackness" rhetoric, and the lines separating "blacks" from "coloureds" are very complexly (and differentially) drawn in each Caribbean instance.

White sectors of Caribbean societies vary in their relative numbers, their social isolation, and their power and rootedness within local life, so much so that it is difficult to generalize usefully about them in any way. Much the same is, of course, true of the nonwhite sectors of these societies, and in each instance the nonwhite sectors are differently divided, differently constituted. The rise of new ideologies of blackness in the Caribbean, comparable to ideologies of this kind in the United States, inevitably becomes linked to significantly different conceptions of reform, based on the different histories and present ethnic compositions of Antillean societies. In fact, it can be argued that such ideologies do not travel well if they fail to become adapted to different cultural values, different codes of social assortment, and different economic settings. In countries such as contemporary Cuba and Santo Domingo, nonwhiteness simply cannot form an effective basis of political organization, except perhaps in expressing on some very general level the anticolonial nationalism of Latin American peoples toward the United States. In societies such as Barbados or Jamaica, the emergence of antimulatto ideologies makes clear that the issue in some Caribbean contexts is really not color but power, and that divisions along color lines—in terms of degrees, that is, of perceived blackness—are politically necessary in order to make "race" an issue. In Haiti, a comparable ideology developed approximately three decades ago, and was firmly revivified under Duvalier; but there is as yet no totally convincing evidence that the main sources of Haitian power have been transferred from tan to black hands. To put it somewhat differently, color has always been intermixed with class and with colonial dependency in the Caribbean region; and it is generally still politically impractical to disengage color from these considerations.

The picture is further complicated, of course, by the presence of substantial populations in some Caribbean societies—such as the Indians in Trinidad and Guyana, the Javanese in Surinam, and the Chinese in Jamaica and Cuba—which are (or are considered) nonwhite, but which are ethnically perceived as different from populations of creole (that is, part-African) origin. The building of mass political movements that transcend such distinctions is still in its beginning stages, and some scholars are, to say the least, pessimistic about the future of such attempts.

Yet, at the same time, it would be ill-advised to argue that national unity can be built without taking into account these differences in appearance and in culture, and the ways they are conventionally perceived by Caribbean peoples. A reform or revolutionary ideology, for instance, that did not consider ethnic and "racial" differences in its analysis of any contemporary Caribbean society (including, I would argue, socialist Cuba) would necessarily leave certain important aspects of the past and present (and perhaps, the future) of that society wholly unexplained. Such differences are not, in fact, readily reducible to class explanations, even if one wishes that they were; and attempts to ignore social facts not so reducible do not necessarily lead to better-informed interpretation.

## The Perception of Difference

What we return to, in this regard, is a fundamental question about social reality: What does perceived cultural and "racial" difference have to do with the forging of national unity and national identity in the Caribbean region, either before or after the achievement of political sovereignty? The question is in one sense unanswerable: we simply do not know enough to be able to answer it fully and with certainty. But in the case of the Antilles, we must attempt some highly provisional answers, if only to sharpen the issue.

In no Caribbean colony or country can it be said that local inhabitants are unaware of physical differences; and in every instance there exists some historically determined (and, I would argue, changeable) system of social assortment, one of the dimensions of which is perceived "race." Physical difference may be perceived in terms of the supposed existence of groups, in that individual perceptions and descriptions of others serve to "assign" persons to a "black" group, a "mulatto" group, or some other such group. But it does not follow either that the boundaries of these "groups" are sharply delimited, or that any of them has internal cohesiveness, identity, or consciousness.

Since in most cases the terminology of description is large and complex, inferences about the number of supposed Caribbean groups are very risky. We even lack an adequate description of how "race" is perceived—that is, of the criteria employed by individuals in any Caribbean society in imputing one or another racial identity to others. Our uncertainty is even greater: to the extent that different criteria are employed (for example, such nonphysical criteria as dress, dialect, class position, etc., and such physical criteria as hair form, nose form, skin color, etc.), we are not yet in a position to order these criteria in any hierarchy of importance for any specific Caribbean society. Thus "race" becomes a significant basis of social assortment, whose dynamics of attribution remains very obscure. This lack of knowledge on our part makes very difficult the task of determining the importance of perceived "race" in the political life of any Caribbean country, even though we may be very sure that that importance is real. Nor is it sufficient to recognize that the distribution of populations of different appearance is very variable in the region—that very dark people predominate in Haiti, for instance, are relatively less numerous in Cuba, and are less numerous still in Puerto Rico—for such observations are made through a lens provided by our own societies and social experiences. We neither know where lines may be drawn by local people, nor according to what criteria—even though our observations about the correlation of lightness with privilege are generally accurate, and reflect readily determinable historical processes.

Thus, in order to make any real sense of the place of "race" in Caribbean national life and politics, we need to learn about local codes of perception, about the history of the societies in question, and about the relevance of physical distinctions to the workings of political life. We may note, as have other observers, that physical identity sometimes expresses itself in political formulations, but not in any fashion generalizable to the Caribbean region as a whole. The white Puerto Rican union leader addressing a largely white audience who speaks of the benefits that the Popular Party brought to "us little black ones" (*"nosotros los negritos"*) is making a class point, first of all—and a color point only in terms of the obvious fact that the rich are usually white or nearly so, while the poor are often black or nearly so. The Trinidadian or Jamaican dissenter who rails against the "Afro-Saxons"—light-skinned men who dominate massive nonwhite (or *perceived* nonwhite) majorities—is making a racial point; but we have no way of knowing how black an "Afro-Saxon" must be—and in whose judgment!—in order to escape the epithet. We are able to observe the ready acceptance of various kinds of separatist or race-based appeals in some Caribbean countries, even while we are quite unable to explain their rejection in other countries where the population is—by United States standards—predominantly "Negro." And we have next to nothing to say, of an analytic kind, about the relationship of local codes of racial ascription for people of African or part-African extraction, to the fit of other populations, nonwhite or perceived as nonwhite, in these same countries—such as the Chinese of Cuba; the Indians of Trinidad, Jamaica, Martinique, and Guyana; and the Javanese of Surinam. Least of all are we able to predict with any confidence the fates of these different populations in the future—their chances of genetic (and cultural) interpenetration, their achievement of a national identity or commonality, their tendencies to replace categories based on physical or ethnic difference with others based on consciousness of a common destiny.

Pessimists may argue that nations do not often form out of physically diverse stocks, and recent world history certainly seems on their side. In the United States, melting pot or no (and the answer is surely negative), the only groups systematically and invariably excluded from ready access to mobility of all kinds have always been nonwhite groups, of which Afro-Americans are the most numerous and the most visible, but not the only, sufferers. In the Caribbean region, divisions along lines of class, religion, ethnicity, and color in various societies have led many to doubt the ultimate political viability of these societies as nation-states. Certainly, "race" as a basis for *nationwide* political organization has not worked well, even though it has been used as an organizing principle for one or another group within these societies, or as an implicit aspect of general anticolonial struggles in the past.

At the same time, the underlying assumption of the more pessimistic observers—that national identity will emerge principally through genetic intermixture of all perceived different populations or by exclusion of one or more such populations—remains unproved. The supposition that national identity is interdicted by the presence of large and seemingly unassimilable ethnic groups implies that national identity hinges on some sort of total social homogeneity or homogeneity of values, on Furnivall's concept of "social will" (Furnivall 1939). If that were the case, the societies with the greatest sense of national identity would be those whose populations are most homogeneous in their values. While this view has a certain commonsense appeal, it is not supported by fact. Societies characterized by marked heterogeneity can exhibit a high degree of national identity, as long as individuals are able to align themselves on bases other than membership in particular ethnic or class groupings. In fact, to the extent that social movement can be randomized institutionally so that individual talents are rewarded differentially, a high degree of social heterogeneity may contribute to greater, rather than lesser, national identity.

An unqualified emphasis on homogeneity—either of population or of values—implies that national integration increases as the number of distinguishable social groups within a society declines. Yet both history and sociological theory qualify this view; not the number of groups, but the extent to which they interpenetrate in the maintenance of communication and in the solution of national issues, may be the critical factor (Kessler 1964). National identity can be built in part on the recognition of conflict as integrating, and does not require cultural (or, for that matter, economic) homogeneity. At the same time, cultural and economic heterogeneity can serve to inhibit the growth of national identity if communication between social segments, and their interpenetration, are hampered.

Group differences in physical type, economic status, and culture are sometimes cited as "explanations" for the lack of political unity in certain Caribbean societies. The argument advanced here is that these differences do not "explain" such a lack, nor even necessarily attest to it. National identity may emerge despite the existence of such differences, and may fail to emerge in their absence. Internal conflict can eventuate in greater or lesser national identity. The decisive criterion is the extent to which the citizens of a particular polity can identify themselves with the society in which they live, and employ the means available to achieve such identification in spite of differences in physical type, economic status, and culture.

It has been argued here that the presence of a long-established creole group which identifies itself primarily in local—that is, Caribbean or insular—terms may make a significant difference in the creation of nationhood. This distinction may have played a more important role in the history of some Caribbean societies than of others. It has further been suggested that a number of interlinking factors may have affected the way such long-established creole groups played a part in the formation of a national identity. Such factors include the workings of the plantation system, the sexual and mating codes controlling the masters and the slaves, and the values of the creole masters and their attitudes toward their respective metropolises. What we have refrained from attempting is a combination of this argument with a discussion of the role of peoples and groups of African (or part-African) origin in contemporary Caribbean politics—simply because, in the writer's view, we lack sufficient knowledge to proceed analytically in that direction at this time. Our ignorance results not only from inadequate field-work among Caribbean peoples on these questions, but also from our inability to weigh the significance of the last century of Caribbean history in these terms. It is one thing to evaluate the long-term meanings of different metropolitan policies, different mating patterns, and different historical experiences in the past; it is quite another to bring such evaluations into meaningful relationship with recent influences in Caribbean history. Such ancient factors influencing Caribbean identity, while still important, have been partly supplanted and deeply modified by events in the past century, particularly the expansive role of the United States in Caribbean international politics, and the continuing pressures for political autonomy or formal sovereignty within those societies that are still formally colonial. As for most of the so-called Third World, but with a special intensity in the case of Caribbean peoples—it will be remembered that I question the label in this case—the colonial problem has been one of escaping the past without tumbling into a future every bit as perilous to national identity.

We cannot, unfortunately, undertake a searching discussion of this issue here. Suffice it to say that the spread of United States power in the Caribbean region has probably done more to create an authentic race-based pan-Caribbean ideology than anything that could have been done by the Caribbean peoples themselves. But the contradictions implicit in the pasts of these selfsame societies continue to exert their influences in the present; it is difficult to imagine, other than in the case of the United States, a reactive transformation of racism into a national antiracist platform, even—or perhaps particularly—in those societies that are, by North American standards of perception, overwhelmingly "black." One may, if one wishes, consider this state of affairs either happy or unfortunate. But there is little doubt that radical political ideologies in the Caribbean region will not be deflected from critiques of world imperialism, of the role of the United States in Caribbean affairs, of class bases for economic exploitation, by any long-term commitment to color as the principal basis for political alignment. Surely those Caribbean politicians, of whatever stripe, who have been most successful in the Caribbean region's recent past—Manley and Bustamante in Jamaica, Castro in Cuba, and Williams in Jamaica, for instance—have not viewed race as such as a basis for struggle. In each case, accession to power has meant—if anything—a deliberate playing down of this theme. As Williams once pointed out, when independence comes, it often turns out that not all "massas" are white and not all whites are "massas."

But does any of this mean that "race" is not an organizing principle for oppression in the Caribbean region? Certainly not. Both as an incidental aspect of Caribbean history, and as a basis for maintaining power, "race" is revealed as a major dimension of power. So, too, is the control of the educational system; so, too, is planned (or unplanned) unemployment; so, too, is ethnic difference; so, too, are many other principles of social assortment that can be creatively employed, through discriminatory recruitment, to defend an existing distribution of power. That "race," and particularly blackness, could be used with such intensity and effectiveness against ordinary people in the Caribbean region is a function of world racism, revealed in all its variability and complexity in this part of the world. Political independence has not, it seems, erased the distinctions—among them, color—by which ancient colonial systems maintained themselves; in some ways, the struggle of too many for too little has, if anything, grown more intense. Nor is it entirely conclusive that even plenty for all will successfully remove ancient divisions among peoples whose consciousness of color and ethnicity has been conditioned by the past. This, however, is a question for the future; it will be a long while before the Caribbean masses will be able to reflect upon their identity while enjoying the luxury of a full belly.

The preceding arguments have flowed from a consideration of "race"—that is, perceived physical identity—as an organizing principle in Caribbean nationhood. We have stressed the difference, however, between the biological or genetic facts, and codes of perception and assortment, which are parts of culture not nature— ways to classify and manipulate reality according to the code by which it is interpreted. In concluding, we may change our tack somewhat.

## Culture and National Identity

It remains to refer to Afro-Caribbean culture in the creation of national (and pan-Caribbean) identity. Throughout our treatment so far, relatively little stress has been laid on African cultural content, in the sense of elements or complexes of culture originating in Africa and continuing to play an important role in the daily lives of Afro-Caribbean peoples. But we have seen that such cultural content takes its importance particularly from the ways in which it has been creatively adapted by Antillean folk to changing needs; and it is not necessary here to document the very massive corpus of cultural substance, social and ideological, that reveals African origins, often remodeled and synthesized.

But since we have concerned ourselves in this chapter with the theme of national identity, it may be useful to relate that theme to Afro-Caribbean culture. Culture, in the sense in which we have employed the term here, constitutes a repository of historically derived beliefs, values, etc., upon which societies may draw, particularly for symbolic purposes. When these processes are primarily political in character, it seems to matter little whether the symbolic manipulation is based upon historical realities—whether an item such as a dashiki is in any representative sense "really African," whether Swahili is the "most representative" African language, whether an "Afro" haircut is "truly symbolic" of Africa. Rather, it is quite enough for such symbols to distinguish one group of persons from another, to become markers of pride, to "summarize" a point of view, a sense of self, a group feeling or sentiment. The same is true of cuisine, dialect, dance, music, folklore, or whatever —what counts is the symbolic association and significance, not the historical authenticity.

The more authentically "African" the culture, it would seem, the less likely that those who carry it will regard it as a political weapon. Thus, for instance, the Bush Negroes of Surinam, sometimes dubbed the "most African" of all Afro-Americans, are almost surely the people most remote from the contemporary political struggles of the Caribbean region. The Haitian peasantry, who carry very substantial portions of the African past, may be subjected to africanist political discourse, but do not seem to interpret it in terms of their own lives. And as one moves from these populations toward the most westernized, the most sophisticated (and often, the lightest) Afro-Caribbean populations, among whom emphasis on the African past is an important principle of political action, it is striking to see how very little, indeed, of that past continues to play a vital part in daily life.

Cultures do not change in a vacuum, and the substances of Afro-American cultures have changed over time, just as have the substances of the African cultures from which they flowed. In the New World, culture contact and interpenetration, as a vital aspect of slavery and the slave trade, the spread of emergent (and then modern industrial) capitalism, and the struggle of Afro-Americans everywhere to escape their oppression or to define themselves creatively within it, accompanied the fundamental economic, political, and social forces at work. Quite expectably, the range of variation of "survivals" or "persistences," the maintenance or loss of specific cultural elements or complexes, is enormously wide, precisely because the range of experience of Afro-Americans was itself so wide. Nor can the earlier assertion that isolation may signify a higher degree of retention of African cultural materials confuse us about the subtleties of such retention. The Bush Negroes of Surinam, or the peasant folk of Haiti, while they may have been able to retain considerable cultural materials from the past, also enjoyed special opportunities to create new cultural forms of their own in the relative lack of contact with Western European cultures—such that much of what appears to be "African" in their cultures has of course been distilled and reworked to fit the new conditions of life they made for themselves after their successes in revolting against slavery and its oppression. Contrariwise, those Afro-American societies which grew in daily contact with Western cultures—isolated at the same time by new forms of economic repression and by racism—developed radically variant cultural forms, often assimilating and "re-africanizing" cultural materials drawn from outside. It is in these terms that the debates over origins have sometimes seemed beside the point; in any particular instance, the culture of a people is like a living fabric, and for those who weave it, origins matter less than the creative acts their behavior involves.

When these assertions are put into a social or political context, however, they suggest that we have not yet specified in any satisfying or convincing way just what we mean when we discuss Afro-Caribbean—or Afro-American—culture, since the links between cuisine, dance forms, music, speech, etc., and the ways social and political alliances are forged and maintained, the ways peoples define themselves as one in cultural terms, the ways behavioral differences are transmuted into political differences, remain too vague. This failure is a real one, even though we have begun to develop the concepts we need to describe such linkages. At present, we are far better able to describe particular cultural elements that have played a role in political self-definition than to specify either the symbolic significance of such elements or the extent to which we may fairly describe them as "African." These are not merely verbal distinctions. One might quite reasonably contend that Haitian rural culture is in important ways "less African" than North American black culture, precisely because North American black culture has had to grow in the face of virulent racism, forced segregation, and economic repression; and one might equally reasonably contend that Haitian rural culture is "more African" than North American black culture in many ways, since the people who created and carry it have undergone very different—and differentially isolating—experiences.

By and large, the political manifestations of Africanism in the Caribbean up to the present have been of a seemingly superficial sort, expressed in clothing, coiffure, music, and other aspects of consumption and taste, rather than in terms of political concepts, institutional forms for building new alignments of power, or philosophies of identity. At the same time, there is not the slightest doubt that the consciousness of the African past has grown quite steadily in Caribbean political life. It is equally apparent that the nourishment of such consciousness springs not only from the positive qualities of derived Afro-American cultures, but also from the persistence of archaic social and political structures employing one or another variety of racism to perpetuate themselves. It may be impossible to predict the specific futures of political movements employing "African" symbolism in their platforms and appeals; but there is not the slightest doubt that such techniques will continue to be viable as long as Caribbean societies fail to satisfy the needs of the common citizens—who are, of course, usually non-white. On a wider canvas, there is every reason to suppose that the ultimate support for such movements will come most powerfully from the United States, which is both the most powerful and the most racist imperialist neighbor of the Caribbean peoples. The presence in the United States of the largest, richest, most westernized, and most political Afro-American population in the Hemisphere is no accident. The persisting inability of the United States as a nation to resolve a contradiction that has gnawed at its very vitals for 350 years expresses and reexpresses itself in all of North America's dealings with Caribbean peoples, white and nonwhite, sovereign and colonial; and there is no sign that this contradiction is about to be resolved.

Thus a discussion of Afro-Caribbean culture in terms of identity inescapably extends to wider questions: of power, wealth, and ideology, set in a field of political maneuver stretching at least from Brazil to the United States, if not from Johannesburg to Peking. Nor is our canvas limited to the nonwhite world, since many Caribbean peoples are tied by a variety of factors to particular European nations. The significance of Afro-Caribbean identity thus reposes not solely in the specification of particular traits, elements, or complexes of culture—in itself an immensely important and difficult task for the historian of cultures—but also in the study of how broad-based political movements founded on sweeping axes of consciousness—pan-Arabism, pan-Africanism, nonwhiteness, etc.—become galvanized and effective, even if only for brief time-spans. One day, perhaps, pan-Caribbeanism may become such a movement. For the present, older definitions of group membership based on color, class, language, and the like will probably prevail. Until we are able to deal with populations that are at once backward and modern, racist and antiracist, European and anti-European, however, we shall have no success in decomposing the nature of Caribbean national identity. These folk are, in their own distinctive ways, very much peoples of the future. The inability of Western observers to detect this strikes the writer as strong evidence of our own equally undetected anachronism in a world we made without knowing it.

# References

ABBAD Y LASIERRA, FRAY IÑIGO. *Historia Geográfica Civil y Natural de la Isla de San Juan Bautista de Puerto Rico*. Mexico City: Ediciones de la Universidad de Puerto Rico, 1954 [1788].

ALLEN, CHARLES H. *First Annual Report of Chas. H. Allen, Governor of Porto Rico, 1901*. Washington, D.C.: Government Printing Office, 1901.

APTHEKER, HERBERT. *Negro Slave Revolts in the United States*. New York: International Publishers, 1939.

APTHEKER, HERBERT. *To Be Free*. New York: International Publishers, 1948.

BAGG, MATTHEW D. *Journal of Two Months' Residence in St. Thomas, Santa Cruz and Porto Rico in 1851–1852*. Typed copy of the original, New York Public Library.

BARNET, MIGUEL. *Biografía de un Cimarrón*. Havana: Academia de Ciencias de Cuba, 1966.

BARTH, FREDRIK. "On Responsibility and Humanity: Calling a Colleague to Account," *Current Anthropology* 15 (1974): 99–102.

BASCOM, WILLIAM. "Acculturation among Gullah Negroes," *American Anthropologist* 43 (1941): 43–50.

BASCOM, WILLIAM. "The Yoruba in Cuba," *Nigeria* 37 (1951): 14–20.

BASCOM, WILLIAM. "Two Forms of Afro-Cuban Divination," *Proceedings of the XXIX International Congress of Americanists* (1952) 1:196–99.

BASTIDE, ROGER. "Nègres Marrons et Nègres Libres," *Annales. Economies-Sociétés-Civilisations* 20 (1965): 169–74.

BASTIDE, ROGER. "Etat Actuel et Perspectives d'Avenir des Recherches Afro-Américaines," *Journal de la Société des Américanistes* 58 (1969): 7–29.

BASTIEN, RÉMY. *La Familia Rural Haitiana*. Mexico: Libra, 1951.

BASTIEN, RÉMY. "Haitian Rural Family Organization," *Social and Economic Studies* 10 (1961): 478–510.

BAUER, PETER T. *West African Trade*. Cambridge: Cambridge University Press, 1954

BAUER, RAYMOND, and BAUER, ALICE. "Day to Day Resistance to Slavery," *Journal of Negro History* 28 (1942): 388–419.

BECKFORD, GEORGE L. *Persistent Poverty: Underdevelopment in Plantation Economies of the Third World*. New York: Oxford University Press, 1972.

BECKFORD, WILLIAM. *A Descriptive Account of the Island of Jamaica*. 2 vols. London: Printed for T. and J. Egerton, 1790.

BECKWITH, MARTHA W. *Black Roadways. A Study of Jamaican Folk Life*. Chapel Hill: The University of North Carolina Press, 1929.

BENOIST, JEAN. "Plantations et Groupes Sociaux à la Martinique," *Cahiers des Ameriques Latines* 2 (1968): 130–154.

BEST, LLOYD A. "A Model of Pure Plantation Economy," *Social and Economic Studies* 17 (1968): 283–326.

BICKELL, REVEREND R. *The West Indies As They Are*. London: Printed for J. Hatchard and Son, 1836.

BIGELOW, J. *Jamaica in 1850*. London: George Putnam, 1851.

BLANCO, TOMÁS. *Prontuario Histórico de Puerto Rico*. Madrid: Imprenta Juan Pueyo, 1935.

BLANCO, TOMÁS. *El Prejuicio Racial en Puerto Rico*. 2nd ed. San Juan de Puerto Rico: Editorial Biblioteca de Autores Puertorriqueños, 1948.

BLOME, RICHARD. *A Description of the Island of Jamaica*. London: Printed by T. Milbourn, and sold by J. Williams, 1672.

*Boletín Histórico de Puerto Rico*. San Juan: vol. 2 (1915).

*Boletín Histórico de Puerto Rico*. San Juan: vol. 4 (1917).

*Boletín Histórico de Puerto Rico*. San Juan: vol. 10 (1923).

*Boletín Histórico de Puerto Rico*. San Juan: vol. 14 (1927).

BOTKIN, H. A. *Lay My Burden Down*. Chicago: University of Chicago Press, 1945.

BOURGUIGNON, ERIKA. "Class Structure and Acculturation in Haiti," *The Ohio Journal of Science* 52 (1952): 317–320.

BOURGUIGNON, ERIKA. "Haïti et l'Ambivalence Socialisée: une Reconsideration," *Journal de la Société des Américanistes* 58 (1969): 173–205.

BOURNE, E. G. *Spain in America, 1450–1580*. New York and London: Harper and Brothers, 1904.

BRATHWAITE, EDWARD. *The Development of Creole Society in Jamaica 1770–1820.* Oxford: Clarendon Press, 1971.

BRAU, SALVADOR. *Las Clases Jornaleras de Puerto Rico.* San Juan: Imprenta del Boletín Mercantil, 1882.

BRAU, SALVADOR. *Historia de Puerto Rico.* Nueva York: D. Appleton y cia., 1904.

BRIDGES, G. W. *The Annals of Jamaica.* 2 vols. London: John Murray, 1827.

BURN, W. L. *Emancipation and Apprenticeship in the British West Indies.* London: Jonathan Cape, 1937.

CARROLL, HENRY K. *Report on the Island of Puerto Rico.* Washington, D.C.: Government Printing Office, 1900.

CASSIDY, F. G., and LE PAGE, R. B. *Dictionary of Jamaican English.* Cambridge: Cambridge University Press, 1967.

CLARK, REVEREND JOHN. *A Brief Account of the Settlements of the Emancipated Peasantry in the Neighbourhood of Brown's Town, Jamaica, in a Letter from John Clark, Missionary, to Joseph Sturge of Birmingham.* Birmingham: n.p., 1852.

CLARKE, EDITH. "Land Tenure and the Family in Four Communities in Jamaica." *Social and Economic Studies* 1 (1953): 81–118.

CLARKE, EDITH. *My Mother Who Fathered Me.* London: George Allen and Unwin, 1957.

COHEN, YEHUDI A. "Interpersonal Relations in a Jamaican Community." Ph.D. dissertation, Yale University, 1953.

COLERIDGE, H. N. *Six Months in The West Indies in 1825.* London: J. Murray, published anonymously, 1826.

COMHAIRE, JEAN. "The Haitian Chef de Section," *American Anthropologist* 57 (1955): 620–23.

COMHAIRE-SYLVAIN, SUZANNE. "Land Tenure in the Marbial Region of Haiti." In *Acculturation in the Americas,* edited by Sol Tax. *Proceedings of the 29th International Congress of Americanists,* vol. 2. Chicago: University of Chicago Press (1952): 180–184.

COMHAIRE-SYLVAIN, SUZANNE, and COMHAIRE-SYLVAIN, JEAN. "Urban Stratification in Haiti," *Social and Economic Studies* 8 (1959): 179–189.

COMITAS, LAMBROS. "Occupational Multiplicity in Rural Jamaica." In *Proceedings of the American Ethnological Society, 1963,* edited by V. Garfield and E. Friedl. Seattle: University of Washington Press (1964): 41–50.

CÓRDOVA, PEDRO TOMÁS DE. *Memorias Geográficas, Históricas, Económicas y Estadísticas de la Isla de Puerto Rico,* 6 vols. Puerto Rico: Oficina del Gobierno, 1831–33.

CORWIN, ARTHUR F. *Spain and the Abolition of Slavery in Cuba,*

*1817–1886.* Austin and London: The University of Texas Press, 1967.

CUMPER, GEORGE. "Labour Demand and Supply in the Jamaican Sugar Industry 1830–1950," *Social and Economic Studies* 2 (1954a): 37–86.

CUMPER, GEORGE. "A Modern Sugar Estate," *Social and Economic Studies* 3 (1954b): 119–160.

CUMPER, GEORGE E. "Household and Occupation in Barbados," *Social and Economic Studies* 10 (1961): 386–419.

CUMPER, GEORGE. *The Social Structure of Jamaica.* Caribbean Affairs. Jamaica: University College of The West Indies, n.d.

CUNDALL, FRANK. *The Governors of Jamaica in the Seventeenth Century.* London: The West India Committee, 1936.

CUNDALL, FRANK, and PIETERSZ, J. *Jamaica under the Spaniards.* Kingston, Jamaica: Institute of Jamaica, 1919.

CURTIN, PHILIP. *Two Jamaicas.* Cambridge: Harvard University Press, 1955.

CURTIN, PHILIP. *The Atlantic Slave Trade: A Census.* Madison: University of Wisconsin Press, 1969.

DALLAS, R. C. *The History of the Maroons.* 2 vols. London: T. N. Longman and O. Rees, 1803.

DAVENPORT, WILLIAM H. *"A Comparative Study of Two Jamaican Fishing Communities."* Ph.D. dissertation, Yale University, 1956.

DAVENPORT, WILLIAM H. The Family System in Jamaica," *Social and Economic Studies* 10 (1961): 420–54.

DAVIDSON, DAVID M. "Negro Slave Control and Resistance in Colonial Mexico, 1519–1650." *Hispanic American Historical Review* 46 (1966): 235-53.

DAVIS, DAVID B. *The Problem of Slavery in Western Culture.* Ithaca, New York: Cornell University Press, 1966.

DAVIS, W. D. *Civil Affairs of Puerto Rico, 1899.* Washington, D.C.: Government Printing Office, 1900.

DEBBASCH, YVAN. "Le Marronage: Essai sur la Désertion de l'Esclave Antillais," *L'Année Sociologique* (1961): 1–112; (1962): 117–95.

DIAZ SOLER, LUIS M. *Historia de la Esclavitud Negra en Puerto Rico (1493–1890).* Madrid: Ediciones de la Universidad de Puerto Rico, 1953.

DIAZ SOLER, LUIS M. "La Esclavitud en Puerto Rico," Ciclo de Conferencias sobre la Historia de Puerto Rico. San Juan: Instituto de Cultura Puertorriqueña, 1957.

DORAN, EDWIN, JR. "The West Indian Hip-Roofed Cottage," *The California Geographer* 3 (1962): 97–104.

EDWARDS, BRYAN. *The History, Civil and Commercial, of the British Colonies in the West Indies.* 2 vols. London: John Stockdale, 1793.

ELKINS, STANLEY M. *Slavery. A Problem in American Institutional and Intellectual Life.* Chicago: The University of Chicago Press, 1959.

ELLISON, RALPH. *Shadow and Act.* New York: Random House, Inc., 1964.

ERASMUS, CHARLES J. "Agricultural Changes in Haiti: Patterns of Resistance and Acceptance," *Human Organization* 2 (1952): 20–26.

FERNÁNDEZ MÉNDEZ, EUGENIO. *Crónicas de Puerto Rico.* Spain: Editorial Universidad de Puerto Rico, 1969.

FINLEY, M. I. "Slavery." In *International Encyclopedia of the Social Sciences* 14. Crowell Collier and Macmillan, Inc., n.p.: 1968.

FIRTH, RAYMOND. *Elements of Social Organization.* London: Watts, 1951.

FREDERICKSON, GEORGE, and LASCH, CHRISTOPHER. "Resistance to Slavery," *Civil War History* 13 (1967): 315–29.

FRIEDERICI, GEORG. *Amerikanistisches Wörterbuch und Hilfswörterbuch für den Amerikanisten.* 2nd ed. Hamburg: Cram, De Gruyter & Co., 1960.

FRUCHT, RICHARD. "Caribbean Social Type: Neither 'Peasant' nor 'Proletarian,' " *Social and Economic Studies* 16 (1967): 295–300.

FURNIVALL, J. S. *Netherlands India: a Study of a Plural Economy.* London: Cambridge University Press, 1939.

GARDNER, W. J. *A History of Jamaica.* London: Elliot Stock, 1874.

GAYER, ARTHUR D., HOMAN, PAUL T., and JAMES, EARLE K. *The Sugar Economy of Puerto Rico.* New York: Columbia University Press, 1938.

GENOVESE, EUGENE D. "Rebelliousness and Docility in the Negro Slave," *Civil War History* 13 (1967): 293–314.

GENOVESE, EUGENE D. *The World the Slaveholders Made.* New York: Random House, 1969.

GOVEIA, ELSA V. "Comment on S. W. Mintz, 'Labor and Sugar in Puerto Rico and Jamaica,' " *Comparative Studies in Society and History* 1 (1959): 281–83.

GOVEIA, ELSA V. "The West Indian Slave Laws of the Eighteenth Century," *Revista de Ciencias Sociales* 4 (1960): 75–105.

GOVEIA, ELSA V. *Slave Society in the British Leeward Islands at the End of the Eighteenth Century.* New Haven: Yale University Press, 1965.

GRAY, LEWIS C. *History of Agriculture in the Southern United States to 1860.* New York: P. Smith, 1941.

GREAT BRITAIN. FOREIGN OFFICE. "Paper Respecting the Abolition of Slavery and the Condition of the *Libertos* in Porto Rico," *Slave Trade,* no. 3. Presented to both Houses of Parliament by Command of Her Majesty. London: Harrison and Sons, 1875.

GREAT BRITAIN. PUBLIC RECORD OFFICE. *Letter from Magistrate Harris to the Governor, 27 July, 1836.* Colonial Office Documents, No. 137/216, Jamaica Apprentices, Pt. 3. London, 1836.

GREAVES, IDA C. *Modern Production among Backward Peoples.* London: George Allen and Unwin Ltd., 1935.

GREENFIELD, SIDNEY M. "Socio-Economic Factors and Family Form," *Social and Economic Studies* 10 (1961): 72–85.

GREENFIELD, SIDNEY M. *English Rustics in Black Skin.* New Haven: College and University Press, 1966.

GUERRA Y SÁNCHEZ, RAMIRO. *Sugar and Society in the Caribbean.* New Haven: Yale University Press, 1964.


HALL, DOUGLAS. "The Apprenticeship Period in Jamaica, 1834–1838," *Caribbean Quarterly* 3 (1953): 142–66.

HALL, DOUGLAS. "The Social and Economic Background to Sugar in Slave Days," *Caribbean Historical Review* 3–4 (1954): 149–69.

HALL, DOUGLAS. *Free Jamaica.* New Haven: Yale University Press, 1959.

HANDLER, JEROME. "A Historical Sketch of Pottery Manufacture in Barbados," *The Journal of the Barbados Museum and Historical Society* 30 (1963): 1–24.

HANDLER, JEROME. "Some Aspects of Work Organization on Sugar Plantations in Barbados," *Ethnology* 4 (1965): 16–38.

HANDLER, JEROME. "Small-Scale Sugar Cane in Barbados," *Ethnology* 5 (1966): 264–83.

HANDLER, JEROME S. "The History of Arrowroot and the Origin of Peasantries in the British West Indies," *The Journal of Caribbean History* 2 (1971): 46–93.

HARRIS, MARVIN. "Labor Emigration among the Moçambique Thonga," *Africa* 29 (1959): 50–65.

HART, ANSELL. "Causeries," *Monthly Comments* 1 (1955): 1.

HENDERSON, GEORGE E. *Goodness and Mercy. A Tale of a Hundred Years.* Kingston, Jamaica: The Gleaner Co., Inc., 1931.

HERSKOVITS, MELVILLE J. "Adjiboto, an African Game of the Bush-Negroes of Dutch Guiana," *Man* 29 (1929): 122–27.

HERSKOVITS, MELVILLE J. "The Negro in the New World: the Statement of a Problem," *American Anthropologist* 32 (1930): 145–55.

HERSKOVITS, MELVILLE J. "Wari in the New World," *Journal of the Royal Anthropological Institute of Great Britain and Ireland* 62 (1932): 23–37.

HERSKOVITS, MELVILLE J. *Life in a Haitian Valley.* New York: Alfred A. Knopf, 1937.

HERSKOVITS, MELVILLE J. *Dahomey.* 2 vols. New York: J. J. Augustin, 1938.

HERSKOVITS, MELVILLE J. *The Myth of the Negro Past.* New York: Harper and Bros., 1941.

HERSKOVITS, MELVILLE J. "Problem, Method and Theory in Afroamerican Studies," *Afroamérica* 1 (1945): 5–24.

HERSKOVITS, MELVILLE J., and HERSKOVITS, FRANCES S. *Trinidad Village*. New York: Alfred A. Knopf, 1947.

HICKERINGILL, EDMUND. *Jamaica Viewed*. London: By E. H. London, Printed for J. Williams, 1661.

HOETINK, HARRY. *The Two Variants in Caribbean Race Relations*. London: Oxford University Press, 1967.

HOGG, DONALD W. "Jamaican Religions. A Study in Variations." Ph.D. dissertation, Yale University, 1964.

HOSTOS, ADOLFO DE. *Ciudad Murada*. Havana: Editorial Lex, 1949.

HUTCHINSON, HARRY W. *Village and Plantation in Northeastern Brazil*. Seattle: University of Washington Press, 1957.

INSTITUTE OF JAMAICA. "Notes and Queries: Early Fairs in Jamaica," *Journal of the Institute of Jamaica* 2 (1895): 146.

JAHN, JANHEINZ. *Muntu: the New African Culture*. New York: Grove Press, 1961.

JAIN, RAVINDRA. *South Indians on the Plantation Frontier in Malaya*. New Haven: Yale University Press, 1970.

JAMES, C. L. R. *The Black Jacobins. Toussaint L'Ouverture and the San Domingo Revolution*. New York: Random House, 1963 [1938].

JAYAWARDENA, CHANDRA. *Conflict and Solidarity in a Guianese Plantation*. London: University of London, The Athlone Press, 1963.

JERNEGAN, M. W. *Laboring and Dependent Classes in Colonial America, 1607–1783*. Chicago: University of Chicago Press, 1931.

JOHNSTON, SIR HARRY H. *The Negro in the New World*. London: Methuen, 1910.

KATZIN, MARGARET. "The Jamaican Country Higgler," *Social and Economic Studies* 8 (1959): 421–40.

KATZIN, MARGARET. "The Business of Higglering in Jamaica," *Social and Economic Studies* 9 (1960): 297–331.

KELLER, ALBERT. *Colonization*. Boston: Ginn, 1908.

KESSLER, CLYDE. "Indians in South and East Africa: Immigrant Minorities and the 'Plural Society.' " B. A. Honours thesis, University of Sydney, 1964.

KLEIN, HERBERT S. *Slavery in the Americas. A Comparative Study of Virginia and Cuba*. Chicago: The University of Chicago Press, 1967.

KLOOSTERBOER, W. *Involuntary Labour since the Abolition of Slavery*. Leiden: E. J. Brill, 1960.

KNIGHT, ROLF. *Sugar Plantations and Labor Patterns in the Cauca Valley, Colombia*. Department of Anthropology, University of Toronto, Anthropological Series, November, 1972.

KROEBER, ALFRED L. *Anthropology*. New York: Harcourt Brace, 1948.

LAHAV, PNINA. "The Chef de Section: Structure and Function of Haiti's

Basic Administrative Unit." New Haven, Connecticut: Yale University Antilles Research Program, 1973. Typescript.

LANDSBERGER, HENRY A. (ed.) *Latin American Peasant Movements.* Ithaca: Cornell University Press, 1970.

LESLIE, CHARLES. *A New and Exact Account of Jamaica.* Edinburgh: Printed by R. Fleming, for A. Kincaid, 1739.

LEWIS, M. G. *Journal of a Residence among the Negroes in the West Indies.* London: J. Murray, 1861.

LEYBURN, JAMES G. *The Haitian People.* New Haven: Yale University Press, 1941.

LIGON, RICHARD A. *A True and Exact History of the Island of Barbados.* London: H. Moseley, 1657.

LIND, ANDREW. *An Island Community; Ecological Succession in Hawaii.* Chicago: The University of Chicago Press, 1938.

LIPSON, E. *The Economic History of England.* London: Adam and Chas. Black, 1945.

LIVINGSTONE, W. P. *Black Jamaica.* London: Sampson, Low, Marston & Co., 1900.

LONG, EDWARD. *The History of Jamaica.* 3 vols. London: T. Lowndes, 1774.

LOPEZ, AMY. "Land and Labour to 1900," *Jamaican Historical Review* 1 (1948): 289–301.

LÓPEZ DOMÍNGUEZ, F. A. "Origen y Desarrollo de la Industria del Azúcar de Puerto Rico," *Revista de Agricultura de Puerto Rico* 19 (1927): 49–55, 103–06, 167–72, 222–23, 287–89.

LOUNSBURY, FLOYD G. "One Hundred Years of Anthropological Linguistics." In *One Hundred Years of Anthropology,* edited by J. O. Brew. Cambridge, Mass.: Harvard University Press, 1968.

LOWENTHAL, DAVID. "The Range and Variation of Caribbean Societies," *Annals of the New York Academy of Sciences* 83 (1960): 786–95.


MADDEN, R. R. *A Twelvemonth's Residence in the West Indies.* 2 vols. London: James Cochran, 1835.

MARSHALL, WOODVILLE K. "Peasant Development in the West Indies since 1838," *Social and Economic Studies* 17 (1968): 252–63.

MARX, KARL. "The Indian Revolt," *New York Tribune,* Sept. 16, 1857.

MARX, KARL. *Capital,* vol. 1. New York, International Publishers, 1939 [1867].

MATHIESON, WILLIAM LAW. *British Slavery and Its Abolition 1823–1838.* London: Longman, Greens, 1926.

MERIVALE, HERMAN. *Lectures on Colonization and Colonies.* London: Longman, Orme, Brown, Green, and Longmans, 1841.

MERRIAM, ALAN P., WHINERY, SARA, and FRED, B. G. "Songs of a Rada Community in Trinidad," *Anthropos* 51 (1956): 157–174.

MÉTRAUX, ALFRED. "L'Habitation Paysanne en Haïti," *Bulletin de la Société Neuchâteloise de Géographie* 55 (1949–51): 3–14.

MÉTRAUX, ALFRED. *Making a Living in the Marbial Valley (Haiti). Occasional Papers in Education 10.* Paris: UNESCO, 1951.

MÉTRAUX, ALFRED. "Rites Funéraires des Paysans Haïtiens," *Arts et Traditions Populaires* 4 (1954): 289–306.

MÉTRAUX, ALFRED. *Voodoo.* Trans. by Hugo Charteris. London: André Deutsch, 1959.

MINTZ, SIDNEY W. "The Role of Forced Labour in Nineteenth-Century Puerto Rico," *Caribbean Historical Review* 2 (1951 a): 134–41.

MINTZ, SIDNEY W. "Cañamelar: The Culture of a Rural Puerto Rican Proletariat." Ph.D. dissertation, Columbia University, 1951b.

MINTZ, SIDNEY W. "The Culture-History of a Puerto Rican Sugar-Cane Plantation, 1876–1949," *Hispanic American Historical Review* 33 (1953a): 224–51.

MINTZ, SIDNEY W. "The Folk-Urban Continuum and the Rural Proletarian Community," *American Journal of Sociology* 59 (1953b): 136–43.

MINTZ, SIDNEY W. "The Jamaican Internal Marketing Pattern: Some Notes and Hypotheses," *Social and Economic Studies* 4 (1955): 95–103.

MINTZ, SIDNEY W. "Cañamelar: The Sub-Culture of a Rural Sugar Plantation Proletariat." In *The People of Puerto Rico,* edited by J. H. Steward *et al.* Urbana: University of Illinois Press, 1956.

MINTZ, SIDNEY W. "The Role of the Middleman in the Internal Distribution System of a Caribbean Peasant Economy," *Human Organization* 15 (1957): 18–23.

MINTZ, SIDNEY W. "The Historical Sociology of the Jamaican Church-Founded Free Village System," *De West-Indische Gids* 38 (1958): 46–70.

MINTZ, SIDNEY W. "Labor and Sugar in Puerto Rico and Jamaica, 1800–1850," *Comparative Studies in Society and History* 1 (1959): 273–81.

MINTZ, SIDNEY W. *Worker in the Cane.* New Haven: Yale University Press, 1960.

MINTZ, SIDNEY W. "The Question of Caribbean Peasantries: a Comment," *Caribbean Studies* 1 (1961a): 31–34.

MINTZ, SIDNEY W. Review of Elkins, Stanley, *Slavery. American Anthropologist* 63 (1961b): 579–87.

MINTZ, SIDNEY W. "Living Fences in the Fond-des-Nègres Region, Haiti," *Economic Botany* 16 (1962): 101–5.

MINTZ, SIDNEY W. "Currency Problems in Eighteenth Century Jamaica and Gresham's Law." In *Process and Patterns in Culture,* edited by Robert A. Manners. Chicago: Aldine Publishing Co., 1964.

MINTZ, SIDNEY W. "The Caribbean as a Socio-Cultural Area," *Cahiers d'Histoire Mondiale* IX (1966): 916–41.

MINTZ, SIDNEY W. "Caribbean Society." In *International Encyclopedia of the Social Sciences* 2. Crowell Collier and Macmillan, Inc., n.p. 1968.

MINTZ, SIDNEY W. "Groups, Group Boundaries and the Perception of Race," *Comparative Studies in Society and History* 13 (1971): 437–43.

MINTZ, SIDNEY W. "A Note on the Definition of Peasantries," *The Journal of Peasant Studies* 1 (1973): 91–106.

MINTZ, SIDNEY W. "The Rural Proletariat and the Problem of Rural Proletarian Consciousness," *Journal of Peasant Studies* 1 (1974): 291–325.

MINTZ, SIDNEY W., and PRICE, RICHARD. "An Anthropological Approach to the Study of Afro-American History." New Haven, Connecticut: Yale University, 1973. Mimeographed.

MORAL, PAUL. "La Maison Rurale en Haïti," *Les Cahiers d'Outre-Mer* 10 (1957): 117–30.

MORAL, PAUL. *Le Paysan Haïtien*. Paris: G. P. Maisonneuve et Larose, 1961.

MORALES MUÑOZ, G. E. "Un Estatuto Jurídico de los Trabajadores Domésticos," *Boletín de Historia Puertorriqueña* 1 (1949): 71–78.

MOREAU DE ST. MÉRY, LOUIS. *Description Topographique, Physique, Civile, Politique et Historique de la Partie Française de l'Isle Saint-Domingue*, 3 vols. Paris: Société de l'Histoire des Colonies Françaises et Librairie Larose, 1958 [1797].

MORSE, RICHARD M. "Negro-White Relations in Latin America," *Reports and Speeches of the IXth Yale Conference on the Teaching of the Social Studies, April 3–4, 1964*. New Haven, Connecticut: Yale University. Mimeographed.

MUNRO, DANA G. *Intervention and Dollar Diplomacy in the Caribbean 1900–1921*. Princeton: Princeton University Press, 1964.

NIEBOER, H. J. *Slavery as an Industrial System*. The Hague: Martinus Nijhoff, 1900.

OLIVIER, SIDNEY LORD. *Jamaica, The Blessed Island*. London: Faber and Faber, 1936.

ORTIZ, FERNANDO. *Contrapunteo Cubano del Tabaco y el Azúcar*. Havana: Jesús Montero, 1940.

OTTERBEIN, KEITH F. "Caribbean Family Organization: A Comparative Analysis," *American Anthropologist* 67 (1965): 66–79.

PADILLA, ELENA. "Nocorá: An Agrarian Reform Sugar Community." Ph.D. dissertation, Columbia University, 1951.

PAGET, HUGH. "The Free Village System in Jamaica," *Caribbean Quarterly* 1 (n.d.) : 7–19.

PARES, RICHARD. *A West India Fortune.* London & New York: Longmans, Green, 1950.

PARRY, JOHN H. "Salt Fish and Ackee," *Caribbean Quarterly* 2 (n.d.) : 29–35.

PARRY, JOHN H. "Plantation and Provision Ground," *Revista de Historia* 39 (1955) : 1–20.

PATTERSON, ORLANDO. *The Sociology of Slavery.* London: MacGibbon and Kee, 1967.

PATTERSON, ORLANDO. "Slavery and Slave Revolts: A Socio-Historical Analysis of the First Maroon War, 1655–1740," *Social and Economic Studies* 19 (1970) : 289–325.

PAYNE, ERNEST A. *Freedom in Jamaica.* London: Cary, 1933.

PÉREZ DE LA RIVA, FRANCISCO. *La Habitación Rural en Cuba.* La Habana: Contribución del Grupo Guamá, Antropología No. 26, 1952.

PHILLIPPO, JAMES M. *Jamaica, Its Past and Present State.* London: John Snow, 1843.

PIERSON, DONALD. *Negroes in Brazil.* Chicago: University of Chicago Press, 1942.

PIERSON, DONALD. "Africans and Their Descendants at Bahia, Brasil," *Les Afro-Américains, Mémoires de l'Institut Français d'Afrique Noire,* No. 27 (1953) : 153–56.

PRICE, RICHARD. "Caribbean Fishing and Fishermen: A Historical Sketch," *American Anthropologist* 68 (1966) : 1368–83.

PRICE, RICHARD. "Studies of Caribbean Family Organization: Problems and Prospects," *Dédalo. Revista do Museu de Arte e Archeologia da Universidade de São Paulo* 3 (1970).

PRICE, RICHARD (ed.). *Maroon Societies. Rebel Slave Communities in the Americas.* Garden City: Doubleday, 1973.

PRICE, THOMAS J. "Estado y Necesidades de las Investigaciones Afro-Colombianas," *Revista Colombiana de Antropología* 3 (1955) : 11–36.

PRICE-MARS, JEAN. *Ainsi Parla L'Oncle. Essais d'Ethnographie.* Paris: Imprimerie de Compiègne, 1928.

PRICE-MARS, JEAN. "Classe ou Caste?" *Revue de la Société Haïtienne d'Histoire de Géographie et de Géologie* 13 (1942) : 1–50.

PUERTO RICO, GOVERNMENT OF. Department of Agriculture and Commerce. *Annual Book on Statistics of Puerto Rico: 1939–40.*

RAGATZ, LOWELL J. *The Fall of the Planter Class in the British Caribbean, 1763–1833.* New York: Century Company, 1928.

RAMÍREZ DE ARELLANO, RAFAEL. "Instrucciones al Diputado Don Ramón Power y Giralt," *Boletín de la Universidad de Puerto Rico,* Serie 7, no. 2 (1936) : 39–41.

REDFIELD, ROBERT. *The Primitive World and Its Transformations.* Ithaca, N.Y.: Cornell University Press, 1953.

RENNY, ROBERT. *A History of Jamaica.* London: J. Cawthorn, 1807.

REVERT, EMILE. *La France d'Amérique.* Paris: Editions Maritimes et Colonialès, 1955.

ROTBERG, ROBERT, and CLAGUE, CHRISTOPHER. *Haiti: the Politics of Squalor.* Boston: Houghton Mifflin, 1971.

SAUER, CARL O. "Cultivated Plants of South and Central America." In *Handbook of South American Indians,* edited by Julian Steward. *Bulletin, Bureau of American Ethnology* no. 143, vol. 6 (1950): 487–543.

SAUER, CARL O. "Economic Prospects of the Caribbean." In *The Caribbean: Its Economy,* edited by A. C. Wilgus, pp. 15–27. Gainesville, Florida: University of Florida Press, 1954.

SAUER, CARL O. *The Early Spanish Main.* Berkeley and Los Angeles: University of California Press, 1966.

SCHMIDT, HANS. *The United States Occupation of Haiti, 1915–1934.* New Brunswick: Rutgers University Press, 1971.

SERVICE, ELMAN R. "Indian-European Relations in Colonial Latin America," *American Anthropologist* 57 (1955): 411–425.

SEWELL, WILLIAM G. *The Ordeal of Free Labour in the British West Indies.* New York: Harper & Brothers, 1861.

SHANIN, TEODOR. "Peasantry, Delineation of a Sociological Concept and a Field of Study," *European Journal of Sociology* 12 (1971): 289–300.

SHERLOCK, PHILIP M. "Editorial Note," *Caribbean Quarterly* 3 (n.d.): 3.

SIMPSON, GEORGE E. "The Nine Night Ceremony in Jamaica," *Journal of American Folklore* 70 (1957): 329–35.

SLOANE, HANS. *A Description of a Voyage to the Islands of Madera, Barbados, Etc. . . . .* vol. 1. London: Printed by B. M. for the author, 1707.

SMITH, MICHAEL G. "Social Structure in the British Caribbean about 1820," *Social and Economic Studies* 1 (1953): 55–79.

SMITH, MICHAEL G. "The Transformation of Land Rights by Transmission in Carriacou," *Social and Economic Studies* 5 (1956a): 103–38.

SMITH, MICHAEL G. "Community Organization in Rural Jamaica," *Social and Economic Studies* 5 (1956b): 295–312.

SMITH, MICHAEL G. *West Indian Family Structure.* Seattle: University of Washington Press, 1962.

SMITH, MICHAEL G. *The Plural Society in the British West Indies.* Berkeley and Los Angeles: University of California Press, 1965.

SMITH, RAYMOND T. *The Negro Family in British Guiana.* London: Routledge & Kegan Paul Ltd., 1956.

SOLIEN, NANCIE L. "Household and Family in the Caribbean," *Social and Economic Studies* 9 (1960): 101–06.

STEWARD, JULIAN, MANNERS, ROBERT A., WOLF, ERIC R., PADILLA SEDA, ELENA, MINTZ, SIDNEY W., and SCHEELE, RAYMOND L. *The People of Puerto Rico.* Urbana: University of Illinois Press, 1956.

STEWARD, JULIAN H. (ed.). *Contemporary Change in Traditional Societies.* 3 vols. Urbana: University of Illinois Press, 1967.

STEWART, JOHN. *A View of the Past and Present State of the Island of Jamaica.* Edinburgh: Oliver & Boyd, 1823.

STREET, JOHN M. "Historical and Economic Geography of the Southwest Peninsula of Haiti." Ph.D. dissertation, University of California, 1960.

STURGE, JOSEPH, and HARVEY, THOMAS. *The West Indies in 1837.* London: Hamilton Adams and Co., 1838.

STURTEVANT, WILLIAM C. "Taino Agriculture." In *The Evolution of Horticultural Systems in Native South America. Causes and Consequences,* edited by J. Wilbert. Caracas: Sociedad de Ciencias Naturales La Salle, 1961.

STURTEVANT, WILLIAM C. "History and Ethnology of Some West Indian Starches." In *The Domestication and Exploitation of Plants and Animals,* edited by Peter J. Ucko and G. W. Dimbleby. London: Gerald Duckworth & Co., Ltd., 1969.

TANNENBAUM, FRANK. *Slave and Citizen.* New York: Alfred A. Knopf, 1947.

TANNENBAUM, FRANK. "Discussion." In *Caribbean Studies: A Symposium,* edited by V. Rubin. Seattle: University of Washington Press, 1957.

TAYLOR, DOUGLAS MACRAE. *The Black Carib of British Honduras.* Viking Fund Publications in Anthropology no. 17. New York: Wenner-Gren Foundation for Anthropological Research, Inc., 1951.

TAYLOR, DOUGLAS MACRAE. Review of Mintz, Sidney W., ed., *Papers in Caribbean Anthropology,* Nos. 57–64. *American Anthropologist* 64 (1962): 179–86.

THOMPSON, EDGAR T. "The Plantation." Ph.D. Dissertation, The University of Chicago, 1932.

TURNBULL, DAVID. *Travels in the West. Cuba; with Notices of Porto Rico and the Slave Trade.* London: Longman, Orme, Brown, Green, and Longmans, 1840.

TYLOR, EDWARD B. *Anthropology.* 2 vols. London: Watson Co., 1946 [1881].

UNDERHILL, EDWARD B. *The West Indies: Their Social and Religious Condition.* London: Jackson, Walford and Hodder, 1861.

U.S. BUREAU OF THE CENSUS. *Thirteenth Census of the United States.* vol. 7. Washington, D.C.: Government Printing Office, 1910.

U.S. BUREAU OF THE CENSUS. *Sixteenth Census of the United States, 1940: Population, 1st Series; Puerto Rico Bulletin no. 1, Number of Inhabitants.* Washington: Government Printing Office, 1942.

U.S. BUREAU OF THE CENSUS. *Sixteenth Census of the United States,* vol. 5. Washington, D.C.: Government Printing Office, 1943.

U.S. DEPARTMENT OF COMMERCE. Bureau of Foreign and Domestic Commerce. *The Cane Sugar Industry,* Miscellaneous Series no. 53. Washington: Government Printing Office, 1917.

U.S. WAR DEPARTMENT. *Report on the Census of Porto Rico 1899.* Washington: Government Printing Office, 1900.

WAGLEY, CHARLES. "Plantation-America: a Cultural Sphere." In *Caribbean Studies: A Symposium,* edited by V. Rubin. Seattle: University of Washington Press, 1957.

WAGLEY, CHARLES, and HARRIS, MARVIN. "A Typology of Latin American Subcultures," *American Anthropologist* 57 (1955): 428–51.

WATERMAN, RICHARD A. "African Patterns in Trinidad Negro Music." Ph.D. dissertation, Northwestern University, 1943.

WEATHERLY, U. G. "The West Indies as a Sociological Laboratory," *American Journal of Sociology* 29 (1923): 290–304.

WILLIAMS, ERIC. *Capitalism and Slavery.* Chapel Hill: The University of North Carolina Press, 1944.

WILLIAMS, ERIC. "The Negro Slave Trade in Anglo-Spanish Relations," *Caribbean Historical Review* 1 (1950): 22–45.

WILLIAMS, ERIC. *From Columbus to Castro. The History of the Caribbean, 1492–1969.* New York: Harper and Row, 1970.

WILLIAMS, JOSEPH. *Whence the Black Irish of Jamaica.* New York: Dial, 1932.

WOLF, ERIC R. "Types of Latin American Peasantry: a Preliminary Discussion," *American Anthropologist* 57 (1955): 452–71.

WOLF, ERIC R. "San José: Subcultures of a 'Traditional' Coffee Municipality." In *The People of Puerto Rico,* edited by J. H. Steward *et al.* Urbana: University of Illinois Press, 1956.

WOLF, ERIC R. *Peasants.* Englewood Cliffs, N.J.: Prentice Hall, 1966.

WOLF, ERIC R., and MINTZ, SIDNEY W. "Haciendas and Plantations in Middle America and the Caribbean," *Social and Economic Studies* 6 (1957): 380–412.

X, MALCOLM. *The Autobiography of Malcolm X.* New York: Grove Press, 1966.

YOUNG, WILLIAM. *A Tour Through the Several Islands of Barbados, St. Vincent, Antigua, Tobago and Grenada, in the Years 1791 and 1792.* London: 1801.

ZELINSKY, WILBUR. "The Historical Geography of the Negro Population of Latin America," *Journal of Negro History* 34 (1949): 153–221.

# Index

CARIBBEAN TRANSFORMATIONS
by Sidney W. Mintz

Alexander J. Morin, *Publisher*
Eugene Zucker, *Manuscript Editor*
Georganne E. Marsh, *Production Editor*
Mitzi Carole Trout, *Production Manager*

Composition by SSPA Typesetting, Inc., Carmel, Indiana
Printing by Printing Headquarters, Inc.,
Arlington Heights, Illinois
Binding by Brock & Rankin, Chicago, Illinois